W9-BQZ-480

ALSO BY MICHAEL SCHUMACHER

Reasons to Believe: New Voices in American Fiction

Creative Conversations: The Writer's Complete Guide to Conducting Interviews

Dharma Lion: A Biography of Allen Ginsberg

Crossroads: The Life and Music of Eric Clapton

There But for Fortune

There But for Fortune

THE LIFE OF PHIL OCHS

MICHAEL SCHUMACHER

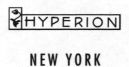

NEW YORK

Frontispiece photo of Phil Ochs: photo by Bernard Gorson,
courtesy of Arthur Gorson.

Library of Congress Cataloging-in-Publication Data

Schumacher, Michael.
There but for fortune : the life of Phil Ochs /
Michael Schumacher.—1st ed.
p.   cm.
Includes bibliographical references,
discography (p.   ), and index.
ISBN 0-7868-6084-7
1. Ochs, Phil. 2. Singers—United States—
Biography. I. Title.
ML420.029S43   1996
782.42162'13'0092—dc20
[B]   96-6340
CIP
MN

Book design by Dorothy S. Baker

FIRST EDITION
2   4   6   8   10   9   7   5   3   1

For Jack Henry Schumacher

Who never marched in the first place . . .

CONTENTS

ACKNOWLEDGMENTS

This book has been a long and, at times, difficult journey, beginning in the late seventies, when I began to collect clippings with the hope of writing a Phil Ochs biography, and ending nearly twenty years after Ochs' death, when I was finally able to finish the task.

However, for as much as I wanted to write this book, it never would have happened had it not been for a strange conversation that I had with two very dear friends.

I will always remember it vividly.

It was early in 1992, and I was sitting in the All-State Cafe on New York's Upper West Side with Carol Edwards and Amelie Littell, two people who had worked closely with me on my Allen Ginsberg biography. I had brought along photographs for the Ginsberg book to show them, and, as the hours stretched on and I had far too many cigarettes and glasses of beer, I began to bemoan the state of publishing. There were so many books crying out to be written, I complained, sounding every bit the misunderstood author. I started rattling off examples, some of which were actually discussed for more than a sentence or two.

"The book that I *really* want to write," I informed them, "is a biography of Phil Ochs. Unfortunately, it's the kind of book that will never get published."

Both women reacted instantly. They knew someone who would want the book, they said. Carol grabbed my manila envelope of Ginsberg pictures and jotted down the name of a publisher and editor. I knew nothing about either, but I promised I'd call. I did, and that's where this book landed.

All this, of course, is a lengthy but very necessary way of thanking two people who are very important to me. Amelie and Carol: Thanks for this and much more. I love you both.

———

I am extremely grateful to the members of the Ochs family for their cooperation and encouragement. It couldn't have been easy for them to backtrack over some of the painful memories, or to deal with my persistent demands for more time and information. Each family member honors Phil's memory in his or her individual way, and all saw that this came through, clearly and immediately, whenever we talked or met.

Sonny Ochs, Phil's sister, sat through countless interviews and telephone conversations, going over point by point, detail by detail, with unflinching honesty and patience. In addition, she helped me line up interviews, blessed me with photos, and even let me use her guest house as a base of operations when I was conducting interviews in upstate New York.

Michael Ochs, Phil's brother and archivist extraordinaire, also sat for numerous interviews and helped me connect with other sources, as well as providing me with valuable photographs. Michael's considerable knowledge of the music business proved to be invaluable, as were his many tapes of Phil's interviews, concerts, and previously unreleased songs.

Meegan Ochs, Phil's daughter, generously permitted me the use of her father's journals and notebooks, as well as many of the previously unpublished photographs included in this book. One of my fondest memories in the writing of this book will always be the day I spent at her home, going through Phil's scrapbooks and clippings collections, seeing some of his possessions (such as his trademark cap and gold lamé suit), and hearing Meegan's thoughts about her father.

Alice Ochs, Phil's former wife, was generous with her time, even though she was initially reluctant to go back over the years that she was hoping to keep behind her. A religious woman who has come to peace with herself and her life, Alice overcame her reluctance and was obliging in providing me with valuable information.

Thank you, all. I hope that you will find this book worth your time and efforts, as I hope that your disagreements with me—and there are bound to be some—are minor.

In piecing together Phil's life, I traveled all over the country and conducted hundreds of hours of interviews. Some of the interviews were actually cathartic in nature, allowing people to express emotions that had been bottled up for nearly two decades. There was a lot of laughing and crying and, in some cases, vocal asides to Phil as if he were actually sitting in the room with us, listening in on the conversations. Never, in all my experiences as a journalist and biographer, have I seen so many people react with such passion when discussing a person's life. This, I take it, is the ultimate measure of Phil's own passion, and the effect it had on others.

My gratitude, then, to: Stew Albert, Peter Asher, Guy Carawan, Len Chandler, Ramsey Clark, Ron Cobb, Lola Cohen, Paul Colby, Sis Cunningham, Henry Diltz, Peggy Duncan, Josh Dunson, Deni Frand, Erik Frandsen, Ian Freebairn-Smith, Allen Ginsberg, Jim Glover, Bernie Grundman, Arlo Guthrie, Sam Hood, Lee Housekeeper, David Ifshin, Erik Jacobsen, Danny Kalb, Paul Krassner, Jack Landron, Harold Leventhal, Jay Levin, Robin Love, Larry Marks, Lincoln Mayorga, Jack Newfield, Robin Ochs, Odetta, Van Dyke Parks, Tom Paxton, Carol Realini, Jerry Rubin, Pete Seeger, Patrick Sky, Larry Sloman, Steven Soles, Studs Terkel, Dave Van Ronk, Mayer Vishner, Cora Weiss, Doug Weston, Andy Wickham, and Jerry Yester.

Special thanks to poet/musician Ed Sanders, whose award-winning liner notes to *Chords of Fame* initially prodded me into exploring Phil's life, and who generously supplied me with clippings and notes he might have used for a biography of his own. Ed's love for Phil lives in his generosity and free spirit.

Thank you, Sammy Walker, for the interview, tapes, and the photograph. When Phil took you under his wing, he saw not only a talent at work, but a kindred spirit who would protect him during difficult times and in the decades following his death.

Arthur Gorson: Beneath your soft-spoken voice lies a toughness that has allowed your survival in a very trying business. I honor your modesty and gentility, which somehow seem to keep you on the level.

When traveling, I was put up (and put up with) by a number of people, many of whom are listed elsewhere in these acknowledgments. I would like to thank Allan Gumbinger, Mike Lovely, and Chris Tunney for their help in California, and Mark Gumbinger for helping to arrange it. My good friends Peter Spielmann and Judy Hansen provided me with a place to stay in New York.

A tip of the hat to other important people, who helped me in large and small ways: Dona Chernoff, Ken Bowser, Dawn Eden, Al and Diane Schumacher, Ken and Karen Ade, Jim Sieger, Glen Puterbaugh, and Simma Holt. Thanks to agents Kim Witherspoon and Maria Massie for all their patience and understanding, and to the staff at Hyperion, for helping see this book into print.

Last, but certainly most important, my love and gratitude to my wife, Susan, and to my children, Adam, Emily (the big Phil Ochs fan in the family), and Jack Henry, for enduring the usual hardships associated with the writing of a biography. You are the people who make all this worthwhile.

Michael Schumacher
March 13, 1996

During the Civil War, a company of singers and entertainers known as the Hutchinson Family moved from Union camp to Union camp, entertaining the troops.

The group had started out as a quartet nearly two decades earlier, and over the ensuing years had expanded to include other family members, their offspring, and various hangers-on. Highly regarded for their musical excellence, the group was even better known for its commitment to the abolition of slavery, as well as to other human rights issues considered radical at the time, including equal rights for women. Much of this material managed to make its way into their performances. To the Hutchinsons, the message was as important as the music.

This approach drew harsh response from some critics, who felt that the Hutchinsons would better serve their audiences by concentrating on music and leaving the editorializing to others. Wrote a reviewer for the Philadelphia Courier in 1846: "It is really time that someone should tell these people, in a spirit of friendly candor, that they are not apostles and martyrs, entrusted with a 'mission' to reform the world, but only a company of common song-singers, whose performances sound very pleasant to the great mass of people ignorant of real music."

Such criticism had no effect whatsoever on the Hutchinsons, who openly acknowledged the controversial nature of their performances, and who made no effort to tone down the political content of their material. If anything, they used the controversy to help sell tickets to their shows.

The group continued to play their topical songs when they per-

formed for the Union troops, enraging soldiers and officers alike with songs that protested warfare in general or, more specifically, President Lincoln for not being a more effective leader in the fight against slavery. After one particularly powerful appearance, the Hutchinsons were summoned before a Union general, who informed them that they could no longer play in front of his troops. The decision was upheld by General George McClellan, who opposed the abolition of slavery to begin with.

The flap was eventually brought to the attention of Lincoln himself. The president was given copies of the songs deemed too incendiary to be sung before the troops. Lincoln read through the material and issued his own proclamation on the Hutchinsons' music.

"It is just the character of song," he declared, "that I desire the soldiers to hear."

PROLOGUE

They came together to honor a life.

Five thousand people—friends, family members, fellow musicians, fans, hangers-on, the media, and the curious—all filing into Madison Square Garden's Felt Forum for what promised to be at least some type of closure to a life that had been so promising yet which had ended so abruptly. Although the event was taking place only a few weeks after the young man's death, there was more of a festive air to the occasion than a sense of mourning. This was a grand re-union.

Phil Ochs,* the folksinger, activist, and, sadly, reason for the gathering, would have loved it, had it occurred under different circumstances. He had always been a catalyst—much more so than a leader—and he loved nothing more than the knowledge that his passion and energy had driven others to action.

And here were the people in his life, greeting each other like long-lost friends—which, in fact, they were. The Movement had sunk several years earlier, its rudder crippled in the bloody streets of Chicago during the 1968 Democratic National Convention, its structure sustaining irreparable damage from the cynicism of the Nixon years, wherein government officials grasped frantically for justification for the murder of four students at Kent State, a CIA-backed overthrow of the government in Chile, and the comic nightmare of Watergate. The Movement had listed heavily for several years—an awkward, unsalvageable vessel—and then it had disappeared unceremoniously

* Pronounced "oaks."

beneath the waters of apathy, its few survivors manning lifeboats, but seeing no rescue ships on the horizon.

The sight had broken Phil Ochs' heart, and from such despair came the loss of his sense of purpose and creativity, his voice, and, perhaps worst of all, the combination of romanticism and determination that had pushed him forward even when things seemed bleak and out of control. Unlike the others, he had been incapable of adapting and moving on.

He had been only thirty-five when he took his life.

———

People hugged and kissed, exchanged pleasantries, caught up on the recent events in each other's lives; some spoke quietly about what, if anything, could have been done to save Phil's life. Abbie Hoffman, still on the lam from police, had somehow managed to slip unnoticed into the hall and sat quietly, sporting the world's worst disguise, hoping to be recognized by everyone except the Law. Allen Ginsberg, wearing Phil's ludicrously tacky gold lamé suit, sat backstage and went over the speakers' carefully prepared texts, tightening grammar and phraseology, making certain that the historic occasion would not be marred by improper prose. Melanie, the folksinger who had made a good first name for herself at Woodstock, tried to amuse her two-year-old daughter with a pet ferret. People wondered aloud, more often than was appropriate, about the whereabouts of Bob Dylan, Phil's friend and Greenwich Village contemporary, and Joan Baez, who had taken home her fair share of loot from her cover of Phil's "There But for Fortune." Jim Glover, Phil's old Ohio State roommate, hooked up with his former wife, Jean Ray, for one final performance as Jim and Jean.

The scene brought back memories of Phil's greatest moment as an organizer, achieved less than two years earlier in this very same hall. Angered over the overthrow of Chile and the murders of President Salvador Allende and folksinger-poet Victor Jara, Phil had put together his ultimate protest, an evening of song and rhetoric condemning the United States' involvement in the coup. The evening's music, bogged down by heavy backstage drinking, had been barely passable, and the speeches, like so many political speeches, tended to be a bit winded, but the fact that Phil had been able to pull it off had been a miracle in itself. Ironically, the success of the event had also hastened his downfall, since he could come up with no way to follow it, either on a personal, creative level or in another large-scale show.

Unfortunately, as his friend Jerry Rubin insisted, it had taken his death to bring everyone together one last time.

For most of his life, Phil Ochs had succeeded through sheer will-power—that, and a forceful personality that could, in turns, be charming or infuriating.

Critics never could understand his success. If you applied the strictest musical standards to his talents, his guitar playing was marginal, and his voice, although pleasing enough—especially in comparison to the fashionably rough-hewn sounds of his contemporaries—sounded far from professionally trained. Yet he had recorded seven albums and performed before SRO audiences at some of the country's finest venues, including Carnegie Hall.

The songs had carried him through. The sincerity of his lyrics, along with the passion of their delivery, more than compensated for Phil's musical shortcomings, and for a while, when topical songs were the rage of the folk scene, Phil Ochs had ranked at the top of the list. He was a classic troubadour, singing the news of the day and applying an editorial spin that urged his audience to get off their hands and move. He hated pretension and hypocrisy, and no political party or philosophy was exempt from his commentary. He could ridicule liberals for paying lip service to their causes as easily as he could rail against the conservatives for dragging their feet when society demanded change.

Politically, he had been anything but a weekend warrior. He had gone to the Kentucky coal mines in support of the underpaid and overworked laborers; he'd risked his personal safety when he had traveled to the Deep South during the voter registration drives. He had spoken out early against the war in Vietnam, and as the conflict dragged on, he had organized or attended countless rallies, sacrificing paying gigs in exchange for gratis appearances at demonstrations. He had been present at the official birthing of the Youth International Party, and he had sung "I Ain't Marching Anymore," his best-known protest anthem, in Chicago's Lincoln Park during the Democratic National Convention.

To no one's surprise, Phil's hard-nosed politics, coupled with his popularity as a performer, caught the FBI's attention, and throughout a career that spanned nearly a quarter-century, the Bureau kept close tabs on Phil's whereabouts, thickening his file with regular updates on his activities, informing other government agencies of the threat that he posed to the common good, and tapping his phone. For those more inclined to live in the real world, Phil was a menace only to the paranoid. In fact, a good portion of his charm, especially in his younger days, could be attributed to his tendency to listen as much as he spoke, to laugh as often as he erupted in anger. He tempered his reality with the political instincts and humor that his adversaries lacked.

———

One by one, the speakers at the memorial took the podium and sang Phil's praises. Ramsey Clark, the former attorney general who had known him and defended him in his dark final days, spoke of Phil's commitment to political and social causes, calling him "a driven man" and wondering aloud about what inspired him to live the difficult life of the activist. Stew Albert, one of the founders of the Yippies, spoke directly to Phil, noting "the world's a little more hypocritical without you"—a sentiment underscored when William Kunstler read Phil's poignant and often very funny testimony from the Chicago Conspiracy Trial. Sonny Ochs and Michael Ochs, Phil's sister and brother, offered biographical sketches tracing his footsteps from his boyhood in Ohio to his rise to the top as a topical singer-songwriter. Emotions ran high, and the music—from Dave Van Ronk's moving rendition of the standard "He Was a Friend of Mine" to Jim and Jean's haunting interpretation of Phil's "Crucifixion"— upped the ante. The evening honoring Phil's life and music was inevitably shaded by a touch of sadness. No one had been afforded the chance to say goodbye, and as a result, people were making their final declarations.

Phil's final year or so had been so horrific, so lacking in grace and dignity that people could only wonder what on earth had happened. What had reduced him to a pathetic street creature wandering around New York, occasionally barefoot and covered in his own filth, often threatening the people he came across? Was it mental illness, alcoholism, a combination of both? It was common knowledge that he was manic depressive and a heavy drinker, but others had suffered similar conditions and walked away alive. Why had he self-destructed?

Perhaps he took his life because, as one of the country's most enthusiastic movie buffs, and as one who often viewed his own life as if it were taking place onscreen, he had the misguided romantic notion that suicide was the only noble ending to a script he had been given to work with. Perhaps he took his life because he had wandered into a darkened corridor from which there was no exit or return to light. Perhaps . . .

Reasons were unimportant.

Phil Ochs ceased to exist, first in his own mind, and then in reality. In the end, there were too many blank calendar pages in his datebook, in the past and in the future.

"So many people have tried to analyze the reasons behind his death," his sister wrote in the memorial concert's program notes. "There's nothing to analyze. He literally could not bear living anymore so he chose to go to sleep. At least he left us a legacy—all the meaningful songs he managed to create while he was with us."

The best of his songs were played at the memorial, but, appropriately enough, it was Phil who managed to steal the show when, with the stage darkened, he was heard singing "Changes," one of his most beautiful ballads, over the hall's sound system. During those few minutes, when his softly lilting voice filled the arena, people were reminded of what was lost and what would be missed.

————

After the memorial, people partied at The Bitter End in Greenwich Village. The get-together lasted until the evening's darkness had passed and the sun was beginning to hit the New York streets again. People got pleasantly drunk, and stories of better days were freely traded.

Phil would have loved that, too.

BOOK ONE

I'm Going to Say It Now

---

*"Ah, but in such an ugly time,
the true protest is beauty."*

—PHIL OCHS

Chapter One

BOY IN OHIO

GERTRUDE OCHS yearned for her native Scotland and the privileged life of her youth, yet for some horrible reason, as if she were being punished by a batallion of angry gods, she had been sentenced to endure her second pregnancy in Columbus, New Mexico.

As far as she was concerned, Columbus was the penultimate stop in the American move westward toward oblivion, the kind of hicktown you'd read about or see in the movies. No one seemed to be doing anything. Townfolk clutching sweaty bottles of Coca-Cola would gather at the general store for the main event of the day—the arrival of the mail truck. On one occasion, when she returned home from a trip to town, Gertrude found a rattlesnake coiled on her front porch; fortunately, her screams brought along a neighbor, who shot the snake as casually as he might have shooed a fly from an apple pie cooling on a windowsill.

Gertrude blamed her husband for her predicament. Two years earlier, Jack Ochs, with his medical degree and his flowery talk of life in America, had sweet-talked her into leaving her homeland. How could she have known what lay ahead? Two of her closest friends in Scotland, Heddy and Dinah, had married American doctors and were living the good life in the States. How could she have suspected that it would be any different for her?

But Jack was nothing if not different. Not only had he struggled to establish a practice in this godforsaken country, but he also had suffered the horrible misfortune of being drafted into the army and shipped off to a CCC camp in New Mexico. Gertrude and their daughter, Sonia, born three years earlier in Scotland, had traveled with Jack to their new home in the Southwest.

In Gertrude's mind, one thing was absolutely certain: she would not be bearing her second child in Columbus. It was bad enough that she had been dragged to the outer reaches of civilization, but she would not hear of having a baby in anything but a proper medical facility, which, in this case, meant traveling to a larger city. The only nearby candidate to meet the expectant mother's qualifications was El Paso, Texas, so in December 1940, with her baby's delivery date rapidly approaching, Gertrude packed a suitcase with books, candy bars, and a single nightgown, and left for the city. She would be on her own, staying in a hotel, until the baby arrived.

Her first son, Philip David, was born on December 19, 1940.

————

Jacob "Jack" Ochs, despite his wife's feelings to the contrary, was actually a product of the American Dream realized, at least to a modest extent. Both of his parents' families had immigrated to the United States in the late-nineteenth century, both coming from the same town, Mlawa, in Russ-Poland. Both families settled in New York City, where some of the Old World traditions could be maintained while the new immigrants settled into a different way of life.

It wasn't easy. Fanny Busky Ochs, Jacob's mother, would never forget the hardship of her early years in America. The entire family— Fanny, her parents, and her four sisters and two brothers—were crowded into a two-room railroad flat on Manhattan's Lower East Side, living on next to nothing and sleeping wherever they could find the space. While Fanny's father tried to eke out a living as the proprietor of a small grocery store, Fanny's mother tried to hold things together at home, taking care of her children while making hats or sewing clothes to supplement the family income. Fanny would recall that her wardrobe consisted of two dresses, one that was worn when the other was being washed, and on her one and only day of school in America, she was ridiculed by her classmates when she turned up without shoes. ("I suppose I looked like something that came from a tree," she reflected, "so they had a good laugh.") She never returned to school, and would never learn to read or write in English.

Instead of attending classes, Fanny went to work, doing whatever she could to earn extra money for the family. For a while, she baked bagels and sold them on the street; she also helped her mother sew hats. The day-to-day trials made her tough and self-sufficient. Although she was barely five feet tall as an adult, she could make it instantly clear, with no room for discussion or argument, that she was not a person to be lightly regarded.

Her future husband, Joe Ochs, was a strong contrast. At nearly six-foot-four, he towered over Fanny, yet he was very quiet and gentle—the kind of individual not given to fighting or raising his voice. This nature of his proved to be beneficial after he and Fanny were married in 1898. Fanny, the dominant force around the house, would order Joe around in even the tiniest of matters, with very little protest from her husband. Joe might come downstairs in the morning, announce that he intended to make scrambled eggs for breakfast, only to hear his wife insist that he soft-boil them; the next morning, Joe would start the water to boil eggs, only to have Fanny chide him for not scrambling them. Joe would simply shrug and take out the skillet.

Jacob Ochs, born in 1910, was the youngest of his parents' four children. At age four, he moved with his family to Arverne (Rockaway Beach), where the Ochs family enjoyed its first home—a brand-new frame house for which Joe Ochs paid the princely sum of four thousand dollars. Joe was justifiably proud of this turn of events: he had no education, very little job training, and had been raised in poverty, yet he had worked himself into the position where he could afford a reasonably good life for his family. He had invested the money he'd earned from his store in Manhattan into a small grocery store and bungalow-building business on Rockaway Beach, and he was holding his own in the business when he moved his family in 1914.

Jack inherited his father's easygoing personality, which definitely set him apart from his two older brothers, David and Sam, who were as hard-nosed as their mother. Unfortunately, Jack had not been handed his father's ambition, and there was very little discussion of his making a career in the bungalow business. Instead, he and his sister Eva would be the first family members to attend and finish college, and with their degrees, both would be afforded opportunities to work as professionals. To someone like Jack, a dreamer if ever there was one, the education was a mixed blessing. He would not have to work with his hands like his father and brothers, but he was also being saddled with the responsibility that accompanied the investment in his degree. He figured, fairly early on, that he would do best as a doctor.

After attending pre-med school at the University of Virginia, Jack was disappointed to learn that he couldn't get into any American medical schools; the quotas for Jewish students had been reached. Undaunted, Jack decided to attend medical school overseas. The University of Edinburgh in Scotland was friendly to Americans wanting to earn medical degrees. Jack's decision to go to school there proved to be fortuitous, at least in terms of his meeting his future wife. Harry Phin, Jack's closest friend at the university, had an older sister that he wanted Jack to meet.

———

For as long as she could remember, Gertrude Phin had been accustomed to the finer things. Her father, George, owned two highly successful tobacco shops in Edinburgh, and he had parlayed his earnings into the kind of life that would see that his wife and five children would never want for a thing. The family lived in a ten-room stone mansion, complete with live-in maid's quarters and a parlor that was never used. Four huge bedrooms, each with its own fireplace, occupied the top floor.

Despite such material wealth, life at the Phin household was less than ideal. George was a cold, domineering presence, rigid in the rules that he set and not given to displays of affection toward his wife and children. Little power plays were the order of the day. When, for instance, it was time for the children to receive their weekly allowances, George would make them stand around and wait until he was finished with a meal or otherwise inclined to dispense the money. Proper behavior was expected at all times.

When Gertrude met Jack Ochs, she was less than impressed. The American, by her estimation, might have been pleasant enough, and there was no doubting that he was a natural-born storyteller, but he lacked the social graces to which she was accustomed. Jack, however, was not to be easily discouraged. He liked his friend's older sister and was determined to win her over. It didn't hurt, either, that Gertrude's parents found Jack agreeable and considered him a good match for their daughter.

Jack regaled the family with tales of New York and America, using his charm to embellish his stories about how his parents owned a string of bungalows by the sea, and how he was going to make a big success of himself as a doctor with his own practice. Gertrude eventually subscribed to Jack's stories, and the two began to plot out the details for their marriage and eventual move to the dream life in the United States that Jack so eagerly described.

They were married on June 24, 1936, and Sonia was born in April 1937. The newly wed mother soon determined that raising a child was not something that came naturally to her. Children could be time-consuming and demanding, and Gertrude, who could barely take care of herself and couldn't cook even the most basic of meals, resented the imposition of having to look after her daughter by herself while her husband was doing his internship in York, England.

In time, the young family boarded a ship for America, Jack with his medical degree, Gertrude with the hope that her life would square itself away in the new land. Neither could have predicted the many turns that would dictate the direction their lives would take.

———

Gertrude was angry and bitterly disappointed when she realized that her life in America was going to be dramatically different from the one she had envisioned. When Jack had spoken of his parents' owning bungalows, Gertrude had pictured exquisite cottages by the sea—the kind she had seen in Scotland—not modest frame units that looked like all the other houses around it and that seemed to be located in the middle of nowhere. When Jack earned his medical degree, Gertrude had anticipated instant success and wealth, not a protracted struggle to establish a practice in post-Depression America. Feeling trapped and betrayed, Gertrude took out her frustration on her husband, berating him as a failure and criticizing his every move around the house.

Upon moving to the States, the Ochs family moved into an apartment in Manhattan, near Seventh Avenue and Fourteenth Street, and Jack found work in one of Manhattan's medical facilities. Then Jack received his call from Uncle Sam. Fierce battles were being fought in both Europe and the Far East, and while American politicians debated over the wisdom of entering the century's second world war, the country's armed forces were gearing up, preparing for what seemed to be inevitable. When the Japanese bombed Pearl Harbor less than two weeks before Philip's first birthday, the family knew that Jack would be in the army for some time to come.

By the time Jack was shipped overseas, the family had grown accustomed to a rather nomadic existence. After a stay in Columbus, New Mexico, Jack had been transferred first to San Antonio, and then to Austin. To Gertrude, who had been raised in rock-solid stability, the moving around represented just another reason to question her marriage to this strange American doctor. For Sonia, there was the challenge of meeting new sets of playmates and learning new terrain. On her first day of kindergarten, she got lost walking home from school and had to be rescued, frightened and sobbing on the street curb, by the ice cream man. Although not gravely affected by the changing locales, Philip had other changes to deal with during this period: a younger brother, Michael, was added to the family in 1943.

Before departing for the war in Europe, Jack moved his family back to New York. Gertrude would need help in raising the children, he decided, and he could think of no better place than with his parents. Little did he know that Gertrude would find life with his mother to be the ultimate confinement, or that his and Gertrude's early years together, trying as they were, would prove to be the least difficult years of his marriage.

———

Jack was sent to England, where he was to await further assignment.

So far, his time in the service had been, at the very best, a mixed bag. During his years of training, Jack had done little to endear himself to his superior officers. He was a bit too moody and rebellious for his own good, and though these traits were not of the sort to get him drummed out of the army, they did cost him the opportunity to gain a decent officer's commission. In addition, when he did finally find himself up for promotion, Jack shrugged off the opportunity, refusing to fill out the paperwork necessary to assure his move up.

There was a reason for Jack's erratic behavior, though it wouldn't be determined until much later, after he had been hospitalized, given a battery of treatments (including shock treatments), and finally diagnosed as being manic depressive. In the army, he was seen as being eccentric—and not always unpleasantly so. In England, he was nicknamed "Charlie"—short for "Goodtime Charlie"—because of his buoyant personality. His paycheck would arrive, and Jack would spend it as if a time limit had been imposed on the contents of his wallet. Nights out with the boys, fine liquor and food, new clothing— Jack would enjoy life to the hilt, only to have to scrimp for the rest of the month to make ends meet until the next paycheck. Then it came time to repeat the procedure . . .

His darker side emerged when he was called upon to apply his medical skills to the fodder of war. Working on soldiers injured in the Battle of the Bulge proved to be a hellish task, and seeing the day-to-day carnage had a profound effect on the good-natured doctor. In no time, he was as shell-shocked as the young men on the battlefront, his depression leaving him hard-pressed to concentrate on his duties. In time, the army realized that he had become another war casualty and, in November 1945, a deeply troubled Jack Ochs was issued an honorable medical discharge and shipped back to the States. He had been in the service for nearly five years.

———

Jack's absence had been rough on his wife, if for no other reason than because Gertrude found life with her in-laws—and particularly Fanny—to be more unbearable than life with her husband. As a guest of Jack's parents, Gertrude had no choice but to accept the ways of the household, which was not always easy. Fanny could be both demanding and critical, and contending with her, as well as trying to raise three children without the physical presence of their father, was difficult for Gertrude. At one point, all three children came down with the chicken pox, one after the other, which was immediately followed by individual cases of the measles. Gertrude was all but imprisoned in the house, looking after her children's needs, unable to escape the constant hectoring of her mother-in-law.

After Jack's return, the family moved to a house in Far Rockaway. The Ochses celebrated Christmas 1945 amidst packed boxes of belongings, a small Christmas tree perched atop the kitchen table, and the presents piled underneath. It wasn't much, but at least they were all together again, living in their own house and looking to the future.

The reunion was short-lived. Jack needed psychiatric treatment, and he had barely unpacked when he was off to a hospital on Long Island. It would be his home for nearly two years.

The long-term effects of his father's absence on Philip, coupled with the many changes of homes that he would go through during his childhood, can never be accurately determined, but there is no doubting that Philip was markedly different from his older sister and younger brother. Sonia and Michael were cheerful and gregarious, both capable of easily making new friends and adapting to the changes of scenery. Philip, on the other hand, was naturally shy and tended to be withdrawn even among his own family. Making new friends was exceedingly difficult and, as a boy, Philip would never have more than one friend at a time. In school, he was quiet and inattentive, more inclined to wander the landscapes of his own imagination than to pay attention to anything a teacher might have to say.

In February 1947, with Jack still gone, Gertrude decided to take her children for an extended stay with her family in Scotland. Traveling by boat in the middle of winter made for a long trip. Philip, Sonia, and Michael filled some of their hours by playing on the ship's deck, which had been glazed by frozen sea spray, their footing made delightfully precarious by the combination of icy floorboards and the pitching ship. The games were brought to an abrupt halt one day when Philip lost his balance and slid across the deck toward the edge of the ship. At the last second, he latched onto a volleyball net that had been left at the side of the deck. As an adult, Phil Ochs would use the imagery of the sea in a number of his songs, but his initial introduction to it as a six-year-old was anything but romantic.

He would also hold a chauvinistic attitude toward Scotland in his later years, though there is very little evidence to indicate that his six months in the country were especially memorable. Every morning, he and Sonia took a bus to the Liberton School, a tiny schoolhouse located just outside of Edinburgh. Philip would carry his books in an old music case his mother had used as a child, and it was not uncommon for him to leave his books behind, either at school or on the bus, his absent-mindedness driving his mother to near distraction.

"He was a dreamer, with a capital D," his sister remarked many years later, noting that this characteristic remained consistent through adulthood. As a child, Philip would lose his school books; as an adult, it would be his wallet. When he began to wear glasses, Philip would lose or break them with a regularity that proved to be humiliating to his mother.

"My mother had bought him glasses at Sears," Sonny* recalled, "and they had some kind of policy in which you were insured if the glasses were lost or broken. It got to the point where my mother was downright embarrassed to walk in because they had replaced or repaired so many pairs of glasses. She felt guilty and wanted to pay, but they wouldn't let her."

Teachers could be equally exasperated with Philip's spaciness. He generally earned good grades, but his instructors were hardpressed to understand why; he never seemed to be paying attention to anything going on in class.

One particular teacher—a Miss Jocelyn—eventually exploded in frustration. She had taught Sonia a few years earlier and deemed her to be a model student, which only meant that Sonia had fallen in step with her teacher's strict, traditionalist approach to learning. Philip, on the other hand, was different; he didn't listen or participate in class. Miss Jocelyn complained about this to Sonia, and to prove her point, she summoned Philip's sister to her classroom one day.

"I cannot stand it anymore," she said, obviously at wit's end. "I cannot teach your brother."

Sitting in the back of the room, Philip stared out the window, oblivious to Sonia's presence in the classroom.

"I'll show you what the problem is," Miss Jocelyn continued. "Philip," she called out.

The youngster did not respond.

"Philip!" she called out in a louder, more insistent tone.

Philip continued to stare off into space.

"PHILIP OCHS!" she shouted at the top of her lungs.

"Huh?"

Miss Jocelyn turned to Sonia.

"I want you to go home and tell your mother that I cannot stand it anymore," she said. "He's this way all the time."

Sonia dutifully reported the incident to her mother, but they both realized that there was no changing the boy. He was incorrigible.

* Sonia began calling herself "Sonny" when she was about twelve years old. She held onto the nickname throughout her life.

———

For a dreamer like Philip Ochs, the ultimate parallel universe was a darkened movie theater and a Western double feature. In the world of cinema, life was as uncluttered and black-and-white as the giant heroic images projected onto the screen. In the real world, life could be complicated and sometimes painful, even for the good guys; in the movie theater, justice always prevailed.

Philip's interest in movies began innocently enough: whenever she needed a babysitter, or just wanted some time to herself, his mother would send him and Michael to one of Far Rockaway's three movie theaters. The boys watched movie after movie, never tiring of the action pictures, taking in as many as nine movies a week. Philip loved *The Count of Monte Cristo, King Kong,* and any movie featuring John Wayne. To Philip, John Wayne—and, to only a slightly lesser extent, Audie Murphy—symbolized everything that America stood for.

Movies quickly became the most important activity in Philip's life. Anything connected to the movies drew his instant attention, from the films themselves to his sister's movie magazines and posters. Whenever he went to the movie theater, Philip brought along his Kodak Brownie camera and took pictures of the theater's marquee; he even attempted to shoot photographs of the movies as they played on the big screen. He collected scores of movie-star postcards that he could purchase for a penny in vending machines.

The obsession would last a lifetime. As an adult, he would attend thousands of movies, quite often as many as three or four a day. Friends marveled at his ability to remember not only titles, release dates, plots, directors, and stars, but seemingly every minor detail connected with every film he saw. Not surprisingly, he often saw dramatic events in his life as if they were scenes in a movie and he was the film's protagonist. Movies gave him his first exposure to the idea of celebrity, and even in his youthful years, he knew that this was a status he wanted to attain.

———

After his release from the hospital, Jack Ochs tried to start a private medical practice in Far Rockaway. He put together a small office and, anticipating extra work if someone happened to step on a piece of glass or other sharp object, he hung a shingle near the beach. Patients, however, were hard to come by.

Life was even tougher at home. Gertrude continued to badger him relentlessly, criticizing his inability as a doctor, husband, and father. At this point, Jack and Gertrude's marriage was totally loveless. Neither showed the slightest affection for the other, and the two slept in separate beds, prompting their children to joke as adults that their parents were either blessed with three immaculate conceptions or had actually had sex a grand total of three times over the course of their marriage. The only thing keeping the two together was Gertrude's uncompromising belief that divorce was simply out of the question.

On a typical day, Jack would come home from work, eat dinner, and immediately retire to his room, where he would either read in bed or go to sleep. Contact with his children was held to a minimum. Every so often, he might take Sonny to a track meet or baseball game, but this kind of bonding was nonexistent between him and the boys, who never showed any interest in sports. As a rule, Jack preferred to keep to himself.

"My father was almost like a phantom," Sonny explained, remembering her father as more of a fixture than a living being around the house. "He was there, but he wasn't there." Significantly, when Sonny and Michael, as adults, were asked what the two of them might have inherited from their father, both offered identical responses: "Nothing."

Jack eventually gave up the hope of practicing medicine in Far Rockaway, and after inquiring about employment opportunities in area hospitals and clinics, he found a job working in a TB clinic in Otisville, a tiny community in upstate New York. Rather than relocate his family, Jack packed his bags and moved alone. Given his state of mind and his problems with his wife, the decision must have felt like an escape.

———

If Gertrude Ochs made one lasting impression upon their children, it was the emphasis she placed on confronting the truth. Throughout their lives, Sonny, Phil, and Michael would be candid to the point of being unsettling, no matter how difficult it was to face up to the truth.

On occasion, Phil's honesty could make him look naive, as if he didn't realize that being forthright could cause him trouble.

However, there was one occasion when he could not bring himself to own up to the truth.

He had just turned nine. The family was going shopping in Jamaica, Queens, and Philip, not wanting to go along, asked if he could stay home. His parents agreed. To amuse himself during their absence, Philip repaired to his mother's clothing closet, which also housed the cardboard box with all the children's toys. The closet was dark, so Philip, unable to find what he was looking for, struck a match to shed a little light on his search. The flame caught the bottom of a piece of Gertrude's clothing, and before he knew what was happening, Philip had a fire going in the closet. He ran to the kitchen, filled a pot with water, and tried to dowse the fire. When this failed to extinguish the flames, Philip tried to think of someone who could help him. He had been expressly forbidden to talk to strangers, and the only people he knew in the area were his former next-door neighbors, who were now living a block away, on Rose Street. Philip ran up the alleyway to their house, let himself in, and reported the fire to the family's teenage daughter. The daughter immediately called the Fire Department, and firefighters were still at the scene when the Ochs family returned from their shopping trip. When questioned about the fire, Philip denied having anything to do with it, claiming he had no idea how it had started—a story he would stand by for years to come.

The fire turned out to be one of very few eventful moments in an otherwise passive childhood. Like his father, Philip preferred to spend his time alone in his room, and on those occasions when he was around Sonny or Michael, a squabble always seemed to take place. Philip would tease or pick on Michael, who was physically incapable of defending himself in a fight, and he thought nothing of taking advantage of his younger brother in other ways. Philip especially enjoyed trading toys with Michael because he knew he could always bargain to his advantage. Sonny, who resented the interest that Philip charged whenever he loaned her money, would jump to Michael's aid, and before long the three would be going at it, infuriating Gertrude with their incessant fighting and teasing.

If he was around, Jack bore the brunt of Gertrude's frustration.

"Take these goddamn kids out of here so I can have some peace and quiet," she'd order her husband, virtually on a weekly basis. Jack would then gather the kids in the family car and take them for long drives in the countryside, giving Gertrude time to cool off. On other occasions, Jack would take them out on his own, using the time for rare moments with his children.

Over the years, the evening meals became a study of how dysfunctional the family really was. Gertrude loved to read, and she insisted on bringing a book to the dinner table with her. That, however, was only the beginning. She also demanded silence while she read, so the typical Ochs family dinner would find four people—or five, if Jack was present—sitting at the table and reading books or comic books, the entire meal taken in silence, unless, of course, the kids were fighting among themselves, which was not at all uncommon.

———

In June 1951, the Ochs family moved from Far Rockaway to Perrysburg, a tiny rural town in upstate New York. Jack had moved on to another job in another TB clinic, and this time he took his family with him. Phil spent a year attending a three-room schoolhouse before he was shipped off to nearby Gowanda, where a larger, central school was located. It was here that he began his musical training.

Gertrude believed that her children would benefit from music lessons, and she urged them to select an instrument to study. Sonny picked the piano, which she learned to play efficiently; Michael chose the saxophone, and Philip decided to go with the clarinet.

"He was incredibly gifted," Michael said of his brother. "I took the saxophone and was good at it, but then he picked it up and topped me in a week. He was so much better that I quit right away. He was a natural."

At first Philip was less than enthusiastic about taking any instrument, but in no time he was attacking his musical studies with a passion that bordered the fanatical. Every day after school, he would head straight to his room and practice for hours, running through his scales over and over, the family dog positioned at his feet and howling along with him. Before long, the endless repetitions unnerved the entire family.

"It was absolute torture," Sonny insisted, noting that such behavior was in keeping with her brother's obsessive nature. In fact, as Sonny recalled, the persistent practicing led to a humorous episode a year or so later, when Philip decided to supplement his musical knowledge by learning to play the drums. The family lived in a four-unit apartment complex at the time, and when Gertrude casually mentioned to her downstairs neighbor—who happened to be married to the assistant director of the hospital where Jack worked—that Philip was thinking of taking up the drums, she received a firm, unenthusiastic response.

"Over my dead body," the woman told Gertrude. "If he's going to learn drums, he's going out in the woods. He's not doing it in that apartment. A person can take only so much."

Nothing ever came of Philip's interest in drums; mastering the clarinet kept him busy enough. He was a standout on the instrument—so much so that he quickly surpassed other students who had been studying it for years. His technical skills went unquestioned, but even more important, he showed a remarkable gift for interpretation. Each year, Philip would go to Fredonia State Teacher's College, where he would have his musical skills professionally analyzed, and every year he would earn A's for his individual performances. "You have exceptional musical feeling and the ability to transfer it on your instrument is abundant," commented one judge, who encouraged Philip to continue his studies.

In just over three years' time, Philip's progress on the clarinet was so remarkable that his teacher, Mr. Navarro, was genuinely upset when the Perrysburg TB hospital closed down and Jack was forced to look for work in another city. Students like Philip didn't come along often, and Navarro wanted to see him through the school term. It would be in her son's best interests, the instructor told Gertrude, if Philip remained behind and finished his course of study. Philip could stay with him. Gertrude, of course, disagreed.

It was December 1954, and the family was off to another part of the country—to Columbus, Ohio, and still another TB hospital.

———

By then, Sonny was no longer living at home. Gertrude had received a modest inheritance when her mother died, and in an effort to provide more poise and polish for a daughter she considered to be too tomboyish, Gertrude sent Sonny to a finishing school in Switzerland. Sonny loved living in rural New York, and she never forgave her parents, first, for sending her to Switzerland against her wishes, and, second, for moving while she was away.

Meanwhile, in Ohio, life followed its familiar pattern for the Ochs clan. Jack took a job at the local TB hospital, the family found an apartment on the hospital grounds and ate the same food served to the patients, and the boys were enrolled in a small country school.

As an adult, Phil Ochs would retain fond memories of his time in Columbus. The city, fairly small in those days, was especially uninhabited on the outskirts of town, where the Ochs family lived, and life was an uncluttered slice from Rockwellian Americana. Philip loved to take his bicycle on long rides down Alum Creek Drive, a rural stretch of road that seemed to accentuate the area's natural beauty. Many of his classmates were country kids who didn't report to school until after the October harvest, and who left school for spring planting.

As one might expect, Gertrude found the scene totally unacceptable. Their apartment, placed in the midst of a hospital complex, an old-age home, and a cemetery, was a far cry from serenity. Jack was again going through a manic phase, manifested by his fighting with the hospital's head nurse; from past experiences, Gertrude could tell that he was not long for his job. As for the boys . . . well, there had to be something better than a country-bumpkin school offering little more than nineteenth-century educational standards.

Gertrude was especially appalled when Philip came home with a friend who appeared to embody everything she disliked about the area. With his unkempt hair and sloppy clothes, Dave Sweazy was anything but the kind of boy Gertrude would have preferred her son to be hanging around with. It didn't matter that this was Philip's first close friend; Sweazy seemed so uncultured to Gertrude that the best she could muster for him was pity.

Philip ignored his mother's objections to his new friend. After years of staying off on his own, having occasional, but never especially close friends, Philip had come across someone he could talk to for hours on end—a buddy who shared his enthusiasm for going to the movies or for just hanging out. Philip enjoyed having Sweazy over at the house as a dinner guest, or for long conversations in his room. Significantly, he took a number of photographs of Sweazy, and on one occasion posed with him in a dimestore photo booth; the pictures were then added to Philip's scrapbook of movie marquees and film stars—an honor bestowed upon no other friend to that point.

Sweazy made an important contribution to bringing Philip out of his shell. After moving to Columbus, Philip had continued his training on the clarinet, studying at the Capital University Conservatory of Music and achieving the unheard-of status of principal soloist in the college orchestra by his sixteenth birthday. Despite his talent and membership in the orchestra, Philip was never really a part of the group. At school, he continued to stay away from the crowd, distinguishing himself in neither academics nor athletics. If anything, his occasional playground fights established him as a moody figure. With Sweazy, Philip could be himself and be accepted for it.

Unfortunately, the friendship was short-lived. Gertrude had every intention of extracting her sons from the small school they attended, and she told Philip and Michael that they would be transferring to the Columbus Academy the following school year. When Philip balked at the notion, Gertrude countered with the suggestion that he come up with an alternative. Phil mulled it over, and after seeing an advertisement in the *New York Times Magazine*, he announced that he wanted to attend the Staunton Military Academy in Virginia's Shenandoah Valley.

As far as Gertrude was concerned, Philip wouldn't be leaving soon enough, especially after his latest bit of mischief with Dave Sweazy. The two had been to another Western playing at the movie theater, and afterward, inspired by the onscreen gunplay, Philip decided to check out his own quick-draw capability with a Sweazy family pistol. The gun went off, and Philip was fortunate to escape with only a flesh wound in his leg.

Philip, Gertrude concluded, might be better off elsewhere.

———

In retrospect, it seems ironic that Phil Ochs, who made "I Ain't Marching Anymore" his signature song, could have enjoyed military school as much as he did. However, he was anything but a rebel when he departed for Staunton, Virginia, in the fall of 1956. If anything, he needed to find a compromise to his conflicting needs of both fitting in and setting himself apart from his classmates.

As he later admitted, he was nothing more than a confused teenager.

"I had no idea what I was going to be," he said. "I was just an American nebbish, being formed by societal forces, completely captivated by movies, the whole James Dean, Marlon Brando trip."

In some respects, military school was an ideal environment for

Philip. All students were subject to the same rigid rules and schedules; everyone marched to the same beat, awoke to the same bell, and could commiserate with each other when academic life became too structured or oppressive. Since he was extremely shy around girls to begin with, Philip found that he could walk more freely in the all-boys school, where guys could be guys without the added distractions of the opposite sex. It was easier to fit in when one was literally living with one's classmates. Guys spoke in a shorthand, hung out together, pulled pranks and stunts, formed their own society. In Staunton, Philip shortened his name to "Phil"—indicative, perhaps, of his new, freer spirit.

Phil found small ways to distinguish himself. Although he had always been awkward and uncoordinated in athletics, he discovered that he enjoyed lifting weights and could hold his own in the weight room; classmates nicknamed him "Mr. Universe." He was also a member of Staunton's marching band, but this proved to be a disappointment. Wearing a uniform and marching in formation offered absolutely no opportunity for creativity, and as the months passed by, Phil considered dropping clarinet entirely.

His attention was now directed to another type of music—the kind being broadcast by a nearby country radio station. Phil loved the voices of Faron Young, Ernest Tubb, Webb Pierce, and Lefty Frizzell, who offered emotional impact in their deceptively simple phrasing. The same could be said about Johnny Cash or Hank Williams, who appeared to have arisen straight from the masses. Then there was Elvis Presley, who filtered every sound that was truly American through a voice that came from an uncharted place and served it to a public thirsty for something new. In Phil's eyes, Presley truly was the King.

For Phil, the music was more than just a casual pleasure; it quickly became another obsession. He listened to it nonstop on his radio. He hummed or sang along. When he returned to Ohio for summer vacation, he bought records at the local record shop and argued about his musical discoveries with Michael, who was also interested in music, though he preferred rhythm and blues to the country-flavored music that Phil liked. Phil entertained the notion of being a singer himself someday.

The family, by now all too familiar with Phil's obsessive nature, humored him, although Gertrude was bothered when Phil talked about giving up the clarinet, for which he had proven talent, and becoming a star, which seemed so far removed from the real world. At one time, Gertrude had listened to a young man's visions of grandeur; now, two decades and numerous problems with her husband later, she knew reality well enough to map its course.

Phil had no idea how he would attain the stardom that he talked about, but he was sensible enough to acknowledge that he would do well to continue his education after his graduation from high school. Ohio State, the local Columbus campus, was a logical choice.

———

Besides his passion for music, Phil had cultivated a strong interest in writing during his two years at Staunton. When the academy sponsored a short-story writing contest for its students, Phil entered "White Milk to Red Wine," a brief yet very effective vignette that took the contest's ten-dollar second prize:

> I had never been so worried in all my life. When I got out of bed that morning a cold sweat came over me. I knew I had to fight him sooner or later, and today was it. He had bullied me so often, and now I had finally reached my breaking point. If a person is stronger than others, he doesn't have the right to pick on people smaller and weaker than him.
>
> He insulted me in front of my friends. I had to make a stand. In a moment of anger, I challenged him to a fight the next day after lunch. When he accepted, he threw back his head and laughed cruelly.
>
> I went to school the following day feeling like David when he went to meet Goliath. Unfortunately, I had no slingshot to cover me. My morning classes seemed to pass too quickly and the lunch I ate had no taste. When I walked towards the meeting place, I knew how a condemned man feels as he walks the last mile. All of a sudden a hand gripped my shoulder. I spun around and there he stood. The only difference was that the triumphant look was gone from his face. He stammered nervously and said that he didn't mean to pick on me, and that he didn't want to fight.
>
> With a sigh of relief I agreed, and we walked back to the school to spend another routine kindergarten afternoon.

The story, with its dramatic presentation and O. Henry–like surprise ending, gave some indication of the artist and person Phil Ochs would become in the future. Phil would always see a much larger picture framed in everyday events, and in "White Milk to Red Wine," he viewed his confrontation with the schoolyard bully as symbolic of the struggle between smaller, weaker people and their tormentors. Further, in citing the David-and-Goliath Bible tale, he acknowledged that his story was hardly new. Nevertheless, in making a passing reference to the epic struggle, he added impact to the ironic, humorous ending.

As an adult, Phil would integrate similar elements of drama and irony in his songs. The idea of showing courage in the face of tough opposition would become a personal credo motivating his political activism and topical protest music.

Of main importance, for the time being, was the recognition that the story brought Phil. After being raised in a household where he had to struggle to be noticed, he had moved away and discovered that he could be honored for what he had to say. For an aspiring star, this was a small but considerable start.

———

Phil had never been comfortable with his physical appearance. He had a long nose, weak eyes, and ears that stuck out too far; his lack of athleticism had left him with a soft yet gangly frame. He realized, as a result of his mother's constantly carrying on about other people's physical appearance, and especially in comparison to his collection of movie-star pictures, that he was, at utter best, plain in his appearance, and he believed that he had to do better if he could ever hope to stand out in the public eye.

His weight-lifting regimen at Staunton had put him on the right track. Contact lenses helped, as did a brand-new, brushed-back, and longer hairstyle. Despite these improvements, Phil was dissatisfied. Something had to be done about his nose.

Shortly after his graduation from Staunton, Phil told his mother that he wanted corrective surgery. He wanted to start college with a new look, and he wanted to give himself at least a decent chance to succeed in whatever he would eventually be doing. Gertrude was not inclined to go along with such foolish vanity, and it took some convincing on Phil's—and, eventually, Sonny's—part to change her mind, but the surgery was finally done. The procedure might have been unnecessary, but there was no doubting that the new Phil Ochs looked better than the old one. After a childhood spent in the background, he was ready to step forward and make his mark.

Chapter Two

THE SINGING SOCIALISTS

OHIO STATE did not agree with Phil Ochs. The studies were challenging, and he found it difficult to make new friends. There had been more comradery among the students at Staunton, a greater sense of unity; at Ohio State, students applied themselves to their individual courses of study, their thoughts geared to future careers.

When Phil enrolled at the Columbus campus, he had no idea what his eventual major would be. He still hoped to find a way into the entertainment field, perhaps as an actor or a singer, but these were not necessarily the kind of careers that one prepared for at a university. There was no specific curriculum for stardom.

After a semester of taking general courses and spending lonely nights in his dorm, Phil decided he'd had enough. College, he reasoned, was a waste of time and money, at least for the time being; he ought to be checking out the real world.

With this in mind, Phil closed out his first semester, took a leave of absence from the university, and told his parents that he was going to head down to Florida to look into the prospects of earning a living as a singer.

This was not the kind of news that Gertrude hoped to hear. By all indications, Phil was turning out to be just like his father. Jack could never settle down or hold a job. He'd been fired from his job in Columbus and had taken another one in Cleveland, hauling Gertrude and Michael to Cleveland Heights in the wake of his decision. He never seemed focused, never able to find his place and grow comfortable with it. Like Phil, Jack had briefly pursued a youthful fantasy. As a teenager, he had left home and roamed around the South for several months, trying to establish himself as a prizefighter. He

had returned home, whipped and penniless. Phil, Gertrude concluded, was destined to similar failure. He was the proverbial chip off
the old block.

Gertrude had good reason to be concerned. Phil's plans for Florida were half-baked. Indeed, he had been collecting records and listening to the radio with such burning enthusiasm that he now knew
the lyrics to scores of popular songs, but he had no formal training
as a singer and could not accompany himself on an instrument. He
had no connections to help him find work in the South, nowhere to
stay while he was trying to establish himself. He had little to rec-
ommend him for *any* kind of job.

Nevertheless, Phil was adamant about going, even when his
mother warned him that the family would not support him while he
was pursuing his foolhardy ambitions. Phil packed his bag and, in
late February, caught a bus to Miami.

————

He had no sooner set foot in Florida than he was picked up for va-
grancy and sentenced to fifteen days in the county jail. To Phil, who
tended to romanticize some of the events of his life as if they were
scenes in an epic motion picture, the jail time was one big adventure.
He was passing his hours with real people, receiving a better education than he could have ever expected back home. The sheriff failed
to share such enthusiasm. As far as he could tell, Phil was just a
clean-cut Midwestern kid completely alone and out of his element,
and there was no telling what effect the other prisoners would have
on him. To isolate Phil from the others, the sheriff gave him a number
of odd jobs to do, including the task of washing his car every day.

The two weeks passed and Phil was back on the streets, in no
better shape than he had been in prior to his arrest. He still had no
job or place to stay, and his efforts to find work as a singer were
predictably dismal. He picked up a couple of jobs, one selling shoes
and another washing dishes, but neither lasted for more than a few
days. He grew sick from the lack of nutrition; his gums bled from
pyorrhea. He finally gave up, called home, and asked his mother to
send the money he needed for return fare to Cleveland.

Had he never become famous for his antiestablishment stance,
Phil's fiasco in Florida might have been written off as a harmless,
youthful mistake—little more than a case of poor judgment. Unfor-

tunately, the FBI would eventually use the arrest as evidence of Phil's criminality, as proof of his instability, as if sleeping in the park had set him off on the road to becoming a clear and present danger to the state.

———

In the heyday of the Beat Generation, when young people on college campuses across the United States wore black and affected a look that they felt jumped straight from the pages of Kerouac and Ginsberg, Phil Ochs was as collegiate as they came, conservatively dressed and always smiling, ending many of his conversations with a cheery "see you around campus." When he began his second semester at Ohio State in the fall of 1959, his attitudes were still relatively straight-laced, his interests still geared more toward the movies than the political goings-on in the world.

All that was about to change.

Prior to enrolling for fall semester classes, Phil shopped around for an off-campus place to live. He found a boarding house on East 15th Avenue in Columbus, and moved in a week before classes began. Phil shared a room with another student, who was none too pleased to see Phil set up his portable record player, stock it with rock 'n' roll and country records, and plop back onto his bed, ready to listen to the music for hours on end. As at home, Phil covered the walls of his room with posters of Elvis Presley, John Wayne, and other heroes, and he showed no inclination whatsoever to clean up after himself. He had no sooner moved in than his roommate started looking for a way out.

One day, early into the school year, a tall, lanky student strolled by Phil's room and, seeing the door open, paused to listen to the music coming from the record player. As usual, Phil was sprawled out on his bed, listening to Elvis. The student introduced himself as Jim Glover.

Like Phil, Jim was a music aficionado, but his tastes were quite different. Whereas Phil liked songs for their stories, Jim listened to songs for their messages. Jim loved the dust-bowl ballads of Woody Guthrie and the politically charged songs popularized by Pete Seeger and the Weavers. Phil knew very little about this kind of music, but Jim's passion for it convinced him that he ought to give it a listen. In addition, Phil was excited to learn that Jim could play guitar and banjo, and that he could sing a wide range of folk and country songs. The two became instant friends, and in no time Jim had replaced Phil's disgruntled roommate at the boarding house.

Jim loved debating politics as much as he liked listening to or playing music, and this interest quickly rubbed off on Phil. Other than a casual interest in the McCarthy hearings, Phil's parents had never shown much enthusiasm for politics. Phil had picked up a basic interest in politics on his own. Like many Americans, he had been captivated by the news reports of Castro's revolution in Cuba, and the larger-than-life Cuban leader represented to Phil a real-life hero in the tradition of his gunslinging matinee idols. Phil read whatever he could find about the revolution, and by the time he met Jim Glover, he could speak with some authority about the events that had taken place so close to the American shores.

Phil spent a lot of time at Jim's parents' house, and he particularly enjoyed the many hours that he, Jim, and Jim's father spent at the dinner table, discussing the issues of the day. Jim's father, an Ohio State alumnus, was as political as they came. An open Marxist, Mr. Glover represented a radical voice quite alien to Phil, and he heard plenty about the investigations of the House Un-American Activities Committee, red-baiting, unionism, and Joe McCarthy. Mr. Glover claimed to know Gus Hall, one of the top-ranking Communist Party officials in America, and he loved to lecture the boys on the oppressed masses and his personal vision for a greater, left-leaning future. Phil took it all in, totally impressed by the man who seemed to know so much more about the important things going on in the world than his own family.

Phil offered his own contributions to the discussions. He had done his homework on the Cuban revolution, and could hold his own whenever the talk turned to Castro's plans for his country. According to Jim Glover, "Phil knew more about Castro and Cuba than my dad did. My dad knew about the persecution of people—of the associations in the country that the government was trying to spy on, the McCarthy period. But he really didn't know much about Castro. He didn't know anything more about Castro than anyone else who reads the papers. But Phil did."

Back at the rooming house, Phil and Jim would discuss politics late into the evening. Although he never read much other than the daily newspapers, Phil now skimmed over books of political philosophy and history, going through texts like a student cramming for an exam. He proved to be a quick study. The United States was preparing for another presidential election, and Phil watched with great interest as the battle lines were drawn between conservative incumbent Republicans, represented by two-term Eisenhower vice-president Richard Nixon, and the decisively more liberal Democrats, to be represented by either Hubert Humphrey, the former mayor of Minneapolis and current senator from Minnesota, or by John Kennedy, the young, charismatic senator from Massachusetts. Phil was delighted when Kennedy seized the Democratic Party nomination, and he and Jim Glover bantered back and forth about the prospects of Kennedy's winning the general election in November.

Jim didn't see Kennedy as having much chance. "I wasn't really too familiar with Kennedy at all," he confessed years later, long after history had run its course and Kennedy had become one of American history's great success stories. "I thought Nixon would definitely win because he had the experience."

Phil disagreed, so much so that he proposed an unusual wager: he would put fifty dollars on Kennedy if Jim would bet his Kay acoustic guitar on Nixon. It didn't matter that Phil was in no financial position to lose the bet, or that he couldn't play guitar. He had every intention of winning, and when he did, he would talk his roommate into teaching him how to play.

———

Returning to Ohio State on the rebound from his disaster in Florida turned out to be an ideal scenario for Phil. This time around, he was much more comfortable on campus, much more prepared to focus on academic endeavors. He excelled in his classes and made himself a familiar figure around campus. To a large extent, this change could be attributed to his conversations with Jim Glover and his father: for the first time in his life, people were listening to what he had to say and taking his opinion seriously. After growing up in a household where all three children would jockey to be noticed—even if it was negative attention garnered from misbehavior—Phil was being treated seriously by his peers.

Thus encouraged, Phil pushed himself to a higher level of campus activity. He helped organize and participated in student affairs, including protests against mandatory ROTC training and the way student government was conducted at Ohio State. He talked politics nonstop with fellow students. Most importantly, he began to write.

Editors of *The Lantern*, the Ohio State student newspaper, and *Sundial*, the campus humor magazine, discovered that Phil was a bundle of opinions, especially on politics and music. With his manic energy, he could jump from topic to topic with no effort at all, and, better yet, he could witness events, analyze them, and write about them at a speed uncommon to other students, whose outside interests and extracurricular activities hindered them from making daily deadlines. In short, editors could see Phil as an ideal candidate to work at *The Lantern* or *Sundial*.

Or so they thought.

Unbeknownst to these editors, Phil also harbored a self-destructive side—one that would never permit him to be satisfied with the status quo. Like his father, Phil was destined to be a wanderer, never content with minor gains or successes, always looking for more. In the beginning, however, he was happy to work for *The Lantern* and *Sundial*, and he applied himself to the task with his customary zeal. To remain close to the action, he moved out of the rooming house and back to a campus dormitory, staying in Steeb Hall with many of his fellow reporters. Journalism became more than just a potential major; it became a way of life. A newshound unsurpassed, Phil studied newspapers with the enthusiasm of a theologian poring over Holy Scripture, reading and taking notes on the events of the day, his commentary making its way into the many pieces that he turned out for *The Lantern* and *Sundial*.

Phil would write on a wide variety of topics in the months ahead, from politics to the arts; he contributed articles on student affairs and government, as well as reviews of concerts and plays. His loose, conversational style—a strong suit later in his life, when he was on-stage and chatting between songs—was ideal for his *Sundial* pieces, regardless of whether he was writing about local appearances of the Kingston Trio or Limeliters, or sending up campus politics in biting satirical sketches. For the *Lantern*, he stayed closer to straight journalism, conforming to a style practiced by the rest of his peers. Either way, his opinions were always close to the surface.

In time, Phil became one of Ohio State's most prolific writers, but he was still dissatisfied. He had far too many ideas for the available creative outlets. In addition, his opinions on some issues were far too radical for his *Lantern* editors, who advised him to tone down his commentary. Phil's continuing defense of Castro and the political affairs of Cuba made his editors and fellow reporters quite nervous, not simply because of political differences of opinion, but also because funding for *The Lantern* originated from highly conservative sources.

Angered by the opposition to some of his ideas, Phil looked for other journalistic outlets. He wrote letters to the editors of the daily newspapers in the area, though this was only a partial success, since there were limits to the number of letters he could publish in any given period of time. In frustration, he started his own newspaper, *The Word*, a sporadically released publication designed to print material deemed too controversial for *The Lantern*.

Phil's friendship with Jim Glover led to one other major outlet for his opinion—a venue he would have never dreamed possible just a few years earlier, when he was playing clarinet and marching in formation at Staunton.

He could speak through his music.

———

Upon winning his election bet with Glover, Phil had talked him into teaching him how to play the guitar. Ironically, Phil did not take to the instrument as quickly as he had learned to play the clarinet or his brother's saxophone, and while his playing on the guitar was average at best, Phil would never treat the instrument as anything other than a means of accompaniment, existing only to complement his voice and ideas.

Jim taught Phil a few basic folk songs, and before long the two were playing together, Jim on banjo and Phil on guitar, Jim harmonizing with Phil's singing of the lead melodies. The two worked well together. Phil learned quickly, picking up new chords and chord progressions almost every night, applying small creative flourishes to compensate for his rudimentary skills on guitar. His voice was pleasing enough, even if it did tend to rise from his throat rather than his diaphragm, creating a natural flutter that future record producers would try to minimize on his recordings. Fortunately for Phil, his vocal weaknesses were easily neutralized by Jim Glover's exceptional harmonies.

As would be the case throughout his life, Phil's main talent was his ability to write songs. His bottomless well of ideas, already evident in his journalism, supplied him with the basis for countless songs, and Phil had barely learned to play the guitar when he began to write lyrics and apply them to folk-influenced tunes that he could make up on the spot. Each newspaper headline seemed to provide the grist for a new song, which Phil would put together and present to an approving Jim Glover.

Boosted by his confidence in his newfound musical abilities, Phil quite naturally started to consider a way to apply them to his long-standing hopes of entering the entertainment field. Folk music, though far from the rage it would become in a year or two, was becoming popular in the area, on campus and in several folk clubs starting up in the Cleveland area, and Phil fancied the idea of making a name for himself. Folk music, he believed, could be both artful and informative.

In no time, he was forging a scheme for a "can't miss" folk duo. As Phil saw it, he would be the brains of the operation, writing songs and overseeing the duo's business affairs, while Jim, with his great voice and good looks, would provide the onstage appeal. Phil outlined his plans to Jim on a number of occasions, his enthusiasm overwhelming any of Glover's skepticism, and the two agreed to give it a shot. Pointing to the heavy political content of their material, Jim suggested that they call themselves The Singing Socialists.

Phil loved it. The idea of the "Singing Socialists" resonated with echoes of Joe Hill and the Wobblies, Woody Guthrie's work songs, Pete Seeger and the Weavers, and the battles against McCarthyism. Phil hoped to follow the same path, as well as continue the tradition of the news-singing troubador. His first two songs had been an angry diatribe against the Bay of Pigs invasion and a caustic commentary on Billy Sol Estes, a Texas millionaire recently involved in a price-fixing scandal.

The part-political/part-chip-on-the-shoulder stance played well on campus, where Phil and Jim found a built-in, sympathetic audience for their impromptu concerts, or at parties thrown by friends. The two were a study of contrasts, Jim loose and affable, never quite taking the music too seriously, Phil somber and entirely focused, playing each song as if it had the power to change people's minds and move them to action.

The differences were never as apparent as when the Singing Socialists were enlisted to play at a private party hosted by a powerful Republican family in Columbus. Phil had set up the engagement—

more than likely without letting the party's hosts in on the precise nature of the duo's material. After singing several numbers, Phil and Jim were approached by an angry guest who demanded to know if they were communists. The confrontation made Jim nervous, but Phil shrugged it off. "Well," he casually told Jim, assuming his posture of always knowing what was best for the duo, "we gotta make waves."

There was a limit, however, to how many waves the Singing Socialists could make, and Phil recognized as much. One could raise all kinds of hell when playing in private, but there were limits to how far you could go if you intended to perform in public.

Such was Phil's argument when, without warning, he decided to change the duo's name just prior to a Singing Socialists appearance at a local talent show. Sensing that a good showing in the competition might lead to an engagement or two in some of Cleveland's folk clubs, Phil suggested that he and Jim call themselves the Sundowners, the name originating from a Robert Mitchum film. Jim had no objection to the new title, and so, without fanfare or public notice, the short career of the Singing Socialists sank below the horizon, never to rise again.

———

Despite his interest in commercial endeavors, Phil never compromised his politics, in either his music or his journalism. In fact, his political stance grew more radical as time went on. The editors of *The Lantern*, bothered by Phil's positions, pulled him from all political stories—a decision that did not sit well with Phil, who was clearly one of the better writers on the paper, and whose opinions could now be published only if he submitted a formal letter to the editor. Rather than force the issue, Phil fulfilled his other assignments for the paper, hoping that his compliance, along with his talent as a journalist, might earn him the position of editor-in-chief of *The Lantern* during his senior year.

He and Jim Glover continued to work on new material for the Sundowners, practicing in the basement of Phil's parents' house and playing sporadically in public, usually for a handful of students hanging out on campus. Phil managed to maintain his grades, but Jim was beginning to struggle. For both, academics were almost beside the point.

Getting established was difficult. The popularity of the Kingston Trio had spawned all kinds of imitators, and encouraged countless teenagers and college students to pick up guitars and learn folk songs. Competition was fierce, even for nonpaying gigs. Phil and Jim would turn up at clubs like the Sacred Mushroom or Larry's, listen to their contemporaries or better known national acts such as the Journeymen or the Country Gentlemen, and occasionally step on-stage for a few numbers of their own. Any opportunity to be seen and heard was important.

The Sundowners' big break presented itself when they auditioned for a paying, headlining gig at a new Cleveland coffeehouse called La Cave. The coffeehouse's management was looking for new, inexpensive entertainment, and college kids like Phil Ochs and Jim Glover were just the type of act they were seeking. The Sundowners performed well during their audition, and they were hired to work on a probationary basis: they would play a weekend at La Cave—the club's *opening* weekend—and if they received a decent response, they would be asked back for another weekend.

This was all that Phil needed to hear. He was certain that the Sundowners would overwhelm management and audience alike with a repertoire of standard folk songs and original tunes; all he and Jim needed to do was polish their act and firm up a solid set list.

Jim, true to form, was nowhere near as worked up as Phil about the La Cave engagement, so when Phil gave him a new song and asked him to learn it overnight, Jim failed to see the urgency in Phil's request. Jim figured that he had plenty of time to learn the song. Such reasoning, he regretted to learn, was incorrect. The next day, when Phil dropped by and wanted to rehearse the song, and Jim told him he hadn't even looked at it, Phil flew into a rage and declared an end to the Sundowners and his friendship with Jim.

At first, Jim was unconcerned. Phil had a way of blowing things out of proportion, especially in matters political or musical, and Jim was convinced that Phil would eventually cool off and come around. Phil could be stubborn, but there was no way that he would jeopardize their first big chance—or so Jim thought. The days passed and Phil held his ground. Nothing that Jim did could mollify him—not the conciliatory words, not the matching shirts that Jim purchased for the Sundowners' professional debut. On the evening of the first scheduled performance, only Jim showed up at the coffeehouse, and he and Phil were promptly fired by the managers of La Cave. As a performing outfit, the Sundowners had gone under faster than the Singing Socialists.

The duo's demise had little effect on Phil, who fully believed that he could make it on his own as a solo act. He had his songs, his guitar, and very little use for Jim Glover. He was anything but shattered when, a short time after the La Cave fiasco, his former best friend called to inform him that he was leaving Ohio State and taking off for New York, where he hoped to build a career as a folksinger. As far as Phil was concerned, Jim Glover was history.

———

Phil would face even greater disappointment within a few months, but for the time being he busied himself with the task of lining up his own club dates. Most places weren't at all interested in signing on either expensive or bargain-rate headliners, even if the singer could boast, as Phil could, of writing original material; too many unknown talents were willing to work for free. After being turned down by a number of club owners, Phil finally latched onto a week-long engagement at Faragher's, a Cleveland Heights club owned by performer Danny Dalton. The club was going through hard times and couldn't offer payment to its performers, but Phil, having exhausted his other options, was willing to work simply for the experience.

As a performer, Phil had a long way to go. His skills on guitar still needed improvement, and as a singer he was no better or worse than any number of other aspiring, unpolished young acts. What Phil had on the others was his undeniable enthusiasm and sincerity: it was virtually impossible for an audience not to be impressed by someone who put such effort into his work. Phil would walk onstage, stutter a few introductory remarks, often in a humorous, self-deprecating style, strumming his guitar to fill the quiet moments, and then he would be off, singing a repertoire of standard folk songs, with one or two originals sprinkled in for good measure. He tried so hard that he would inevitably win over an audience in a matter of two or three numbers.

Phil was ready to try anything to break through. In one of his most unusual career moves, he wrote a theme song for the Cleveland Indians baseball team and sent it to the local radio station that broadcast the team's games. Not surprisingly, the tape was returned, along with the kind of encouraging note intended to let the young songwriter down lightly.

"Your song shows a lot of originality and much fine spirit," the letter read. "It might make a fine specialty number. I would suggest that you send this tape directly to the ball club."

The song was never recorded.

Phil's association with Faragher's paid off in a big way. The club staggered through the early portion of the summer of '61, barely meeting expenses and finally suffering the indignity of having its electricity cut off. Dalton somehow managed to keep the club open, running operations by candlelight when he had to, and just when it seemed as if he had no alternative but to close its doors, he contacted Tom Smothers, an old friend, and asked if the Smothers Brothers would appear at the club as a personal favor. The Smothers Brothers, in Cleveland to tape a television show, were one of the fastest-rising new comedy acts in the country, and their appearance before an SRO crowd at Faragher's reversed the club's fortunes, giving it a badly needed shot of credibility. Suddenly, Faragher's was one of the most prestigious places to play in the Cleveland area.

Phil opened for the Smothers Brothers, as well as for other well-known acts playing at the club that summer, including the Greenbriar Boys, Judy Henske, and the Knob Lick Upper Ten Thousand. For Phil, the exposure was minimal, usually involving his playing a couple of songs before introducing the headliners, but the contacts that he made were important. In time, he would become good friends with Judy Henske and Erik Jacobsen, the latter a member of the Knob Lick Upper Ten Thousand and eventually the producer for such popular national acts as the Lovin' Spoonful, Tim Hardin, and Chris Isaak. Talking shop with these and other professionals meant a lot to a college kid with hopes of making his own name in the business.

"Everybody came through that particular summer," Phil recalled nearly a decade later, in a radio interview with Studs Terkel. "It was really a fantastic experience," he noted, "because I had literally only been playing guitar for a couple of months, doing these little ditties."

One performer spent extra time encouraging Phil that summer. Bob Gibson, a well-respected folksinger who had seen his career threatened by his political beliefs, was impressed by Phil's music and sincerity, and during his stint at Faragher's, Gibson went out of his way to take Phil aside and offer him the benefit of his experience. Topical songwriting was risky business, he told Phil, detailing his own problems finding work on television or radio as a result of the HUAC investigations. Not only could you find trouble when expressing unpopular beliefs, but doing so could lead to unrealistic results: friends and enemies alike would judge a person on the basis of the music alone, the friends pumping up the artist because they agreed with his political stand, the enemies trying to destroy him because they hated it. Neither was good for one's career, and both could have very negative effects on the artist.

Phil listened carefully to what Gibson had to say. It all rang true enough to him. In just a brief period of time, Phil had seen the effects of his political beliefs on others. Around Ohio State, he had attracted a small following of students who hung on his every word—people who were hearing his message but not his music. Conversely, he had already been penalized by the editors of the campus paper for his unpopular opinions. Neither side really understood him or knew who he was, any more than Jim Glover had been able to puzzle out his utter, uncompromising devotion to the self-discipline needed to make music.

Bob Gibson's influence on Phil went far beyond his words of advice; the two even collaborated on a couple of new songs. Gibson, Phil discovered, was a man of countless melodies, but he struggled with lyrics. This, of course, was no problem for Phil, who could write lyrics by the hour. Gibson carried around a tape of his favorite melodies, and after listening to some of the tunes, Phil set out to write lyrics for them. The final products—"One More Parade" and "That's the Way It's Gonna Be"—were more mature and fully realized songs than Phil's earlier efforts.

In the development of his songwriting and guitar-playing skills, Phil owed more than a passing nod to Bob Gibson's influence. If Jim Glover was Phil's teacher, Gibson was his first true musical mentor, even if their first encounter lasted only a few days.

"I don't think Gibson gets nearly the credit he should for being not *a*, but *the* seminal musical influence on Phil," noted Dave Van Ronk, another well-established singer and musician who would meet Phil a few months later. "I thought Phil was a very interesting extension of Bob Gibson. He really assimilated a great deal of what Bob was doing musically. Of course, he had harnessed all of this for his political commentary, which Bob never really was interested in doing.

It was marvelous that he and Bob collaborated on songs. It was like Bob collaborating with his political self, or Phil collaborating with his nonpolitical self. It was perfect."

————

Phil's senior year at Ohio State found him at a crossroads: he was obviously gifted enough to work as a journalist after his graduation, but he had also grown confident enough in his musical ability to seriously consider a career as a singer. He was now in demand at several of the local clubs, and he even mended fences with Jim Glover during one of Jim's return visits to Ohio, the two making a reunion appearance onstage at Larry's. Gertrude urged Phil to take the more responsible, stable route of the journalist, but Phil wasn't sure which way to go.

In the end, fate had as much to do with Phil's ultimate decision as anything.

When he began his final year of college, all that Phil had to look forward to, other than finishing his work for his diploma, was landing the editor-in-chief position at *The Lantern*. He was certain that his work over the past two years had earned him the title. What he didn't figure, however, was the bottom-line effect that his politics had had on the newspaper's editorial board. When it came time to choose the new editor, Phil was passed over in favor of someone with less talent but, more important in the university's eyes, a much less radical view.

Phil was crushed by the decision, and he could see no point in continuing to write innocuous reviews and profiles for the paper. He had something to say, and if he couldn't say it through his journalistic writings, perhaps he ought to look into something else. When he had been in Ohio visiting, Jim Glover had spoken of the modest success he was enjoying as a folksinger in New York. The brief Sundowners reunion had gone well enough for Phil to consider reviving the act in the country's biggest city. As Phil saw it, he had nothing to lose.

Gertrude, not surprisingly, disagreed. It was sheer folly, she argued, for Phil to be leaving school during his final quarter to pursue a dream that was bound to fail. What difference did a couple months make? Why not stay in school and graduate? Hadn't he learned anything from his miserable experiences in Florida? Had he no idea of the odds against his making a name for himself in the music business? What was he going to do when it all fell through?

Phil was hearing none of it. He dropped out of school, bought a one-way bus ticket to New York City, and headed out to what he felt was his inevitable future in show business.

Chapter Three

BOUND FOR GLORY

PHIL LOOKED UP Jim Glover as soon as he arrived in New York. Not only did he need a place to stay, but he was eager to resume the Sundowners partnership for what he hoped would be a long, successful run in the Greenwich Village folk clubs.

Glover, however, had gone through significant changes since he and Phil had parted ways, and he was in no position to resurrect their old Ohio State days. Almost immediately after moving to New York, Jim had met Jean Ray, a drama student from California. Jim ran into Jean when he dropped by the Cafe Raffio, one of the city's lesser known folk establishments, during his job search. Jean worked as a singer at the club, and after Jim was hired as a solo act, the two would practice together. They soon discovered that they operated more effectively as a duo, and a new stage act was developed. "Jim and Jean" quickly turned into one of the more popular folk acts in the area. A romance blossomed from the partnership, and the two were living together in Jean's tiny Greenwich Village apartment when Phil Ochs blew into town from the Midwest. Seeing that Phil had no place to stay, Jim invited him to move in with them.

Anyone else in Phil's position might have noticed that he was disruptive to his hosts' daily routine, but Phil was too focused on his own agenda to notice or care. It was going to be just like old times in Ohio, he insisted, and for a while it looked as if that was how things were going to turn out. Phil brainstormed with Jim until all hours of the night, showing him new songs, talking politics, and re-establishing their friendship. Phil had big plans for the Sundowners—plans that definitely did not include Jean.

Both Jim and Jean were at a loss over what to do about Phil.

When he had taken Phil in, Jim had figured that his guest would crash at their place until he found work and an apartment of his own, but as the days started to add up, Jim wondered if Phil was ever going to leave. He enjoyed having Phil around, but he was underfoot in such cramped quarters, and Jim worried when Phil ignored his often re-peated insistence that he was now a part of Jim and Jean, not the Sundowners. Jean, too, was fond of Phil, but she resented the way he monopolized her boyfriend's time. Phil was always hanging around, either at the apartment or at the Raffio, where he would show up to watch Jim and Jean at work. For some reason, Phil didn't seem to understand that things had changed. The apartment was not a college dorm room, even if, with two sloppy young men around, it was starting to look like one.

Jean gave the problem a lot of thought. One solution, she figured, was finding Phil a woman.

———

Under the usual circumstances, Jean's matchmaking plans might have been welcomed by someone like Phil, who was new in town and shy around women to begin with, but Phil had never shown much interest in women. He had rarely been seen in the company of a young woman while he was in high school or college, and as a young adult he showed very little propensity for establishing the type of lasting relationships with women that most men his age took for granted. Even later, after he had reached the pinnacle of his fame and might have found himself in the position to take part in the one-night stands enjoyed by so many performers, Phil generally avoided the traffic, prompting his manager at the time to joke that the only people attracted to him were the "Earth Shoe groupies."

Through Jean Ray, Phil met Alice Skinner, an attractive eigh-teen-year-old who, like Jean, attended the Sanford Meisner School and hoped to eventually act on Broadway. Alice had an apartment in the same building as Jim and Jean, and to complete the scenario of ever-crossing paths, Alice worked at the Raffio.

Phil and Alice were mismatched from the start. Alice had been raised by a wealthy aunt in Philadelphia, and had attended private schools, whereas Phil had come from a nomadic and struggling middle-class background. Alice had nowhere near Phil's education. Neither had spent much time in the real world.

"What you had here," observed Sonny Ochs, "were two basically good people who needed somebody to lead them. They were two followers looking for a leader, and neither one of them could lead. That was the tragedy of the relationship."

Phil certainly needed someone to direct him in matters of the heart. His work kept him totally occupied day and night, and most evenings, when Alice was in bed, hoping that Phil might just once spend a little time with her, Phil would be in the next room, sitting at the kitchen table and feverishly working on his next song.

Neither showed an interest or aptitude for domestic chores. Dustballs gathered in the corners of the rooms, newspapers accumulated into a sea of scattered or stacked sections of the *New York Times*. Stalactites formed in the freezer compartment of the refrigerator. Cockroaches were so abundant that Phil made a game out of suddenly turning on a light, attacking them with a fly swatter, and keeping a running tally of the body count.

Phil's sloppiness would always be a bone of contention between Phil and his family, and even Phil and his friends. At times, he seemed totally unaware or unconcerned about his personal appearance or hygiene—a problem that became more pronounced as time went on. Shirt buttons would go undone, and Phil's bare belly would peek out at people; his hair, naturally oily to begin with, would look downright greasy if he let too much time pass without washing it. None of it seemed to bother him. All that mattered was the music.*

Phil could not have planned a better time or place to take up his musical career: folk music was surging in national popularity, es-

---

* Anecdotes about Phil's sloppiness are plentiful, but one particular story not only illustrates this aspect of his character, but also acts as a poignant commentary about the nature of Phil's relationship with another contemporary—Bob Dylan.

"We were in the apartment," a friend recalled, speaking of a time later in Phil's life, "and Phil was looking for something. He started emptying his pockets onto the couch and it was repulsive. It was shit—dirty, filthy garbage—coming out of his pockets. I started commenting on it: 'How could you be such a pig, such a slob, so filthy?' Dylan was there, and he started screaming at me, telling me to shut up and not put him down: 'How can you talk this way to Phil? He's an *artist*. Artists can't be thinking about what they have in their pockets.' Dylan stuck up for Phil tremendously."

pecially on the East Coast, where it had taken a stronghold in New York City, as well as in the Boston-Cambridge area. There were the inevitable disputes between older, hard-line purists and the new, younger camp of singers, and from the debates came a greater range in music, best typified, perhaps, in the differences between two of folk music's rising stars—the sweet-voiced, traditional-sounding Joan Baez, who had drawn national attention during her carefully orchestrated debut at the 1959 Newport Folk Festival, and Bob Dylan, the young singer-songwriter from Minnesota, who had arrived in New York in 1961 with tall tales about his past, a voice so rough that it appeared as if he were trying to sing badly, and a gigantic talent and presence that belied his age and experience. Baez had a manager and recording contract, and she performed on college campuses and at the higher-paying New York clubs such as the Village Vanguard; Dylan, though establishing an enormous reputation among his peers, was still struggling to break through, playing in the smaller Village outlets and backing better known folk and blues acts.

Bars and clubs featuring folk music were popping up all over the Village, especially around the coffeehouse strips on MacDougal and Bleecker Streets, where NYU students flocked to pass inexpensive hours of conversation and entertainment. The names and owner-ships of the clubs would change—the Fat Black Pussycat became the Commons, the Cock 'n' Bull became the Bitter End—but just-in-town folkies and tourists alike knew how to find such establishments as the Cafe Wha? or the Gaslight. On any given night, you could hear some of the best new performers just by hopping from club to club.

When Phil Ochs hit town, one of the most coveted establishments to play was a bar and restaurant known as Gerdes Folk City. Like many of the clubs in the Village, Folk City had an illustrious history, complete with a rise to prominence that, in retrospect, seems purely accidental.

William Gerdes, the original owner of the place, had run a suc-cessful restaurant on West Third Street in the first half of the twen-tieth century, his patrons coming mostly from the surrounding Italian and German neighborhoods. Over the passing decades, the long-established ethnic configuration changed, and the neighbor-hoods along with it, and by the time Gerdes decided to sell his business, the area around the restaurant had deteriorated badly and the octogenarian owner could no longer depend upon his old clientele to support him. He sold the establishment in 1952 to Mike Porco, his brother John, and Joe Bastone, a cousin of the Porcos. All three were Italian immigrants.

With his thick Calabrian accent and Old World values, Mike Porco would have fit well into the neighborhood several decades earlier. He had a natural gift of gab, along with a true empathy for the hardships of the working stiffs living in the neighborhood. He managed to maintain a good business for several years after buying Gerdes, but the changing times were imposing new demands. The city had condemned much of the property in the area, and residents were forced to relocate when the heavy equipment was brought in to knock down the old, decaying buildings—all to be replaced by new high-rises. It was obvious to the owners of Gerdes that the restaurant would never survive in its present location.

Porco looked around and found a place at 11 West Fourth Street—a nineteenth-century brownstone that had once served as a spray-gun factory. This, he decided, would be the site of the new Gerdes. Business, however, continued to sag, and in an effort to pick up new customers, Porco obtained a cabaret license and hired bongo players and small jazz combos to cater to the weekend beatniks that flooded the Village. Unfortunately for Porco, the heyday of the Beat Generation was rapidly fading, and he had to find a new form of entertainment to save a restaurant that was barely scraping by.

The answer to his problems arrived late in 1959, when Porco was approached by two young men with a compelling proposition. Israel G. "Izzy" Young, who ran the Folklore Center a short distance away, on MacDougal Street, and Tom Prendergast, a local businessman, were looking to stage folk nights in Greenwich Village, but they needed to find a regular location for these concerts—a place similar to Gerdes. There was a burgeoning interest in folk music, they told Porco, and all he had to do was run his bar and restaurant; they would take care of booking and paying the talent. Porco would be able to keep the profits from what was sure to be a lucrative bar business, and the two entrepreneurs would keep whatever was left from the gate receipts after the acts had been paid. Young suggested that Porco rename the club the "Fifth Peg"* to attract the folk crowd. Porco complied, and the new business opened in January 1960.

* The "fifth peg" is in reference to the tuning peg on a banjo.

The plan worked. Young and Prendergast booked some of the best talent around, and once word about the club began to circulate, Porco found himself serving large, thirsty crowds. His bar business thrived. Young and Prendergast, however, had a difficult time realizing a profit at their end of the business, mainly because, in booking some of the better and more popular acts in the area, they were taking on performers whose wages were barely met by the club's gate receipts. The two eventually approached Porco about changing the arrangement, but Porco would hear none of it. Why should he offer a percentage of his bar profits to the two promoters? If they couldn't earn a profit for their efforts, that was their problem. Young and Prendergast dropped out of the partnership, leaving an inexperienced bar owner the task of booking his own entertainment.

Porco may not have known a folk song from a show tune, but he was a shrewd enough businessman to keep his establishment rolling along. After the departure of Young and Prendergast, Porco renamed his place Gerdes Folk City and began staging open-mike nights on Mondays, which had always been the slowest evenings for business. The talent show experiment succeeded better than Porco ever could have imagined: young folk artists lined up for the chance to play, even if there was no payment involved, and customers jammed Folk City to capacity. Robert Shelton, a *New York Times* music critic, whose review of a Bob Dylan performance had launched Dylan's career, began to drop in to see who was around, as did Charlie Rothschild, a folk manager always on the lookout for new acts. Shelton and Rothschild proposed that Porco give his talent night a catchy title: "Call it a hootenanny."

Porco had never heard the word before—nor had most people outside of folk circles. This would change in a hurry: in a year or two, most of the country would not only be familiar with the word, but people would be using it in casual everyday conversation.

————

"Hootenanny": the four syllables rolled easily off the tongue. The word had a playful sound to it, and when hearing it for the first time, you had a sense, even before learning its meaning, of something homey and folksy.

Woody Guthrie, generally acknowledged as the person responsible for bringing the word to the East Coast, claimed to have first heard the word "hootenanny" in his travels through the Pacific North-west, where ghosts of the IWW (International Workers of the World) still hung in the air of old union halls. It originally referred to union singalongs, but by the time it was being bandied about the Greenwich Village folk clubs a couple of decades later, it applied to any gathering of folk musicians and singers—the more informal the assembly, the better.

Singalongs had been around forever, and Guthrie had been to a good many of them in all parts of the country. He had helped popu-larize them as a member of the Almanac Singers, arguably the best agit-prop group making the rounds in the 1940s. Now, just as folk music was enjoying its burgeoning popularity on the East Coast, Woody Guthrie lay dying an excruciatingly slow and inhumane death in a New Jersey hospital, victim of Huntington's chorea. Despite his physical absence from the folk scene, he was as important a presence as anyone who was there in the flesh, his place in American folk mu-sic's family tree absolutely assured.

Guthrie may not have been in the position to help push the new folk movement forward, but two of his contemporaries, Pete Seeger and Sis Cunningham, both former members of the Almanac Singers, played significant roles in fueling the popularity of folk music. Through his work as a solo artist, as well as his membership in the Weavers, Seeger had become the best known folksinger in the coun-try. Tough and brilliant, unrepentant about his unionism (which had landed him in trouble during the era of McCarthyism), and encyclo-pedic in his knowledge of folk music and history, Seeger brought in-telligence and passion to a scene ripe for commercial exploitation. Seeger had enjoyed enviable commercial success—the Weavers' "Goodnight Irene" had been one of the best-selling recordings of the 1950s—but he had done so without compromising the integrity of his music. He willingly accepted his position as elder statesman to the new generation of singers and songwriters, though there would come a time, in the not-so-distant future, when his traditionalist at-titudes would be called into question.

Agnes "Sis" Cunningham's contribution to the movement was a modest mimeographed publication called *Broadside*. The magazine, Cunningham recalled, came together as the result of conversations that she and her husband, Gordon Friesen, had had with Malvina Reynolds and Pete Seeger.

"Malvina Reynolds thought it would be a good idea to have a magazine devoted just to topical songs," said Cunningham. "*Sing Out!* contained topical songs, but it was a general folk song magazine. They'd dig up old folk songs and print them. Malvina wanted to do her own thing."

Reynolds, author of a number of classic songs, most notably, "Little Boxes," was too involved in her songwriting and performing career to work on the proposed publication, so she suggested that Cunningham, with her topical music background, and Friesen, a journalist who had once been blacklisted for his leftist sympathies, try their hand at it. Pete Seeger felt likewise. Seeger had recently been in England and was delighted to see that country's interest in topical music, but like Reynolds, he was too busy to edit a new publication in the States.

With Seeger's assistance, Cunningham and Friesen enlisted the assistance of Gil Turner, who was acting as emcee at Folk City. Not only was he younger than Sis and Gordon, but Turner also had the connections that assured the magazine plenty of new material.

"The three of us went to work," said Cunningham. "We got ahold of a mailing list of three hundred people, and we sent out a letter, just to feel out what people thought about the magazine. We got mostly good responses. So we just went right ahead. We came out every two weeks for quite a while, just cranking them out on a mimeograph machine. It was slow going at first, and we always had financial troubles, but sure enough, it took hold."

––––––

Phil plugged into the Village folk scene with manic energy. This, he told himself, was where he would make his mark. He darted from club to club, taking in countless shows, convinced that his talent was the equal to anything he was witnessing in the different clubs. He was poignant, insightful, witty, and entertaining—all qualities that made the others stand out. All he needed were the right breaks and proper connections.

He became a familiar performer at the folk clubs. He haunted the Village "basket houses," playing for free or next to nothing, picking up the change dropped in the baskets passed around after his short sets. He was a regular at The Third Side. He could often be found standing in line and taking numbers for a possible appearance at the overcrowded Folk City hootenannies. He landed a gig at the Palisades

Amusement Park. None of these jobs paid enough for much more than coffee, drinks, sandwiches or, on an extremely rare occasion, a sack of groceries, but this was of no great concern to Phil. Alice was earning enough money to pay the rent and cover their bills, and if being flat broke all the time was really a matter of paying your dues, as most folkies claimed, at least he wasn't paying them alone. Very few folksingers kicking around the streets of Lower Manhattan had shine on their shoes.

Phil became a regular at Gordon Friesen and Sis Cunningham's Upper West Side apartment, where regular *Broadside* meetings brought together some of the city's best folksingers and journalists. Friesen had taken quite a liking to Phil, and he encouraged Phil to pursue his obvious gifts as a topical songwriter. Phil never let him down.

"He would dig into his jacket pocket and bring out scraps of paper on which he had scribbled new songs on the subway ride up to our place," Friesen recalled. According to Friesen, Phil habitually dropped by with two or three new offerings, and on one occasion, he amazed everyone at the *Broadside* offices by walking in with seven new works, all written on the subway ride uptown. "When I asked him where he got the ideas for his lyrics," Friesen said, "he would respond, 'From *Newsweek*, of course,' and hold up a copy of the latest issue. Then I asked where he got his tunes and he would reply, half-laughing, 'From Mozart.' "

Phil had a great distance to travel before he could even begin to skirt, let alone walk in, Mozart's shadow, but the *Newsweek* part of his statement was easy to understand: all of his material was coming directly from the headlines of the day. However, most of his early lyrics, if judged from a strictly critical standpoint, left much to be desired. Phil's passion for his subject matter bubbled at the surface of every new song, but in all but a couple instances, his lyrics seemed forced and often derivative, bogged down by the kind of sloganeering that sounded good at the moment, when emotions ran high and an issue was fresh, but which ultimately robbed a song of a durability that extended much beyond yesterday's headlines.

Of course, longevity was not a high priority to Phil, who, at least in the early goings, aspired to nothing more than scratching a day-to-day living. Nor was he especially concerned that he was young and inexperienced and getting most of his information from secondhand sources. With any luck at all, he would have plenty of future opportunity to travel and witness history in the making. For the time being, he wanted to register his thoughts on the issues of the day.

Broadside provided him with an outlet for such opinion, and he took full advantage of the opportunity. His first entry, "Billy Sol," one of the early numbers he had written while he was still at Ohio State, appeared in *Broadside #13*, and from that point on, Phil had a song in every one of the magazine's biweekly issues. Phil would turn up at Gordon and Sis's apartment and play his latest songs for the *Broadside* reel-to-reel tape recorder. Sis Cunningham would then listen to the playbacks and make up lead sheets for publication in future issues of the magazine. Phil's contributions began to pile up, and he soon found himself in the same position he'd been in during his early tenure at *The Lantern*, when he had more material on his hands than he could possibly see published.

———

In April, Phil headed down to Florida for a two-week series of gigs in a Fort Lauderdale club called the House of Pegasus. The Florida dates, which found Phil backing the Knob Lick Upper Ten Thousand, meant a great deal to the young folksinger. Beside being paying gigs, which were still far and few between, the appearances also gave Phil the opportunity to work his material on audiences far removed, at least geographically, from the predictably supportive East Coast audiences he had grown accustomed to.

Not that he had reason to worry: his performances were well received, and Phil, now being billed in newspaper ads as "a Will Rogers of Folksinging," was given a strong review in the *Ft. Lauderdale News*. "His social protest material," offered the reviewer, "is excellently-written stuff, with rhyming and rhythm bringing across his barbs with deadly accuracy."

Erik Jacobsen, the driving force behind Phil's backing the Knob Lick Upper Ten Thousand in Florida, shared a hotel room with Phil, and was amazed by his self-discipline.

"He was up every day at dawn, sitting with his guitar, working and writing for hours everyday, just sitting in a chair or cross-legged on the floor, playing and writing lyrics," Jacobsen remarked. "He was so young and enthusiastic. In his later years, he'd make me retell this very story. He'd say, 'Tell me how I used to be,' because he couldn't believe that he had worked so hard."

Phil's time in Florida represented one final gasp of life as it "used to be." On a professional level, Phil's life was constantly moving forward, even if not as rapidly as he would have hoped. From a personal standpoint, however, his life was about to change suddenly and significantly. Phil learned as much one day when Jacobsen handed him a telegram from New York: Alice was pregnant, and she would be coming to Fort Lauderdale to discuss the situation in detail with Phil.

For Phil, this was the worst possible news. He had to stay free, available to travel on a moment's notice, if he ever expected to move up in his profession, and having a child around would certainly put the clamps on his mobility. Furthermore, Phil wasn't certain that he loved Alice enough to make the marriage commitment she was seeking. There was something imposing and even frightening about making their relationship legal and tidy.

The two spent many hours talking over their options after Alice arrived in Florida. Alice intended to have the child, one way or another, but she would have preferred to have Phil around, ideally as her husband, participating in the child's upbringing. She hated the idea of pressuring Phil into marriage, so rather than push him, she told him to think everything over and come up with his own plan of action.

Phil waffled on his decision, and he asked Alice for more time to make up his mind. Alice agreed, vowing to keep her pregnancy a secret until Phil had figured out what he was going to do. Phil promised to deliver a decision when he returned from Florida.

———

Phil agonized over Alice's pregnancy, and for another opinion on the matter, he called his sister in Far Rockaway. Sonny had been through her own family crisis when she had married against her mother's wishes, only to see the marriage end in divorce. She had recently moved back to the hometown of her youth.

"I don't know what to do," Phil told Sonny. "Alice is four months pregnant and she wants me to marry her, but I don't think I want to marry her."

Sonny had already spoken to Alice, and as far as she was concerned, there was only one proper course of action.

"She wants to have the baby," Sonny said, going back over what

Phil already knew, "but she won't do it without being married. I think you owe her at least that much."

Still fearing the commitment, Phil told Sonny that he needed more time to think it over.

"What's there to think about?" Sonny demanded. "What the hell's the big deal? I mean, it's not the rest of your life. All you're doing is giving the baby a legitimate name. If it works out, fine. If it doesn't, so what? You can always get divorced. At least she'll have the baby. You could at least do that much for her."

Phil listened to what Sonny had to say, and when she was finished, he insisted that he had to give the matter more thought. Although frustrated by the conversation, Sonny could do nothing but reiterate her position.

Once again, fate played a large role in helping Phil make an important decision when, only a few days after his talk with Sonny, Phil received a return call from his sister, this time to inform him that his father had died suddenly from a cerebral hemorrhage.

"You don't have a week to think about it," Sonny said, bringing up the topic of Alice's pregnancy. "You have twenty-four hours."

"Why?"

"Phil, your father just dropped dead. They're bringing his body to New York. The funeral is tomorrow and Ma's going to be here. You better decide what you're going to do right now."

"Why do I have to be there? What's the difference if I'm there or not?"

Sonny could not believe what she was hearing.

"Phil," she said, "this is your *father*. Regardless of the feelings you have or don't have, you must be at the funeral, and it's tomorrow. So you get your ass out here, and you make your decision by tomorrow, because Ma's going to be here and you're going to have to tell her."

Phil waited until the most inappropriate moment to drop the news about Alice's pregnancy. The family was sitting in the funeral limousine, riding out to the cemetery to put Jacob Ochs' body in the earth, when Phil turned to his mother.

"Ma, I have something to tell you."

"What?"

"Alice and I are getting married."

"Why?"

"Because Alice is pregnant."

"Why?"

Thirty years after the fact, Sonny could laugh about the conversation.

"It was something out of an Abbott and Costello movie," she said, noting that Phil's behavior was completely in character, consistent with her brother's ignorance of social convention, while Gertrude's clipped responses were the result of her still being in shock over Jack's death. "I mean, I'm sitting there and listening to this, and I'm very upset because my father's dead, and I'm very upset about the whole thing that's going on with Phil and Alice, and in the meantime, the way it's coming out is so funny."

Phil's announcement caught Gertrude completely off balance. She was just beginning to accept her son's choice of careers, and all of a sudden he seemed to be doing his damnedest to undermine his future. Tying himself to a family would only slow him down. Despite these feelings, Gertrude said nothing to Phil or Alice to discourage them.

In the wake of the strange chain of events preceding their marriage, Phil and Alice's wedding was anticlimactic, as much a postscript as anything else. Jim Glover stood in as Phil's best man, and Jean Ray served as the bridesmaid at a private ceremony at City Hall. At one point during the proceedings, the justice of the peace halted the ceremony and scolded Phil for giggling off and on throughout the service. Alice reassured the judge that she and Phil were snickering because they were nervous, not because they disrespected the ceremony or the institution of matrimony.

In fact, neither had a clue about what marriage was all about, which, given the family history of both bride and groom, was only natural. Ultimately, it made little difference. The union may have been doomed before the ink had dried on the marriage license, but the wedding had served its purpose.

———

One day, not long after Phil and Alice's wedding, Gertrude and Sonny visited the couple in their apartment. After her husband's death, Gertrude had moved back to Far Rockaway, supposedly to gather her family around her for support. Sonny now lived a short walking distance away, and Michael was still living at home, although he planned to enroll for fall classes at Adelphi University within a few months. Jack's funeral had brought the family together in an unsteady truce, particularly between Sonny and Gertrude, who still had to resolve issues dating back to Sonny's adolescence.

Gertrude was horrified by the sloppy condition of Phil's apartment, but in the spirit of keeping the peace, she said very little. In all likelihood, Phil wouldn't have noticed if Gertrude had brought in a Marine Corps drill sergeant to dress him down: throughout his mother and sister's visit, he sat off by himself, strumming the same four-chord progression over and over on his guitar, oblivious to the fact that he was being rude to guests who had gone to some trouble to visit him. Sonny listened in silence for a while, and, finally, when she could take the repetition no longer, she demanded to know what Phil was doing.

"I'm playing the greatest song I'll ever write," he replied in a matter-of-fact manner.

"Well then," Sonny said, "sing it. What are the words?"

Phil continued to strum his guitar. "I haven't written them yet," he said.

When the words finally did come to him, they constituted his most powerful, mature lyrics to date, combining, in three brief verses, Phil's sense of social conscience with heartfelt patriotism:

> *C'mon and take a walk with me through this green and growin'*
> *   land,*
> *Walk through the meadows and the mountains and the sand,*
> *Walk through the valleys and the rivers and the plains,*
> *Walk through the sun and walk through the rain . . .*

It was a new anthem, complete with a chorus that could easily compete with Irving Berlin's song of a few decades earlier.

> *Here's a land full of power and glory*
> *Beauty that words cannot recall*
> *Oh her power will rest on the strength of her freedom*
> *Her glory shall rest on us all, on us all.*

"Power and the Glory"—a title that Phil had lifted from the Graham Greene novel—had a melody that owed more than a nodding debt to Bob Gibson, and lyrics that might have been written by the great Woody Guthrie himself. Phil had enormous respect for both songwriters.

Like so many putative folksingers, Bob Dylan included, Phil visited Guthrie in the hospital. Unfortunately, Guthrie's health had deteriorated to such an extent that Phil was unable to converse with him or play music for him, as Dylan had done during his earlier visit, but Phil's homage to Guthrie, "Bound for Glory," written shortly after his visit and at about the same time as "Power and the Glory," was arguably a better tribute than Dylan's "Song for Woody":

> *Now they sing out his praises on every distant shore.*
> *But so few remember what he was fightin' for,*
> *Oh why sing the songs and forget about the aim.*
> *He wrote them for a reason, why not sing them for the same.*
> *And now he's bound for a glory of his own,*
> *And now he's bound for glory.*

For the blossoming songwriter, the long hours of work were beginning to pay off.

———

By the summer of 1963, interest in folk music was hitting a new peak. In recent months, there had been chart successes and television controversies, magazine cover stories, and SRO concerts at universities across the country. There seemed to be a new topical song for every issue of the day: the civil rights movement alone led to dozens of memorable new entries.

At the white-hot center of all the attention was Bob Dylan, whose "Blowin' in the Wind," as covered by Peter, Paul, and Mary, had become the music sensation of the season. Dylan's second album, *The Freewheelin' Bob Dylan*, released in May to overwhelming critical acclaim, featured three songs ("Blowin' in the Wind," "Masters of War," and "A Hard Rain's A-Gonna Fall") destined to become classics. People outside of the East Coast folk hub might not have seen Dylan or heard him play—many could not even pronounce his name correctly—but they were familiar with the name.

No one was happier about this turn of events than Phil Ochs. He and Dylan had become very close over the past year, and Phil was genuinely pleased by Dylan's good fortune. Dylan had set a standard for the rest of the folk community, and as Phil saw it, the entire folk industry stood to benefit from all the attention directed at Dylan.

Nowhere was this as apparent as at the 1963 Newport Folk Festival, which Robert Shelton would later term "a dress rehearsal for Woodstock nation . . . the cocoon of an alternative culture." The event, held between July 26 and 28, saw nearly fifty thousand people convert the small Rhode Island town into what Dave Van Ronk would jokingly refer to as "a convention minus only the bags of water," with folkies playing the role of "shriners with guitars."

"There was a definite pandemonium right from the beginning," recalled Tom Paxton, another young folksinger performing at the festival. Much of the brouhaha, he noted, was swirling around Bob Dylan, who gave the performance of his life on the first evening of the festival, bringing the crowd to its feet when, as a grand finale to the opening night's performances, he locked arms onstage with Joan Baez, Pete Seeger, The Freedom Singers, Theodore Bikel, and Peter, Paul and Mary, and sang a moving version of "We Shall Overcome."

The three-day affair, called "Dylan's crowning moment" by biographer Anthony Scaduto, produced numerous lasting images for the participants: Dylan's wandering around the grounds with a twenty-foot bullwhip coiled around his shoulder . . . Tom Paxton distributing postcards calling for a general boycott of television's *Hootenanny* program . . . workshops finding a heady combination of old-timers and new faces . . . countless after-hours parties in hotel rooms.

Arlo Guthrie, just fifteen years old at the time, remembered Newport '63 as a time of great fun and comradery, with an underlying seriousness that gave it an added sense of importance. "I loved the spirit of the festival which, in a way, held the promise of a new world, where all of these diverse performers from around the world, from all these different traditions, could spend a few days together." Like so many in attendance, Guthrie enjoyed the accessibility of people who previously had been only faces on album covers.

For Phil, Newport '63 was a mixed bag. He was thrilled when he was asked to take part in one of the weekend's workshops, but by the time he made it to Newport's Freebody Park, he had worked himself into such a state of anxiety that he was almost unable to perform.

His problems began during the drive from New York to Rhode Island, when he developed a headache so severe that it literally reduced him to tears. To alleviate his suffering, Phil sprawled out across the back seat of the car, but he was still in sorry shape when the group arrived in Newport. On two separate occasions, he was rushed to the hospital—one time in his own car, and once by ambulance—where he was treated, given medication, and advised to cancel his performance.

That, of course, was not about to happen, and when it came time for him to play, a badly weakened Phil Ochs took the stage, hoping only to survive the ordeal. He opened the set with "Too Many Martyrs," a ballad he had written with Bob Gibson about the murder of Medgar Evers. His singing and playing were in less than top form, but he was picking up strength by the time he reached the song's penultimate verse:

> They laid him in the ground while the bugle sounded clear.
> They laid him in his grave when victory was near.
> While we waited for the future with the wisdom of our plans,
> The country gained a killer, and the country lost a man.

The crowd ate it up. The civil rights movement had inspired many of the protest and topical songs featured at Newport that year, and Phil's entry was symbolic of the movement's great passion and sense of commitment. Phil's second number, "Talking Birmingham Jam," was another indictment of Southern segregationist practices, and Phil delivered it confidently, showing no sign of the illness he'd experienced only a short time earlier, when he was preparing to go onstage. Like his other spoken songs, "Talking Birmingham Jam" was a scalding commentary delivered in a wry, almost offhanded manner:

> Well, I've seen travel in many ways,
> I've traveled in cars and old subways,
> But in Birmingham some people chose
> To fly down the street from a fire hose,
> Doin' some Hard Travelin'
> From hydrants of plenty.

Throughout his career, Phil used his sense of humor to win over crowds and ease his own nervousness onstage, and his performance of "Talking Birmingham Jam" served both purposes well at Newport. Phil concluded his set with "Power and the Glory," receiving a standing ovation when he had finished. Emotionally spent, Phil left the stage and collapsed under a tree.

Phil's headaches at Newport were just the beginning of what appeared to be strong bouts of performance anxiety that would plague him throughout his life. Severe headaches, constricted throat, dry mouth—the symptoms would vary, but they would render him all but useless before a show. Not that performance anxiety was all that rare: many singers grew frightened or even ill before stepping out into the onstage lights.

"A lot of them suffered like that," said Harold Leventhal, who represented some of the biggest names in the folk scene, including Woody Guthrie and Pete Seeger. "I had to push some top artists onstage when it was time to go out, because they froze going out from the curtain."

In Phil's case, the attacks were almost legendary. Sis Cunningham remembered him complaining to her on a number of occasions of having "something funny happening in my head . . . like there's a bubble in my head." Erik Jacobsen cited an occasion where Phil's anxiety was so pronounced that he went numb in his fingers and toes, and had to be soothed with massages before he was able to perform. Sam Hood, owner of The Gaslight, recalled a time when Phil was so worked up that he asked if he could play his club date lying down on the stage.

Such attacks, however, were infrequent, and Phil never missed a show in his career as the result of his anxiety.

Chapter Four

WHAT'S THAT I HEAR?

NEWPORT '63 —particularly the talented young folksingers christened "Woody's Children" by Sis Cunningham—received a lot of attention from the media, and the singers and songwriters had barely returned to their homes when they began to hear from business interests eager to market them. Agents rushed to add them to their client lists; record companies scouted around for the next new Dylan, Baez, or Peter, Paul and Mary; and television producers began to include folk acts in their programming. *New York Times* critic Robert Shelton, viewed by some as an oddball for all the time he had been spending in Village folk clubs, was suddenly looking like nothing less than a visionary.

The folk scene, deemed the various powers that be, had much to offer. From a recording standpoint, the folk artist was ideal: since so many of the acts involved just a singer and his or her guitar, studio setup was simple, and an entire album's worth of material could be (and often was) recorded in a day or two. The folksingers appealed to the youth market, which was good news to television producers constantly searching for ways to boost ratings. Club owners liked the acts because they were still inexpensive to book but always seemed to bring in throngs of customers.

The folksingers, however, were anything but pushovers. Bob Dylan proved as much when he walked off the *Ed Sullivan Show* rather than submit to the popular CBS variety show host's request that he substitute another song for his "Talkin' John Birch Society Blues," the number that he originally intended to sing on the program. The publicity from the incident was an embarrassment for Sullivan, who, for his part, had been reluctantly following a network censor's orders, and a boon to Dylan, whose actions seemed noble in the eyes of the public.

For all the attention it received, the Sullivan flap paled in comparison to the dispute brewing over ABC's *Hootenanny* program—a controversy that some of the folkies waved off as little more than a "tempest in a teapot," but that nevertheless had a profound effect on a program designed to showcase all types of traditional and contemporary folk music.

The controversy had flared up in spring 1963, when rumor began to circulate that Pete Seeger had not appeared on the program because he had been blacklisted for his left-wing politics. ABC officials vigorously denied the allegation, published in *Broadside* and *Sing Out!* magazines, but the network was hard-pressed to offer a credible explanation as to why it so adamantly refused to invite Seeger or his group, the Weavers, to appear on the show. According to the program's producers, Seeger was not popular enough to include in *Hootenanny*.

The explanation failed to impress Harold Leventhal, Seeger's agent, or any number of folksingers, journalists, and music aficionados, who found something malodorous about the entire affair. Joan Baez, scheduled to appear on the show, declared that she would not perform on the program if Seeger wasn't welcome on it. Judy Collins and Carolyn Hester took matters a step further when they organized an official boycott of the show. Phil Ochs liked the idea, and by the time he appeared at the Newport festival, he was fully involved with the boycott, attending informal meetings and trying to talk people into supporting the cause.

Pete Seeger, interestingly enough, opposed the boycott idea. He was embarrassed by all the publicity, and he disliked the notion of setting up a form of blacklisting to protest a form of blacklisting. Far better, he argued, for people to appear on the show and strengthen interest in folk music as a whole.

Two distinct viewpoints began to take shape, one side favoring a boycott of the show, even if it meant running it off the air, the other holding the position that while it was admirable for well-established acts like Joan Baez, Bob Dylan, or Peter, Paul and Mary to refuse to appear on the program, it would only be harmful for lesser known or new acts to follow suit, especially since, in some cases, it might mean trading their careers for a principle.

Phil, clearly enjoying the battle, stood fast, even though it eliminated any chance he would have of appearing on national television. In the end, ABC decided that the program wasn't worth the hassle, and *Hootenanny* was taken off the air.

————————

Convinced that it was only a matter of time before he would need someone to oversee his career full-time, Phil set out to find a manager.

Harold Leventhal, Phil's first choice, wasn't interested. Leventhal had seen Phil perform, and he had heard more about him from some of the other folksingers, but he wasn't altogether sold on Phil's ability. From what he had seen, Phil displayed very little stage presence, and nothing about his voice or guitar playing predicted a bright future. On top of this, Leventhal was more than a little put off when Phil walked into his office and started rambling on about his abilities as if he was Woody Guthrie, Pete Seeger, and Bob Dylan rolled into one package.

What really interested Leventhal was Phil's songwriting. There was good money to be made on the publishing end of the music business, and a solid, prolific songwriter like Phil could prove to be very profitable. Leventhal declined to represent Phil as a performer, but he and Phil did reach an agreement about the publishing. Leventhal established Appleseed Music as Phil's official publisher.

Phil shrugged off Leventhal's disinterest. There were other managers available, and from what he could see, Leventhal's loss would be someone else's gain.* There was, after all, reason to be optimistic. The Newport festival had been taped, and a couple of his songs were being considered for a forthcoming album of the festival's highlights. He had recently signed for an appearance at a Carnegie Hall hootenanny, and his services were in as much demand as ever, in New York City and out of town. An issue of *Broadside* didn't appear without a Phil Ochs contribution.

Unfortunately, the upswing in Phil's professional life had a pronounced effect on his marriage. Phil was now spending very little time around the apartment other than to eat or sleep, yet in his absence he expected Alice to hold onto her regular job, as well as take care of all domestic duties and act as his business secretary in the event

* Phil eventually signed on with Albert Grossman, Bob Dylan's manager.

that the phone would ring with career offers. It didn't matter that her pregnancy sapped her of her energy, or that the sweltering summer heat exacted a toll of its own. Alice's main obligation, as Phil saw it, was to be there for him.

All this was challenging enough, but it became even more difficult for Alice after she gave birth to a daughter on September 4, a month before her expected delivery date. Phil, fittingly enough, was out of town when Alice went into labor, and the responsibility of getting her to a doctor fell upon Erik Jacobsen, who happened to be visiting when Alice went into labor. Erik accompanied Alice to the Lenox Hill Hospital, and after a relatively short labor, the child was born. The baby, named Meegan, was so tiny and frail that she remained behind in a clinic incubator for several weeks after her birth.

Less than two weeks after the birth of his daughter, Phil reached another professional peak when he performed in highly publicized hootenannies at Town Hall and Carnegie Hall, two of New York City's most time-honored concert venues. At Town Hall, Phil found himself in a lineup that included Buffy Sainte-Marie, a Native American folksinger who had become very popular on the East Coast, and Guy Carawan, one of the important freedom singers in the civil rights movement. In the program for the September 13 event, advertised as a "99¢ Hootenanny for Students and Working People," Phil offered a lofty yet succinct statement about what he hoped to accomplish in his topical songs. "A lot of people say my songs sound alike," he wrote. "What I'm trying to do is write one endless song called truth, painting this world exactly as I see it without compromise, always questioning."

The September 21 Carnegie Hall event, sponsored by *Sing Out!* magazine and featuring Theodore Bikel and Izzie Young as masters of ceremony, presented an impressive range of folk, blues, bluegrass, and jug band music from the likes of Len Chandler, Dave Van Ronk, John Hammond, Jr., Peter LaFarge, Jim Kweskin, and others, giving many performers urgently needed exposure in a field that was rapidly becoming extremely crowded and competitive. Phil regarded his Carnegie Hall appearance as a monumental step forward, even if, as part of a large group, he was only allowed to sing several songs. Only a few months earlier, a newspaper ad had marked the appearance of a singer named "Phil Oake" at a benefit concert; having his name properly spelled and placed in a Carnegie Hall program would certainly help see that such a mistake wouldn't be repeated.

To establish his name, Phil took a two-pronged attack. First, there was the music itself, and by the end of 1963, Phil had secured his reputation as one of the brightest new songwriters on the horizon. He wasn't yet Dylan's equal, as either a poet or tunesmith, but he was quickly closing the distance between them. Then there was Phil's unflagging commitment to any and all political or social causes that he deemed to be worthwhile. Whenever an advertisement for a benefit concert appeared in the papers, be it in a large publication such as *The Village Voice* or *The New York Times*, or in small student publications, Phil's name always seemed to be included—and given prominent mention to boot.

These were heady times. John F. Kennedy had become the youngest chief executive in the country's history, and in the nearly three years he had been in office, he had suggested, by his words and actions, that the United States would be leading the way in a boldly changing world. Phil idolized Kennedy, even if he strongly disagreed with the president's position in the invasion of Cuba and the resulting Cuban missile crisis, or in the country's growing involvement in the civil war in a small Southeast Asian country called Vietnam. Phil regarded Kennedy with a passion not unlike his love of John Wayne: there was something powerful in these men and their bigger-than-life public images, a mythology that towered over political ideology and cast a large shadow of its own.

For Phil, a part of the dream ended as abruptly as the speed of a bullet when, on November 22, 1963, Kennedy was murdered in Dallas. Badly shaken by the news, Phil joined millions of other Americans in watching the television accounts of the event and its aftermath. Here was the president, smiling, waving at the throngs of people who had gathered to see him, squinting in the midday sun. Then it was suddenly over, a country's hopes slipping away, starkly symbolized in the bloodstains on his widow's dress. Phil sat at the kitchen table in his apartment and wept, his body wracked by sobs of depression, anger, and a sense of futility.

"I think I'm going to die tonight," he told his wife.

Part of him did.

———

In the wake of the events in Dallas, Phil's emotions, like those of an entire nation, appeared to be governed by a hair trigger. Within days of the assassination, he had written a heartfelt eulogy to the slain president ("it seemed as though a friendless world had lost itself a friend"), but even as he sorted through his feelings, Phil refused to become involved in the brand of revisionist history that now suggested that Kennedy was worthy of canonization. He made as much clear when, appearing at the Gaslight in early December, he and the club's manager, Sam Hood, argued bitterly over Phil's decision to play a couple of songs critical of Kennedy. The two numbers in question, "Cuban Missile Crisis" and "Talking Vietnam," were a standard part of Phil's stage repertoire, but Hood asserted that Phil's performing the song so soon after Kennedy's assassination might be regarded as disrespectful and lead to the kind of uproar they could all do without. Phil vehemently disagreed.

"Phil was absolutely right," Hood admitted, thirty years after the fact. "I was out of line. I was concerned about the reaction that Phil would get from the audience if he were to perform some of that material, and I rashly presented my feelings on it to Phil without giving a whole lot of thought as to what the implications were."

Hood, it should be noted, was not being arbitrary in his judgment of the material that Phil was proposing to play. Only a short time earlier, Dave Van Ronk had infuriated Gaslight patrons with a scathing, over-the-top parody of Kennedy. Van Ronk had been lucky to leave the club in one piece.

Nevertheless, in recalling the events, Hood was not prepared to give his decisions at the time the benefit of the doubt. He was, he said, thinking like a businessman, but that did not excuse his actions.

"I wasn't just flying off the handle," he said. "Dave had very nearly caused a riot—to the extent that a riot is possible with a hundred people. Still, I don't believe a club owner has the right to have it both ways, to benefit from a person's appearance *and* have an influence over what is being said onstage. You pay your money and you take your chances. Phil saw that immediately. As he saw it, his two-week performance at the Gaslight at that particular time was critically important to his career, but he wouldn't give a moment's thought to accommodating the wishes of the club owner, even if it meant that these dates weren't going to come off for him. We went at it tooth-and-nail, and I learned so much from that experience with Phil."

After all the bickering had ended, Phil won the day. He sang the songs at the Gaslight, with very little protest from his audience.

Never one to walk away from his convictions, Phil was in his best position yet to stand by them. *Broadside #36*, on newsstands in early December, featured a cover story on Phil, as well as the lead sheets for two songs ("That Was the President," "It Must Have Been Another Country") memorializing John Kennedy and Medgar Evers. *Broadside Ballads, Volume 1*, an album featuring an assortment of new and established songwriters, including Pete Seeger, Happy Traum, Peter LaFarge, and Bob Dylan (appearing, for contractual reasons, under the nom de plume of Blind Boy Grunt), presented "The Ballad of William Worthy," marking Phil's first appearance on record.

The song, heavily influenced by the work of Woody Guthrie, the Weavers, and other agit-prop performers dating back to the old union organizing days, was a strong representation of Phil's best topical work of the period. Worthy, a journalist, had ignored a State Department ban on Americans traveling to Cuba, and he had been arrested when he tried to re-enter the States with what officials considered to be an invalid passport. Phil, who was by nature sympathetic to journalists—particularly those covering the revolution and issues in Cuba—found the United States' position both ironic and infuriating, and he lampooned it in the chorus of his song:

> William Worthy isn't worthy
> To enter our door
> He went down to Cuba
> He's not American anymore
> But somehow it is strange to hear
> The State Department say
> "You are living in the Free World
> In the Free World you must stay."

When informed that a song had been written about his passport case, William Worthy contacted Ochs, and Phil suggested that they get together. The two discussed the case over dinner at Phil's apartment, and afterward Worthy accompanied Phil to his performance at the Third Side. Phil made a special point of introducing Worthy to his audience before he played the song.

The absurdity of the case was not wasted on the songwriter, the subject of the song, or just about anybody who had heard of Worthy's predicament. "Dick Gregory has told me that he plans to start cracking jokes about the case on his circuit," Worthy wrote in a letter to Phil shortly after the Third Side show. "Perhaps between Ochs and Gregory this whole sorry business can be laughed out of court."

Phil was certainly doing his part to ridicule the situation. "The song," he wrote sarcastically, "has been taped by three major recording companies dealing in folk music: Elecktra, Folkways, and the FBI."

Worthy was convicted in a lower court, but the verdict was eventually overturned in appeals. Phil would include his song about the case on his first album, *All the News That's Fit to Sing*, showing how journalism and music could be united for a higher cause.

———

Phil's work on the *Broadside Ballads* album had one negative offshoot: during the recording sessions, a serious rift had developed between Phil and his brother Michael. Not surprisingly, the problem might have been avoided had Phil been at all sensitive to the effect his career was having on Michael.

Michael, as one might expect, was getting a vicarious thrill from his older brother's growing success. Not only was Phil making a name for himself, but he was also spending time with some of the most interesting people in the music business. Michael, who knew as much if not more about popular music as Phil, loved to attend the performances at the Village clubs or, better yet, sit as an observer at the Kettle of Fish, where folkies would gather and drink, discuss politics and music, or play cards when they weren't performing. Good-sized groups got together on those nights when Dylan held court at the Kettle, and on those occasions, the conversations were fast and furious—and often biting.

Michael was dying to attend the recording sessions for the *Broadside Ballads* album, but Phil told him it wasn't possible. The recording studio, he said, wasn't large enough to accommodate a lot of guests—which may have been true enough, although in all likelihood, Phil was orchestrating his own little power play, engaging in an adult version of ditching the clinging younger sibling. Michael was disappointed by the explanation, but he had no alternative but to go along with Phil's decision.

He was shocked, then, when Phil later ran into a musician friend and invited him to sit in on the recording sessions. All of a sudden, there appeared to be all kinds of room in the studio. Michael left the Kettle and wandered around the Village, trying to decide what he should do. If Phil wanted to play the role of hotshot star around his own family, Michael wanted nothing to do with him.

The next night, he confronted Phil in his apartment and, in typical Ochs fashion, stated his case without mincing words.

"I wouldn't have you as a friend," he told Phil, "so I won't have you as a brother."

And with that he was gone—out of Phil's life and away from the entire folk scene. He dropped out of Adelphi and left the East Coast, reasoning that he would be better off completing his college education at Ohio State. It would be years before he and Phil patched up their differences.

———

Rather than spend the holiday season with his wife and infant daughter, Phil spent Christmas in Hazard, Kentucky, performing for the families of the area's striking coal miners. Phil's actions, indicative of the way he sacrificed his personal life for his political beliefs and professional career, only led to the further erosion of a marriage that, by now, was crumbling badly.

The Hazard story was rich in dramatic texture. The miners and their families, as sympathetic as figures in a John Steinbeck novel, appeared to be in a no-win situation. Modernization was replacing many workers with machinery, and the decline of the coal industry was threatening them all. At best, the miners' leadership was suspect, their political allies few; at the worst, corruption and apathy threatened to reduce a bittersweet history to dust.

Phil's sensibilities, from his interests in writing what he was now calling "social realism," to his romanticism of epic drama in the John Ford tradition, had drawn him to the struggle, and he had been one of the first young folksingers to become involved. His participation was due largely to the efforts of two men: Scottish filmmaker Hamish Sinclair and an American activist-organizer named Arthur Gorson.

Sinclair, who has heavily involved in the National Committee for Miners, hoped to film a feature-length documentary of the coal miners' struggle in Kentucky, and he worked tirelessly in an effort to convince others to join his cause. Phil needed little persuading, and through Sinclair he met Arthur Gorson, a young activist who was busy organizing benefit concerts for the miners at the Village Gate.

Gorson was an interesting study. As a student at Jamaica High School in New York, Gorson had fallen in love with the very early folk scene in Greenwich Village. He and his friends had attended concerts by Pete Seeger and others, and at one point, an inspired Arthur Gorson had actually gone out and made field recordings of fiddle and banjo players in the North Carolina hills. He learned to play banjo and guitar, and for a time he entertained the notion of becoming a professional musician himself.

Instead, he went off to study economics at New York University. While there, he was swept up in Kennedy politics, working first for Students for Kennedy, and eventually becoming chairman of NYU's Americans for Democratic Action. He rose to the position of national chairman of Campus ADA, which led to his involvement with such groups as Students for a Democratic Society and the Student Nonviolent Coordinating Committee. His experience and enthusiasm made him a top-notch, if not totally idealistic, activist.

"I organized a lot of civil rights demonstrations out of New York," he recalled. "The first ones involved the National Council of Churches—big marches on Baltimore and the Glen Oaks Amusement Park."

Gorson's involvement with the Hazard miners developed as a spin-off of his work with the civil rights movement. The Kennedy administration was launching an all-out battle against poverty, which tied in naturally with the civil rights movement, but the SNCC wanted to work on a project without the racial undercurrent. The Hazard case seemed to be ideal.

When Arthur Gorson met Phil Ochs, he knew instantly that he had hooked up to someone who could be very useful to his organization: Phil took in information like a sponge, and he was passionate about his convictions. In no time, Phil was performing regularly at the Village Gate benefit hoots, and he even traveled to Kentucky for an extended weekend of benefit shows with Tom Paxton, Carolyn Hester, and others.

Phil was galvanized by what he saw in Hazard. It was one thing to stand on a comfortable stage in New York City and sing Guthri-esque songs about the oppressed masses, quite another to travel to a region where people carried guns and had their guests sleep on floors to stay out of the way of company goons who might drive by at night and shoot up the house.

"We met an awful lot of miners and got to hear what life in East-ern Kentucky was like," remembered Tom Paxton, adding that, while the performers were never directly threatened, life in the region "was not nonviolent." Phil had his own wry assessment of the situation: "Minin' is a hazard in Hazard, Kentucky."

Three decades after making the trip, Arthur Gorson still smiled at the memory. "We were hot," he said, chuckling at the youthful idealism that had driven them to action. "Not only were we politically correct, but we were a genuine movement. Can you imagine singing in Hazard, Kentucky, in an abandoned United Mine Workers hall, in front of a bunch of cheering miners? It was a great high."

Phil called the experience "the most satisfying thing that has happened to me as a folksinger."

"It's an all-enveloping feeling of accomplishment that's worth more than any concert or TV appearance," he said. "I have come to believe that this is, in essence, the role of the folksinger . . . I feel that the singer almost has a responsibility with political and social in-volvement. You can't look at folk music as simply an element of show business, because it's much deeper and more important than that."

For Phil, the experience precluded dramatic struggle he would see only a few months later, when he traveled to the Deep South to witness and contribute to the civil rights movement. He was getting his social realism firsthand. Not surprisingly, a poignant topical song rose out of his experiences. Titled "No Christmas in Kentucky," the song addressed the enormous poverty and hunger that Phil had en-countered during his holiday stay in mining country:

> *Let's drink a toast to Congress and a toast to Santa Claus*
> *There's no Santa in the chimney when there are no minin' laws*
> *And back in old Kentucky they're all goin' for a ride*
> *On a Christmas sled that's fallin' down a jobless mountainside.*
>
> *No, they don't have Christmas in Kentucky*
> *There's no holly on a West Virginia door*
> *For the trees don't twinkle when you're hungry*
> *And the jingle bells don't jingle when you're poor.*

On December 5, 1963, the Federal Bureau of Investigation filed a four-page report on Phil—the first of a lengthy series of reports and memorandums that would continue even after Phil's death in 1976.

Described in the document as a "beatnik type," Ochs had initially caught the FBI's attention when he published the lyrics to "Bound for Glory," along with an essay on Woody Guthrie entitled "The Guthrie Legacy," in the August 1963 issue of Mainstream magazine. The FBI, nothing if not persistent, was keeping a close eye on Guthrie, even though the legendary folksinger was so incapacitated by Huntington's chorea that he could barely speak or light a cigarette, let alone pose a threat to the government. Phil, presumably, was guilty by association, suspect for showing so much as an interest in Guthrie.

The FBI's special agent in New York pored over Phil's Mainstream contributions and deduced the following:

> OCHS does not specifically describe himself in these writings, but their context shows that he has conversed with guitarists and folk singers. The reader is drawn to conclude that OCHS himself is a guitarist and folk singer. An article on page 42 of the same issue of "Mainstream" entitled "Off the Record" by JOSH DUNSON describes PHILIP OCHS as a "topical song writer." NYO Indices reflect no information concerning PHILIP OCHS. Central records of Selective Service System, 205 East 42nd Street, NYC, were checked on 10/28/63, by SA [name blacked out] and reflected no Selective Service registration in the New York area for PHILIP OCHS.

The Bureau, however, was not about to let a potential security risk slip from their grasp so easily. By checking American Federation of Musicians records, the FBI was able to ascertain Phil's Social Security number, and from there the agent checked Phil's records with the Credit Bureau of Greater New York, the Bureau of Motor Vehicles, the Bureau of Special Services of the New York Police Department, and the Board of Elections. In addition, about a dozen "security informants" were contacted for any information they might have on Phil.

Such vigilance brought very little reward. No one seemed to know

*much about Phil, other than the fact that he was a folksinger living in
Greenwich Village.*

———

The new year brought Phil his best career news yet: a recording contract for his first album.

Upon returning from Kentucky, Phil had resumed his usual
schedule of one-nighters in Village clubs. After one of his performances at the Gaslight, he was approached by Paul Rothchild, a young
producer and A & R man for Elektra Records. Rothchild, at one time
an aspiring conductor, had been a fixture around the Cambridge folk
scene before moving to New York and frequenting the Village clubs.
He and Elektra owner-founder Jac Holzman were looking to expand
the label's folk catalogue to the point where it could compete with
Vanguard Records, which currently boasted of the industry's largest
roster of promising folksingers.

Although Rothchild was impressed with Phil's music, particularly the new topical songs, he was not prepared to sign him after
their initial meeting at the Gaslight. A veteran of record company
rejections, Phil went right to work on Rothchild, filling the producer's
ears with his self-promotional spiel, telling him how, as folk music's
next big star, he could make Elektra a lot of money. Finally, after
several subsequent meetings, Rothchild relented.

Phil recorded the album in February. When he entered the studio, he had enough material for three or four albums, including a
long list of topical songs, a couple of numbers he had written with
Bob Gibson, and an excellent interpretation of "The Bells," the Edgar
Allan Poe poem that he had set to music. To compensate for Phil's
guitar-playing inadequacies—still the weakest part of his act—Elektra brought in Danny Kalb, a fine musician who would eventually
work in The Blues Project, to play second guitar on the album.

All the News That's Fit to Sing, as the album was called, was badly
flawed by Phil's tendency to dash through his songs, speeding up
their tempo substantially from the way he performed them onstage.
In years to come, Phil would be known for his high energy level in the
studio, and this, along with the excitement and nervousness that he
felt in recording his first album, may have led him to move through
his songs more quickly than he might have liked.

Nevertheless, *All the News* was a worthy representation of Phil's talents as a modern-day troubadour. The title, a spin-off from *The New York Times*'s motto, promised an album addressing the important topics of the day, and Phil delivered on the promise with a fourteen-song assortment that leaned heavily on the news, as seen through Phil's unique perspective.

All the News was not the type of album destined for the top of the popular music charts. In early 1964, American record buyers were anything but interested in singing headlines, editorializing, or self-examination. The British Invasion was in full swing, and American airwaves were clogged with the kind of pop-music hooks that enabled a nation to distance itself from its recent troubles. While Phil was busy at work on his first album, the Beatles were entertaining huge audiences on *The Ed Sullivan Show*, their "yeah yeah yeahs" infinitely more marketable than topical song lyrics confronting important social or political issues.

Reviews of Phil's album were mixed, as they tended to be throughout his career. Whereas some critics objected to the quality of Phil's untrained voice, others found it charming and perfectly suitable for the populist underpinnings of his music. In a number of reviews, critics complained that Phil's lyrics lacked strong poetic imagery, while others praised him for directness of style. In some cases, the contradictory reviews proved to be amusing. "Phil Ochs has the intellectual capacity to put his ideas forward," offered one critic in a negative review, "but he needs to mature." Wrote another: "In his first record, Phil Ochs has reached a maturity as a singer and writer that few acquire in a lifetime of work."

The notices had little effect, one way or another, on Phil. He was willing to concede that it might take years to find acceptance among the record-buying public, but he was not about to alter his style in order to appeal to a broader-based audience. He clearly relished the controversy that his songs created. At any given performance, he noted in an interview, he could look out and find Goldwater Republicans in the audience. This alone rewarded him with a measure of victory. "There is great satisfaction in having someone who disagrees with your political ideas humming your melodies," he said. "You might call it musical brainwashing."

———

Phil spent the early months of 1964 in constant motion, bouncing from New York to Boston and back, playing a heavy club schedule that enabled him to preview his forthcoming album's songs and talk up its release. No venue was too small or insignificant. One night he would be playing alongside Tom Paxton, Peter LaFarge, and others before a packed house at Town Hall; a few days later, he would be appearing at the New York City College bookstore, strumming songs for unsuspecting students who happened to drop by. He continued to pepper his schedule with appearances at benefit concerts.

It was a great time, not only for Phil but also for the Village performers in general. A sense of comradery still existed among the folksingers, with each night of the week becoming a combination of business and pleasure, when musicians would hang out, perform their new material for each other, play all-night games of cards, drink, and pull practical jokes.

"Some of the early scenes in the Village were just fabulous," recalled Len Chandler, one of the seemingly endless number of young folksingers trying to break into the business. "In the summer, the sidewalks would be so crowded that you would have to walk in the street. There was the Gaslight, and across the street from the Gaslight was the Fat Black Pussycat . . . and then there was the Bitter End, the Cafe Wha? Raffio's . . . all these little places were happening. We would just run back and forth between them. You would do a set and then run across the street to hear somebody else. Then, after everything closed, after the regular scene was over, the Gaslight started holding court real late in the evening. Everybody from all the other clubs—all the other players—would come by and just play for each other. Jim McGuinn—who later changed his name to Roger—came into the Gaslight one of those late sets and did 'I Want to Hold Your Hand' eighteen times in a row. People kept yelling, 'One more time,' and he'd do it—literally eighteen times in a row. It was kind of an open set. That's when Dylan first did 'Hard Rain.' It was unbelievable. People were standing up on chairs and yelling, 'It's a hard, it's a hard, it's a hard rain's a-gonna fall.' "

Quite often, the informal gatherings spilled over into the musicians' apartments. Henry Diltz, then playing with the Modern Folk Quartet, shared an apartment with Erik Jacobsen, and on any given night, their livingroom would be filled with folksingers playing new songs.

"It was a real nice, carpeted, air-conditioned apartment on the first floor, right off the street," said Diltz. "We had no furniture. We had only a mattress in each bedroom and a Chinese coffee table in the livingroom. That's all—the rest was just carpets. All these people would just drop in. Tim Hardin would come by, or Phil Ochs. John Sebastian would come over just about every day—sometimes before we were even up—and he would play the songs he'd just written. We'd sit on the edge of a mattress sort of like sitting around a campfire, only the campfire would be the ashtray with all these roaches and matches in it."

"We were young guys, full of piss and vinegar, not to mention bourbon," remarked Dave Van Ronk, who fondly remembered the club-hopping and fraternizing. "The worst audience you could possibly imagine," he said, "was an audience of your singer friends, because they'd all come down to see you, but they'd wind up seeing each other. By ten o'clock on any given night, everybody was at least half-loaded, and God only knew what kind of mischief you could get into."

Some of the mischief took the form of outrageous practical joking. For a while, the favorite trick involved goosing a singer while he was performing onstage. Anyone was fair game, and the more serious the song, the better the time for the goosing.

"We were goosing everybody," said Len Chandler, "and Phil was in on this. We would go to outrageous lengths to goose people onstage with sticks and umbrellas and stuff, from behind the curtain at the Gaslight. It was hilarious."

"Van Ronk used to tease me about going bald," offered Tom Paxton, who loved to engage in the antics. He said he couldn't wait for the day when I started wearing a hairpiece. He was going to get a fishing pole and come up behind me and snatch it off."

"This was a very lively group of people," commented Arthur Gorson, who was quick to point out that the folksingers were not as dour in real life as the lyrics of their songs might have indicated them to be. "These were Peck's Bad Boys. These were not serious, intense scholars. There were constant, hysterical things going on—witticisms and double-entendres. We took over wherever we went."

Phil unwittingly became a part of Village lore when, one evening before a performance at the Gaslight, he accidentally swallowed a contact lens. With no time to retrieve another set of lenses before going onstage, he chose what he considered to be his only option: he stuck his finger down his throat and vomited out the contents of his stomach—contact lens included. Phil fished out the lens, cleaned it off, and took the stage as if nothing unusual had occurred. The folkies laughed about the story for weeks.

———

Somehow, in the midst of such activity, Phil found time to begin writing prose again. In March, he contributed a scathing attack on the now all-but-dead *Hootenanny* television program to the Second Anniversary issue of *Boston Broadside*. His essay, ridiculing the program's producers for their blacklisting policies, may have been an instance of preaching to the already converted, but he hammered home his points nonetheless. "Ironically," he wrote, "the formation of this show on folk music may turn out to be one of the most powerful blows ever struck against the blacklist by giving it so much unwanted publicity and making so many people aware of a well-disguised problem. It has also forced many singers to analyze their principles and their roles as folk performers. If the show is renewed for another thirteen weeks, there is a good chance that the original dissenters and those who were later disillusioned will combine in signed statements and other levels of action against the blacklist."

Other pieces followed, including a couple of essays on topical music. When Pete Seeger saw Phil's piece in *Boston Broadside*, he wrote him a brief note soliciting contributions to his "Johnny Appleseed" column in *Sing Out!* Other publications requested Phil's work as well.

As compelling as some of this writing was, it ultimately had a mixed effect on Phil's career. As an insider, Phil's observations and opinions about the folk scene carried special weight. In addition, the articles and essays made Phil seem more accessible than those contemporaries who came across as young *artistes*. This accessibility, however, could work against him. In writing about the scene—especially when he expounded on Bob Dylan, which he did repeatedly throughout his career—Phil risked coming across as an apologist, which was the last hat that he needed to wear.

All the work—the time away from home, on the road or in the Village clubs and bars—finished off what little remained of Phil's marriage. From the beginning, Phil had treated Alice more like a maid and a secretary than a wife, and now that she had a baby to care for,

Alice was as tied down to the apartment as ever. Her status in the marriage, understandably enough, was unacceptable to Alice, who had creative urges of her own. Phil had dabbled in photography as a hobby, and during one of his road trips, Alice had started learning how to use the camera herself, ostensibly to shoot pictures of Meegan. She quickly discovered that she had a talent for taking good photographs, and she began to shoot the many musicians that stopped by the apartment. When he was around, Phil was an obvious, favorite subject, even if the resulting photographs represented, in their own peculiar way, the gulf that had developed between husband and wife. Phil wasn't interested in being depicted in candid shots; it was image that could boost your career. Alice's photos of Phil, though slick and professionally polished, captured a subject who seemed self-absorbed, far removed from the person holding the camera.

Both Phil and Alice realized that their marriage was in trouble, and both discussed the possibility of splitting up. Phil, however, was reluctant to make a clean break when Alice suggested it, and the two continued to slog along, their marriage a shaky truce interrupted by occasional bursts of angry bickering. Even when Phil had finally had enough of such co-existence and had moved out of the apartment and into a room at the Chelsea Hotel, he was bothered by indecision. Were they really finished, or could something be worked out? Maybe, he told Alice, they should give their marriage another chance; maybe they should both try a little harder. Phil even went as far as to suggest that their having another child might help strengthen their relationship.

Alice was skeptical. Phil could sound very convincing when he spoke of wanting to jumpstart their marriage, but his actions said otherwise. For all his talk to the contrary, he showed little inclination of changing his behavior. Only convenience held husband and wife together.

————

Phil would never forget the time he heard a knock on his door in the wee hours of the morning, not long before sunrise. The visitor, Bob Dylan, rushed into the apartment, eager to play a new song for Phil and David Cohen, who had just concluded another typical all-night session of drinking and singing and talking. Dylan insisted that each of the two play a song before he presented his new one. Phil obliged with "Power and the Glory." When his turn finally came around, Dylan picked up a guitar and sang "Mr. Tambourine Man." It was the first time he had played the song for anyone.

Phil, a huge fan of Dylan's work to begin with, was thunderstruck by this latest composition. Dylan's wild, juxtaposed images harkened back to the rhythmic, jazz-inspired works of the Beat Generation poets; they could have been lifted directly from Allen Ginsberg's early San Francisco poetry, or from Jack Kerouac's *Mexico City Blues*. Dylan, already being labeled a spokesperson for his generation—a title he was very reluctant to accept or acknowledge—had suddenly, in the course of one song, come dangerously close to becoming a generation's poet. "Mr. Tambourine Man," in Phil's judgment, was nothing short of a masterwork.

Not that Phil was especially surprised by the song: he had been hanging around Dylan long enough to expect virtually anything. He had witnessed Dylan's remarkable metamorphosis from lost but talented Midwestern singer to folk music's new *cause célèbre*. If anything, "Mr. Tambourine Man" was another signpost on an amazing artistic path. Dylan still wrote powerful statements on topical issues, yet more and more the words to his songs were moving away from traditional lyricism and closer to postmodern poetry; at times, it seemed almost coincidental that his words were set to music at all.

Still, for all that he admired in Dylan's work, Phil was not willing to totally embrace Dylan's new direction; he was not ready to accept the idea of making art for its own sake. Ever the idealist, Phil insisted that popular music could—and should—change the world.

"One good song with a message can bring a point more deeply to more people than a thousand rallies," he had written in 1963. A year later, with an album of topical songs and countless folk club appearances behind him, Phil had seen enough that he was able to state that "the commercial folk boom has reached its peak and is now on the decline." He also contended, perhaps a bit self-indulgently, that topical songs were legitimate, lasting artforms."Whether topical songs can be considered folk music right after they are written is a controversial point," he proposed, "but one thing is sure: Many of the topical songs written now will work their way into oral tradition and become a permanent mirror of the folkways and social issues of our time."

Dylan disagreed. He was growing skeptical of the actual influence of topical songs, including his own. In his opinion, it was better to aspire to a higher form of art.

"The stuff you're writing is bullshit," he told Phil, "because politics is bullshit. It's all unreal. The only thing that's real is inside you. Your feelings. Just look at the world you're writing about and you'll see that you're wasting your time. The world is, well . . . it's just absurd."

Dylan was equally emphatic in his interviews with the press. He was changing, he insisted. In the past, he had been writing what others wanted to hear, what they expected from him; in the future, he would be writing for himself.

In time, Phil would come around to accepting many of Dylan's ideas. Unfortunately, by the time he did, he would be lost in the maze of his own artistic purpose, running into the barriers of his personal limitations, political vision, and, perhaps most damaging of all, his disenchantment with America.

And Dylan would still be moving on.*

———

The overwhelming success of the 1963 Newport Folk Festival all but assured a strong interest in the gathering the following year, and a record number of people journeyed to the tiny Rhode Island town to see and hear the biggest names in the industry. As usual, there was an impressive selection of performers representing all types of music. Johnny Cash turned in a memorable performance, as did blues giant Muddy Waters. Joan Baez and Judy Collins returned, while such newcomers as Richie Havens and Eric Andersen made their first appearances at the festival.

Once again, the Bob Dylan performances—and there were three in 1964—drew the largest crowds. This time, however, audience response to Dylan was guarded. The singer featured works from his

---

* True to form, Phil was gracious in his analysis of his differences with Dylan. In the program for the 1964 Newport Folk Festival, he wrote:"I think he's slowly drifting away from song-writing because he feels limited by the form. More and more of his work will probably come out in poetry and free verse, and I wouldn't be surprised if he stopped singing altogether considering the over-adulation of his fans and the lack of understanding of audiences that identify with him."

forthcoming *Another Side of Bob Dylan*, and though some of the new numbers, such as the beautiful "Chimes of Freedom," sounded like the Bob Dylan that people come together to hear, entries like "It Ain't Me, Babe" and "All I Really Want to Do" left people grumbling that they hadn't ventured to Newport to hear Dylan sing about his love life.

Phil's performance, on the other hand, was widely embraced, leaving little doubt that he was taking over as folk music's premier topical singer-songwriter. Besides playing material from *All the News*, Phil served up a sampling of new selections that he hoped to include on his second album. The savage wit of "Draft Dodger Rag," a tune that lampooned the Selective Service and people's attempts to avoid the draft, was gracefully balanced by the patriotic "Power and the Glory"; "Links on the Chain," a recently written song chiding American labor unions for not taking a stronger stance in the civil rights movement, was offset by "What's That I Hear," an anthem extolling "the sound of old ways a-fallin'." To keep things loose, he called Eric Andersen onstage and the two ran through the Beatles' "I Should Have Known Better," much to the delight of a crowd that screamed and wailed like the British band's most ardent teenage followers.

Critical response to the Newport shows was pointed, with much of the focus on Bob Dylan and Phil Ochs. Folk hard-liners attacked Dylan for abandoning the type of music that had established his reputation, some critics going so far as to accuse him of selling out to the interests of commercialism. *Sing Out*, in an open letter to Dylan written by editor Irwin Silber, presented a eulogy for a man who, in Silber's opinion, "had somehow lost contact with people." Paul Wolfe, writing for *Broadside*, offered a lengthy essay comparing Phil and Dylan, praising the former while condemning the latter. "The Festival's most significant achievement," argued Wolfe, "was specific and twofold: it marked the emergence of Phil Ochs as the most important voice in the movement, simultaneous with the renunciation of topical music by its major prophet, Bob Dylan . . . The difference between the two performers became manifest: meaning vs. innocuousness, sincerity vs. utter disregard for the tastes of the audience, idealistic principle vs. self-conscious egotism. And even in his attempts at seriousness Dylan was bewildering."

Phil, in an admirable but highly questionable (in terms of its value to his career) move, defended Dylan in a blistering *Broadside* editorial of his own, chiding "Professor Silber and Student Wolfe" for dissecting Dylan as if he were a "rare, prize frog" in a biology class. "To cater to an audience's taste," suggested Phil, "is not to respect them, and if the audience doesn't understand that, they don't deserve respect."

The battle between Dylan's defenders and detractors, reflective of the schism developing between folk purists and the new songwriters, was only beginning to heat up. Newport '64 was a mere skirmish in comparison to what would occur a year later at the same festival. Then it would be all-out war.

———

As part of its efforts to promote voter registration, the Council of Federated Organizations assembled the Mississippi Caravan of Music, a troupe of folksingers that traveled from town to town, playing benefit concerts and meeting with local activists. Veterans such as Pete Seeger and Gil Turner were natural selections to headline the shows, which were rounded out by a group of younger, lesser known singers. When invited, Phil leapt at the opportunity to be part of the caravan.

Although well intentioned, the singers occasionally let professional interests cloud the main purpose of their mission. Squabbles broke out over the order of appearance, the length of a set, or the songs that were to be performed during a show; egos were bruised. Phil, who tended to treat any given performance, regardless of where it was held, as if it were an appearance at Carnegie Hall, was as susceptible as anyone to the petty bickering.

In all likelihood, a number of the singers, Phil included, underestimated the risks they were taking in the South. To some, the caravan was a glorified field trip of sorts: they would roll into town, talk to a bunch of the locals, play their concert, and move on. They had seen television reports or read about the violence in the South, but they had not been personally affected by it. In Phil's case, the element of danger only added a romanticized sense of purpose to the epic struggle playing in his mind's private movie.

These attitudes, such as they were, changed quickly. During the summer of 1964, Northern liberals and civil rights activists were given a practical education of the traditions of the South. Folksingers, all too quick to write songs critical of a region they had never visited, were suddenly confronting a political powder keg. Human rights, they learned, meant little to the people opposing their movement; freedom of speech meant even less.

Len Chandler, part of the caravan tour, witnessed the battle from a unique perspective. As one of only a few prominent young black folksingers, Chandler not only saw the confrontation from an activist's perspective, but as a minority he also felt the heat of racist hatred directed at him. "It was very intense," he recalled. "On the first day I was there, people drove by and shot up the porch where we were sitting."

This proved to be only one of numerous incidents. On another occasion, while riding through town with two others, Chandler found himself in the midst of an ugly scene when a car pulled up next to Chandler's at a stoplight, and a passenger in the other car leaned out the window and tried to beat the people in the car with a nightstick. Fortunately, no one was hurt. At the next stoplight, the car again pulled alongside Chandler's, and the passenger beat on the car with his club.

"We turned at the corner and got away from the car," said Chandler. "That was a policeman's nightstick, and the guy was trying to irritate us into doing something. He was probably sitting there with a gun in his other hand, or in his lap. We would have been dead if we had made the wrong move. Things like that were happening constantly."

For Phil, the Mississippi caravan tour became a harrowing experience. Prior to his jaunt through the state, his worst concert experience had been an occasional encounter with a heckler or angry audience member. It was much more menacing here. He had barely driven into the state when he heard the news that the bodies of James E. Chaney, Michael Schwerner, and Andrew Goodman, three young civil rights workers, had been found in the swamps. Suddenly, there could be actual danger in singing a controversial topical song, and Phil was convinced that somebody was going to kill him while he was onstage—a fear that would stay with him for the endurance of his career as a performer.*

---

* It was not uncommon for Phil to station friends or family members in key areas of a concert hall, to watch for potential assassins. Sonny Ochs recalled a time when she saw a short-haired man in the audience and became convinced that he was someone out to kill her brother, only to have her fears alleviated when the concert-goer laughed

Phil approached his week in Mississippi the way a journalist gathers information for a news story. He carried around a notebook and jotted down his impressions of the people and events around him. He met with the locals and asked them endless questions about their day-to-day lives. The more he saw and heard, the more alarmed he became. A year earlier, he had written "Talking Birmingham Jam," a sarcastic bit of work about what he perceived to be the South. Now, having seen firsthand the effects of racial discrimination and hatred, and feeling his initial shock being replaced by anger and outrage, he was more inclined to indict than to ridicule. In "Here's to the State of Mississippi," a seething new song written immediately upon his return from the South, Phil devoted eight lengthy verses to damning the racist society he had seen:

> *Here's to the State of Mississippi*
> *For underneath her borders*
> *The devil draws no line.*
> *If you drag her muddy rivers*
> *Nameless bodies you will find.*
> *Oh, the fair trees of the forest*
> *Have hid a thousand crimes.*
> *The calendar's lyin'*
> *When it reads the present time.*

And, in the song's chorus, he brought home his anger with the power of a hammer driven into an anvil:

> *Oh, here's to the land*
> *You've torn out the heart of,*

---

uproariously at "Draft Dodger Rag." Tom Paxton, aware of Phil's worries, decided to play a prank while he was standing on the wings of the stage, while Phil performed at one of the Town Hall hootenannies. Paxton found a two-by-four, and he snapped it off the stage sending off a crack that sounded like a pistol report.

"It scared the shit out of him," Paxton laughed. "I forget what he was singing at the time, but it was one of his 'out there' political songs. I thought, 'This is the one to do it on' and got the board."

Dave Van Ronk, also present at the concert, also laughed at the memory. "Tom dropped the two-by-four and Phil hit the deck," he said. "But he hit the deck in such a way that he did not fall on his guitar. He was a pro."

> *Mississippi find yourself*
> *Another country to be part of.*

"Here's to the State of Mississippi" instantly became one of Phil's most controversial songs. It drew shouts of approval whenever he performed it in the New York clubs, although some of Phil's friends argued that, in singling out just one state, he was taking an obvious, overly simplistic approach. Racism was not confined to one state— or to one region—of the country.

A number of Mississippi blacks stated objections of their own. They appreciated Phil's involvement with the cause, they said, but they were as much a part of Mississippi as their persecutors, and they were committed to saving the state, not providing it with a decent burial.

Phil was unaffected by either praise or protest. As a journalist, his job was to get to the truth as he saw it, even if it meant, as it occasionally did, that arrows would be slung at the messenger.

————

The fall and winter of 1964 found Phil writing at a torrid pace, turning out reviews and essays for the New York and Boston *Broadside* magazines, and composing some of his finest songs to date. He recorded five songs for a compilation album called *New Folks*. Club dates brought him a steady, if somewhat meager income. As if caught in the vortex of a hurricane, he seemed incapable of sitting still.

An ambitious recording project, *The Broadside Singers*, caught Phil at the height of his manic energy. The album, described by Phil as "a continuation of the spirit of the Almanac Singers of the forties," was a vinyl edition of *Broadside* magazine, full of the kind of topical and agit-prop songs that made Sis Cunningham and Gordon Friesen smile. All told, nine of folk music's best young talents, including Bob Dylan, Eric Andersen, Buffy Sainte-Marie, and Patrick Sky, contributed work to the album, making it the most impressive group effort to rise out of the New York folk scene. Phil sang and played on the album, composed some of its songs, produced it, and wrote its liner notes.

His leadership role could not be overlooked. In two years' time, he had advanced from the ranks of the unknown to the upper echelon of the country's folksingers, and he was still moving up. What he needed now was an album that would break him out on a national scale.

Chapter Five

I AIN'T MARCHING ANYMORE

PHIL'S SECOND ALBUM, *I Ain't Marching Anymore*, was released by Elektra in February 1965. Most of the recording's fourteen songs had been part of Phil's stage repertoire for the better part of a year, but for those who had not seen him during that time frame, the collection displayed a subtle shift in approach. Phil was still the patriot, still dedicated to the cause, but he was showing signs of weariness. The new album, like the first, opened with an antiwar song, but the voice on the second album was more direct—more activist and less journalist: he wasn't marching anymore.

> *Oh, I marched to the Battle of New Orleans*
> *At the end of the early British war,*
> *A young land started growin'*
> *The young blood started flowin'*
> *But I ain't marching anymore.*

The song's bridge broke away from the litany of bloody historical episodes and asked the question on the lips of everyone protesting the war in Vietnam:

> *It's always the old to lead us to the war,*
> *Always the young to fall,*
> *Now look at all we won with a sabre and a gun,*
> *Tell me, was it worth it all?*

The man who had written "Power and the Glory" had grown disillusioned, perhaps not with his country, but certainly with its leaders, and in "I Ain't Marching Anymore" he was taking his protest as far as to suggest the unthinkable:

> *Call it 'Peace' or call it 'Treason,'*
> *Call it 'Love' or call it 'Reason,'*
> *But I ain't marchin' anymore.*

"This borders between pacifism and treason, combining the best qualities of both," Phil offered in explanation of his new album's title song, allowing that his stance was not likely to win him friends in commercial radio markets. This, however, did not bother him in the least. If anything, he was feeling militant about his position. "The fact that you won't be hearing this song over the radio is more than enough justification for the writing of it," he said.

He would create better melodies and lyrics, but few, if any, of his songs would cut closer to the heart of self-definition, at least self-definition as an activist. "I Ain't Marching Anymore" instantly became his signature song.

Phil may not have been marching, but he couldn't help hearing the drumbeats. A lot had happened in the world since his first album had been released, and Phil, performing in his role of late-twentieth-century troubadour, had much to report in the new recording. The previous year's Harlem riots inspired "In the Heat of the Summer," a song of surprising durability, featuring one of Phil's most gripping melodies. Reflections on the assassination of John Kennedy ("That was the President") and the execution of murderer Caryl Chessman ("Iron Lady") were balanced by Phil's commentary on nameless, everyday people battling to survive poverty, racism, and corrupt or ineffective politicians. The civil rights movement and the Vietnam War were still major obsessions.

Evident everywhere was Phil's continued growth as a songwriter, even if, as on the first album, he ran through some of the songs too quickly. "The Hills of West Virginia," written after one of Phil's trips to Hazard, was a series of striking visual images. ("I was taking pictures with my mind," Phil commented. "When the trip was over, I set down these images, which really don't have any special messages.") As in "The Bells" on *All the News*, he took a favorite poem from his youth (Alfred Noyes' "The Highwayman") and assigned it a beautiful, haunting melody.

I Ain't Marching fared better than *All the News* at the marketplace. The new album, like its predecessor, received mixed reviews, although, significantly, the criticism was beginning to register from all over the country, rather than just from those regional markets where Phil performed regularly. A Wichita reviewer, conceding that the recording would not "win any fans among the American Legion and the DAR," called *I Ain't Marching* "one of the finest albums of topical music available." A Denver critic, agreeing that "you have to be in tune with this kind of music to like it," congratulated Phil on his convictions. "Don't be fooled by the title," he wrote. "Mr. Ochs is still marching, against war, against intolerance, against the South, and nearly everything else that troubles people today."

By now, Phil was all too familiar with the reaction to his work, pro and con, and in a humorous preemptive strike, he went as far as to list many of the most common complaints in his album's liner notes. Humor, he had discovered long ago, could disarm his harshest critic:

> And so people walk up to me and ask, "Do you really believe in what your songs are saying?"
>
> And I have to smile and reply, "Hell, no, but the money's good."

———

The money, in fact, was not very good, and Phil was growing impatient. He and Alice had separated for good about a month before *I Ain't Marching* was issued, and he now had more complicated financial obligations to address. On a professional level, he felt as if he was running in place—recording and performing at a steady clip, but never moving ahead. Albert Grossman, he complained, was ignoring him in favor of Bob Dylan, Peter, Paul and Mary, and other better known acts. It didn't matter to Phil that others were presently covering his songs, or that he had become one of the most highly respected topical songwriters in the business; he wanted to be a star.

It was time to gamble, and in a move that was perhaps as foolhardy as it was bold, Phil dropped Albert Grossman and replaced him with Arthur Gorson. In the short time that he had known him, Phil had grown very close to Gorson, who had taken such an intelligent and aggressive approach to organizing the Hazard benefits in the Village. Phil and Arthur shared the same political beliefs and commitment to activism—an essential ingredient for what Phil had in mind for his career.

Then there was the ironic simularity between Gorson's and Grossman's names, right down to the initials.

"I didn't know what I was stepping into," Gorson reflected years later. "I was stepping into competition with Albert Grossman because Phil wanted that. The name of the new company would be Arthur H. Gorson Management. So Phil had left ABGM to go to AHGM. It was all Phil's creation."

Phil immediately put Gorson to work, testing his negotiating abilities by sending him to Grossman's office to wrestle back his publishing contract. Phil had hoped to control his own copyrights—a radical concept in those days—and he was asking a lot when he sent Gorson to negotiate with someone as tough and seasoned as Grossman.

Grossman, though a bit surprised by Phil's leaving him for someone as inexperienced as Gorson, listened to what the young manager had to say, and to Gorson's amazement, he turned the publishing rights over without a fight.

"It's the right move," Grossman said to Gorson of Phil's switch in management, "but it's a mistake."

Phil and Arthur immediately established Barricade Music, Inc., a company which, in Phil's words, was dedicated to "revolution in songwriting." There was certainly little question that the company's distribution of wealth was unorthodox: Phil and Arthur were equal partners and, as such, they were to divide all publishing revenues equally. Phil's confidence and ability, said Gorson, were reaching new heights.

"I've never met anyone more ambitious than Phil," Gorson recalled, reflecting on the days when both he and Phil believed that anything was possible. "I came in at a point where Phil was fully up to speed. He would come in every day with songs, and a high percentage of it was really good stuff. It partially had to do with the scene, partially with Phil's ambition, and partially with the time in history and the events that were happening all around us. It was incredible."

One day, not long after establishing their partnership, Phil and Arthur found themselves walking down the street near Carnegie Hall. Although he had played in the hall as part of large hootenanny ensembles, Phil had fantasized, almost from his first day as a performer, about appearing there as a solo act. To Phil, playing Carnegie Hall signified an arrival.

Phil and Arthur tried the doors and, finding one open, snuck into the empty hall. The two made their way up the aisles to the front of the hall. Standing on the edge of the darkened stage and looking up at the tiers of seats above them, both felt a rush of excitement.

"Someday," Phil told Arthur, "we'll have this place."

Of that he was certain.

Phil buried another part of his past, though this time much more reluctantly, when Alice and Meegan moved to California. Alice had recently received a substantial inheritance, and she used the money to purchase a house in Mill Valley. Phil saw them off with mixed emotions. He and Alice would still bicker from time to time, but their relationship had been mostly cordial since their separation. As for Meegan . . . Phil recognized that he was less than an ideal father, but Meegan was the only person in his life that he had ever—and would ever—love unconditionally. He hated seeing her moving to a place so far away.

No one needed to remind Phil of his shortcomings as a husband or father. The breakup with Alice, though mutually agreed upon, had bothered Phil more than he let on. In "First Snow," an unreleased ballad, he expressed some of his feelings of regret:

First snow, down you dart,
Cold as the winter,
Cold as my heart.
Fall from the sky,
Please tell me why
I let her go
And lost her, first snow.

Phil would never get it right with women. A couple of months after his separation from Alice, he was introduced to a young Australian folksinger named Tina Date. Absolutely smitten, Phil made a number of awkward advances. Tina was attracted to Phil's intelligence and humor, but she was also repulsed by his sloppiness. In the months ahead, the two would see each other off and on, but nothing much would come of it.

It was just as well. With his career chugging ahead, Phil had little time for stops, romantic or otherwise, along the way.

———————

Joan Baez recorded "There But for Fortune," and while it was only a minor hit when it was eventually released as a single in the United States, it enjoyed solid success in England, where it eventually rose to the Number 13 slot on the charts. Phil might have enjoyed his song's success a lot more had he been able to place some of his own recorded material on the charts, but as it was, he had to be content in watching someone else score a hit with one of his best songs.

In fact, Phil was lucky that Baez had recorded his song in the first place. Baez had never been overwhelmed by Phil or his music, and she would have never recorded "There But for Fortune" had it not been for Jack Landron, who was then performing under the name of Jackie Washington.

"I knew Phil rather well," Landron recalled. "I used to stay in his apartment when I came into New York, and he used to stay in my house in Boston when he was in town. One time, while he was staying with me, he showed me 'There But for Fortune.' I liked the song, but I didn't like the line about my face being pale—which it isn't—so I changed it to 'Show me a prison, show me a jail/Show me a prisoner whose life has grown stale.'

"I was playing at the Club 47 one night when Joan came in. She used to play the spot, and I was playing the same night she had used to play. She came in with a tape recorder and said, 'Show me something new. I liked that song you were singing.' And I said, 'Oh, yeah, Phil wrote that.' She learned the song from me, and she used the version that had my changes in it."

Phil's music was being performed and recorded by others as well. Jim and Jean, now working on the West Coast in television, continued to feature Phil's songs, including "There But for Fortune," as part of their repertoire. The Modern Folk Quartet, a group popular with the collegiate set, recorded "The Bells." The Weavers had broken up, and Ronnie Gilbert, recording as a solo act, did "Power and the Glory." Frankie Valli and his group, on an album of folk songs, cut "New Town," an early number that Phil never got around to putting on record himself.

The popularity of the topical song was waning, at least in terms of its commercial rewards. Dylan, Baez, and Peter, Paul and Mary, among others, though still working topical and protest songs into their performances, were expanding their musical ranges, maintaining their already established followers while exploring new and—especially in Dylan's case—more daring forms. Their political commitment remained, but the folksingers seemed to have arrived at a collective conclusion that they risked losing their impact if they were too didactic in their music, or if they were perceived to be capable of performing only one type of song.

The immense of popularity of Barry McGuire's "Eve of Destruction," released the previous summer and easily the most commercially successful song to rise out of the folk movement, raised a lot of questions about the relationship between protest music and chart success. Folk purists universally condemned the song as a transparent attempt to cash in on both the growing national concern over the Vietnam War and the popularity of protest music at the time. Others argued that, while the song was far from being an artistic wonder, "Eve of Destruction" was valid for its ability to get listeners to focus on a crucial issue—the greater the sales figures, the more people reached.

When asked for his thoughts on the topic, Phil took a diplomatic stance. "Eve of Destruction," he said, contained "some very good lines," and it was important that a protest song reach a lot of people the way this song did. Still, in Phil's opinion, the song was a bad imitation—"like tenth-rate Dylan"—and its success would only encourage future imitations of an imitation.

"It's going to give a lot of people a bad impression of protest songs," he concluded. "So it'll be a good and bad thing. It will be an introduction of protest songs to many people, but it's a bad introduction. Better things have to happen. Better songs have to get on the charts."

Phil was doing his best to write a better song. He was again in the midst of a very fertile creative period, in which words and music came to him in flashes. This time around, Vietnam was his obsession.

His interest in the war had intensified in recent months. The Johnson-Goldwater campaign rhetoric had heightened the nation's awareness of events taking place in the Southeast Asian country, and Phil was convinced that his public opposition to the war was well-founded. These feelings were fortified when Phil audited some lectures at the Free University and subsequently met Stew Albert, a young civil rights–antiwar activist, and *Realist* magazine publisher Paul Krassner.

Phil and Krassner had corresponded a couple years earlier, after Krassner published an article by William Worthy about his controversial passport case. Phil had seen the piece, and wanting to write a song that was essentially based on the article, he contacted Krassner. The two discovered that they shared an irreverant sense of humor and a passion for politics.

"He was very down-to-earth, witty, dedicated, and uncompromising," said Krassner of his first impressions of Phil, pointing out that he was especially attracted to the way Phil could bring a sense of play to a topic or event that was deadly serious. "He wanted to sing 'I Ain't Marching Anymore' on *The Ed Sullivan Show*," Krassner recalled.

Through Krassner, Phil met Jerry Rubin, a fiery West Coast activist who was using his considerable organizational skills to mount a huge campaign against the Vietnam War. The outspoken and charismatic leader was planning a series of teach-ins and demonstrations in Berkeley, complete with lectures, demonstrations, and entertainment, culminating in the biggest rally yet against the war. During the event's planning stages, Paul Krassner recommended Phil as an ideal performer, and though he had never heard of Phil Ochs or his music, Rubin went along with the suggestion.

According to Krassner, Phil's job was to act as "a slab or mortar between all the bricks of speakers," which meant playing a song or two whenever there was danger of the event's being bogged down by too much speechifying. Rubin would simply give Phil a signal, and Phil would step up to the microphone and sing. A song like "I Ain't Marching Anymore" could entertain but also say more in a few verses than a speaker could get across in a half hour of lecturing.

Phil loved the idea. "A demonstration should turn you on, not turn you off," he told Krassner, stating an attitude adopted by numerous sixties activists. At the teach-in, Phil seemed to be everywhere, performing at the lectures, talking politics with the organizers, meeting with students. A year earlier, Phil had tried to connect with people at this level in Mississippi, but political tension had made it difficult and uncomfortable. In Berkeley, Phil was given a hero's welcome.

"They responded to him because he was unique," said Krassner.

"Phil was always accessible. If he was going to perform at a college, he'd get there early, just to get the feel of a place. You know, he would talk to the waitresses. So he was not only articulating their consciousness in his songs, but he was accessible, too. It made a big difference."

The Berkeley teach-in had a major impact on Phil's career. Phil, who had canceled a couple of paying gigs in order to appear in Berkeley, was convinced that he had found a new way to reach an audience. Prior to Berkeley, he had been reaching people on a limited basis. In his club performances, he was singing to a couple hundred people. His journeys to Hazard and Mississippi, although effective and valuable experiences, were also small-time affairs when compared to the way he was touching base with thousands of people at a demonstration or rally. His future, he decided, would have to include more of these bigger events.

———

Somehow, for reasons that would be greatly debated, Phil was not invited to play at Newport '65. Frustrated and insulted by the omission, Phil vowed to be part of the event, even if it meant having to sneak backstage to be with his friends.

In the meantime, he maintained his busy schedule of performances and benefits. Some, like his appearances at the "End the Vietnam War" demonstration at Haverford College, or his triumphant return to Ohio State, at a rally sponsored by the Free Speech Front, extended the good feelings of the Berkeley teach-in. At these performances, he heard hosannas shouted by thousands of students who hung on his every note and cheered his lambasting of government officials, warmongers, and even fellow liberals. He couldn't hit a sour note.

This, however, was not always the case. The larger audiences at higher-profile events also meant greater media coverage, and with the exposure came a deeper focus on the controversial nature of Phil's material. Phil might have been saluted by ovations on college campuses, by students who were at a prime age for the draft, but he was less likely to be embraced by their parents, who still regarded World War II as "the good war," and who, after watching Hitler conquer Europe with relative ease, were more likely than their children to subscribe to domino theories. Working-stiff taxpayers were not inclined to offer blanket endorsements to upstart folksingers hell-bent on making waves on their rather tranquil middle-class waters.

This much became clear when Phil signed on to perform a Hazard benefit in Baltimore. The benefit, sponsored by the Committee for Miners and the local Foghouse Folk Center, was to be held in Baltimore's Polytechnic Institute, but tickets had no sooner gone on sale than the show was jeopardized by two citizen complaints to the school board. Phil Ochs, said the complainants, was a "Communist" and could not be supported in any way by the school system.

The charges didn't bother Phil, who relished any controversy created by his music, and who tended to dismiss negative publicity as "a reverse kind of recognition." If anything, he said, the notoriety would make more people aware of his music.

"I don't want to make it like Belafonte or Bobby Darin," he insisted. "I want to make it in a more special way—with songs that don't pull punches, that don't go on television or make 'Top-40' radio stations."

Part of Phil's statement was indicative of his uncompromising nature, yet part of it was pure posturing. Phil would have loved nothing more than to have an enormous hit (or, better yet, a string of enormous hits), big-name recognition, and television appearances. For all of his public naysaying, he still wanted to be a star. He longed to be music's answer to James Dean.

———

The first annual New York Folk Festival, held on June 17–20 at Carnegie Hall, featured eight hootenanny-style concerts, two seminars, and a special performance for children. Noteworthy for their absence were Bob Dylan, Joan Baez, Pete Seeger, and Peter, Paul and Mary, but the talent-rich festival attracted bluesmen Muddy Waters, Son House, Mose Allison, and Eric Von Schmidt, along with such folk artists as Buffy Sainte-Marie, the Greenbriar Boys, Eric Andersen, and, to Phil's delight, Jim and Jean.

Phil turned in a sterling performance, his set opening with "I'm Going to Say It Now," a relatively new number that had become a favorite on college campuses, and continuing with selections from his two albums. In "Love Me, I'm a Liberal," another recent composition, he turned the sharp focus of his caustic political commentary on the hypocrisy of people who talked the liberal party line only if it was about issues that didn't affect them personally:

> *I cried when they shot Medgar Evers,*
> *Tears ran down my spine.*
> *And I cried when they shot Mister Kennedy,*
> *As though I'd lost a father of mine.*
> *But Malcolm X got what was coming.*
> *He got what he asked for this time.*
> *So love me, love me, love me,*
> *I'm a liberal.*

The song would always elicit a strange mixture of laughter, from nervous twittering from those who recognized themselves in Phil's indictment, to open roars of approval from the radical factions in the audience. The loudest was applause reserved for the song's penultimate verse:

> *Sure, once I was young and compulsive,*
> *I wore every conceivable pin.*
> *Even went to Socialist meetings,*
> *Learned all the old union hymns.*
> *Ah, but I've grown older and wiser,*
> *And that's why I'm turning you in.*
> *So love me, love me, love me,*
> *I'm a liberal.*

As always, the patter between songs became a major part of Phil's show, his humorous, self-deprecating style acting as an effective buffer for hard-hitting punchlines.

"Now, for a change, here's a protest song," he told his New York Folk Festival audience, speaking in his rapid-fire, staccato voice. "A protest song," he instructed, "is a song so specific that you cannot mistake it for bullshit." He paused briefly for effect, and to allow the laughter to die down. "Good word, bullshit," he continued. "Ought to be used more often, especially in Washington." Another pause. "Speaking of bullshit, I'd like to dedicate this song to McGeorge Bundy." And with that, he launched into the opening notes of "I Ain't Marching Anymore."

Phil's sarcasm was not for everyone. Disgusted audience members walked out of his shows. Others, feeling that they had come to hear music and not a sermon, shouted out their displeasure. Reviews of his performances were often laced with criticism of his onstage style. *Variety* magazine was not atypical in its review of his Folk Festival performance:

> Phil Ochs, who writes and sings semi-literate protest songs (one a taunting anti-liberal number) uttered a word probably never delivered in Carnegie Hall before. Seeing that it got a laugh, he said it again. Another laugh. The third time he realized he was playing to diminishing returns and like a kid who finds it no longer shocks the adults, he desisted.

Phil could only laugh when such reviews were brought to his attention. Accusing him of trying to shock his audiences was like accusing a cow of trying to give milk. Jolting people into a response—or, God forbid, *action*—was nothing less than a gadfly's sacred duty.

———

Phil drove with Arthur Gorson and Paul Krassner to Rhode Island for what proved to be the most controversial Newport Folk Festival in the event's short history. There had already been plenty of discussion as to why Phil and Tom Paxton, arguably topical music's top two songwriters, had not been invited to perform, with concert organizers claiming that there was only room for so many performers. The roster, they said, was already filled with "citybillies," and they were hoping to include as wide a variety of music as possible. Skeptics argued that the purists on the organizing committee were uncomfortable with the biting nature of some of the topical songs, that organizers wanted more affirmative music on the Newport stages.

Phil's only public response to his exclusion was a humorous aside published in *The Village Voice*: "As for the reasons for my not being invited to Newport, I wouldn't presume to guess their motivations, but I couldn't help but wonder, perhaps it's my breath?"

The festival was doomed from the outset. What had begun as a means for musicians, singers, and songwriters to gather, talk shop, and play for people who might otherwise never see them perform, was now sullied by feelings of resentment and competition. In one of the most bizarre occurrences in Newport history, Albert Grossman and Alan Lomax Jr., both hulking presences, wound up fighting and rolling around on the ground in a comical battle after Lomax slighted the Butterfield Blues Band, a group represented by Grossman, in his introduction to the Butterfield set.

Phil was appalled by the negativity that he witnessed at the festival. "The trouble with Newport '65," he commented afterward, "was that too many people forgot that it was supposed to be a festival. The cops were ridiculously harsh and rude. Many city performers were uptight about how well they would do professionally. And juvenile gossip seemed to be on too many people's tongues. It should have been called the Newport Fuzz Festival. If people don't take it so seriously next year it should turn out to be a whole lot better."

Phil had good reason to resent the festival's strict formality and security policies. After arriving at Newport, he had quickly discovered that, as a nonperformer, he did not have the kind of access to the event that he had enjoyed the previous two years. When he, Arthur Gorson, and Paul Krassner tried to enter the backstage area of the main stage, they were stopped by Ronnie Gilbert, who told them they would have to leave. When Phil asked for passes, he was refused.

"It was like a war zone to get into the festival, where Phil should have been embraced anyway," remarked Gorson. "Phil, Krassner, and I snuck in the back like we were in a commando movie or something. We climbed fences and crawled under fences until we got in backstage. Phil was very insulted that he wasn't invited that year, and then the insult became worse when Ronnie Gilbert wouldn't give him any courtesies."

Phil's treatment, however, paled in comparison to the rude reception meted out to Bob Dylan during his evening performance. When Dylan took the stage on July 25 for his highly anticipated concert, he was dressed like a rock star and had members of the Butterfield Blues Band behind him, and all hell broke loose when he broke into a highly amplified version of "Maggie's Farm," followed by an equally loud and distorted reading of "Like a Rolling Stone." Folk purists booed and shouted catcalls; others sat in stunned silence. *This was folk music?* Backstage, Pete Seeger, overcome in a purple rage, grabbed an ax and threatened to cut the power lines. People screamed at each other, angrily debating whether the music was appropriate for such a venerable gathering. When Dylan finally left the stage after beginning but failing to complete a third song, only to return with an acoustic guitar for two final numbers ("Mr. Tambourine Man" and "It's All Over Now, Baby Blue"), the crowd felt vindicated, as if it had driven him back to the kind of music he was supposed to be playing in the first place.

Phil was utterly blown away by the spectacle. Not only had Dylan shown enormous courage in his performance, but he was also redefining the direction his music would be taking in the future. Phil just shook his head and laughed in amazement.

"Some people saw fit to boo Bob Dylan after each song," he wrote in defense of Dylan's performance,

> and I think they were getting a needed dose of musical shock treatment. Dylan, as usual, was doing the unexpected, but was quite responsibly doing what any real artist should, that is, performing the music he personally felt closest to and putting his own judgment before that of his audience. . . . The people that thought they were booing Dylan were in reality booing themselves in a most vulgar display of unthinking mob censorship. Meanwhile, life went on all around them.

Dylan was badly shaken by the hostile response to his music. He had not taken the stage to upset his audience, and he was both angered and depressed when he was rebuffed. "It's all music, no more, no less," he told Robert Shelton. "I know in my own mind what I'm doing. If anyone has imagination, he'll know what I'm doing. If they can't understand my songs, they're missing something . . . What I write is much more concise now than before. It's not deceiving."

From the moment Dylan had walked onstage, Newport '65 had taken on the atmosphere of a circus, with Dylan standing in the center ring. Folksinger Patrick Sky recalled a moment when he, Dylan, and Donovan were walking across a field and suddenly found themselves being pursued by a mob of reporters and fans.

"A herd of people were running after us," he said, "so we started running across the field. When we got to this fence, Donovan and I made it over, but Dylan couldn't. We reached over and grabbed him by the seat of the pants and dropped him over just as the crowd got there. It was frightening."

In retrospect, Dylan's "going electric" at Newport should not have been that much of a surprise. Earlier in the year, the Byrds had charted a huge hit with an electric version of "Mr. Tambourine Man." Dylan's most recent album, *Bringing It All Back Home*, released in March, had featured an electric side and an acoustic side, the former presenting a stunning new poetry set to music that combined the best elements of folk, blues, and rock 'n' roll. His new single, "Like A Rolling Stone," found him playing with a rock band backing, and was rising up the charts at the time of the Newport festival. Dylan had always been a volatile presence on the music scene, so his plugging a solid-body guitar into an amplifier should have surprised no one.

To his most severe critics, Dylan might have seemed similar to the main character of his first big commercial hit—out on his own, with no direction home. They might have even taken a jaded satisfaction in watching what they presumed to be Dylan's fall from grace. Ultimately, the critical attacks would bother Dylan personally, but they would have little effect on his art.

He was mapping out his own newly discovered territory.

And others, Phil included, would follow.

———

Newport '65 changed everything. Although his performance drew nasty, high-minded rejections from the likes of *Sing Out!* and *Boston Broadside*, Dylan saw his influence fan out to a new roster of musicians playing folk-rock. Groups such as the Turtles, the Mamas and the Papas, Simon and Garfunkel, and the Lovin' Spoonful—some boasting of members who had toiled in obscurity during the heyday of the Village folk scene—were embraced by large national followings. In perhaps the greatest irony of all, the Byrds recorded an electric arrangement of Pete Seeger's "Turn, Turn, Turn" and enjoyed another major hit.

The critical salvos had done their damage to Dylan, and his tight circle of friends, including Phil, felt the immediate effects. Dylan still held court at some of his old Village haunts, but he was now turning his anger and resentment on his friends, engaging them in cutting games of dirty dozens that, on any given night, could reduce a victim to tears. It was not uncommon to find Dylan seated at a table in the Kettle of Fish, winged by friends Bobby Neuwirth and David Cohen (now calling himself David Blue), who egged him on as he launched verbal missiles at Phil, Eric Andersen, Dave Van Ronk, Tom Paxton, and others.

"Hey, maybe you think you're gonna make it like me," he would taunt, mocking their desire for fame or wealth. "Nobody's gonna make it. Maybe you think you're gonna do what I did. Nobody's gonna do it."

In hindsight, the tongue-lashings were probably as much self-directed as they were intended for other targets. Dylan had never aspired to be a leader; he had never written lyrics with the intention of their being analyzed by the academics. If he was guilty of inventing himself over and over again, it was largely to accommodate his immense artistry, as well as to act as a defense mechanism against the attacks on his ever-changing musical direction. Dylan had drunk success to the dregs, and he was familiar with its bitter aftertaste. For the life of him, he could not understand the ambitions of someone like Phil Ochs, nor did he need Phil to act as his apologist when times were rough.

"You ought to find a new line of work, Ochs," he'd tell Phil. "You're not doing very much in this one." On another occasion, he lashed out even more viciously: "Why don't you just become a stand-up comic?"

Phil took it all in, feeling the effects of the parrying, fighting back when he believed the attacks were going too far. In arguments, he could hold his own with Dylan or anyone else. Others, like Eric Andersen, took the criticism and sarcasm more to heart.

"Dylan was always brutal," noted Len Chandler, who was rarely one of Dylan's victims. "Dylan had a real hatchet mouth, and it was always very competitive between him and Phil. There was a kind of competition going on about who wrote what, and what was better— that kind of stuff."

"In retrospect," offered Tom Paxton, "I strongly think that the stuff happening with Bob and Phil at the Kettle of Fish was about eighty-percent *shtick*. Some of it was real. Phil was very envious of Bob. *All* of us were envious of Bob's success. What the hell? We all started out with the same equipment—guitars and voices—and one of us was suddenly a comet. It's unsettling, and nobody's going to handle that perfectly."

One thing was indisputable: after being punched around and analyzed to death by the critics, Dylan was not up to taking a lot of guff from his friends. He demanded absolute support from those around him, and there were dire consequences for those who did not understand this.

Phil learned as much one evening after he, Dylan, and a host of others performed at a "Sing In for Peace" at Carnegie Hall. Dylan had a new song—"Can You Please Crawl Out Your Window?"—that he wanted to play for Phil and David Blue. Dylan was especially proud of the number, calling it "the one I've been trying to do for years." After hearing the song, Blue knew better than to offer anything but an unqualified endorsement, but Phil volunteered a straightforward, honest appraisal.

"It's okay," he said.

"What do you mean?" Dylan challenged Phil, instantly angry at him. "Listen to it again."

Phil listened as Dylan ran through the song a second time, but another hearing did not alter his initial reaction.

"It's okay," he told Dylan, "but it's not going to be a hit."

Dylan went through the ceiling. "You're crazy, man," he raged. "It's a great song. You only know protest, that's all."

Dylan fumed, unable to accept Phil's failure to see the song's hit potential. A limousine arrived to take Dylan, Phil, and others to an uptown club. It had only gone a few blocks up Sixth Avenue when Dylan ordered the driver to pull over. When the limo had pulled up to the curb, Dylan demanded that Phil get out of the car. Phil thought Dylan was joking.

"Get out, Ochs," Dylan said a second time, making certain that Phil did not misunderstand him. As Phil stepped from the limousine, Dylan delivered his final blows. "You're not a folksinger," he snarled. "You're a journalist."

Phil was on the mark with his assessment of the song's commercial potential. "Can You Please Crawl Out Your Window?" went nowhere when it was released as a single a short time later. Dylan, not surprisingly, had the final say, not only to Phil, but to all the people he felt were putting him down or holding him back, when he issued "Positively Fourth Street," one of the most vitriolic attacks ever put on record. The times were indeed a-changin'.

In a year that had seen him constantly on the move, performing non-stop in folk clubs and university theaters, at political rallies and folk festivals, and at all points in-between, Phil drew some of his greatest satisfaction from several brief excursions to Canada. Canadian audiences, he was happy to discover, were well informed of the political goings-on in the United States, and his topical songs were as well received as they might have been if he had been writing about events taking place in Canada. Phil was especially pleased when the Canadian Federation of English Teachers went so far as to nominate "Here's to the State of Mississippi" as "Song of the Year."

The country appeared to bring him new sources of inspiration. He basked in the debates generated by the controversial content of some of his songs; he thrived on the discussion about whether he was a socialist or a communist. Each newsclipping and editorial, pro or con, was carefully taped into the pages of his expanding scrapbook of career highlights.

He was in Toronto, on the very first day of his very first trip outside of the United States, when he came up with the words and music to the song that would easily become his most popular:

Sit by my side, come as close as the air,
Share in a memory of gray.
And wander in my words, and dream about the
Pictures that I play of changes.

The ballad featured Phil's most beautiful melody to date, with lyrics that were pure poetry:

Scenes of my young years were warm in my mind,
Visions of shadows that shine.
Till one day I returned and found they were the
Victims of the vines of changes.

By staying abstract, Phil had a song that worked on many levels. At the time of the song's writing, he still had Alice very much on his mind. It had not been long since she and Meegan had moved to the West Coast. Phil's bittersweet memories of his and Alice's relationship, coupled with the feelings he had on being out of the country and away from his friends, left him in a nostalgic mood, edged with

the kind of sadness that anyone feels when going through changes
that are not entirely welcome:

> *Passions will part to a strange melody,*
> *As fires will sometimes burn cold.*
> *Like petals in the wind, we're puppets to the*
> *Silver strings of souls of changes.*
>
> *Your tears will be trembling, now we're somewhere else.*
> *One last cup of wine we will pour.*
> *And I'll kiss you one more time and leave you on the*
> *Rolling river shores of changes.*

Phil realized, the moment he had finished the song, that he had
something special on his hands. He had written a work of great passion, combining a simple but memorable melody and lyrics in a way
that had both artistry and commercial potential. He called Alice in
California and sang the song to her over the telephone. He then
phoned Arthur Gorson in New York.

"He called to tell me that the earth had changed," Gorson recalled, laughing. "That was one of the things that set Phil Ochs apart
from most of the others: there was no moderation. Everything was
the best, the most incredible, the most important. When he called
me, he was freaking out. He had just written the best song in history."

———

As it turned out, that judgment would be short-lived.

At the end of November, Phil and Arthur embarked on an abbreviated tour of the United Kingdom. Arthur had visited England earlier
in the year to set up a UK publishing deal for Phil. He had been impressed by the enthusiasm for folk music in London, and had subsequently arranged, through British promoter Tito Burns, for Phil to
appear in London, Manchester, and Nottingham.

The concerts were well received, finding Phil serving up such old
chestnuts as "Talking Plane Disaster" and "What's That I Hear,"
along with such fresh-off-the-press entries as "Changes" and "Flower
Lady." The British press offered respectful write-ups of the concerts,
comparing him to Bob Dylan, who had toured the country earlier in
the year, and who had himself spoken favorably of Phil. "I just can't

keep up with Phil," Dylan had told London reporters, "and he just keeps getting better and better and better."

Phil was delighted to discover the appreciation for topical music in England, but in his interviews, he offered hints that his music, like Dylan's, would be taking a new direction in the near future.

"I'm at the point in my songwriting," he declared, "where I give more consideration to the art involved in my songs rather than the politics." By his estimation, far too many bad songs were being accepted because they supported the right causes or had acceptable messages. "As bad as it may sound," he insisted, "I'd rather listen to a good song on the side of segregation than a bad song on the side of integration."

England, like Canada, sparked Phil's creativity, and he filled scraps of paper with lines and titles for potential songs. One evening, as he and Arthur were returning to London from a concert in Manchester, Phil began working on a new song. He and Arthur were traveling by lorry, Arthur sitting at the wheel while Phil slouched in the back and looked up at the stars:

> *And the night comes again to the circle-studded sky*
> *The stars settle slowly, in loneliness they lie*
> *Till the universe explodes as a falling star is raised*
> *The planets are paralyzed, the mountains are amazed*
> *But they all glow brighter from the brilliance of the blaze*
> *With the speed of insanity, then, he dies.*

The words came to him in a rush, as if all of his experiences in recent years, all the sensory detail and every scrap of conversation, everything he could store in his songwriter's mind, had come bursting out.

> *In the green fields of turning a baby is born*
> *His cries crease the wind and mingle with the morn*
> *An assault upon the order, the changing of the guard*
> *Chosen for a challenge that's hopelessly hard*
> *And the only single sign is the sighing of the stars*
> *But to the silence of the distance, they're sworn.*

The chorus resounded with the voices of people throughout history, all waiting to be saved.

So dance, dance, dance,
Teach us to be true
Come dance, dance, dance,
'Cause we love you.

It was the story of Jesus, an account of the life and death of John F. Kennedy, and a commentary on every heroic leader who had passed under the sun.

Images of innocence charge him to go on
But the decadence of history is looking for a pawn
To a nightmare of knowledge he opens up the gate
A blinding revelation is served upon his plate
That beneath the greatest love is a hurricane of hate
And God help the critic of the dawn.

Years later, in an interview with Studs Terkel, Phil called the song "a study of the process." In ancient times, he explained, people sacrificed a healthy young male in his prime to the gods. In modern times, it was no different.

"The Kennedy assassination, in a way, was destroying our best in some kind of ritual," Phil said. "People say they really love the reformer, they love the radical, but they want to see him killed. It's a certain part of the human psyche—the dark side of the human psyche."

The sacrifice was inevitable:

They say they can't believe it, it's a sacrilegious shame
Now who would want to hurt such a hero of the game
But you know I predicted it, I knew he had to fall
How did it happen, I hope his suffering was small
Tell me every detail, I've got to know it all
And do you have a picture of the pain?

All ten verses of "Crucifixion" were essentially written in one sitting, during the two-hour ride from Manchester to London. In years to come, whenever he discussed the composition of what he himself would call his greatest song, Phil would be hard-pressed to pinpoint exactly how he had come to write it on that particular night, under those particular circumstances, but he was quick to reiterate that

"Crucifixion" was not a piece that just materialized as a fully realized work, out of nowhere.

"I don't know where the songs come from," he insisted, saying that most of his songs rose from his subconscious. "You know, you talk about things, you discuss the assassination and read about it—all those things. Then you go to see a movie, you meet a girl, you get drunk . . . and somehow, out of all that, comes a subconscious process."

Arthur Gorson had seen Phil at his most creative, and he agreed with his overall explanation. "Phil wrote ['Crucifixion'] very quickly," he recalled. "There were ideas and thoughts and bits and pieces, and the idea of the assassination and how to deal with it, and all he had been laboring with for quite a while. When it came, it just poured out. It was the culmination of a lot of ruminating, thinking about this particular subject matter and how to express it in a universal way."

"Crucifixion" was the daring, poignant, disturbing, and brilliantly passionate kind of song that Phil had been aspiring to write; a work maddeningly beautiful and terrifying. If, over the span of a couple of hours in England, he had found himself at the beck and call of true genius, he was now obligated to keep it nearby, in all the work that he would be doing from that point on. Like those before him, he would learn how difficult that could be.

Chapter Six

CHANGES

ON FRIDAY, January 7, 1966, Phil Ochs made his solo debut before a capacity crowd at Carnegie Hall. The show represented not only the realization of a longstanding dream; it also marked the end of a lengthy, trying journey for Arthur Gorson.

For the better part of a year, Gorson had attempted to find someone to produce the concert, but nobody was interested. Concert promoters were skeptical of Phil's ability to bring in a crowd large enough to earn a profit. He would be a good draw as part of a package deal, they argued, but he didn't have the following to pull off the show by himself. Harold Leventhal, who knew more than a little about concert production, suggested that Phil test the waters by staging a solo concert at Town Hall. If there was a substantial ticket demand for that show, he might be willing to produce a program at Carnegie Hall.

Phil dismissed the idea outright. Leventhal, he felt, was being too conservative. As far as Phil was concerned, his career was not moving along quickly enough. Others had broken through to national recognition; now it was his turn.

Arthur Gorson agreed, although he, like others before him, was put off by Phil's persistent impatience. Gorson was not, by nature, anywhere near as ambitious as Phil, nor was he inclined to assert himself as forcefully as his client. He would get defensive when Phil accused him of not pushing hard enough, even though he knew that Phil had a valid point when he insisted that he was as good as other contemporaries enjoying greater success.

Eventually, when it became apparent that they weren't going to find someone to produce a Carnegie Hall show, Phil and Arthur decided to put it together themselves.

"Everyone said it was way out of reach," Gorson recalled. "Well, we didn't know much about producing big concerts at Carnegie Hall, but we knew how to produce concerts."

Only Phil and Arthur could have concocted a scheme for staging a concert designed *not* to make money, but that's exactly what they did. Their main objective, they decided, would be to fill the hall and use the sold-out performance as a publicity tool in the future. To accomplish this, they kept ticket prices low enough to stimulate sales, yet adequate enough to cover the expenses of renting the hall and paying advertisers. To publicize the event, they blanketed Manhattan with signs, posters, and handbills, and took out daily ads in *The New York Times* and other newspapers. People may not have heard of Phil Ochs or his music before, but they knew for certain that he was playing at Carnegie Hall. The ploy worked: every seat in the hall was sold three weeks prior to the show.

"Promotion was our main concern," said Gorson, "and we targeted our audience properly. We knew Phil's audience, and we advertised in places where they were. We priced the tickets so low that no one could say no. Then we kept running ads. There were three weeks of ads in *The New York Times* that said, 'Phil Ochs at Carnegie Hall' with 'Sold Out' running across the ads. It was a big career move."

According to the plan, the concert would be taped for eventual release as a live album. Record buyers across the country were familiar with Carnegie Hall's reputation, and an album recorded in that venue would have built-in credibility. Phil had a wealth of new material to play—more than enough for an album. "There But for Fortune" and "Changes" would act as cornerstones for the recording, which would be fleshed out with selections of his more recent topical songs.

The night of the concert finally arrived. Gertrude Ochs, along with her mother-in-law and daughter, came to New York City for Phil's big moment. Outside the hall, Phil posed proudly next to a concert poster announcing the show's sold-out status; he was now officially a serious artist and a star. Inside, Fanny Ochs took a look around and, seeing all the young, longhaired college kids, declared, "A barber could clean up in this place."

Unfortunately, Phil was hit with another case of performance anxiety shortly before the show. His throat constricted and his mouth went dry, reducing him to a raspy-voiced, backstage wreck. He repeatedly cleared his throat and drank glass after glass of water. Noth-

ing helped. The more he tried to straighten himself out, the worse he
seemed to become.

The show itself, although well received by those in attendance,
was largely forgettable. Phil's voice never returned entirely, and each
song became a struggle. You didn't have to be a Phil Ochs fanatic to
realize that the man onstage was not the same singer who had built
an enviable reputation in the New York club scene. Robert Shelton,
an Ochs booster from the early days, tried to give Phil the benefit of
the doubt in his mixed review of the show: "Mostly, one suspects, it
was a bad case of nerves that kept the boyish, charming, touseled-
haired, 25-year-old former journalism student from bringing the
many fine things he has in his verbal-musical arsenal to the auditorium."

The show had its better moments, more often when Phil was talking than when he was singing. His between-songs patter and song
introductions remained as sharp as ever, drawing laughter and applause from the Carnegie Hall audience. Phil's wit and sense of co-
medic timing served him well, especially when he was directing them
at such a hot, controversial topic as the recent American military
intervention in the Dominican Republic:

> There's been a drastic change in American foreign policy in re-
> cent months. Take the Dominican Republic—which we did . . .
> a little while ago, killing a few people here and there—mostly
> there . . . saving the day for freedom and democracy in the West-
> ern Hemisphere once again, folks. I was over there, entertaining
> the troops. I won't say which troops. Over there with a USO
> group including Walter Lippmann and Soupy Sales . . . I played
> there in a small coffeehouse called The Sniper . . . and this was
> my most unpopular song . . . with the poetic, symbolic title,
> "The Marines Have Landed on the Shores of Santo Domingo."

There was nothing funny about the song that followed—not a
single humorous line. Phil was as adept as anyone in using a punchline to set up the knockout blow.

If Phil's voice betrayed him during his Carnegie Hall outing, his
passion carried the day. His messages burned at the center of his
songs, and his followers were happy to accept them, no matter how
they were delivered. In the evening's final number, Phil played a new
song that offered a concise explanation of his purpose as an artist

and a man. It was as strong a personal credo as his "revolution in songwriting" motto:

> *And I won't be laughing at the lies, when I'm gone.*
> *And I can't question how or where or why, when I'm gone.*
> *Can't live proud enough to die, when I'm gone.*
> *So I guess I'll have to do it while I'm here.*

Both Phil and Arthur were stung by reviews of the concert. It was bad enough that the show itself came under fire. Phil had endured enough negative criticism to know better than to take a bad review to heart, and he knew, when he looked at it honestly, that the show had been less than an unqualified success. What really hurt was the suggestion, brought up by both *The New York Times* and *The Village Voice*, that he might have played Carnegie Hall before he was ready. That kind of criticism slashed at something vital.

––––––––

The tapes of the Carnegie Hall concert confirmed the critics' comments; after listening to them, Phil and Arthur concluded that there was very little usuable material for the projected live album. Another show would have to be recorded.

The second taping fared only slightly better. This time, the concert took place in Boston's Jordan Hall. Over the past couple of years, Phil had built a sizeable following in Boston, and a concert there was seen as an ideal place for him to work before a receptive audience. Phil, however, was so worked up about getting things right the second time around that he worked himself into a frenzy, and by the time he walked onstage, he was so overwrought with anxiety that he was barely able to get through the performance.

Neither artist nor recording company knew what to do. By this time, Elektra had invested a fair amount of money in the live-album project, and Phil was artistically committed to the concept. It had been nearly a year since the release of Phil's last album, and all parties were eager to get a new product on the market.

Rather than attempt still another taping, which would have been expensive and could offer no promise of better results, Phil, Arthur, and Elektra producer Jac Holzman decided to use the existing material, along with newly recorded music, to piece together the album.

In a New York studio, Phil re-recorded many of the songs he had performed onstage, as well as vocal overdubs to enhance some of the others. His stage patter, audience response, and applause were skillfully spliced into the studio material, giving the album the feeling of a live Phil Ochs performance.

After completing the recording, Phil turned his attention to the album's packaging. In the liner notes to his first two records, Phil had written explanatory notes about the songs themselves. This time around, he had a different plan—something that would address his disgust with the Vietnam War and the attendant anti-Asian sentiments that he heard everyday. Instead of writing statements of his own, Phil selected eight short poems by Mao Tse-tung, all to be placed on the back cover, under which Phil posed a simple question: *Is this the enemy?*

"That's not a practical question," Phil said at the time. "It introduces something many people are not aware of: that this man is more sensitive than Lyndon Johnson. It's an esthetic question."

Not surprisingly, Elektra was opposed to the idea, esthetics or no esthetics. Given the raging national debate over the escalation of the war in Southeast Asia, Phil's confrontational album jacket was ill-advised. Record stores and distribution companies were almost certain to balk at carrying the album, and from an artistic standpoint, Phil risked seeing discussion of the coverwork overshadow the music itself. Elektra asked Phil to consider using different liner notes, but Phil held fast. One of his purposes as an artist was to challenge the status quo and force his listeners to think about topics that otherwise troubled them; changing the notes was a concession he was not prepared to make.*

Phil Ochs in Concert may not have been a true live album, but it ranked as Phil's finest effort as a recording artist to that point. The album's eleven songs included "Changes" and "Love Me, I'm a Liberal"—two of Phil's most popular concert staples—as well as the usual assortment of commentary on the issues of the day. "Bracero," Phil's ode to the overburdened and underpaid immigrant workers,

* In its review of *Phil Ochs in Concert*, *Variety* magazine posed a question of its own— one that Phil himself would have been hard-pressed to answer: "Could he sing this type of song in China?" Chairman Mao may have written some poetry, but he was hardly a friend of cultural or artistic expression, regardless of what Phil thought of his sensitivity.

was a standout, as was "There But for Fortune," which he was finally putting on record nearly three years after its writing. Of all the songs that Phil would ever write, none would show his humanity as brilliantly as the four brief verses of "There but for Fortune":

Show me a prison, show me a jail,
Show me a prison man whose face is growing pale,
And I'll show you a young man with many reasons why,
And there but for fortune may go you or I.

When the album was released in March 1966, critics praised *Phil Ochs in Concert* as "vicious, brilliant dynamite" and "a good sampling of [Phil's] songwriting and opinions." *Billboard* magazine gave it a "Special Merit Pick" listing, while *Cash Box* recommended it as "a fast-moving set." Most important of all, record buyers picked up the record, eventually making it Phil's first entry on the *Billboard* charts.

———

The Federal Bureau of Investigation had little trouble answering Phil's rhetorical question about whether Mao Tse-tung was the enemy; what FBI agents wanted to know was if Phil Ochs was an enemy.

By 1966, he had an expanding file in the Bureau offices, and had been brought to the direct attention of J. Edgar Hoover. The FBI director, who had once called beatniks one of the country's biggest threats, was as busy as ever, working overtime to keep his eyes on such national security risks as the civil rights and antiwar movements.

Phil was now under regular FBI surveillance. When he performed in Canada in 1965, a legal attaché from Ottawa saw to it that a report fell into the hands of the Bureau. When he played at an antiwar rally in Philadelphia in October 1965, special agents in the city made certain that his participation was duly entered into his file. When he became involved with Disaster Relief to Cuba, contributing to help victims of a hurricane, agents noted his concern in his file.

Was Philip David Ochs a communist? A national security risk? Inquiring FBI minds needed to know.

Reports on Phil contained appendixes connecting the folksinger to such organizations as the Progressive Labor Party, the Progressive Labor movement, and the Greater New York Labor Press Club—all organizations suspected by the FBI as being communist in nature. In digging into Phil's past, the FBI determined that he had performed a benefit for Rosenberg co-defendant Morton Sobell—a sure sign that his heart was in all the wrong places.

Despite such damning evidence, the FBI decided that Phil's activities were not serious enough to demand further action. Keeping a file in Washington D.C. would suffice.

As of February 16, 1966, Phil Ochs was officially classified as an FBI "Security Matter."

———

New songs were coming to Phil at a pace that was amazing even by the songwriter's prolific standards. Anything, it seemed, could inspire a new number. A spat with Tina Date led to "I've Had Her," a solid bit of poetry with a particularly nasty punchline. A viewing of *The Long Voyage Home* prompted the wistful "Pleasures of the Harbor." A fragment of overheard conversation ("It wouldn't interest anybody outside a small circle of friends") ended up as the title and theme of a wicked commentary on American apathy. By early summer, Phil had enough material for another album.

The new record, Phil decided, was going to be a radical departure from the voice-guitar format of his first three albums. He envisioned an album of complex musical arrangement, in which each song would be treated as if it was a short film. Some of the songs would require full orchestration with carefully layered arrangements; others would be stripped back, giving his lyrics maximum impact. The album, as Phil envisioned it, was going to take plenty of time and money to produce.

The problem was finding someone to do it. Elektra was not enthusiastic about underwriting the costs of the album, partly because, as a small company, it could not easily produce an album of such ambition, and partly because the sales figures for Phil's previous three albums did not justify the expense. Phil's albums sold reasonably well by folk standards, but to be profitable in the kind of project he was now proposing, he would have to cross over into pop audiences, and Elektra was not at all convinced that he had the ability or appeal.

With nowhere else to turn, Phil vented his frustration on Arthur Gorson, browbeating his manager for the way things were going around the office. Barricade had been steadily adding new clients to its roster, and Phil accused Arthur of paying more attention to the careers of David Blue, Tom Rush, Eric Andersen, and others than he did to his original client and partner. "Changes," Phil insisted, should have been his breakthrough hit, but it was never issued as a single. Instead, Barricade clients Jim and Jean turned their interpretation of the song into a minor hit. Then, when Arthur formed Wild Indigo Productions as a record-producing branch of Barricade, his first production was a Jim and Jean album containing the duet's arrangement of "Crucifixion." Phil voiced no objection to the way the song was recorded, though he privately complained that he should have at least had the opportunity to record his own song before someone else covered it.

Despite his frustrations, Phil decided to hold off on taking any action. He and Elektra were due to discuss a new contract, and these negotiations would have as much to say as anything about his future with his record company and manager.

———

Phil spent much of the year touring in support of *Phil Ochs in Concert*, playing almost all of the album's contents and even reciting some of Mao's poetry from the stage. He worked some of his new songs into the shows, but with the exception of "Changes," a crowd-pleaser from the beginning, audiences preferred his topical material, particularly the antiwar songs. "Cops of the World," a sarcastic number depicting the United States as a global bully, drew approving cheers every time Phil performed it. "White Boots Marching in a Yellow Land," another Vietnam commentary, and "I Ain't Marching Anymore" elicited similar response.

It was more of the same when, after a year's absence, Phil played at the Newport Folk Festival. The furor over Dylan's defection to the ranks of rock 'n' roll had calmed down, but sentiment toward topical music still ran high. At Newport, Phil was greeted as if he were one of the few remaining bastions against the invading heathens of commerce; his new material would be accepted, or at least tolerated, as long as he continued to play the topical songs.

For the first time in his life, Phil was facing a powerful artistic dilemma, brought on, no doubt, by a division in his public persona. His political self had changed very little over the past couple of years, even as his music was significantly evolving. He still played political rallies, especially antiwar assemblies, and he was as outspoken as ever in his opinions. Such endeavors, though welcomed by activists and folk music buffs alike, were not enough. As the numbers of topical songwriters continued to dwindle, fans expected Phil to seize the moment and wear the crown that Bob Dylan had abandoned. Ironically, had he chosen to accept this role, Phil might have achieved the stardom he wanted so badly.

Phil's decision to move on was not motivated by pure artistry alone. Indeed, he was inspired by Dylan's *Highway 61 Revisited* and the Beach Boys' *Pet Sounds*, which stood as dramatic proof of the way established musicians could change creative direction. Like the rest of the world, Phil had been bowled over by the Beatles' 1966 American chart entries, *Rubber Soul* and *Yesterday and Today*, which had raised the artistic ante in commercial pop. In addition, there were signs that folk-grounded acts had made adjustments to reach spots on the charts. Throughout the summer of 1966, Phil witnessed successful albums launched by the Mamas and the Papas, the Lovin' Spoonful, Simon and Garfunkel, the Byrds, We Five, Chad and Jeremy, and Peter, Paul and Mary.

From a purely commercial standpoint, Phil was also intrigued by the overwhelming success of movie sound tracks, which dominated the market throughout the year. The sound tracks for *The Sound of Music*, *Fiddler on the Roof*, *Zorba the Greek*, and *My Fair Lady* had been listed on the charts for over a year, and the new entry for 1966, *Dr. Zhivago*, moved quickly to the head of the pack; even an album with the theme for television's *Batman* found a spot in the *Billboard 150*.

Phil's love of the movies had only grown over the years. He would take in a movie—or sometimes two or three—whenever he had the chance, and he still harbored the faint hope, which he would bring up from time to time, of acting in the movies himself.* Writing for the

---

* At one point during this period, Phil was offered the lead role in *Wild in the Streets*, a feature film about a rock 'n' roll idol who is elected President of the United States. Arthur Gorson had disapproved of the movie's right-wing message, and had discouraged Phil from accepting the part. The movie went on to become a major hit, and twenty-five years after the fact, Michael Ochs still stewed about his brother's rejecting the opportunity to star in the film.

"I was not managing him at that point," Michael stated, "but if I had been, I would

motion picture industry presented an interesting challenge, for while Phil had no illusions of becoming the next Lerner and Loewe, or Rodgers and Hammerstein, writing smash Broadway plays that were eventually converted into big-screen successes, he did believe that he had the capability to work in the business, as either a screenplay or sound-track writer, if not as an actor. Doing so would probably demand relocation to the West Coast, but Phil was ready to consider any option.

————

On November 24—Thanksgiving evening—Phil made his second appearance of the year at Carnegie Hall. As before, the show had been sold out in advance, but on this occasion, Phil was in much better form, with steady nerves and a vastly improved voice. The critics took notice. "Ochs has gained performing poise since January," said *The New York Times*. "While one had to bend to find the makings of a stage personality then, the firm outlines of one are now clearly apparent . . . Ochs is growing and has the talent to grow even further." "The best test of a creative talent," offered *The Village Voice*, "is whether his gift stagnates or grows richer . . . Ochs continues to grow."

Phil would not have disputed these assessments, but as the year drew to a close with numerous issues about his management and record company yet to resolve, he was certain that he wasn't growing fast enough, and that his lack of growth was due to a lack of effort on the part of others. He instructed Arthur to quietly look into other record labels, but the early indication was that other companies were no more likely to produce the new album than Elektra. Companies wanted Phil Ochs, but not under his unconditional terms.

Once again, Phil turned on Arthur Gorson, accusing him of not taking an aggressive enough approach to promoting his career. Arthur, Phil sputtered, was far too busy managing the careers of others and producing their records than in taking care of his Number One client. Phil was especially galled by the amount of time that Gorson

———————

not have let him turn it down. Yes, it was right wing, and it was against everything he believed in but he still should have done it. He loved the movies and wanted to be in them, and this was his chance. Once you're in, you're in."

was spending in the recording studio. He seethed whenever he called the studio to talk to his manager, only to learn that Arthur was working on a recording and was unable to come to the phone.

For his part, Arthur was growing weary of listening to Phil's complaints. Wild Indigo Productions was faring well enough to justify its existence within the Barricade framework. Furthermore, Arthur felt that he was growing into his role as a producer. After working with Jim and Jean on their *Changes* album, Arthur had gone on to produce Tom Rush's critically and commercially successful *Circle Game* album. "I loved it in the studio," said Gorson. "I felt more comfortable in the creative give-and-take of the studio than sitting behind my desk and being a businessman. Perhaps my interests strayed in terms of taking care of Phil's business. He resented the fact that, if you're in the studio, you're not a manager because you're not available on the phone every minute."

Still, Arthur was not about to take a lot of guff from Phil about the way the Barricade offices were run. As a businessman, Phil was no better than Arthur—a fact that became painfully apparent when Phil managed to talk Arthur out of pursuing the publishing rights to a talented young folksinging duo named Chuck and Joni Mitchell. Phil's concept of a songwriting revolution was beginning to look like just another dictatorship.

Nor did it help that Arthur's duties often resembled those of a full-time babysitter. Phil could be terribly absent-minded, and at any given moment, day or night, Arthur would hear from his client, who had lost his glasses or contact lenses, a wallet or passport, or other important personal papers. Phil expected Arthur to handle these matters as if they were part of his regular duties. As a rule, Arthur didn't object too strenuously to Phil's outrageous demands, but he did begin to bristle when Phil turned the tables on him and complained about minor mistakes made around the office.

"He was very, very demanding of everybody," said Gorson, "and he was somewhat hypocritical in that he would be unforgiving of everyone's errors except his own. He was very intolerant of other people's mistakes, and he could be cruel."

Most damaging, by Gorson's estimation, was the toll his and Phil's professional relationship took on their friendship. When they first started out, they had adopted an us-against-the-world approach; they were young and sharp and ready to answer any call. However, as the months passed and Phil grew more disenchanted with the direction his career was taking, the manager-client relationship began to overshadow the friendship, and Arthur found himself in an increasingly subservient role. Tension developed when Arthur and another Barricade worker struck up a romantic relationship that eventually fell apart. Phil was unsympathetic. Arthur's problems with the woman, he felt, could only disrupt Barricade.

Arthur was hurt by Phil's lack of concern, and by the way he tethered his manager's personal life to the business. "We started out as friends," he said, "but then one became reluctant to talk about personal problems because Phil would get nervous about the office."

Finally, after months of working in what he felt was a professional stalemate, Phil decided to take action. He and Arthur sat down and discussed where they had been and where they were going, and both concluded that it would be best to go their separate ways. In a move symbolic of the value he placed on their friendship, Arthur surrendered his fifty-percent share in Barricade, even though he realized that it would mean his losing a significant amount of money in the future. Barricade had never been about money, Arthur insisted, and Phil agreed. As a final gesture, they poured two glasses of wine and raised a toast to the past, as well as to their uncertain futures.

———

Once he and Arthur had parted company, Phil had a major problem on his hands: Who was going to manage him now? He had already been through two of the best in the business in Harold Leventhal and Albert Grossman, as publisher and manager respectively, and while he might have been able to catch on with Manny Greenhill, who represented a number of well-known folk acts, Phil was reluctant to become just another name in a large stable of clients. What he really wanted was someone who would devote total attention to him.

Phil mulled it over and decided to call his brother in California.

"What are you up to?" he asked Michael. It was the first time they had spoken since their falling out three years earlier.

"I'm out here working as a photographer," Michael responded. He could not have been more surprised if he had been hearing a voice from the grave.

A lot had happened since Michael had sworn Phil off as a brother and moved back to Ohio. He had graduated from Ohio State with a degree in video and television writing the previous summer and, despite warnings that he was wasting his time, he had moved to Los Angeles to find work. Nothing was available.

Good fortune intervened, just when Michael was beginning to wonder if he was going to spend the rest of his years working odd jobs. "I was at a concert one night," he remembered, "and the photographer didn't show up. I had my camera equipment with me, and they asked me to shoot the concert. 'How much?' I asked them. 'Fifty bucks,' they said. Well, fifty bucks was a lot of money to me then. The next day, I went out and had business cards printed up: 'Mike Ochs— Professional Photography.' "

Other assignments followed. Through Columbia Records, Michael secured photo shoots with Taj Mahal, the Chambers Brothers, Ray Coniff, and others. Erik Jacobsen, Phil's old friend from the Knob Lick Upper Ten Thousand, now managing acts rather than performing, helped Michael secure a job shooting an album jacket of Sopwith Camel for Buddah Records. When Bob Kravnow, president of Buddah, learned that Michael was Phil's brother, he approached Michael with a different sort of proposition.

"What's up with your brother?" Kravnow asked. "I heard he's leaving Elektra. Can you get word to him, please, that I'm interested in signing him at Buddah."

"Sure," Michael said. "No problem."

But there *was* a problem. Although Michael didn't want to jeopardize his chances of future work with Buddah by turning down its president, he didn't want to talk to Phil, either. To keep his word, Michael called Alice and asked that she pass along the message the next time she spoke to her ex-husband. Alice not only gave Phil the message, she also gave him Michael's telephone number.

Now, all of a sudden and without any warning whatsoever, Michael had Phil on the line.

"How are you doing?" Phil asked when he heard of Michael's new career as a photographer.

"Just barely surviving."

"Look," Phil went on, "I want you to manage me. You're the only one I can trust."

Michael was shocked by the offer. "What are you talking about?" he asked. "We don't get along, Phil. You know that. We hate each other."

"No," Phil countered. "You're the only one I can trust, and I need somebody I can trust totally."

The two talked on, Phil explaining the way his life had gone since he and Michael had split three years earlier. Over the course of the conversation, Phil's tone became almost desperate. His career was stagnant, he told Michael; his love life was a shambles. He needed someone to look after him. Michael's college degree, along with his newly established connections in the music business, were perfect for the job. Most important of all, Michael was honest. They might have their disagreements, but Michael had always been forthright with him.

Michael wasn't certain as to how much of Phil's argument he was buying.

"I don't think we'd get along," he insisted. "You treated me like shit in New York when you were making it. How's it going to be any different now?"

"I've totally changed," Phil shot back. "Trust me. I'm really different now."

Michael asked for time to consider the offer. Taking the job would not be a simple matter of packing his bags and moving to New York. Only a month earlier, Michael's girlfriend from Ohio had quit her job and moved to Los Angeles to live with him in his rented house. He couldn't just up and leave her on the spur of the moment, on what seemed to be a whim.

To Michael's amazement, his girlfriend was all for the move. "You can't turn this guy down," she told him when he explained Phil's telephone call. "It's too good an opportunity. I'll keep the house, quit my job in six months, and join you in New York."

———

Phil wanted his brother to work as more than a business manager, and he was willing to pay extra for the additional service.

"I'll give you twenty-five percent," he told Michael. "Most managers get fifteen or twenty percent. I'll give you twenty five. But I want you to be my *personal* manager."

Michael wasn't sure he knew the difference between a standard business manager and a personal manager, but he learned as soon as he moved to New York.

"Find me an apartment and a girlfriend," Phil instructed him.

"Is that what a personal manager does?" Michael asked.

Phil nodded.

Priorities thus established, Michael went immediately to work. The best place for Phil to live, he figured, would be in Greenwich Village, and he started his search for an apartment in the area bordering the old folk clubs. He didn't have to look for long. He found a large duplex at 156 Prince Street—well within walking distance of Phil's favorite haunts. The street-level apartment had a second floor, and its spacious rooms received plenty of light. Phil loved it.

Finding Phil a girlfriend proved to be less difficult than Michael had anticipated. A girl that Michael knew from Ohio State had moved to New York, and Michael looked her up. After asking if she wanted to attend a club opening with him, Michael asked if she could arrange a date for his brother on that same evening. The girl had a friend named Karen, who was bright, attractive, and available.

At first, Phil was less than taken with Karen. She was too quiet and serious for his tastes, and as someone who was awkward around women to begin with, Phil found himself fumbling to keep up a conversation. Their first night out was something to forget, but subsequent dates went well. Karen enjoyed Phil's sense of humor, and she was attracted to his celebrity. Like Alice, she had an aura of innocence that Phil found very appealing—especially after his dealings with more sophisticated New Yorkers. In a matter of a few weeks, he asked her to move in with him.

———

Phil might have been interested in the *personal* side of Michael's personal-management career, but as far as Michael was concerned, their main responsibility was to establish an office and get Phil's business interests rolling again.

He found an office suite available in the Ed Sullivan Building at 1697 Broadway. Ever the music buff, Michael looked forward to establishing his fledgling management company—Aquarian Age, Inc.—in the old Tin Pan Alley district of New York, and he was thrilled to learn that a number of music figures, including the Tokens, had offices in the Sullivan Building. The management business, he decided, could turn out to be as much fun as it was work.

Although he had Phil's checkbook at his disposal, Michael took a frugal, creative approach in furnishing the office. He and Phil haunted Manhattan's secondhand stores, where they found used office supplies for next-to-nothing. Wooden wastepaper baskets could be obtained for a dollar a piece. A gigantic, wall-sized map of the world, already framed, cost them all of two dollars. Office furniture, Michael discovered, could be picked up at the Sullivan Building itself, just by bribing a janitor into giving him what other tenants threw out.

"I was sitting in my office one night," he remembered, "and the janitor came in to clean up. And I said, 'By the way, does anybody leave anything in the basement?' He said, 'Sure,' and we went down there. It was all junk, obviously, but in the corner was this desk. It was covered with dirt and boxes, but I could see right away that it would work out. I said, 'I'll bet that's been here for a long time,' and he said, 'Oh yeah, that's been here forever.' 'What would it take to get that in my office?' 'What do you have?' 'Fifty bucks.' 'You got it.' So I took it up. I have it in my office today."

Michael's main contribution—and Phil's favorite piece of "furniture" in the office—was an antique pump organ, circa-1880, that Michael had purchased in Ohio and taken with him wherever he moved. Phil loved to play the organ whenever he was sitting around the office, and it quickly became the centerpiece of what was one of the more unusually stocked business offices in the city.

Michael could poke fun at himself for being tight when it came to supplying the office, but there was nothing conservative about the way he set out to find Phil a recording contract.

He realized that it was not going to be easy. With three albums under his belt, Phil believed that he was overdue to cash in on the escalating royalty schedules that were now becoming the industry norm. However, such expectations were not totally realistic. Like many artists, Phil had an inflated sense of his importance to his label, his feelings based more on his popularity on the concert circuit than on album sales. He had always enjoyed his greatest support in New York City, and he had done well in Boston and Philadelphia, which had large folk followings. His popularity had soared over the past two years in Canada. In these areas, his record sales were good. Conversely, he sold poorly on the West Coast, where he rarely appeared.

Phil was convinced that the failure of his albums to sell better was the result of poor promotion and distribution on Elektra's part, and some of this contention was accurate. Record companies, like publishing houses, tend to advertise and promote products already destined for large sales figures; advertising and promoting small or mid-range sellers is regarded as a waste of money.

Nevertheless, Phil's complaints disregarded or ignored the fact that folk and topical music did not enjoy pop music's broad base of appeal and, by nature, topical albums were bound to do less at the cash register, regardless of the promotion they received. Even after the release of three albums, Phil felt that stardom was only one good break away.

Elektra disagreed, and in its early negotiations with Arthur Gorson, the company had tried to show Phil and his manager how their demands—greater royalty schedule, better promotion money, and higher recording budgets—were economically unfeasible. The company was a *business*, not a patron of the arts, and Phil's demands, pitted against his sales track record, were excessive. Phil countered with the angry accusation that Elektra, in signing rock 'n' roll bands, most notably The Doors, was foresaking its commitment to folk acts, and, for all of its claims to the contrary, was paying out big dollars to these acts. After a fair amount of bickering and negotiating, Elektra decided that it simply could not afford to meet Phil's terms, and company and artist went their separate ways.

Phil was unconcerned. Michael had some record company connections that they could explore, and Phil himself had put together his own short list of companies he wanted to work for. Dylan's label, Columbia Records, topped the list, and Warner Brothers, which had shown interest back in the Arthur Gorson days, was second.

Michael knew two people at Columbia from his photography days in Los Angeles: Dave Swayse, who had been head of publicity prior to his transfer to New York, and David Rubinson, a producer who had worked with Taj Mahal. Both had been involved in Anita Bryant's recent recording of "Power and the Glory"—a project that, given Bryant's ultraconservative reputation, amused Phil to no end. Phil admired Rubinson and was eager to have him produce his next album.

Phil, Michael, and the two Columbia representatives met at The Tin Angel in Greenwich Village. Over dinner, Phil spoke of his plans for his new album, which he was calling *Pleasures of the Harbor*, and of his hopes for a lasting relationship with Columbia. There was, Phil said, one hitch: he didn't want to go through tedious and time-consuming negotiations with the usual assortment of record company underlings; he wanted to deal with the company president himself.

"If you're Columbia's ace producer," he challenged Rubinson, "can you get us Clive Davis right now?"

"What do you mean?"

"I want to go over to Clive's place right now and sing him *Pleasures of the Harbor*. I want to speak to him tonight."

Michael watched in disbelief as Rubinson called Davis and the record company executive invited the group to his apartment. "I was in seventh heaven," he recalled, admitting that he had his doubts about his ability to pull off the record deal. "It was *too* easy."

At Davis' apartment, Phil played all of the songs he had written for the new album on an acoustic guitar. Davis was impressed.

"I love it," he told Phil. "How much do you want to sign with Columbia?"

Michael didn't hesitate. "Twenty-five thousand," he said. The figure, high by industry standards, was significantly more than the signing bonus Phil had been previously offered by Warner Brothers.

"You've got it," Davis said.

Phil and Michael's elation over the deal was short-lived. The next day, when Michael spoke to an attorney for Columbia Records, he was informed that the twenty-five-thousand-dollar figure was more than the company would pay. At best, Phil could expect a contract in the ten-to-fifteen-thousand-dollar range.

"Wait a minute," Michael told the attorney. "We met with Clive Davis and he said twenty-five thousand was fine. We want twenty-five and not a penny less."

Negotiations were terminated at that point. Phil, though totally supportive of Michael's hard-nosed stance, was disappointed that he would not be recording for Columbia. Michael, on the other hand, was secretly pleased. He had felt all along that Columbia was the wrong label for his brother, that Phil would be lost in the huge corporation's list of recording artists. As far as Michael was concerned, the contract negotiations were proof positive of the way Phil might have been buried in a big corporation.

The Ochs brothers moved on to other companies. They talked to Buddah, but neither Phil nor Michael was enamored with the label. They met again with Mo Ostin, president of Warner Brothers, but Michael, still worried that the label, like Columbia, was too large, delayed agreeing to a final deal. MGM's Verve-Forecast, a smaller label with an impressive list of folk artists, met Michael's twenty-five-thousand-dollar asking price, but Phil refused to sign the contract.

Michael was getting desperate. "Let's forget the New York labels and go to the West Coast," he suggested to Phil. If nothing worked out in California, he said, they could always sign with Warner Brothers.

The two flew to Los Angeles and took a room at the Tropicana Hotel. Phil immediately came to life. Los Angeles, he discovered, had its own music community. On his first day in town, he ran into Ed Sanders and the Fugs, who were staying in rooms across the hall. Later, when he and Michael went to a little greasy spoon for a sandwich, they came across Dave Guard of the Kingston Trio, Judy Henske, and her husband, Jerry Yester. Los Angeles, Phil decided, might not be so bad after all.

Michael set up a meeting with Jerry Moss, president of A & M Records. In Michael's opinion, the label was perfect for Phil. It was relatively small and, even more important, as far as Michael and Phil were concerned, it had no major folk acts. The company specialized in such middle-of-the-road acts as Herb Alpert and the Tijuana Brass, Burt Bacharach, Liza Minelli, and the Baja Marimba Band. At one point during the summer of 1966, Herb Alpert, the company's co-owner, had five albums in the top fifty *Billboard* spots. The company could certainly afford to commit to an all-out effort behind Phil's next album.

Moss was very interested in signing Phil. He was willing to meet Phil's demands for artistic control, as well as the twenty-five-thousand-dollar signing bonus, but negotiations hit a snag when Moss required that the publishing rights to Phil's music be thrown in as part of the deal. Michael adamantly refused, and when A & M wouldn't back down, Michael again found himself at an impasse.

Meanwhile, Phil began to push for a signing with Warner Brothers. He liked the company not only because, at the time, it was taking chances on smaller acts such as Randy Newman and Van Dyke Parks, but also because of its connection to the movies. Mo Ostin was known to be fair with his artists, and the company was skillful in marketing its product.

Michael still wasn't convinced: "I was still leaning toward A & M," he said. "I thought Warner's was too big, and that A & M would give Phil a better shot. But when A & M wouldn't back down on the publishing, I figured there was no choice but to give Phil his wishes."

To Michael's great relief, Jerry Moss called at the last minute, just as Michael and Phil were about to finalize a contract with Warner Brothers. Phil, said Moss, could keep his publishing rights.

Chapter Seven

THE WAR IS OVER

NOW THAT he had secured a new record label, Phil was eager to go to the studio and cut his new album. A & M had other plans. It might be better, the company suggested, for Phil to build interest in the forthcoming album by hitting the road and playing some of the new songs for people unfamiliar with his work. They could record later in the year, after Phil had completed his tour.

Throughout the spring, Phil played in clubs and halls, at folk festivals and occasional demonstrations or rallies. He was well received wherever he went. In the past, in their reviews of his concerts, critics had often expressed surprise at Phil's popularity. Here was a singer, they said, who had limited vocal and guitar-playing ability, and whose songs often sounded alike, yet he had one of the most fervent, loyal followings in the business.

If his critics had bothered to examine Phil in any depth whatsoever, they would have had little difficulty in determining the source of his popularity. Phil truly loved people. He sang of their concerns; he remained accessible to them. Unlike other performers, who could not wait to be whisked away from a hall after an engagement—or who, if they did manage to stick around, were very selective about the people they allowed into their backstage inner sanctums—Phil relished contact with his fans. Anyone was welcome backstage, and when he met with people, Phil didn't give them the impression that they were part of a privileged audience. He would ask about what was on their minds, and any kind of political discussion was welcome, especially if it had anything to do with Vietnam.

The war was now a national obsession. It had long ago become clear that the United States was not going to simply roll over the

North Vietnamese army in a show of military might. The casualty figures were adding up to staggering figures, and with no end to the war in sight, the American public was slowly beginning to withdraw its support. The presidential primaries were only a year away, and leaders from both political parties were scrambling to find positions to take on an increasingly unpopular war.

Phil, perennial news junkie that he was, followed the day-to-day events with extreme interest. He was still technically eligible for the draft, although as a highly visible critic of the war, he was an unlikely candidate for the army. The Selective Service had made some rumblings about drafting him in the past, but nothing ever came of it. Phil was supporting a young daughter, he had poor eyesight, and his attitudes were definitely not what Uncle Sam was looking for.

———————

On March 1, Phil ran into Jack Newfield, a young journalist, folk enthusiast, and antiwar activist he had met a couple of years earlier in one of the Village clubs. Newfield had written a number of pieces about Phil and the folk scene for *The Village Voice*, and he and Phil had become friendly when they realized that they shared many of the same political views. Newfield was presently working on a book-length profile of Robert F. Kennedy, and he had a compelling proposition: would Phil like to fly to Washington D.C. with him to meet Kennedy and watch him deliver an historic speech on the floor of the Senate the following day?

Phil jumped at the opportunity.

As Newfield recalled, Phil wanted to meet Kennedy "for literary as well as political reasons." The Kennedy name, dating back to the 1960 presidential elections, had carried almost mythological meaning to Phil, and the chance to meet the young New York senator carried symbolic as well as real political importance to Phil. "I think Phil was very interested in Robert Kennedy," said Newfield, "not just as a political figure, but as a kind of pop culture icon, in the way he was interested in Elvis Presley or Che Guevara."

At the time, Kennedy was at a political crossroads. Democratic Party insiders, fearing that President Johnson was losing his support, were nudging Kennedy into taking a larger leadership role within the party, with perhaps the outside chance that he might run for the presidency the following year. The issue of Vietnam—and, more specifically, the relentless bombing of North Vietnam—had become a point of focus and division within the party. Kennedy realized that a majority of voters still backed the bombings, but he was deeply troubled by the war. Complicating the issue were his well-publicized battles with the president. Thus far, he had made no public proclamations condemning the bombing, but that was all about to change. On March 2, he was scheduled to address the Senate floor.

Phil and Newfield flew to Washington D.C. with expectations of witnessing a momentous occasion. Both were gripped by the drama surrounding the speech: in denouncing the bombing, Kennedy would be confronting—and criticizing—some of his own brother's actions.

"He had to deal with his brother's ghost," Newfield commented, "because he knew this was a war his brother had helped to start. Lyndon Johnson had been picked by his own brother to be vice-president, and he was now president in 1967. It was almost Shakespearean, where Robert Kennedy was the legitimate heir to the king by blood and biology, and Johnson was the usurper, but Johnson had been picked—and therefore legitimized—by his own brother. By giving this speech, Bobby had to admit to himself that his brother had been wrong in supporting the war, and that his brother had been wrong in picking Lyndon Johnson to be his vice-president and successor. So the whole thing was tremendously heavy for him."

Kennedy's speech on the Senate floor delivered on every promise. Newfield had introduced Phil to Kennedy before the speech, and then they had both taken places in the gallery to watch. In one of his finer moments as a statesman, Kennedy confronted his brother's ghost, but rather than pass the blame, he included himself in the decisions that had led to the war, as well as in the decisions that allowed it to continue.

"It is we who live in abundance and send our young men out to die," Kennedy said. "It is our chemicals that scorch the children and our bombs that level the villages. We are all participants." The United States, he continued, should not be in the war to act as an avenging angel punishing an oppressive government; the troops were there to help a nation in self-determination. North Vietnam had recently sent forth signals that it was ready to negotiate a solution. Why not halt the bombing and see if this was possible?

Later that day, Phil and Newfield caught a shuttle back to New York. Kennedy was aboard the same flight. Kennedy was familiar with Phil's music, as well as with the popularity of folk and protest music on college campuses across the country. Was it true, he asked Phil, that Bob Dylan had changed his name to boost his career? Yes, Phil answered, that was indeed the case. "You think it would help," quipped the senator, "if I changed mine?"

Phil, Newfield, and Kennedy talked for a while. Kennedy was endlessly curious about attitudes on college campuses, and Phil, as a regular university performer, was a good barometer. Kennedy asked Phil to sing one of his songs. Newfield suggested "Crucifixion" but Phil declined, saying that he needed a guitar to do the song. Newfield persisted, and Phil finally agreed to sing it a capella.

Phil offered Kennedy no explanation about the song's origins, but it was not necessary. Phil had only sung a few verses of "Crucifixion" when Kennedy began to shake his head slowly, his eyes brimming with tears. He, like his brother before him, knew something about leadership's tolls. The song left Kennedy speechless.

"It was an extraordinary, dramatic moment, both for Phil and for Bobby," recalled Newfield. "It was very meaningful to Phil because he was an artist and could see the guy who would be most affected by the song being mesmerized by it. And for Bobby, who had just come out against the Vietnam War, and who understood that the song was about the assassination of his brother . . . it was an electric experience. I felt like a voyeur."

Kennedy, of course, would take on an even heavier burden of leadership when, less than a year later, he would attempt to follow his brother into the White House. His death would leave Phil and Newfield stunned by the incredible, almost prophetic irony of Phil's singing "Crucifixion" a year earlier to yet another victim of history's ritualistic sacrifices.

———

Phil moved to Los Angeles in May. He had no idea how long he would be staying on the West Coast, but he knew that he needed a change of scenery. "It was a very bad time," he explained in an interview conducted at the time. "I was going through some emotional changes and very bad scenes. I had an idea for an album and everything else had to stop for it."

The move was not intended to be permanent. Phil kept his Prince Street apartment in New York, and he told friends that he would be staying on the West Coast for several months—long enough to cut the new album and see it into production.

He was not exaggerating, however, when he said that he had grown tired of New York. Nothing much seemed to be happening there, in the Village or elsewhere, and Phil suddenly found himself without a rudder. By contrast, the West Coast was thriving. It was the Summer of Love, the era of the hippie and psychedelic music, and while most of the action was taking place further up the coast from Los Angeles, in the Bay Area around Berkeley and San Francisco, Phil was happy for any change of environment. Perhaps the greatest bonus in his moving was the opportunity to spend time with Meegan. He had not seen his daughter for any length of time since Alice had left New York, and he had missed her more than he ever would have predicted.

As for stopping everything for the new album . . . Phil never sat still for any notable period of time, album or no album. He had no sooner checked into his small rental house in Laurel Canyon than he was hitting the bricks, checking in with friends, establishing new contacts, and learning the lay of the land. Getting around Los Angeles, he quickly determined, was going to take some effort. The city was enormous, and its mass transit system was vastly different from New York, where you were only a quick subway or cab ride away from any given destination. Phil was a terrible driver—inattentive and heavy-footed. Rather than immediately buy a car, he purchased a secondhand bicycle. That, along with the assistance of friends who drove, would be enough to get him from place to place on most occasions.

———

Earlier in the year, while he was still in New York, Phil had met and befriended a young Englishman named Andy Wickham. The two had hit it off well, and Wickham had urged Phil to look him up when he was in California. Phil called Wickham as soon as he had settled in, and before long, the two were seeing each other regularly.

At first glance, they could not have been a stranger couple. Pale and bone-thin, Wickham was as mannered as a British country squire, yet when he turned his razor-sharp intellect on a subject, he could be overbearingly arrogant, his running commentary turning off all but the most tolerant. Many of Phil's friends disliked him as soon as they met him.

"He was like an old aunt," commented one of Phil's friends of Wickham, adding that his appeal to Phil was his dissimilarity from any other acquaintances. "Andy was a bit of the forbidden world of self-indulgence and bitchiness and gossip. He and Phil would sit there and cluck away about everything. Andy wasn't a pleasant fellow, but he really had Phil's ear." Another friend was much less kind in his assessment: "Andy Wickham was a stuck-up, snobbish little British brat."

What infuriated a good number of Phil's friends, even more than Wickham's abrasive personality, was his politics: Not only was Wickham ultraconservative, but he exuded an upper-crust intolerance for the very people that Phil cared the most about. Wickham was especially vocal in his opinions about the New Left. He had nothing but contempt for middle-class college kids who protested the war while making certain they maintained their student deferments, or who joined hands and sang "We Shall Overcome" shortly before speeding past the ghettos to return to their comfortable homes in suburbia. As far as Wickham was concerned, liberalism was the flavor of the day, and not a very tasty one at that. Thumbing his nose at the New Left was a sport.

Phil's attraction to Wickham was similar to his friendships with other people of differing political views. No one relished a good argument about politics more than Phil, not just because he enjoyed the exchange of ideas, but also because such arguments helped him fine-tune his own opinions. When he was with people who thought like him and agreed with his political positions, Phil was nowhere near as intellectually stimulated as he was when he was with someone like Wickham.

"Our friendship was based on opposites attracting intellectually," Wickham admitted, although he maintained, as did other close friends of Phil's, that Phil was more conservative than his political activism would have led you to believe. "His values," said Wickham, "were basically to the right."

It was Phil's humanity, rather than his talents as a musician or political activist, that had initially attracted Wickham. On the night of their first meeting at the Kettle of Fish in New York, Phil had shown more interest in Wickham than any of his friends, who were less inclined to welcome a stranger into their midst.

"With Phil," noted Wickham, "there was lots of laughter when the others were serious. He was open, warm, friendly, and curious—a natural journalist. He had tremendous understanding of human nature. Dylan had said that Phil was a better journalist than songwriter, and I would agree with that. His persona was the work of art."

Wickham brought other attributes to the friendship that others sometimes failed to see. He was fiercely loyal—a trait Phil could really appreciate, having recently moved from a scene where competition and jealousy had poisoned friendships, sometimes beyond antidote. Wickham may have ridiculed the effectiveness of a protest song as a tool for political change, but he always stood beside Phil's artistic decisions. In public, Wickham supported Phil without reservation.

Finally, Andy Wickham came into Phil's life at a time of turmoil, when Phil was making significant changes in his personal and professional lives. Under the best of circumstances, Phil was sloppy and undisciplined; under the current circumstances, he was in danger of drifting out of control. Wickham, conversely, was very organized, and much of his self-discipline rubbed off on Phil when he really needed it.

In New York, Phil had enjoyed a number of significant friendships. He had been close to Arthur Gorson, and for periods of time he had been tight with Bob Dylan, David Blue, Eric Andersen, and others. Their friendships would continue, even if time, geography, circumstances, and careers weakened or altered them. In Andy Wickham, Phil had found his closest friend since he had met Jim Glover, and the friendship, like the one with Glover, would endure.

Shortly after moving to the city, Phil ran into Paul Krassner at the *Los Angeles Free Press* offices. Krassner, now one of the major voices of the West Coast counterculture, was scheduled to appear on ultra-conservative Joe Pyne's television program, and Phil offered to drive him to the studio.

Pyne's confrontational style had earned him a huge following, and he was at his nasty, insulting best when he brought Krassner out for his spot on the show. However, as the studio audience quickly learned, Pyne had all he could handle in Krassner, who deftly matched him, point by point, insult for insult. Under the usual circumstances, Pyne would not allow his guests the opportunity to present their side of an argument, let alone verbally spar with him, but Krassner's jabs seemed to knock him back a step.

"Why," Pyne asked Krassner, "are you for the repeal of abortion laws?"

Replied Krassner: "Because I don't think that a woman should have to bear an unwanted child as punishment for an accidental conception."

"Do you edit your magazine," Pyne continued, "because you were an unwanted child?"

"No, Daddy."

Krassner continued to embarrass Pyne in front of his minions until finally, in frustration, Pyne lashed out with a vicious remark about the acne scars on Krassner's face.

"Well, Joe," Krassner fired back, "if you're gonna ask questions like that, then let me ask *you*: Do you take off your wooden leg before you make love with your wife?"

Pyne's jaw dropped and his audience gasped. He tried to stammer out a response, but his composure was gone. As Krassner knew, Pyne had lost a leg when he was in the Marine Corps during World War II.

The program deteriorated quickly. Pyne cut off the Krassner interview and turned the show over to his "Beef Box" segment of the show, in which audience members could question guests or make comments of their own. People lined up for a turn at the microphone, each attacking Krassner for his comment.

Phil took a place at the end of the line, and when he had finally reached the front, he praised Krassner and his magazine. "What Paul Krassner does is in the finest tradition of American journalism," Phil insisted.

Pyne had been embarrassed enough for one program.

"Isn't it true," he said, turning to Krassner, "that the man that is now in the dock is known to you as one of the leaders of the hippie revolution?"

"No," Krassner replied. "He's known to me as a folksinger."

"Uh-huh." Pyne now turned his attention back to Phil. "Mr. Ochs," he said, "are you a hippie?"

"No."

"Do you play for hippies, mostly?"

"No, I play for everybody. . . ."

Krassner would never forget the incident. "Phil stood his ground because he thought Joe Pyne was putting me out of context. He was trying to defend me in the midst of a lion's den. I really didn't mind it personally—it was just a game, and I have given him a taste of his own medicine—but Phil was diligent about speaking out."

———————

Phil's move to Los Angeles coincided with the early planning stages of the city's largest antiwar demonstration to date. According to the plan, people would gather in Cheviet Hills Park, the largest park in west Los Angeles, for an afternoon be-in, complete with music, dancing, and speeches. In the early evening, the demonstrators would march to the Century Plaza Hotel, where they would picket President Lyndon Johnson's appearance at a $500-a-plate fundraiser.

Phil swung into action as soon as he heard of the event. In recent months, as the Vietnam War dragged on and the U.S. bombing of North Vietnam continued without letup, Phil had become more and more convinced that the only way to attack the war would be to ridicule it through absurdist politics. What would happen, he wondered, if everyone simply declared an end to the war? The action would be deliciously ironic, given the fact that Vietnam was an undeclared war to begin with, plus it would be an effective, positive protest against the powers that refused to recognize the people's opposition to the war.

The idea was not entirely original. A year earlier, Allen Ginsberg had made a similar war-is-over declaration in his epic poem, "Wichita Vortex Sutra." When talking about the origins of his poem, Ginsberg cited Walt Whitman's fear that the United States would fall as a result of its own inhumanity. In "Wichita Vortex Sutra," Ginsberg was taking seriously his poet's role as unacknowledged legislator and declaring an end to the war. If enough people followed his example, democratic society would win out over the masters of war.

Phil knew of Ginsberg's poem and ideas, and he was intrigued by the notion of placing Ginsberg's concept within the framework of absurdist politics. He would declare an end to the war, celebrate it in Cheviet Hills Park and, as the crowning touch, hold a penny-a-plate dinner to coincide with Johnson's Century Plaza Hotel fundraiser. Rather than condemn Johnson, Phil suggested that people praise him for being a great peacemaker. It would be great political theater.

"The old standbys of the Left and the attitudes they encompass should be avoided," he insisted, reflecting, perhaps, some of his conversations with Andy Wickham. "Classics like 'Hey, hey, LBJ, how many kids did you kill today?' are as dated as the M-16. Since the war is over, we should have positive signs, like 'Johnson in '68—the Peace President,' 'Welcome Hanoi to the Great Society,' or 'Thank you, Lyndon, for ending the war.' "

For all of his claims to being an absurdist, Phil's approach was clear-eyed and reasoned. He was tired, he complained, of his debates with people about the war. "It's beyond argument," he contended, "beyond rational, logical right-and-wrong argument. It's so obviously immoral, and it was obviously immoral two years ago. It was just a farce from the beginning, and now it's a suicidal farce for the country." Declaring an end to the war, he believed, would be a form of meaningful mental civil disobedience.

"It sounds like a silly step to take," he proposed, "but it makes sense to me. It makes an infinite amount more sense than saying the war is wrong. To wake up in the morning and walk out and say, 'The war is wrong' says absolutely nothing to me because I've heard it too many times. The soldiers have heard it too many times and the Viet Cong have heard it too many times."

Phil worked feverishly on his contribution to the rally. He wrote a manifesto, "Have You Heard? The War Is Over," for the *Los Angeles Free Press*. He enlisted cartoonist Ron Cobb's help in designing the rally's official handbill, a take-off of the famous World War II photo of a sailor kissing a young woman in Times Square. On Phil's poster, the legend "VD Day" was emblazoned across the top.

Ron Cobb had become one of Phil's valued new friends. Phil had seen Cobb's editorial cartoons in the *Free Press*, and not long after moving to Los Angeles, he turned up, unannounced, at Cobb's door, wanting to introduce himself to the artist who was doing some of the most imaginative work in the business. Cobb, who had gone straight from high school to work as an animator for Walk Disney, and who would go on to contribute to the sets of *Star Wars* and *Alien*, was creating highly original cartoons that drew on his fascination with theology, science, and politics. After seeing Cobb's work, Phil decided that he had to meet the man. The two hit it off, and the friendship, like Phil's friendship with Andy Wickham, would be a lasting one.

To commemorate the upcoming rally, Phil wrote a special song entitled, appropriately enough, "The War Is Over." A year earlier, Sgt.
Barry Sadler had scored the year's biggest commercial hit with "Ballad of the Green Beret," a hyper-patriotic song that sounded as if it
had come from another era; John Wayne, Phil's favorite actor, was
slated to appear in the film based on the song. In "The War Is Over,"
Phil began with a passing nod to all of the propagandistic war movies
ever made, the homage strongly contrasting the reality of the war
being broadcast daily on television news reports across the nation:

> *Silent soldiers on a silver screen,*
> *Framed in fantasies and drugged in dreams,*
> *Unpaid actors of the mystery,*
> *The mad director knows that freedom will not make you free.*
> *And what's this got to do with me?*
> *I declare the war is over.*
> *It's over, it's over . . .*

In a sense, the song was a continuation of all that Phil had
started in "I Ain't Marching Anymore"; it borrowed heavily from its
predecessor thematically and musically. In another sense, it rejected
the earlier song's aura of passive resistance. The word "treason" was
used in both numbers, but in different ways. In "I Ain't Marching,"
"treason" was an alternative word for "peace" ("Call it peace or call it
treason . . ."), whereas in "The War Is Over," Phil was pulling no
punches:

> *So do your duty, boys, and join with pride;*
> *Serve your country in her suicide;*
> *Find a flag so you can wave goodbye.*
> *But just before the end even treason might be worth a try—*
> *This country is too young to die.*
> *I declare the war is over . . .*

The song's final verse addressed the walking wounded—the GIs
who would return from the war, battered and broken—in a way that

was part *Johnny Got His Gun*, part "When Johnny Comes Marching Home." In retrospect, it stands as a grim prediction of the horrors of the Vietnam veteran:

> *One-legged veterans will greet the dawn,*
> *And they're whistling marches as they mow the lawn,*
> *And the gargoyles only sit and grieve,*
> *The gypsy fortune-teller told me we've been deceived—*
> *You only are what you believe.*
> *I believe the war is over . . .*

In the months ahead, Phil would try to make clear the idea that the song was an indictment of a country's actions, not of the country itself. Like a parent disciplining a child, Phil could condemn his leaders' actions without losing his love for his country.

"The war in Vietnam," he stated, "is an amphetamine trip, a reflection of the spiritual disease that has gripped this country and distorted every principle on which it was built. This generation must make a choice between the total rejection of the country and the decision to regain a spiritual balance. I believe there is still something inherent in the fibre of America worth saving, and that the fortunes of the entire world may well ride on the ability of young Americans to face the responsibilities of an old America gone mad."

Although "The War Is Over" may have seemed, to an angry nation confronting an uncertain future, like a "When Johnny Comes Marching Home" shot in negative, it also stood as one of the most patriotic songs written by an American since World War II. If "I Ain't Marching Anymore" was Phil's ultimate statement of defiance, "The War Is Over" was his greatest act of bravery as a topical songwriter.

———

Unbeknownst to those organizing the demonstration and the march to the hotel, an employee of International Investigation Systems, a private firm retained by lawyers for the Century Plaza Hotel, had infiltrated a planning meeting and filed a report with her employers. The infiltrator, an attractive young woman named Sharon Stewart, had gained the confidence of the organizers with a tale of how her brother had been killed in Vietnam; a second brother, she claimed, was about to enlist, and she was desperate to do anything she could to stop the war before it claimed his life.

In her report, later recorded in court, Stewart offered detailed information about what she had heard at a meeting of parade monitors held on June 19 at the First Unitarian Church In Los Angeles. At that meeting, organizers discussed a number of civil-obedience tactics that could be used at the demonstration. Members of the audience, given the opportunity to address the organizing committee, offered a wide variety of suggestions, from the unleashing of mice or cockroaches in the hotel, to a takeover of the hotel lobby.

Every one of these suggestions was immediately rejected. As it was, there had been great debate between the Peace Action Council (PAC), the demonstration's sponsoring organization, and the Student Mobilization Committee on the topic of civil disobedience, with the PAC eventually deciding to officially disassociate from any and all individual acts of civil disobedience. The PAC made it unmistakably clear that it would not endorse or encourage outrageous tactics of any kind.

Nevertheless, in her report Sharon Stewart painted a grim portrait of what the demonstrators had in mind for the march to the hotel. She brought up the radical actions proposed by the audience members and, in general, outlined a proposal in which demonstrators would go to extraordinary measures to disrupt the dinner and embarrass the president and the hotel.

On June 21, attorneys representing Century Plaza Hotel and Century City, Inc., prepared papers for a suit seeking a temporary restraining order prohibiting the march. A Santa Monica judge scheduled a hearing for the morning of June 23—the day of the demonstration. Neither the demonstration organizers nor their attorney was informed of the hearing.*

————

The Los Angeles Police Department prepared for the worst, assigning thirteen hundred officers to duty at Century City on the evening of June 23, with another two hundred in reserve; it was the greatest

* On the morning of the march, phone calls were placed to the PAC office and the attorney's office. The calls were placed at 8:00 A.M.—an hour before either office opened.

amassing of police in Los Angeles since Paul Robeson's visit to the city two decades earlier. Three huge lines of defense were planned for the front of the hotel, and officers armed with high-powered rifles were assigned to building tops throughout the area. A military helicopter, equipped with a 20-mm cannon, was to patrol overhead. In describing the measures taken by the police to protect the president, Los Angeles Mayor Sam Yorty declared, "We will take all precautions we feel are necessary," promising to "use only such force as is necessary to enforce the law."

> *Angry artists painting angry signs,*
> *Use their vision just to blind the blind.*
> *Poisoned players of a grisly game,*
> *One is guilty and the other gets to point the blame.*
> *Pardon me if I refrain.*
> *I declare the war is over . . .*

———————

On the morning of Friday, June 23, Los Angeles Supreme Court judge Orlando H. Rhodes held an *ex parte* hearing to consider the request for a temporary restraining order prohibiting the march. Unaware of the hearing, neither members of the PAC or the group's attorney, A. L. Wirin, were on hand, to present their side of the argument. Judge Rhodes listened to the hotel's attorneys' case, based almost entirely on the Stewart report, and issued the restraining order. The inevitable confrontation between the police and demonstrators was now in motion.

———————

It was supposed to have been Phil's big day. Although his "War Is Over" rally was only a small part of a much larger demonstration, he planned the event as if it were the only program of the day. He had no idea what to expect, although, when the day dawned sunny and hot, he was all but assured of a good turnout and, consequently, a large contingency of news reporters and photographers. Never one to take chances, Phil made certain that Ron Cobb brought along a camera to record this snippet of history in the making.

Phil's segment of the rally was scheduled to take place in a vacant lot near the Century Plaza Hotel. When he arrived, folksinger Judy Henske at his side, Phil was a bundle of energetic optimism, his mood unaffected by the presence of police officers everywhere. If anything, the police were a necessary ingredient: Phil would have been disappointed if his rally had failed to generate controversy.

He had led his own impromptu parade to the rally site, his group picking up demonstrators and well-wishers as it made its way along the Avenue of the Stars, the marchers chanting "The war is over! The war is over!" The police watched but did nothing.

At the rally site, Phil hopped onto the back of a flatbed truck and sang "The War Is Over." The crowd roared its approval. When Phil had finished the song, the police announced over a bullhorn that the crowd had to disperse immediately, that the rally constituted an illegal assembly. When the demonstrators showed no inclination to move, the police moved in, many swinging their nightsticks at anyone in their paths. People ran everywhere, some screaming as they were beaten by the police, others pushing and shoving their way out of the vacant lot. Phil escaped without a scratch, as did Ron Cobb and Judy Henske. In an instant, Phil's big absurdist rally had fallen victim to those sworn to serve the people and protect the laws of the Constitution—including, presumably, the document's First Amendment.

———

The setting was much more pleasant at Cheviet Hills Park, where thousands assembled in what was nothing less than a summertime festival. Young mothers brought babies in carriages; youthful hippies handed out flowers, flew kites, and sang songs. Hotdog vendors made their way through the throngs of people. Children, veterans in wheelchairs or on crutches, elderly couples, businessmen dressed in suits, large antiwar groups displaying colorful banners, political activists of every stripe—all gathered for what was to be a major declaration against the country's policies in Southeast Asia. Muhammad Ali, a last-minute surprise guest, autographed draft cards.

After the aborted "War Is Over" rally, Phil and Ron Cobb had made their way back to the park, where they linked up with Paul Krassner. All three intended to listen to the speeches in the park, and then march with the demonstrators to the hotel.

At six o'clock, the official program began. Speakers for the evening included Dr. Benjamin Spock, the pediatrician and best-selling author who had become one of the leading activists against the war; H. Rap Brown, the outspoken leader of the Student Non-Violent Coordinating Committee; and Muhammad Ali. The heavyweight boxing champion, recently stripped of his title for evading the draft, warned the thousands of people in the park to remain calm during the march. Copies of the restraining order were now being circulated, and a decision had been reached to march anyway. Ali, like some of the organizers, feared a violent confrontation. If there was to be trouble, Ali cautioned, let the police be the ones to instigate it.

Ali's words turned out to be prophetic. After an uneventful march, an estimated fifteen thousand people wound up in the area around the Century Plaza Hotel, many bottled up by police who narrowed the line of demonstrators just north of the hotel. Spontaneous sit-ins further broke the flow of the march. When the chief of police gave the order to disperse, thousands of people found themselves caught in a human traffic jam with nowhere to go.

The police, on edge to begin with, moved in, suddenly and without warning. In the melee that followed, people were severely beaten, thrown onto the hoods of cars, prodded with nightsticks, pushed and shoved, dragged on the ground, and kicked and stomped. No one was spared. The elderly, teenage kids, women with small children—reports of the beatings were all but impossible to believe. Said one witness:

> My son is a hemiplegic—that is, he has partial paralysis on his right side and can walk by dragging that foot, which is supported by a brace. He also wears a brace on his arm. The paralysis is caused by a malignant brain tumor and surgery . . .
>
> The police charged into us. The crowd went back as far as possible and my son and I began to walk south as the police desired, as fast as we could. A man on crutches was on my left, my son on my right. Three policemen followed us, poking with their clubs. The man on crutches was jabbed viciously in the back, again and again. I told the policeman, "He is moving; he's going as fast as he can on crutches," but he just said, "He came in on crutches, he'll go out on crutches."
>
> My son turned and told the officer who was poking me not to hit his mother. He responded by hitting my son on the left side of the head—the side where his tumor is—knocking him to

the ground and breaking his glasses. Then he and several officers began swinging their clubs at him and kicking him. I
screamed, "Please don't hit his head, please don't hit his head,"
because any blow could kill him. I threw myself on top of his
head to protect it, and they kicked him in the side and stepped
on his hand.

A Los Angeles schoolteacher, acting as a monitor during the rally
and march, spoke of the attitudes of those attacking the demonstrators.

The police were swinging wildly at anyone who approached; they
seemed thoroughly frightened, but quite excited by the violence.
One standing off to one side was grinning broadly, obviously
pleased at what had transpired.

Such accounts, offered afterward in an official report on the violence, were all too common. Dozens of people were arrested, countless others beaten senselessly. Phil and his group, once again
fortunate enough to escape the worst, were nevertheless caught up
in the mayhem.

"The cops chased us into this grassy area," Paul Krassner remembered. "They were vicious. They were attacking people in wheelchairs with billy clubs. It was a power thing, a territorial thing."

"The police did a flying wedge right into the crowd," said Ron
Cobb. "People were being chased up and down the street, with waves
of cops sweeping people here and there. A lot of kids were badly
beaten. It was very shocking. I think it was the first time that kind of
thing around the Vietnam War had occurred. It went on into the
night."

Phil was utterly transfixed by the violence. At times, he would
edge closer to the action, as if to confirm what was really happening.
Then he would jump back, concerned about his own safety. As Ron
Cobb recalled, Phil was unable to sleep that evening. He stayed up
all night, electrified by the events of the day.

"Phil just couldn't believe it had happened," said Cobb. "We
hadn't personally experienced anything like that in our lives. Phil
thought it was the beginning of something really big and really bad.
It was like a movie to him, a Fellini movie."

He would see much worse fourteen months later at the Democratic National Convention in Chicago, where a full-scale police riot would be televised from coast to coast. The events in Los Angeles had been a learning experience. They taught him that the war was far from being over. If anything, the real battles were just beginning.

Chapter Eight

PLEASURES OF THE HARBOR

IN AUGUST, Phil entered the recording studio to begin work on his long-delayed fourth album. Larry Marks, a highly regarded, classically trained producer, oversaw the project.

From the moment he began writing songs for the album, Phil wanted *Pleasures of the Harbor* to be a breakthrough work, a bold move from his folk and topical music background into the realms of pop, classical, jazz, and even avant garde. He was eager to experiment, to prove that he was much more than a singing newspaper; he wanted to display his artistry, to be accepted as a poet as well as a journalist. The new recording would propel him into another phase of his career.

With the exception of "Outside a Small Circle of Friends," a song inspired by the well-publicized Kitty Genovese murder in New York, there were to be no topical songs on the record. This meant that "Joe Hill," a longtime concert favorite that Phil had written in England during the same period that he wrote "Crucifixion," and the antiwar songs "White Boots Marching in a Yellow Land" and "The War Is Over," would have to be saved for a future project. *Pleasures of the Harbor* would be chock-full of messages, but they would be more subtle and personal, and less overtly political, than Phil was accustomed to putting on record.

Before heading to the studio, Phil met with Larry Marks, along with Ian Freebairn-Smith, who had been hired by Marks to work out the arrangements for the individual songs. Phil played the entries on his guitar and explained, as well as he could, what he had in mind for them. After hearing Phil's plans, both producer and arranger realized they had their work cut out for them.

"We made a conscious decision to overproduce the material," said Marks, "and see if we could expand his audience." This, Marks conceded, would prove to be difficult, given Phil's formula for writing songs. "Phil wrote verse-chorus-verse-chorus-verse-chorus," he recalled, "so we had to do a song where there would be something different each time we came into a new verse."

Freebairn-Smith, who had worked with Marks on a number of projects, including Liza Minnelli's first recording, shared the producer's concerns about how, in light of Phil's limitations, he would meet Phil's expectations for the album.

"He was an unsophisticated musician," Freebairn-Smith said of Phil. "His songs had only two or three chords, and some of the tunes were very similar. Phil used his basic guitar skills and harmony skills as a kind of framework to support the lyrics and ideas he was trying to put across. He didn't come out there to dazzle you with his musicianship or guitar playing. He came out there to try to affect the way you feel and think about your surroundings.

"I remember thinking that these songs were extremely simple, and that it would be a major project trying to do what he wanted to do with them—to flesh them out and find substitute harmonies, countermelodies, orchestral colors, and so on, to put it together and make it sound bigger than it really was to start with. It became a kind of structural challenge to make the songs grow and have a form to them. It was like musical architecture."

Phil had his own ideas about the musical structure for the individual songs. Prior to his departure for California, he had worked out rudimentary arrangements and countermelodies for "Pleasures of the Harbor," "Flower Lady," and several other songs. He had charted the arrangements on manuscript paper and brought them with him to Los Angeles. Freebairn-Smith judged the countermelodies "a little awkward" when Phil sang them for him, but Phil felt strongly enough about them that Freebairn-Smith had no other choice but to work with them.

Phil's instincts may have been difficult to translate in the studio, but there is little doubting that his ambitions spurred the album on. Each song, he insisted, had to be a separate, independent production, yet somehow, in the end, the songs had to lock together as an overall statement. Phil had seen this idea executed almost flawlessly by Brian Wilson on the Beach Boys' 1966 *Pet Sounds*, and his ambitions were only underscored when he heard the Beatles' *Sgt. Pep-*

per's *Lonely Hearts Club Band*, which was released at the time Phil was entering the recording studio. On both albums, each song was dramatically different from the others. Still, when looked at in their entirety, the albums boasted a strong thematic unity. Phil would settle for nothing less on his new album.

––––––––

All of the songs for *Pleasures of the Harbor* had been written on guitar, in Phil's usual fashion of finding melodies to match his lyrics. This approach had worked well in the past, when Phil could walk into the recording studio, strap on his guitar, and play the songs the way he was accustomed to playing them onstage.

It was entirely different with *Pleasures of the Harbor*. The arrangements called for very little guitar, and in recording the album, Phil would essentially be singing into a microphone while he was accompanied by piano, orchestra, or whatever combination of instruments required by the arrangement. He had not given this much thought when he, Larry Marks, and Ian Freebairn-Smith had planned out the album, but once he had begun the actual recording process, he found it virtually impossible to work without a guitar.

"In a way, Phil was a true Pete Seeger type of traditional folk-singer," noted Freebairn-Smith. "He played guitar and he sang his songs. He never sang without his guitar. That's what he did up to the point where we did this album.

"When we did the first recording session, Phil walked in with a guitar around his neck. I had the whole orchestra there, and Phil was going to play his guitar and sing while the orchestra played. He always sang live with the orchestra—we didn't make tracks and have him sing over them—and during this first session, he was reluctant to take off the guitar. He needed that guitar strap around his neck; he had to have something to do with his hands. It was kind of a security thing."

The early going was quite awkward. Seeing how uncomfortable Phil was without his guitar, Marks and Freebairn-Smith tried to find ways to accommodate him. They asked him to play his guitar very softly; they repositioned the vocal microphone with the hope that his guitar would not be picked up. Nothing worked. No matter what they attempted, the sound of Phil's guitar bled into his vocals and the orchestra.

Finally, after a number of aborted attempts, Marks persuaded Phil to remove the instrument and put it on a nearby chair, where he could see it but would not be actually playing it. According to Freebairn-Smith, "It was a real strain for Phil to take that guitar off and stand in a studio with an orchestra and sing a song. He was very uneasy. The first couple of takes weren't very good because he kept coming in too soon, or he wasn't in the rhythm because he wasn't making the rhythm with his right hand. He was having to listen to it coming from the orchestra. What surprised me was how quickly he adapted to it. The further we got into the album, the more comfortable he became."

As Phil had suspected, the recording process was more demanding now than anything he had worked on previously. In the past, he had been working with a producer, an engineer and, on the first two albums, a second guitarist. *Pleasures of the Harbor* was truly a collaborative adventure, and at any given time, Phil would find himself in the studio with a group of total strangers, all contributing to his effort. The previous albums had been cut in a day or two; with the new one, he was lucky to record two complete songs in a day.

Fortunately, he possessed an energy level that only seemed to increase when he was in the studio. "He was indefatigable," said Larry Marks. "In fact, he had to be told when he could no longer sing, when it was just becoming a matter of diminishing returns. Phil had a very distinctive, lyrical voice, with a built-in vibrato, and when it worked, it worked great. It would work for a period of time, and then it would slowly but surely go on him. We'd work all day, and I'd finally have to say, 'So, Phil, the last hour and a half you've just been driving your voice crazy. You can't sing anymore.' And we'd wrap it up for the night. You would get the feeling that Phil was at loose ends if he wasn't doing something, regardless of whether it was productive or not. When he was making a record, he was absolutely manic. He could go on forever."

————

When he was planning the arrangements for *Pleasures of the Harbor*, Phil had decided to feature piano on most of the songs. Although he could not play the instrument well enough to accompany himself, Phil believed that piano offered him the greatest options for the variety of songs he had written for the album, especially the numbers with classical motifs.

Lincoln Mayorga, an exceptional young pianist with experience in the television and film industries, as well as in the recording studio, was hired to play throughout the album. Mayorga was comfortable working in all forms of music, from classical to pop. As a teenager, he had hooked up with the Four Preps, working on their arrangements in the studio and going on the road with them; he eventually went on to doing arrangements for Vikki Carr, Johnny Mathis, Mel Torme, and others. He had never heard of Phil or his music prior to their meeting shortly before the Los Angeles sessions, but he took an immediate liking to him and was intrigued by the musical possibilities for his album.

"He spoke to me about coming up with classical approaches to these songs," Mayorga said, "so I improvised around some of the songs that he showed me. He played them on a guitar and I came up with ideas. On one song on the album, I would play in the style of a different composer each time we did the chorus. I played it like Bach, I played it like Beethoven, I played it like Schumann. Then there was a little gag in 'The Party' that most people did not get: each time we would do a chorus, at the end of the chorus I would misquote a standard song. I would play three or four bars wrong, with a bad melody or a change or whatever. I mangled 'Stardust' and a couple others. It was a spoof of the cocktail piano player."

Of all his contributions to the recording, Mayorga will probably be best remembered for his ragtime piano on "Outside of a Small Circle of Friends." The lyrics to the song—some of the best of Phil's career—were excoriating, and Phil wanted a bouncy, upbeat melody for ironic effect. Mayorga came up with the perfect selection.

"We actually used a tack piano—a piano with thumbtacks in the hammers—on that song," he said. "The piano belonged to the famous ragtime piano player, Phil 'Fingers' Carr. I knew of its existence, so we rented it for the session."

Like the others, Mayorga spoke of the way Phil struggled to overcome his shortcomings during the making of the album. Phil, said Mayorga, was very respectful but not particularly knowledgeable of classical music. He was, however, a quick learner open to suggestion. In the long run, his lack of knowledge may have worked out to his benefit: in combining familiar musical forms with unfamiliar ones,

Phil wandered into new creative territories. Doing so meant working harder than he had ever worked on an album, but it ultimately led to a work that, to this day, stands as his greatest musical achievement.

———

Pleasures of the Harbor was not, by any stretch of the imagination, a perfect album. Two of the recording's eight songs are only average, and, despite the best efforts on the part of the creative minds in the studio, the arrangements detracted from some of the songs, particularly "Crucifixion." The strengths and weaknesses of Phil's voice are evident throughout. When the album is at its best, the songs are true works of art; at its worst, the material sounds forced or, worse yet, pretentious.

"Cross My Heart" Given the album's powerful theme of contemporary yearning for personal and spiritual fulfillment, "Cross My Heart" is a natural selection to open *Pleasures of the Harbor*. In a world gone mad, an individual's dreams, plans, actions, and even sense of security are never as certain or stable as they might seem:

> *I don't know, but it seems that every single dream*
> *Is painting pretty pictures in the air,*
> *Then it tumbles in despair*
> *And it starts to bend, and by the end it's a nightmare.*

In such times, it would be easy to become cynical, but in twisting an old cliché, Phil shows guarded optimism:

> *But I'm gonna give all that I've got to give,*
> *Cross my heart and I hope to live.*

The song has a nice pop hook, and at the time he was recording it, Phil believed "Cross My Heart" had a chance to become a hit single. However, when compared to the rest of the songs on the album, it comes up short. Phil's voice sounds strained on any number of occasions, and he seems lost in the song's arrangement. It was not one of his stronger songs to begin with, and even Phil seemed to acknowledge as much: when the total playing time of *Pleasures of the Harbor* came in too long, Phil trimmed several verses from "Cross My Heart." The song does not suffer from the loss.

"Flower Lady"   This song represents, more than any other entry on the album, the marriage between classical and contemporary that Phil envisioned. Exquisitely arranged, with strings and oboe providing ornate countermelodies to Lincoln Mayorga's piano track, "Flower Lady" seems too beautiful for its message of despair, loss, and broken dreams:

> *Millionaires and paupers walk the hungry street,*
> *Rich and poor companions of the restless feet.*
> *Strangers in a foreign land, strike a match with a tremblin'*
>   *hand,*
> *Learned too much to ever understand.*
> *But nobody's buying flowers from the flower lady.*

The use of strings was critical: Phil wanted a sense of pathos in the song, but not at the risk of slipping into crass melodrama, which would have cheapened the number's overall effect. "He wanted to have something very cultured behind that song," Ian Freebairn-Smith recalled, "to contrast what the lyrics were talking about—this old flower lady."

Throughout *Pleasures of the Harbor*, Phil sings of moments when one can experience flashes of beauty in a bleak society, where a person can find a moment of contentment or safe harbor from the storm. In "Flower Lady," people refuse (or cannot) see even the simplest forms of beauty. To them, the flower lady is a reminder of failure, or even potential doom (or, as Phil sang in another song, "There but for fortune go you or I . . ."), not the bearer of momentary pleasure. She is ignored, life goes on:

> *And the flower lady hobbles home without a sale;*
> *Tattered shreds of petals leave a fading trail.*
> *Not a pause to hold a rose, even she no longer knows.*
> *The lamp goes out, the evening now is closed.*
> *And nobody's buying flowers from the flower lady.*

The sweetness in Phil's voice, a negative quality in some of his earlier topical songs, works to his advantage in "Flower Lady," giving the song an edge of innocence that offsets the lyrics' bleak message. However, Phil struggles with, and never entirely succeeds in overcoming, his vocal limitations when he tries to stretch the word "flower" into an incredible six notes. His voice is not flexible enough to handle it gracefully, and this mars an otherwise flawless performance.

"Outside of a Small Circle of Friends"   In an interview conducted six years after the release of *Pleasures of the Harbor*, Phil spoke of the origins of "Outside of a Small Circle of Friends," one of his most popular songs:

> [It] came out of a chance remark, late at night in a coffeehouse. I was talking to a Canadian guy, and he said, "Oh, I'm sure it wouldn't interest anybody outside a small circle of friends." I said, "What'd you say?" and I picked a guitar and ZOOM, the chords came right away. I said, "That's a song. Here are the chords." And from there it [was] just a matter of writing the verses. It's just that simple. You hear it or you grab it, wherever it comes from.

As an artist, Phil had always been deeply troubled by the apathy he saw every day on the street; it was inconceivable to him that people could see but not react to crime, violence, racial discrimination, or any number of social maladies that plagued modern life. Phil had been horrified by the story about a young woman who, over the span of a half hour, had been repeatedly attacked and stabbed while dozens of people nearby refused so much as to lift a finger in response to her cries for help:

> *Look outside your window, there's a woman being grabbed.*
> *They've dragged her to the bushes and now she's being*
>   *stabbed.*
> *Maybe we should call the cops and try to stop the pain,*
> *But Monopoly is so much fun, I'd hate to blow the game.*
> *And I'm sure it wouldn't interest anybody outside of a small*
>   *circle of friends.*

Lincoln Mayorga's tack piano, along with a banjo and rhythm section, give the song a ragtime sound so incongruous with its lyrics that you could imagine the song being played at a party and going unnoticed by all but a few paying close attention. This, of course, was precisely the point of the arrangement, and rarely in modern music has an arrangement so perfectly fit a songwriter's intentions: while Phil slices apart apathy and hypocrisy with surgical precision, the very people he is addressing could be going about their merry ways, oblivious to the attack.

Oddly enough, Phil found himself in the center of controversy when "Outside of a Small Circle of Friends" was issued as a single. Radio stations across the country, either missing the point or fearing reprisals from their advertisers or the FCC, refused to play the song because of the drug references in its fifth verse:

> *Smoking marijuana is more fun than drinking beer,*
> *But a friend of ours was captured and they gave him thirty*
> > *years.*
> *Maybe we should raise our voices, ask somebody why,*
> *But demonstrations are a drag, besides we're much too high.*
> *And I'm sure it wouldn't interest anybody outside of a small*
> > *circle of friends.*

The objections were the ultimate in hypocrisy. Drug use was a way of life in the music industry, and drug references could be found in songs everywhere in 1967, including on the biggest album of the summer, on which the drummer for the world's most popular band sang about getting high with a little help from his friends. Ironically, Phil rarely used marijuana, mainly because he thought it brought out his paranoia, and he couldn't believe the objections raised over his lyrics. A & M responded to the controversy by releasing three different versions of the song: a complete, unedited version; a version in which the objectionable verse had been edited out completely; and a version that included the fifth verse, with the edited first line, "Smoking is more fun than drinking beer."

"I've Had Her" By far the weakest song on the album, "I've Had Her" borders on mysogyny, particularly in the last line of each verse ("But I've had her, I've had her, she's nothing"), rather than promulgating its intended theme of longing for an ideal, almost mystical lover. The song, written on the heels of a nasty fight with Tina Date, speaks volumes about Phil's lifelong inability to experience anything but

short-term happiness in a relationship, and only a handful of good lines and an interesting arrangement prevent this number from being a total throwaway. Significantly, Phil would write very few love songs over his career, and none would be about happy relationships. "Changes," his most memorable effort, was about the breaking up of a love affair.

"Miranda"   A pure pop song, enhanced by a Dixieland combo, "Miranda" continues the album's subtext of survival in a tough, often cruel world:

> *Do you have a problem, would you like someone to solve them?*
> *Would you like someone to share in your misery?*
> *Now I don't know the answer, but I know a flamenco dancer*
> *Who will dance for you, if you will dance for me.*
> *Her name's Miranda.*
> *She's a Rudolph Valentino fan,*
> *And she doesn't claim to understand.*
> *She bakes brownies for the boys in the band.*

"Miranda," the character and the song, is the flip side of "The Flower Lady." Whereas Phil had employed strings to elicit pathos in the flower lady's story, he used an upbeat backing, not unlike the effect in "Outside of a Small Circle of Friends," to tell his story of a woman who always manages to make the best of a poor situation. "The tune itself didn't exactly fit the Dixieland style," noted Lincoln Mayorga, speaking of the song's arrangement, "but the guys were able to make something of it. We got a wonderful little Dixieland group that consisted of old-timers who had worked with Bob Crosby's Bobcats, Andy Madlock, and others."

The choice of which Dixieland players to use, noted Ian Freebairn-Smith, was critical to the song's authentic sound. "I wanted to get that real, New Orleans quality on the record," he recalled. "I remember very distinctly saying, 'I can think of a million guys I know who work at film studios and can play anything, from jazz to Dixieland to classical music. But I want to get guys who just play Dixieland, who have never done anything else—the old mouldy figs from New Orleans. There are people in town like that.' I didn't want slick musicians playing Dixieland. That was fun because it took a little research to do it."

"The Party" Presented from the point of view of a lounge pianist, "The Party," with its skewering of upper-class pretention and snobbery, ranks as one of Phil Ochs' funniest songs. Phil knew, from the moment he finished the song, how he wanted it presented on record.

"He had strong feelings about it," said Larry Marks. "He wanted to see if he could get away with just piano—somebody playing at a party—and the sound effects of clinking glasses."

Phil's hopes of creating miniature movies in his songs is fully realized in "The Party": one can easily picture the enormous hostess greeting her guests, the wallflower shrinking from the center of activity, or the ladies' man looking over the crowd for his next sexual conquest; one feels the daggers behind the phony smiles, the egos hard at work:

> *They travel to the table; the host is served for supper.*
> *And they pass each other down for salt and pepper.*
> *And the conversation sparkles as their wits are dipped in wine.*
> *Dinosaurs on a diet, on each other they will dine.*
> *Then they pick their teeth, and they squelch a belch, saying,*
> *"Darling, you tasted divine."*
> *And my shoulders had to shrug as I crawled beneath the rug*
> *And retuned my piano.*

"Pleasures of the Harbor" Over the years, "Pleasures of the Harbor," the title song and centerpiece of the album, would be issued in three different forms: as it appears on *Pleasures of the Harbor*, with full orchestral accompaniment; as it appears on *Gunfight at Carnegie Hall*, with Phil singing over Lincoln Mayorga's piano accompaniment; and as it finally turns up on the posthumously released *Then and Now: Live in Vancouver 1968*, with Phil accompanying himself on guitar. There would be all kinds of discussion and disagreement about which version worked best, including an argument between the Ochs brothers shortly before the album's release, Phil defending the lushly orchestrated version while Michael wrote it off as being "too overdone." Even Larry Marks, though standing by the production decisions, admitted, almost two decades after the album's release, that this was a tremendous departure for Phil—and not one that would be embraced by everyone. "We sat down and decided together to overproduce it, to really treat it as a kind of epic or saga," he said.

One thing is certain: Phil worked harder on this number than on any other song on the album. The vocal track was extremely difficult for him, and it had to be wiped from the tape and redone in a number of places. The orchestration and countermelodies threw him off, and he was constantly thwarted by his tendency, effective onstage but unusable in these recording circumstances, of slowing his own tempo to create emphasis on lyrics.

"That's okay when you're singing by yourself with a guitar," Ian Freebairn-Smith said of the tempo changes, "because you are your own rhythm section. You can slow down or speed up, and it becomes part of the feeling of the tune you're singing. But when you have an orchestra out there, you have to be with the conductor. The orchestra, conductor, and singer have to be together."

The recording suffered from numerous false starts and repeated takes, and at one point Larry Marks wondered if it might be best for Phil to record the song in a simpler arrangement. Phil, however, was determined to record it with the orchestral arrangement. "It was tricky," Phil admitted in an interview published shortly after the album's release. "I wanted to really get into musical boundaries. I was far more concerned than any listener could be about losing any of these songs. I was determined not to lose one song through arrangements, which happens oftentimes when you get ambitious like that."

As an album, Phil explained, *Pleasures of the Harbor* was "an attempt to match lyrics as a sound experience. My old work was a documentary of a writer's thoughts. The idea for this one was to round out songs and make them a complete entity."

As a story, "Pleasures of the Harbor" tells the tale of a shore leave during which sailors seek to relieve loneliness and monotony through the temporary pleasures of prostitutes and alcohol. By this point of the album, the theme of temporary solace has been well established, though in "Pleasures of the Harbor," Phil seems more gentle, more reassuring. As if in counterpoint to "I've Had Her," in which dream lovers are waved off as being "nothing," Phil treats his ladies of the evening with something bordering on kindness. They aren't the solution, he seems to be saying, but they can make the problem more bearable:

> *In the room dark and dim, the touch of skin, he asks her of her*
> *   name.*
> *She answers with no shame and not a sense of sin.*

The fingers draw the blind, the sip of wine, the cigarette of
   doubt
Till the candle is blown out, the darkness is so kind.
Oh! Soon, your sailing will be over
Come and take your pleasures of the harbor.

The orchestration, which rises and falls like the movement of the ocean itself, achieves its intended effect: the song not only takes on an epic sense, it also assumes, in its classical arrangement, a feeling of timelessness.

"Crucifixion" This song, Phil's all-time best, should have been the album's crowning touch. Instead, it ranks as the biggest recording failure of Phil's career—a song lost in a flavorless stew of experimental electronic sound, with Phil's voice (and, therefore, his lyrics) buried in the instrumental arrangement. In this one instance, Phil let his ambitions cloud his better judgment.

Not that Phil's intentions were anything but the best: he wanted a contemporary, perhaps even futuristic, arrangement to contrast with the other arrangements used on the album. The decision, however, was not based solely on the need for contrast or variety. The assassination of John Kennedy was a sacrifice that society could ill afford to make. Nuclear holocaust threatened the existence of civilization, war and racial strife tore open the fabric of American life, and a cold war continued to divide superpowers. Leaders of Kennedy's vision were rare, and his violent death only underscored the future's uncertainty. To bring this feeling across in a song demanded an arrangement that reflected the chaos of the times, as well as the passage of time, from ancient to modern days.

Rather than have Ian Freebairn-Smith write the arrangement for "Crucifixion," Phil contacted Joe Byrd, who was working with such bands as The Incredible String Band and the Electric Flag, producing work that Phil thought was on the cutting edge of contemporary music. "Crucifixion" was quite different from anything Byrd had been doing, although, in fairness, Byrd wrote exactly the kind of arrangement that Phil wanted: by combining such old sounds as harpsichord with modern, electronic sounds, the arrangement had a timeless yet totally contemporary sound to it, giving the song an eerie, almost psychedelic feeling.

Unfortunately, this was not what "Crucifixion" called for. The song was structurally simple and not easily given to such complex arrangement. Larry Marks told Phil as much, but to no avail. "Crucifixion" cried out for a simple arrangement—perhaps just singer and guitar, which would have been a suitable ending for Phil's trip through musical history—but Phil was hearing none of it. To make matters even more complicated, Phil struggled mightily with the vocal track on the song. When it became apparent that he would not be able to sing along with the instrumental track, Marks wrote a chart for a moving click track that he described as "an absolute nightmare. It was endless," said Marks. "It must have been 165 pages."

Phil would defend the arrangement when *Pleasures of the Harbor* was released, but he would change his mind over the ensuing years. According to Michael Ochs, Phil eventually admitted that the song had been a failure and spoke of re-recording it on a future album. It never happened.

————

Pleasures of the Harbor left both artist and his production team totally exhausted. Many of the sessions had lasted all day and well into the night, and that, along with Phil's perfectionism, had placed quite a strain on all parties involved. As soon as he had wrapped up the recording sessions, Larry Marks jumped on a plane bound for Connecticut, where he hoped to relax and spend some time with his wife's family, but the vacation was not to be. A message was waiting for him when he arrived on the East Coast.

"Phil was unhappy with a little section of 'Pleasures of the Harbor'—a vocal performance," Marks recalled. "We were up against the wall because we had a release date, so I turned around and went back. We went in and overdubbed the vocals."

The end of the recording sessions did not spell the end of the concerns about the album: by the standards of the day, the album's playing time ran far too long. In 1967, the average playing time for any album side was fifteen to eighteen minutes; the sides for *Pleasures of the Harbor* were running in excess of twenty-five minutes each. Phil, understandably enough, did not want to edit or eliminate any of the songs, but getting the album out the way he had recorded it was going to take special measures in the mastering process.

Luckily, A & M sent most of its tapes to Contemporary Records for mastering. Contemporary Records was universally respected for its excellent work on jazz albums, which tended to run long, and which tended to feature a wide range of sound dynamics similar to those on *Pleasures of the Harbor*. Much of the company's success could be directly attributed to the efforts of Bernie Grundman, a young mastering wizard who was setting new standards for cutting album lacquers. As Grundman recalled, the mastering process was still relatively primitive in 1967—usually involving no more than setting levels and letting a machine do the work.

"In those days," he said, "practically all the engineer did was sit there and read a magazine—set a level and cut. When I came along, the studio was open to all these producers looking for a place to put some finishing touches on their product. I was getting in on the ground floor, and people really appreciated what we could do."

Grundman had worked on a number of jazz recordings, as well as on rock albums, including *The Doors*, which, like Phil's album, checked in at well over the usual playing time constraints. To fit everything on the record, Grundman would analyze each cut on the record, noting sound dynamics and adjusting the grooves on the lacquer by hand. On quieter songs, such as "The Party," he could cheat on the standard spacing by moving the grooves closer together, confident that a turntable's needle would not jump during these passages.

"I would watch the grooves under a microscope," Grundman explained, "and see as best as I could what was going on and how close I was when I would tighten it up. It was time-consuming because you couldn't see very much under the microscope, and a lot of times we actually had to vary it within each cut. When one of the quiet passages came, I would actually fudge the system and bring the grooves even closer, and when it started to get louder, I would just gradually open it up. A lot of that was done by hand in those days."

Grundman's efforts paid off. When it was released, *Pleasures of the Harbor* was one of the longest-running single-disk pop albums in history, and with the exception of a little editing on "Cross My Heart," the recording was issued exactly the way Phil had recorded it.

———

As always, Phil oversaw all aspects of the album's packaging, from selecting the front and back cover photos to writing the jacket copy. For the cover, Phil used a photograph, shot in subtle earth tones, depicting him standing on a dock, wearing a flat cap and battered suede jacket, looking every bit the sailor or immigrant. The jacket had once belonged to Lenny Bruce, one of Phil's heroes, and Phil was ecstatic about having it for his cover photo.

"I remember when he got Lenny Bruce's jacket," said Larry Marks. "It was an unbelievable day—one of the most important days. It was torn, but he wouldn't have it fixed. He was ready to take the cover shot."

For the back cover, Phil selected a photograph of him and Meegan, taken by his former wife. One of the highlights of Phil's four-month stay in California had been the time he had been able to spend with his daughter. He would grow depressed when she left after a visit, his mind riddled with the "what-ifs" that torment so many people after a divorce. One evening, while he was still recording *Pleasures of the Harbor*, he had made an unannounced visit to Ian Freebairn-Smith's place in Studio City.

"I had just separated from my wife and had three young daughters," said Freebairn-Smith, "and it was very difficult for me at that time. We didn't talk about music or his life story or anything else. We talked about how hard it is to be away from your children when you're divorced. He was just so devastated by the fact that he wasn't going to be with his little girl all the time anymore, and it touched me because I was having these same feelings."

The back cover photo effectively complemented the front cover shot of the expressionless young man standing on the dock. For Phil, Meegan was one of life's wonderful havens from a day-to-day existence that could be so challenging and heartless.

———

When it was issued in October 1967, *Pleasures of the Harbor* garnered the largest number of reviews of any of Phil's albums. Critics accustomed to Phil's simple voice-guitar albums were as surprised by the complex musical arrangements on the new recording as they were by Phil's new emphasis on lyricism.

For folk purists, *Pleasures of the Harbor* was the proverbial last straw, proof positive that Phil Ochs had followed Bob Dylan down a gilded road to oblivion. Reviewers and publications once supportive of Phil's topical music now yammered on about his shortcomings as a singer, musician, and songwriter, as if somehow, in his former life, such limitations had been forgivable—or, God forbid, part of his charm.

Boston's *Broadside* staged an all-out assault in one of the most vitriolic reviews Phil would ever receive, running through the album song by song and dismissing the overall effort as being "of no consequence." Phil Ochs, wrote the reviewer, knew how to write protest material; on this record, he was clearly out of his league. "The record jacket depicts the artist as an immigrant," sniffed the reviewer, "and to the land of the art song he is certainly a stranger."

Sing Out! editor Irwin Silber, writing for *Guardian*, bemoaned the backslide of the topical song revolution, calling it "a memory—not quite nostalgia yet, but an echo from another time which serves to remind us of intervening battles waged and miles traveled." Although he judged Phil to be "the most interesting" of "the more important luminaries of the ever-dimming folk music scene," Silber believed Phil to be more effective when writing topical songs, and not the kind of material on *Pleasures of the Harbor*: "Ochs deals consciously in ideas—and sometimes, as in 'Outside of a Small Circle of Friends' or 'The Party,' both from his new album PLEASURES OF THE HARBOR, they seem contrived, manufactured for the occasion." Unlike the critics from *Boston Broadside*, which had grown increasingly hostile toward Phil over the last year, Silber seemed willing to give Phil his blessing in the future—provided, of course, that he return to the fold.

Other reviews, though mixed, approached the album from a less biased perspective. "Ochs is destined to become one of the most celebrated composers and poets of our age," gushed a critic for *The Hartford Times*, calling *Pleasures of the Harbor* "a biting and beautiful protest drenched in the matrix of subtle satire." *The New York Times* was less convinced. Phil's efforts "to move from social criticism to a more personal, introspective expression," wrote the reviewer, resulted "in very muddled and maudlin poeticizing." *Cash Box* called the album "a milestone for Ochs," while *The Florida Times-Union* praised Phil as "a lyrical James Joyce, compressing a whole universe of emotional responses, all uniquely his own."

Phil's favorite review, written by a critic he had befriended, and published in *Esquire*, was a vicious attack that Phil found hysterically funny.

"The thing about Phil Ochs," the reviewer began, "is that he's unquestionably a nice guy. He's so sincere, you know? It's impossible to dislike someone who can annotate his own record with eight poems by Mao Tse-tung and the inscription: 'Is This the enemy?' Too bad his voice shows an effective range of about half an octave, almost no dramatic quality, and a built-in vibrato that makes it sound warped; too bad his guitar playing would not suffer much were his right hand webbed."

Pleasures of the Harbor would never hit the Number 1 position on the charts, as Phil brazenly predicted when it was released. In fact, it would barely crack the Top 100 on the *Cash Box* and *Record World* charts, and would only climb as high as the 168th position on the *Billboard* survey. Nevertheless, in time, the album became Phil's most commercially successful venture, surpassing the sales figures of *In Concert*, his previous best.

From the moment he began planning the album, Phil had hoped to make *Pleasures of the Harbor* his magnum opus. That he succeeded in creating his finest album was both a blessing and a curse. He could revel in his artistic achievement, but in time, especially in his later years, it would serve as a haunting reminder that he had hit his peak and could do no better.

Chapter Nine

TAPE FROM CALIFORNIA

MICHAEL OCHS felt that it was going to take some heavy-duty promoting for Phil to get *Pleasures of the Harbor* off the ground. Michael was not a big fan of the album, to say the least. He was furious with Phil for recording "Pleasures of the Harbor" and "Crucifixion" in their present arrangements, and he was very vocal with Phil about his opinions. "Miranda," he felt, sounded too much like a Beatles imitation, and he was not fond of "The Party." As far as he was concerned, the only redeeming numbers on the album were "Outside of a Small Circle of Friends," which he liked very much, "Flower Lady," which he deemed to be "not a disaster, but not great," and "Cross My Heart."

"I was very disappointed when I got the first acetates," Michael said. "I thought, 'Oh, God, he's overdone it. It's overkill.' I thought Side Two was unplayable—one play and you file it. I was ready to kill him over 'Crucifixion.' I told him, 'You killed your best song.' He couldn't believe I'd said that. 'I don't care what you think,' he said. 'You're wrong. This is going to be the next thing.' "

While his criticism might not have endeared him to his brother, Michael was fully prepared to back the album in his capacity as Phil's manager. If the record was going to have any chance at all, Phil would have to hit the road and play every hall he could book. Michael was convinced that *Pleasures of the Harbor* would be getting very little, if any, radio airplay, so the only way to put the music in front of fans would be through an extensive tour.

Phil stubbornly disagreed. The record was too good to be ignored, he countered, and once people had heard some of its songs on the radio, they would flock to his concerts. Touring now would be a disaster. He wouldn't pull anywhere near the attendance that he would enjoy once the album was a hit. Besides, he wanted to get back to New York. He missed Karen, and he hadn't seen his friends all summer. He needed time to rest from the tedium of recording.

Michael had no choice but to follow Phil's wishes. The tour would have to wait.

———

There was, however, one concert venue that Phil insisted on playing: Carnegie Hall. His last show there had been a success, and Phil reasoned that it would be the perfect place to introduce *Pleasures of the Harbor* to his hometown.

Michael wasn't so sure. It had been a year and a half since Phil's last album, and Michael worried that his brother might have trouble filling the hall. He was still learning the business, he told Phil, and he really didn't know any booking agents.

"We'll book it ourselves," Phil proposed.

"We will?"

"Yeah," said Phil, "with our money."

"With *our* money?" Michael responded. "It's *your* money, Phil."

Phil remained confident. He reminded Michael that he had gone from small Greenwich Village clubs to Carnegie Hall without a hitch. He and Arthur Gorson had bucked the system and won.

"Everybody said I couldn't do it," Phil said, "but I did it. I booked Carnegie Hall myself."

Michael went to work on it. "I was terrified," he later admitted, "because I signed a paper saying that I was liable for all the money, but I took Phil's word for it. Sure enough, Phil sold it out. It was close—we pulled it out right toward the end—but we ran a 'Sold Out' ad in *The New York Times*. Phil was so proud."

The October 1 concert wound up being one of the strangest public appearances of Phil's career. The show itself went well, with Phil offering a lineup of fifteen old songs and four new works ("Outside of a Small Circle of Friends," "The Party," "Pleasures of the Harbor," and "Crucifixion") from *Pleasures of the Harbor*. He was in top form, displaying none of the nervousness that had spoiled his first appearance at the hall, prompting one concert reviewer to remark that "Ochs has finally found his own voice, finally escaped the shadows of Dylan and Pete Seeger."

The concert would have been a whopping success had Phil chosen to end it at that point, with his audience giving him a standing ovation. Phil, however, had other plans. When the applause died down, he announced that he had two speakers who wanted to address the audience about plans for a gathering at the Democratic National Convention the following summer.

After Phil's brief introduction, Jerry Rubin and Abbie Hoffman took centerstage. Phil had renewed his friendship with Rubin while he was in California, and he had learned of the plans being made for a large antiwar demonstration in Chicago, where Lyndon Johnson would undoubtedly be nominated for a second full term in the White House. Phil was totally in favor of the idea of a demonstration. The "War is Over" rally was still fresh in his mind, and he was ready to do his part to help move the antiwar demonstrations to the next level.

What Phil did not count on was Abbie Hoffman's theatrics at his Carnegie Hall concert. Hoffman, as volatile a presence as anyone involved in the antiwar movement, seized his moment onstage. Rubin had barely begun his formal announcement when Hoffman tore the microphone away from his partner and started shouting, "Fuck Lyndon Johnson! Fuck Robert Kennedy! And fuck you if you don't like it!"

Phil could only watch the ensuing pandemonium. His audience, cheering him only moments ago, now booed Hoffman as he leapt off the stage and ran frantically up the aisles, shrieking obscenities at startled concert-goers. The Carnegie Hall management quickly cut the power to the microphones and stage lights. People shouted at Hoffman and Rubin, ordering them to leave. When the two finally did leave, Phil found himself standing alone onstage, looking like a lost, embarrassed ringmaster. What had started out as one of his finest onstage moments had disintegrated into a nightmare. He muttered a short speech about how one didn't have to be vulgar to battle a vulgar system, but the lecture was coming too late. He would be fortunate if he was ever allowed to perform on the Carnegie Hall stage again.

———

In extending an invitation to Rubin and Hoffman to speak at his concert, Phil had hoped to show the world that he was still very much involved in the protest against the Vietnam war. When introducing his guests, he had joked that the Left was starting to accuse him of abandoning the cause in favor of commercial recording adventures. Even a critic for *The New York Times*, in his review of *Pleasures of the Harbor*, had noted that there was a conspicuous absence of antiwar songs on Phil's latest album. Such criticism cut deeper than Phil liked to admit.

As it was, he was putting together another "War Is Over" demonstration, this one scheduled to take place in New York City on Saturday, November 25. As Phil conceived it, the rally would commence in Washington Square Park and proceed uptown, via a large group march, to the army recruiting station on 42nd Street; from there, the assembly would move on to the United Nations building. It would be, Phil decided, the ultimate declaration of peace.

The number of antiwar rallies was now increasing nationwide on college campuses, in city parks, at recruitment centers and draft board offices. As casualty figures piled up, announced every evening on the news with accompanying footage from the battle lines, more and more people, once supportive of the war, were moving to the other side. It had not been that long since senators voted their overwhelming support of the Gulf of Tonkin resolution; now they were abandoning what appeared to be a sinking political ship, leaving Lyndon Johnson and his allies in a losing struggle to stay afloat.

On October 21, an enormous antiwar demonstration was held in Washington D.C., beginning at the Lincoln Memorial and culminating with a mass march on the Pentagon. Phil, who would not have missed the rally for anything, attended the early portion of the proceedings, addressing an estimated crowd of 150,000 people before returning to New York later that same day to honor a radio show appearance. In recounting the experience, Phil initially took a rather jaded approach. "The weather was great and the speeches were dull, as always," he quipped. "It was the same old morality question being raised in the same phraseology, and nobody [was] really listening." When pressed to elaborate, he grew serious. "It's always good to have shows of strength," he said. "It helps people in their own personal commitment to the peace movement, and it scares Washington. And it could lead to other things."

Although he had been humiliated by their antics at his Carnegie Hall show, Phil embraced many of Jerry Rubin and Abbie Hoffman's ideas about staging a demonstration. Rather than spout angry words that only alienated potential recruits to the antiwar cause, Phil believed that it was much better to keep humor nearby and take a positive approach to demonstrating. He kept all this in mind when he offered an open invitation to his "War Is Over" rally in *The Village Voice*:

Does protesting the war leave you tired and upset? Does civil disobedience leave you nervous and irritable? Does defending liberalism leave you feeling friendless and perhaps wondering about your breath? Does defending the need of repelling communist aggression leave you exhausted and give you that generation gap feeling?

On the other hand, are you tired of taking drugs to avoid the crushing responsibilities of a sober world? Do you want to do something about the war and yet refuse to bring yourself down to the low level of current demonstrations?

Is everybody sick of this stinking war?

In that case, friends, do what I and thousands of other Americans have done—declare the war over.

That's right, I said declare the war over from the bottom up.

This simple remedy has provided relief for countless frustrated citizens and has been overlooked for an amazingly long time, perhaps because it is so obvious. After all, this is our country, our taxes, our war. We pay for it, we die for it, we curiously watch it on television—we should at least have the right to end it.

Now I enjoy violence as much as the next guy, but enough is enough. Five seasons is plenty for the most exciting of series.

On Saturday, November 25, we are going to declare the war over and celebrate the end of the war in Washington Square Park at 1 P.M.

For one day only, you and your family can achieve that moment you've all been waiting for. Ludicrous as this may appear, it is certainly far less so than the war itself. I am not recommending this as a substitute for other actions; it is merely an attack of mental disobedience on an obediently insane society.

This is the sin of sins against an awkward power structure, the refusal to take it seriously. If you are surprised the war is over, imagine the incredulity of this administration when they hear about it. . . .

The lengthy essay was Phil's most brilliant moment as a journalist, a passionate plea for sanity through peaceful, absurdist action. The incongruity of it was pure Phil Ochs: it was the man who wrote "Power and the Glory" *and* "I Ain't Marching Anymore," the patriot willing to consider treason if it meant saving his nation. It was the spirit that eventually led Phil to participate in the founding of the Youth International Party.

The rally was a huge success, free of the violence that had ruined the Los Angeles demonstration. The cool but sunny weather brought out a large crowd, and by noon Washington Square Park was teeming with people of all ages. Allen Ginsberg, author of "Pentagon Exorcism," the poem used during a theatrical exorcism during the march on Washington a month earlier, made an appearance with fellow Beat poet Gregory Corso. Several dozen demonstrators posed near the edge of the park for a group photograph for *The Village Voice*. People rattled and spun noisemakers, adding to the festive environment. Curious passersby paused on the sidewalks and watched. Phil, decked out in a replica Civil War uniform, mingled among his troops, thrilled that his party had attracted so many people.

The New York rally, unlike its Los Angeles counterpart, met little resistance from the authorities. Permits had been easily secured, and the event was publicized by handouts distributed by the Diggers, a countercultural group with ties to the Wobblies. Phil maintained a light-hearted stance throughout the planning and publicizing of the rally, making certain that the public perceived it as a peaceful and nonthreatening gathering. When, for example, a police captain attended a press conference and asked Phil how people were going to be celebrating, Phil replied, "They'll do a lot of kissing and hugging."

"What would you call it?" the police captain wanted to know.

"Counterabsurdity," Phil responded. The idea for the march, he had pointed out earlier, was not new. A similar rally had taken place in California earlier in the year.

"How did the idea get here from California?"

"Through the mails."

The parade itself could not have come off better. After singing "The War Is Over" in Washington Square Park, Phil led a huge mass of people on a march through what must have seemed like half of Manhattan. Writer Larry Sloman, covering the event for the Queens College newspaper, remembered the rally as "an amazing event."

"There must have been a couple thousand people," Sloman remarked. "We were just this ragtag bunch of people running in the street, saying, 'Did you hear? The war is over! The war is over!' Buses were stopping and people would get off and go, 'What?' And we'd say, 'Yeah, the war is over.' People were hugging and kissing each other. Store owners came out. We went by this cinema, and the movie they were playing at that time was *La Guerre Est Finie*. Everybody started cheering. It was one of the most brilliant demonstrations ever."

Phil might not have gone that far in sizing up the success of the rally, but he was thoroughly pleased with the way things had turned out. Not only had he mobilized a large number of people for a worthwhile cause, but in doing so, he had also proven, in the wake of his Carnegie Hall debacle, that demonstrations could be conducted with dignity.

———

After months of trying, Michael was finally able to persuade Phil to tour the West Coast in support of *Pleasures of the Harbor*. "Outside of a Small Circle of Friends" had been released as a single, and was enjoying modest success in Los Angeles and Sacramento, while up in Seattle the song had been listed in one of the radio surveys as a breakout hit. Both Phil and Michael agreed that there could be much to gain through appearances in the West, where Phil had never enjoyed any noteworthy success in the past.

The trip started out well enough, with Phil playing several dates in the Pacific Northwest, but it quickly unraveled in California, where Phil once again stumbled over his ballooning ego. The success of his Carnegie Hall concert and "War Is Over" rally, coupled with the sales figures for "Outside of a Small Circle of Friends" in California, had led Phil to believe that he was capable of filling the larger halls in Los Angeles and the San Francisco Bay Area.

Once again, Michael found himself at odds with his brother. There was no way, he told Phil, that he would fill the bigger venues. "We fought like cats and dogs," he recalled. "I knew he was wrong. I told him he couldn't do it."

Phil's first show in Los Angeles was almost cancelled before it was staged. Michael was aware of a popular nightclub called The Troubadour, and he was eager to book Phil a performance at the club. Doug Weston, the Troubadour's owner, was one of the most astute judges of talent on the West Coast and, as a sideline to his work at his club, he had successfully promoted a number of concerts into larger halls in Los Angeles and San Francisco. When Michael called about Phil's playing at the Troubadour, Weston was agreeable, even though he knew very little about Phil or his music. Phil could play at one of the Troubadour's Monday night hootenannies, Weston suggested. There would be no payment involved, but if Phil was well received, they might be able to work out something for the future.

Weston never advertised his hootenanny performers, but he made an exception in Phil's case, putting a "HOOT NITE TONITE—PHIL OCHS" notice on the Troubadour's marquee. Phil and Michael reacted angrily when they arrived at the club and saw the sign, both believing that Weston was trying to cash in on Phil's name while staging a nonpaying gig. Phil ordered Michael to confront Weston and inform the club owner that there would be no performance if his name stayed on the marquee.

As Weston recalled, the conversation was brief but very tense. "They demanded that I either pay him or take his name off the marquee, and I got into a big argument with them. I said, 'Is Phil going to sing tonight?' and Michael said, 'Yes.' I said, 'Well, then, the name stays.' "

Weston, who had helped launch the careers of a number of acts on the West Coast, could not believe that someone was threatening to pull out of a show because he was *getting* publicity. The complaint was usually the reverse.

"What does it hurt him?" Weston asked Michael. "Nobody knows him here. He's getting his first exposure in town."

Michael held his ground, and Weston finally told one of his assistants to take Phil's name off the marquee—not to mollify Michael and Phil, but because Phil would no longer be playing at the club. Michael thought about it for a moment.

"Leave it up," he told Weston. "He'll play."

———

From such improbable origins sprang another enduring friendship. Phil loved Weston's stories of his early days as a bartender in Los Angeles. Weston had known a large cast of colorful characters, from mafiosi to street-corner pimps, from high-rollers to nickel-and-dimers. Weston would listen to customers' stories of their problems, hold gambling winnings and debts, and pour countless drinks for people who could have just stepped from the pages of a Charles Bukowski tale. People came to Weston because, in a town on the take, he could be trusted.

Of all the stories, there was one that Phil begged Weston to repeat, again and again and again, until Weston could no longer bear to tell it.

"I worked at a fine Italian restaurant," Weston remembered, beginning the story he had told Phil so many times, "and there was one customer, a moody, silent kid, who would come up to the bar, buy a drink, and go sit at a huge round table right next to the bar. He'd sit at that huge table by himself, have one or two drinks, and all of a sudden you'd turn around and he'd be gone. Then you'd hear tires screeching and he'd be heading out to the freeway. That," said Weston, pausing a beat for effect, "was James Dean."

Phil loved the story, and he pumped Weston for as much information about the movie star as Weston could provide. Phil would settle for anything—no description or detail was too small. He was appalled when Weston told him that he didn't even know who James Dean was at the time he was serving him, that he had stopped paying any attention to the movies after he'd quit his job as a theater usher years earlier in New York. In Weston's eyes, Dean had been just another in a series of oddball customers. To Phil, the connection was one more reason to add Weston to his list of friends: anyone who had served drinks to James Dean was good enough for him.

Against his better judgment, Weston agreed to promote two large Phil Ochs concerts on the Coast, one in Los Angeles and one in Berkeley. Weston shared Michael Ochs' opinion that Phil would do better by breaking in at smaller venues before taking on the larger halls, but Phil adamantly refused to take what he considered to be a step backward. He had paid his dues in the Village clubs, toiling for nothing or next-to-nothing in basket houses and closet-sized nightclubs; he had cut four albums, sold out three appearances at Carnegie Hall, and played before tens of thousands of people at rallies and demonstrations across the country. He was not about to start over on the West Coast, regardless of how well he was known.

He should have listened to his brother and Doug Weston. His Los Angeles concert, staged at the Santa Monica Civic Auditorium, found him playing in a hall that was about one-fourth filled—a scenario that certainly did not impress a group of A & M executives attending the performance. To make matters worse, Phil suffered through another episode of performance anxiety. His voice cracked and he forgot the lyrics to his songs; his guitar went out of tune during his performance of "I Ain't Marching Anymore." "Sometimes," he remarked while retuning the instrument, "I suspect this guitar is fascist." A critic for *The Los Angeles Times*, in a mixed review appearing the day after the show, was less than impressed with Phil's songs, and totally put off by his forgetting his lyrics, but he had to concede the singer's appeal: "His charm is so disarming that he had the audience with him all the way, even over those rough spots."

Phil's performance at the Berkeley Community Theater was a bigger disaster yet. As Doug Weston and Michael had predicted, ticket sales were abysmal, despite Weston's best efforts to promote and advertise the concert. At show time, there were only a few dozen people in the auditorium. Facing the ultimate humiliation, Phil turned to his brother for help.

"He made me go out and give tickets away on the street," Michael remembered. "I said, 'Is that what a manager does?' And he said, 'Yes. Stop anybody and give them tickets. We can't afford to do the same thing we did in Santa Monica.' I was too sheepish to say, 'Phil, you should have listened to me.' It was a disaster, but he never learned. Phil was never wrong—the *public* was wrong. He never listened to anybody."

Despite the show's being a major defeat, Doug Weston was impressed with Phil's professionalism. "He was wrong," said Weston. "He wasn't as popular in Berkeley as he thought he was. But he played the show as if he was singing to a hall full of people, and when it was all over, he shook hands and everything was fine. That kind of thing did not really affect him."

———

Phil used the California shows to work on new material that he hoped to include on his next album. In recent months, he had grown fond of jotting down poetry and song ideas into pocket notebooks that he carried with him everywhere, and while the new batch of songs did not come along as easily or as readily as the topical songs of his early days in New York, Phil had several new works by the end of 1967. One, entitled "The Harder They Fall," was an account of lost innocence and corruption, in which Phil twisted fairy tales into nightmarish modern fables:

> *Jack and Jill went up the hill. They were looking for a thrill,*
> *But she forgot to take her pill. Gimme my pill, gimme my pill,*
> > *gimme my pill.*
> *Through our fantasies we fly. In the prison of our dreams we*
> > *die.*
> *Praying in an apple pie.*
> *Though you won't believe a word I say,*
> *Gonna say the words anyway.*
> *The poems are pretty, the tales are tall.*
> *Only the witches recall:*
> *The bigger they are, the harder they fall.*

By early 1968, Phil was obsessed with the theme of America's fall. His years of political activism had left him battered but still hopeful. Convinced that the country's leaders were taking people down a path to madness, he lashed out with a series of songs that found him acting as both gadfly and soothsayer:

> *Half the world is crazy, the other half is scared.*
> *Madonnas do the minuet for naked millionares.*
> *The anarchists are rising, while we're racing for the moon.*
> *It doesn't take a seer to see the scene is coming soon.*

Phil had strong ideas for what he wanted to accomplish on the new record. *Pleasures of the Harbor*, he admitted, had alienated some of his old fans, and though he was still standing by the album, he was ready to try something a little different—something that found a middle ground between the old Phil Ochs and the new one without compromising the integrity of his music.

"In my new album" he told an interviewer, "I'm going to make the next step, which will be a comment on the spiritual decline of America, with some of the musical elements I had in *Harbor* but somewhat played down. And the words are coming to the fore again. Essentially, I'm going to try and get a balance between the *Harbor* record and the *Concert* one that preceded it."

Finding the middle ground was not going to be easy, especially if Phil intended to follow the tough critical guidelines he set in a meandering, cranky, three-part interview published in *Broadside* in the early months of 1968. In the interview, Phil blasted what he felt was a decline in the quality of music issued over the past few years. The problem, he stated, was a decline in aesthetic standards that seemed to run parallel to the moral decline of the nation. Even his old heroes had let him down. Dylan, he said in an uncharacteristic criticism of his fellow songwriter, had not moved ahead after *Highway 61 Revisited*; songwriters such as Donovan and Tim Hardin, after recording wonderful songs early in their careers, had hit artistic plateaus. The psychedelic movement had not produced any valid or important music.

One of the most telling symbols of the decline, Phil went on, could be found in the direction that his idol, John Wayne, was taking in his movies:

> In watching an old John Wayne-John Ford western movie, "Rio Grande," recently, and thinking about Wayne's new movie about to come out called "The Green Berets," it occurred to me that the contrast between these two films was making a similar comment, in some sense, to mine, in that here we have John Wayne, who was a major artistic and psychological figure on the American scene, since he was a very great film star widely popular, who at one point used to make movies of soldiers who had a certain validity in that they were based on a certain view of nobility, a certain sense of honor [about] what the soldier was doing. Even if it was about what the soldier-hero was doing. Even if it was a cavalry movie doing a historically dishonorable thing to the Indians, even as there was a feeling of what it meant to be a man, what it meant to have some sense of duty, let us say. Now today we have the same actor making his new war movie in a war so hopelessly corrupt that, without seeing the movie, I'm sure it is perfectly safe to say that it will be an almost technically-robot-view of soldiery, just by definition of how the whole country has deteriorated. And I think it would make a very interesting double feature to show a good old Wayne movie like, say, "She Wore a Yellow Ribbon" with "The Green Berets." Because that would make a very striking comment on what has happened to America in general.

Though he would have hated to admit it, much of Phil's cynicism could largely be attributed to sour grapes—to his own inability to achieve the commercial success of people with considerably less talent. He longed to see his name at the top of the pop music charts, or to be invited to appear on the prestigious television variety and talk shows. He had played on a number of small local programs, as well as rarely on a nationally broadcast television program, such as Walter Cronkite's *CBS Evening News* program, for which he sang "Draft Dodger Rag," or ABC's *Dissent or Treason* special, on which he sang "I Ain't Marching Anymore," but he had been turned down by variety shows hosted by Ed Sullivan, the Smothers Brothers, and Merv Griffin. *The Tonight Show* found him too controversial.

"It wants snide jokes about the pill," Phil said of *The Tonight Show*, sounding every bit the topical songwriter of old, "but it's not to their interest to have someone say what a large portion of this generation is saying, and that is that this country is falling apart."

Phil could complain all he wanted about falling standards and lost opportunities, and he could train his sights on what he felt were less than superior poetic images in the lyrics of Bob Dylan or Jim Morrison, but as the new songs and lyric fragments in his notebooks indicate, he was struggling with imagery of his own. "The Doll House," a new composition boasting a beautiful melody, was bogged down by lyrics that *sounded* interesting and poetic, but which, in reality, said very little:

> *The flower fled from my feet,*
> *Tom Sawyer voice through the hole of the key,*
> *Landed so gently.*
> *The castles cover the cave,*
> *I had no choice, the visions were brave*
> *And the phantoms were friendly.*
> *And Pirate Jenny was dancing for pennies,*
> *Knucklebones tossed in a spin.*
> *There were silver songs on her skin.*
> *And she wasn't caring when the ship came in.*
> *And the lady of the lake,*
> *Helped me to escape,*
> *And led me to myself at last,*
> *Tho' I danced with the dolls in the doll house.*

As a tunesmith, Phil was writing better and more complex melodies all the time, often in the neoclassical styles that he favored. His lyrics, as always, depended on sparks of inspiration that, even he had to admit, had occurred more frequently when he was writing topical songs and finding subjects for them in *Newsweek* articles. He could write wonderful lines of poetry, but they did not come to him as naturally as they did for Dylan or Morrison, and all of Phil's grumblings would not alter that fact. If he was going to judge his own work by the standard he used for the songs of others, his new material would have to improve greatly to earn a passing grade.

————

New York did little to improve Phil's spirits or creativity. The artistic community, he felt, was dying a slow, agonizing death. The folk scene was a memory; Sam Hood was talking about closing the Gaslight and moving upstate. Many of the singers and musicians were migrating to the West Coast, where they were setting up a community similar to the one of five years ago in New York. *Broadside* still carried the torch for the topical songwriters, but most of the city's critics, formerly sympathetic to Phil and his peers, had turned their attention elsewhere. The Aquarian Age offices, once the gathering place for Phil's musician friends, had lost its sense of fun. The people closest to Phil were as disenchanted as anybody: Michael wanted to move back to Los Angeles, and Karen hated the cold, snowy winters and the time she would be spending alone while Phil recorded his albums in California.

As weary as he had grown of New York City, Phil was equally reluctant to leave. He had lived in the city longer than anywhere else in his life, and it held many fond memories. He had made a name for himself in the country's largest city, and he still had many friends living there. He loved the fast pace of the city and the buzz of sensory overload that he could get, on any given day, when he walked down the streets of the Village. For all his complaints about New York, he still considered it his base of operations. Even Michael's announcement that he was pulling up stakes and moving back to Los Angeles failed to nudge him.

What finally did the trick was a memorial concert for Woody Guthrie held at Carnegie Hall. The show, one of the events of the season in New York, saw an impressive assembly of Guthrie cronies and disciples playing some of the folk hero's greatest songs onstage. Pete Seeger was there, as was Guthrie's son, Arlo; actor Will Geer read narrative passages from Guthrie's autobiography. Bob Dylan, who had not appeared in public since a motorcycle accident in 1967, came out of seclusion to perform.

Phil badly wanted to play at the show, but when the lights dimmed in Carnegie Hall the night of the memorial, he was sitting out in the audience, bitterly depressed, wondering why he had not been invited. Something was terribly wrong with the selection process, he felt, when Richie Havens was brought in to sing but Ramblin' Jack Elliott, one of Guthrie's most visible protégés, had been excluded, when Judy Collins was given a number while he, author of one of the best Woody Guthrie tribute songs in the business, was a spectator.

"He blamed me for it—and correctly so," said Harold Leventhal, one of the organizers of the program. "He felt neglected or pushed away. I felt bad about it, but when you do these things, somebody just doesn't make it."

Phil did not accept the explanation, even after talking over his disappointment with Leventhal after the show. He was convinced that show-biz politics were somehow involved, and he told friends that it was his old manager, Albert Grossman, who had kept him off the roster. Grossman was known to use his bigger clients, particularly Bob Dylan, as leverage to secure gigs for some of his other lesser-known clients, and Phil was certain that Grossman had approached the memorial concert organizers with the promise to deliver Dylan *if* they included Richie Havens—a new Grossman client—in the lineup. Phil bought Leventhal's explanation of his being a victim of the numbers game, but he couldn't help but wonder if those numbers had been stacked against him.

Others, including Izzie Young, Sis Cunningham, and Gordon Friesen, voiced concern about the way the concert had been presented. In a *Broadside* editorial, the irrepressible Cunningham and Friesen questioned the selection process. "There were [some] who felt the people really connected with Woody—like Alan Lomax, for instance—were slighted, and the spotlight given to people who never had anything to do with the Oklahoma folk bard," they wrote. "There was some feeling that Woody himself might have walked out on the whole proceedings, in the sense that the ESTABLISHMENT, which he had resisted with all his strength while he was able, took him over when he was dead and couldn't do a thing about it."

The controversy was unfortunate, for it tarnished an otherwise

brilliant evening. The performances, eventually issued on two albums, did justice to one of America's musical legends and helped
raise funds for Woody's survivors.

None of this mattered to Phil, who sat miserably in the audience,
tears filling his eyes when the entire ensemble gathered onstage and
sang "This Land Is Your Land." Unable to take it any longer, he
walked out before the end of the song.

————

He and Karen were packed and on their way to Los Angeles a short
time later.

The move from New York had been hasty. Unable to completely
cut his connection with the city, Phil subleased his Prince Street
apartment to Jerry Rubin with the specific understanding that he
could stay at the apartment whenever he was in town. Needing some-
where to stay in Los Angeles, Phil looked up Jim Glover, who generously invited Phil and Karen to stay with Jean and him until they
found a place of their own.

Phil was now obsessed with the presidential primaries and the
plans for a mass demonstration in Chicago. At his concerts, he encouraged audiences to travel to the Windy City in August. He began
to campaign actively for Eugene McCarthy, who was basing his
candidacy on bringing a halt to the war in Vietnam. In March, Phil
flew to New York, where he performed benefits for the Minnesota
senator, and he appeared at a press conference formally announcing the Festival of Life taking place in Chicago during the week of
the Democratic National Convention. As Phil saw it, the forthcoming months would spell the future of a country on the brink of self-
destruction.

The primaries fueled countless arguments between Phil and his
friends. Andy Wickham was characteristically skeptical of all the revolutionary talk; the power structure, he predicted, would have its way
in the end. Jack Newfield had thrown his support to Robert Kennedy
who, the journalist believed, was the only true grass-roots candidate.
The Yippies were battling the electoral process itself and had little
inclination to endorse any candidate. When Lyndon Johnson
stunned the nation by announcing that he would not seek or accept
re-election, the real debates began: Could Vice-President Hubert
Humphrey, who had endorsed Johnson's position on the war in

Southeast Asia, withstand the challenges presented by McCarthy and Kennedy?

Phil puzzled over the question. Common sense told him that Robert Kennedy, with his name and experience, was more electable than Eugene McCarthy, but Kennedy still represented the old political machine. Phil could easily endorse Kennedy over Humphrey, but he vacillated over supporting Kennedy over McCarthy. After giving the issue a lot of thought, he decided to continue to campaign for McCarthy— for the time being, at least.

For all his antiestablishment reputation, Phil was still considerably more moderate than some of his fellow Yippies. This much became clear when Phil and Jerry Rubin engaged in a lively—and occasionally heated—public debate on the political candidates and upcoming convention in Chicago. From the onset, Rubin argued that Kennedy was no better choice for the presidency than Johnson; if anything, he said, the race would be less interesting with Johnson gone.

"The battle in America," declared Rubin, "is not between Johnson and Kennedy, or Democrats and Republicans, but between children and the machine. Kennedy represents the basic evil of America, not Johnson. Johnson was just doing all he could in his own way to live up to John Kennedy's memory. I hate all rich bastards."

Phil, who described himself during the debate as a "semi-Yippie," was not about to stand by idly and listen to Rubin connect Kennedy, who had spoken out against the Vietnam War, with Johnson, who seemed determined to keep it going. Furthermore, Phil contended that the Yippies were underestimating the power of their opponent; angry rhetoric and nose-thumbing was not going to effect significant change.

"You radicals are all alike, lashing out at the approaching armed tractor with yo-yo's," Phil told Rubin. "I agree with an essential part of what you're saying, but I also sense the machine is developing a rather apparent emotion, that of survival."

Survival, Rubin countered, was precisely the issue. "I do not want the system to survive," he admitted to Phil. "You do. I want to help destroy America's military domination of the world, and her cultural imperialism. To me, the essence of America is viewing man as a material, not a spiritual, object. In other words, the Death Society. America at her essence is irrational to man's freedom. Kennedy would rationally protect this irrationality. Kennedy is the enemy of the

South American peasant, the Detroit black, and the dropped-out Long Island white teenager."

Rubin's attack placed Phil in an awkward position, for while he was still stumping for McCarthy, he suddenly found himself defending Kennedy's position. Phil had no more use for the upper class than Rubin, but he wanted to approach the war from a moral, rather than economic, perspective. Martin Luther King Jr. had recently come out strongly against the war, largely because it was being fought by minorities unable to buy their way out of the draft through influence or student deferments, and while Phil was fully supportive of King's position, he was also astute enough politically to realize that this approach was not going to gain the votes of the middle and upper classes. The immorality and insanity of the war had to be brought to the forefront.

The debate illustrated the division in the line of thinking of those planning to go to the Chicago convention. Rubin, who would later admit that he went with the intention of inciting a full-scale confrontation with the police, had given up all hope of working with or within the system; he viewed himself as nothing other than a revolutionary prepared to overthrow the present form of government.

Phil, on the other hand, was not ready to give up on America. The country, as he saw it, was "a beautiful shipwreck," yet the people on board could be saved. Perhaps even the ship itself could be salvaged. The months ahead would decide.

———

Phil was devastated when he heard the news of Martin Luther King's assassination on April 4. Here was a man who had devoted his life to nonviolent civil disobedience, and now he, like John Kennedy before him, had been gunned down before he could realize his dream.

Riots tore the nation's major cities apart in the wake of King's murder. Phil watched news reports depicting cities in flames and police attacking rioters and looters. In Chicago, Mayor Richard J. Daley, already troubled by the reports he was hearing about plans for the Democratic National Convention, decided to take extreme measures to quell the rioting. Shoot to kill, he ordered his police force.

———

Somehow, in the midst of all the politicking, Phil found time to work. Earlier in the year, he and Michael had worked on a songbook, *The War Is Over*, a miscellany that included the guitar charts for the Barricade-controlled songs, along with photographs, poetry, cartoons by Ron Cobb, essays written by Phil, and even one of Phil's early interviews with *Broadside*. Judy Henske wrote a humorous introduction, and Phil poked fun at himself by including lines from some of his nastiest reviews. Overall, it was an impressive package—by far more interesting than most of the songbooks on the market.

The big project was *Tape from California*, Phil's fifth album. By his own account, Phil was "wavering back and forth between politics and lyricism" in his songwriting, and the new album, recorded over a five-day period in May, reflected Phil's intention of finding a compromise between the guitar-vocal arrangements of *In Concert* and the classically orchestrated arrangements of *Pleasures of the Harbor*.

The approach was not entirely successful, mostly because the diversity of the songs themselves, along with the huge difference in arrangements, gave the album the feeling of a hodgepodge rather than a unified whole. This was unfortunate, for *Tape from California* contained some standout songs, including the thirteen-minute "When in Rome," another of Phil's mini-movies, and "Joe Hill," a twenty-two-verse biography of the IWW hero.

The recording sessions featured a number of familiar faces from the earlier *Pleasures of the Harbor* sessions. Larry Marks was once again at the production helm, and Ian Freebairn-Smith was brought in to write the charts for "The Floods of Florence," one of Phil's most sensitive works. Lincoln Mayorga was back on the keyboards, most noticeably playing harpsichord on the title cut.

Compared to the recording of *Pleasures of the Harbor*, putting together *Tape from California* was easy. Larry Marks, for one, was grateful for the simpler routine: "It was a little retrogressive, back to the way Phil used to work," he commented. "We organized the album, walked in, and did it in a couple of days."

Oddly enough, the album's simplest arrangement turned out to be the most difficult to get on record. For "Joe Hill," a basic guitar-vocal arrangement, Phil decided that he had to have Ramblin' Jack Elliott as the song's guitarist. Phil told Marks that he wanted Elliott because Ramblin' Jack was the best flat-picker around, but in all likelihood, Phil's decision was at least partially based on the recent Woody Guthrie memorial concert fiasco. "Joe Hill" borrowed its melody from Guthrie's "Pretty Boy Floyd," and by having Elliott record the song with him, Phil would be making his own subtle statement.

Regardless of the motive, Phil's decision to include Elliott proved to be problematic.

"He was a real character," Larry Marks said of Elliott. "He was drunk when he walked in the door. He basically flat-picked his way through 'Joe Hill,' but when he was wasted he just kind of went downhill; he could no longer flat-pick. Phil wasn't going to do the song without Jack. He was going to work his way through it, one way or another, so we started it in the morning, to see if we couldn't get him alive and well."

As a rule, the song arrangements were kept simple. A trumpet in "White Boots Marching in a Yellow Land," a harpsichord flourish in "Half a Century High," a touch of violin in "The Harder They Fall"—just enough to add color to Phil's guitar. If any song suffered from excessive arrangement, it would be the title track: the classical backdrop, offset by some heavy-handed rock drumming, detracted from Phil's poignant lyrics about society gone haywire:

> *The draft board is debating if they'd like to take my life.*
> *I'd sooner take a wife and raise a child or two, wouldn't you?*
> *Peace has turned to poison, and the flag has blown a fuse.*
> *Even courage is confused, and now all the brave are in the*
>   *grave.*
> *The century is bending, have a very happy ending.*
> *To the victor go the ashes of the spoils, the seeds in the soil.*
> *Sorry I can't stop and talk now,*
> *I'm in kind of a hurry anyhow,*
> *But I'll send you a tape from California.*

Tape from California was greeted with considerably more enthusiasm than *Pleasures of the Harbor*. Critics seemed relieved that Phil had returned to the basics and was using his passion and dedication to energize his music.

"Phil Ochs may well be the last of the really angry young men," offered one critic pleased with the album. "In a time when most of the 'protest' singers have turned to introspection, Ochs continues his assault on the senses via his assault on the hypocrisy that punctuates modern life."

Calling the album Phil's "most powerful package so far," *Bill-board* singled out "Tape from California," "The Harder They Fall," and "Half a Century High" as album highlights. "Ochs," wrote the magazine's reviewer, "mixes a warm, credible voice with brilliant lyrics and memorable melodies." The Associated Press, in a review that ran over the wires, caught onto Phil's hopes of writing appealing visual poetry: "Ochs is a master of vignette descriptions. One line will describe something so clearly the picture is complete . . . No added words are needed."

Unfortunately for Phil, the timing for the release of *Tape from California*—the summer of 1968—could not have been worse: Phil might have been singing "The War Is Over," but in real life, Vietnam plodded on. In addition, in the aftermath of the Democratic National Convention in Chicago, the public did not need "When in Rome" to be reminded that America was in danger of crumbling like the Roman Empire. At a time when the worst could—and did—occur, Phil's album seemed almost anticlimactic.

———

Phil could not get Robert Kennedy out of his mind, even as he campaigned for McCarthy. Kennedy was rapidly advancing to the forefront of the race, and his candidacy was looking more attractive to Phil everyday.

"I sang in Indiana for Eugene McCarthy," Phil wrote in an essay for *The Village Voice*, "although my first instinct was for Kennedy, even after New Hampshire. It isn't easy to drag my guitar past the sensual photographs of a displaced prince (better-looking than Paul Newman; I'd like to see a shirtless candidacy shot of him saying, 'Robert Kennedy is Hud'—then I'd vote for him).

"In the meantime, McCarthy has been CONSISTENT in his philosophical attack on militarist America. He has also been more SPECIFIC about the bad guys . . ."

Phil's dilemma was much more complicated than a mere opportunistic jump on a political bandwagon. His belief in the country was slipping steadily, and he was counting on the upcoming election not only to restore his faith, but also to revamp the Democratic Party. The only way this was going to happen, he felt, was with McCarthy or Kennedy in the White House.

"Hubert Humphrey is a disgrace to his party and his country," he declared. "If he bargains his way into the Democratic nomination, that will be the final moral death of that crusted party, the last old questionable cause of old men."

On May 30, Phil flew to Los Angeles with Jack Newfield. Michael had lined up a three-week European tour beginning in early June, but before leaving the States, Phil wanted to relax and see how the California primary turned out. Newfield had been one of Phil's main sounding boards throughout the primaries, and their cross-country flight proved to be one final Kennedy vs. McCarthy debate.

"We argued the whole flight from New York to California," said Newfield. "I was one hundred percent for Kennedy; Phil was for McCarthy, but he was slipping. He kept saying, 'Well, if Kennedy wins in California, I'll switch to Kennedy.' Phil had a practical side, and he wanted to win. He wanted to beat Humphrey. I think Kennedy's losing in Oregon really made him more of a tragic figure to Phil. He was no longer this invincible figure; he could lose.

"My argument to Phil was partly that Kennedy had all the poor people, that he was going to win in California because he had all the blacks and hispanics, as well as working-class whites. That was the real coalition that could change America. McCarthy's base was narrow. In fact, he was in the pocket of special interests, particularly the oil industry. I think I was making headway with Phil with that argument."

As it turned out, all of Phil's agonizing over which candidate to support was for nothing. On the evening of June 4, he stayed in his hotel room and watched the primary results filtering in on television. By the end of the evening, it was apparent that Kennedy had pulled off a stunning victory. Kennedy, now the favorite to seize the party's nomination, was exuberant in his victory speech at the Ambassador Hotel.

Moments later, it was over. As he left the celebration, ducking through the kitchen to avoid the crushing mob of supporters in the hall, Kennedy was shot to death by an assassin awaiting him. Any hopes for another Camelot had been dashed, and the race for the Democratic nomination was again up for grabs.

Phil watched in horror as the reports of Kennedy's murder were telecast on the news bulletins. He wept uncontrollably, just as he had mourned the death of the candidate's older brother less than five years earlier. The country had indeed gone insane. First it had sacrificed John Kennedy, then Malcolm X, then Martin Luther King Jr., and finally Robert Kennedy—and these were only the famous names. There had been too many martyrs, far too many martyrs.

————

Over the passing months, many of Phil's friends had warned him that Chicago could be a terrible trap. The Festival of Life organizers had run into roadblock after roadblock when they tried to obtain the necessary permits for their assemblies and demonstrations. There had been a great deal of chest-thumping on both sides, the Yippies vowing to take over the city if necessary, Mayor Richard Daley promising to meet them with whatever force he deemed necessary to prevent it. Violent confrontation seemed probable, if not inevitable.

Phil recognized this, but unlike the pessimists who believed there was very little to gain and a lot to lose in this particular battlefront, Phil remained guardedly optimistic. The hour for the revolution had arrived, and Phil wanted to be there to witness it. To Phil, the Chicago convention stood to be an epic drama, a real-life movie in the John Ford tradition, with high stakes and monumental winners and losers; he would be one of the characters.

In typical fashion, Phil had taken the larger picture and applied many of its meanings and implications to his own life. If things did not go well in Chicago, Phil stood to lose as much as the nation. He had put all of his personal markers down on one week in August, and it was now time to see if the wheel of fate would reward him.

BOOK TWO

Critic of the Dawn

"*Now I'm an actor on the streets*
And I do it for no pay. . . ."
—JOHN TRAIN

Chapter Ten

CHICAGO

MAYOR RICHARD J. DALEY, known as "Boss" in the city he governed, had no intention of allowing masses of what he considered to be hateful, longhaired, aspiring revolutionaries the opportunity to disrupt the Democratic National Convention. The convention meant a lot to the city in terms of business revenue and national exposure, and Daley was eager to show the world that he could not only help orchestrate a prestigious convention, but that he could also control the radical factions that had wreaked havoc in large cities elsewhere. The riots following the assassination of Martin Luther King had been damaging to Chicago, but nowhere near as devastating as in other cities, and Daley had made it quite clear, in proclamations issued over the four-month interval between the rioting and the convention, that he believed in the concept of fighting force with force.

Phil Ochs was on the money when he accused the Yippies of lashing out at armed tractors with yo-yo's: the activists from the Youth International Party and the National Mobilization Committee to End the War in Vietnam ("the Mobe") might have envisioned a second American Revolutionary War in the making, but Daley was preparing more for another shootout at the O.K. Corral.

The sheer numbers in Daley's forces were staggering. Twelve thousand Chicago police, along with six thousand army troops and fifty-six hundred national guardsmen, were on assigned duty during convention week—and these figures do not include the thousands of federal and local intelligence agents working undercover, many as agent provocateurs. Nearly every activist group had been infiltrated by intelligence agents, with CBS News estimating, in a report issued after the convention, that one of six demonstrators in Chicago during convention week was employed by the government.

By comparison, the demonstrators arriving in Chicago were a ragtag, unorganized lot representing the gamut of leftist philosophy and activism. Jerry Rubin and Abbie Hoffman had hoped to attract at least a hundred thousand—or better, yet, a half a million—demonstrators to the city, but fear had kept most people away; only about five thousand actually made the trip. It didn't take a bookmaker or mathematician to calculate the odds stacked against the demonstrators. Daley was ready and willing to squash any form of uprising.

———

Phil, like so many of the festival organizers, was deeply disappointed by the turnout in Chicago. He had been certain that, given all the advance publicity, the city would be overrun by activists. Still, he tried to maintain an upbeat attitude when he met with the press in Chicago. He liked the city, he said, adding that he thought Chicago had the "best architecture in America."

"There's a poetry to this place," he stated. "It excites me in exactly the way California excited me when I got out there a year ago. I could do a record, maybe, on the ashes of Chicago."

Phil could afford to be engaging in his analysis of the city's comforts. Throughout the week, he stayed at the Conrad Hilton, one of the city's finest hotels, as a guest of the McCarthy campaign, and he spent much of his time bouncing back and forth between the Hilton and Grant and Lincoln Parks, hanging out with McCarthy delegates and watching news reports in the comfort of the hotel, and then flying down to the scene of the action itself. With Robert Kennedy out of the picture, Phil had no choice but to pitch his final battle in the McCarthy camp. Abbie Hoffman and Jerry Rubin chided him for trying to be both a McCarthy supporter and a Yippie, but Phil insisted that he could wear both hats. "You don't have to accept those restrictions," he said of Hoffman's and Rubin's criticism.

He continued to hold out hope for a miracle. McCarthy, he optimistically told reporters, was going to win the nomination. The realist in him knew otherwise, and in some of his statements to the press, he hinted that he would have to leave the country if either Hubert Humphrey or Richard Nixon was elected in November. Maybe, he said, he would move to Scotland and open a pub called The Flower

Lady; it could be the kind of place where you could retire for a lazy evening of beer and darts.

"The truth is," he confessed, "I have much less sense of career than I did a year ago. To have a career you need a society to have it in. You go off and you make works of art and you present them *here*. You're glad to be making a contribution. America doesn't provide that society anymore."

For some time, Phil had been trying to address conflicting ideas in his own mind. He possessed enough political savvy to recognize that the political world was hyperkinetic and complex, yet by nature he was a dualistic thinker who saw things in terms of black and white, good or bad, us versus them. As a general rule, he could intellectualize and deal with his feelings, but during convention week in Chicago, with the sides so polarized and the violence so extreme, he found himself backed into the proverbial corner. He had to chose a side, and it certainly was not going to be with Daley's forces.

His own side, however, was fractured beyond belief or repair. For every Allen Ginsberg or Ed Sanders, who abhorred violence and had ventured to Chicago to help keep peace, there were radical members of the Students for a Democratic Society or the Motherfuckers, who came to the city to provoke a confrontation with the hope that, in the aftermath of the violence, people would be driven to their more radical agendas. For every David Dellinger, who implored people to take a nonviolent path in their demonstrations, there was a Bobby Seale or Abbie Hoffman, whose inflammatory rhetoric egged on clashes between police and demonstrators.

Phil was Dylan's Mr. Jones, wandering through a park littered with the movement's broken skulls, carrying his own battle-torn banner, backlit by flashing blue police lights that gave form to tear gas rising like a mist over Lincoln Park. In choosing his side, Phil had also determined his fate.

————

The Festival of Life's initial activities occurred on Friday, August 23, two days prior to the official opening of the Democratic National Convention. Since the Yippies had decided that they could not support any of the formal candidates in their protest of the selection process, they opted to introduce a candidate of their own—a pig that would represent their "Garbage Platform." The pig candidate's official nomination, the Yippies believed, would be an ideal bit of theater to open the week's activities.

Earlier in the week, Abbie and Anita Hoffman had purchased a small pig at a farm auction, but Jerry Rubin scoffed at their contribution, complaining that the pig was too small and too cute. The ideal candidate, he argued, had to be big and ugly—similar to the average politician. With this in mind, he, Stew Albert, and Phil borrowed a jeep and set off to find a candidate of their own. The group drove around rural Illinois until they found a farmer willing to part with a pig for the grand sum of twenty dollars, which had been raised through the sale of Yippie buttons and posters. The new entry, nick-named Pigasus, was nominated through a run-off vote.

A press conference was announced for 10:00 A.M. on August 23. Phil, Rubin, Albert, Abbie Hoffman, Paul Krassner, and others assembled in an alleyway near the Civic Center, and with two hundred people looking on, Rubin formally announced the Yippies' "Pigasus for President" campaign. "Why vote for half a hog," Rubin posed, "when you can have the whole thing?"

The police assigned to the area were not amused. The large group was clogging up traffic, and the demonstrators had no permits for their assembly. The police ordered the group to break up immediately and disperse.

As political theater, the gathering was wonderfully effective. Ignoring the order to disperse, Rubin continued to deliver the pig's nominating speech, even as paddy wagons and squad cars pulled up and police poured out from all sides. Phil, Rubin, and five others were promptly arrested and the pig confiscated. As the police seized Pigasus, Phil drew howls of laughter by loudly protesting that the police were being too rough on the pig and were therefore guilty of police brutality. News cameras captured the entire fiasco.

Phil and the others were taken to the State Street station and charged with disturbing the peace and bringing livestock into the city. All agreed that the demonstration had been a whopping success, and Phil could not have been happier about his first arrest for civil disobedience. While being booked at the police station, he acted unconcerned about his brush with the law, talking on and on about his career and the albums he had made, leading one witness to conclude that "he was acting more or less like a careless 15 year old."

Stew Albert, one of the seven arrested, remembered a more serious discussion that took place in the back of the paddy wagon.

"Jerry Rubin was concerned that they might get rough with us," he said, "but I told him I didn't think so, that it was just too public. We were held in one big jail cell, and at one point a cop came to our cell and said, 'Boys, I have bad news for you. The pig squealed.' That certainly indicated to me that we weren't going to be beaten up."

———

The Pigasus incident, filled with action and irony and humor, not to mention a handful of well-known names, was a reporter's delight—an ideal kickoff to what could prove to be an eventful week. The media, like the forces of the law, had heard every conceivable rumor about the Yippies' plans for the convention. Most of the rumblings, such as those about the Yippies' spiking Chicago's water supply with LSD or mixing poison in the convention delegates' food, were utterly preposterous, although they made for interesting reading. Columnist Jack Mabley repeated the worst of the rumors in the *Chicago American*, sounding a warning knell that must have put every reactionary in Cook County on instant alert. If one could believe Mabley, the Yippies planned to kidnap delegates, aim stolen gasoline trucks at police stations and hotels, and poison the air conditioning system at the convention site—and this was only the beginning. "How many other sophisticated schemes of sabotage exist can only be imagined," Mabley wrote.

Such hysterical reporting might have been dismissed as laughable, or as yellow journalism, had it not added to an already tense situation. The police had heard many of the same stories themselves, and seeing them in print only added to their fear and loathing of the youths invading their city. If Mayor Daley needed to justify his turning Chicago into an armed camp, he could list his reasons in reports such as Mabley's. If, in days to come, the citizens of Chicago required an explanation to understand the violence they saw on the streets or on their television sets at home, they could always fall back on reports published before and during convention week.

However, the blame for the mass of misinformation could not be placed entirely upon the media. The Yippies—particularly Jerry Rubin and Abbie Hoffman—were masters of media manipulation, and they loved to use reporters and television news teams to rile up the establishment. Almost any tactic was fair game, from Rubin's wearing of war paint to Hoffman's calculated use of obscenities. If wild rumors lit a fire under the opposition, so be it. Unfortunately for the Yippies, far too many members of the press took their antics seriously, and news cameras tended to flatten out their theatrics, making Hoffman, Rubin, and company appear more threatening than they really were. The media would sort through the truth and fiction as the week progressed, but by then they had painted such a dark portrait of the Yippies that some people initially sympathized with the brutal overreaction to their presence in the city.

————

One of the major battles waged between police and demonstrators throughout the week focused on the curfew regulations in the city's parks. The city had refused to issue permits allowing people to stay in the parks after their eleven o'clock closing time, leaving countless demonstrators, who had traveled to Chicago with intentions of sleeping in the parks, with no place to go. A power struggle quickly developed, with the police determined to clear the parks and the Yippie followers equally set on staying.

As usual, the different voices of leadership were divided on the course of action to take. Some believed that a confrontation with police would be the best measure, while others argued that the parks weren't worth the violence that would occur if such a confrontation took place. Abbie Hoffman likened the struggle for Lincoln Park to the Revolutionary War battles for Lexington and Concord, and he warned of violence and vandalism on the streets if people were drummed out of the park. Others, such as Allen Ginsberg and Ed Sanders, tried to discourage the inflammatory talk. Sanders, for one, worried that the weekend warriors—the hundreds of thousands of demonstrators inexperienced in police confrontations, who had come to Chicago unaware of the potential violence—would be getting their heads cracked for nothing.

On Saturday, August 24, the people in Lincoln Park were given their first taste of what the police had in store for curfew enforcement. The day had gone smoothly, with very little hostility between Yippies and the police, but as eleven o'clock approached and larger forces of police assembled in Lincoln Park, tension began to build. Fighting broke out when the police attempted to clear the grounds; tear gas cannisters were launched. Allen Ginsberg and Ed Sanders, seeing the escalating violence, began to walk slowly from the park, chanting "om" in a calm, even manner. Hundreds of Yippies joined them, all chanting, all moving away from the violence.

The next night was much worse. On Saturday, the demonstrators had been chased out of the park and into the streets, where the police, unprepared for this eventuality, had a difficult time containing them. Sunday, the police had set up defense lines outside the park. They had learned an additional lesson the night before: people beaten by the police had taken their assailants' badge numbers, making disciplinary or legal action easier. On Sunday, the police removed their badges and name tags and, as if to further cover their bets, charged into the ranks of the press, clubbing reporters and destroying camera equipment. The beatings were savage, and no one was exempt, including area residents, the media, and hospital medics on hand to help victims of the brutality.

And so it went, with the violence intensifying every night. Frustrated by the Yippies' determination to hold Lincoln Park, the police dispatched greater numbers and heavier equipment to the area on each succeeding night. Jeeps armed with barbed wire, garbage trucks specially fitted with search lights and tear gas hoses—the police used whatever they needed to vacate the premises. The weekend was ugly, but the worst was yet to come.

———————

Despite the mayhem in the streets, Phil continued to hold onto his slim hopes for the convention itself. By the time the convention opened, Hubert Humphrey's nomination was a foregone conclusion, but McCarthy backers, joined by the old Robert Kennedy forces, were trying to introduce a peace provision into the official Democratic Party platform. Such a platform, Phil felt, would at least make the Humphrey selection more bearable.

Tuesday, August 27, was Lyndon Johnson's birthday, and to commemorate the occasion the Yippies and the Mobe gathered at the Chicago Coliseum to stage an "un-birthday" for the president. The event was an enormous success, with an estimated six thousand people turning out to hear speeches by comedian-activist Dick Gregory and writers William S. Burroughs and Jean Genet, along with Abbie Hoffman, Paul Krassner, and David Dellinger. Allen Ginsberg was also scheduled to speak, but he was so hoarse from his chanting in the park that he asked emcee Ed Sanders to read his statement.

As befitted the mood of the entire convention week, Phil performed several of his antiwar and antiestablishment songs at the rally, the high point coming when he sang "I Ain't Marching Anymore." He had just begun to sing when a young man in the audience stood up and set fire to his draft card. People cheered in encouragement. Others followed suit, and before long the Coliseum twinkled from draft cards burning like votive candles. In a matter of just a few moments, Phil's signature song had become a sound track to one of the ultimate acts of antiwar demonstration.

"It was very emotional," recalled Paul Krassner, who had the unenviable duty of following Phil onstage. "People were cheering and standing up, and they were still cheering when Phil left the stage. We embraced, and he said, 'This is the highlight of my career.' "

The euphoria was short-lived. Later in the week, buoyed by his power to move people to action, Phil tried to talk a group of national guardsmen into laying down their arms and joining the Yippies. He was standing outside the Hilton, talking to a small gathering of people, when he suddenly directed his attention to the guardsmen standing in formation nearby. Shouting through a bullhorn, he implored them to break away from the ranks and join the new guard, the peacemakers of the future.

"Will you put down your weapons and join us?" he asked, over and over again. When no one moved, Phil walked over to the line of guardsmen and asked each member individually to put down his weapon and join the Yippies. This time, he actions weren't just theater; Phil was absolutely serious, desperate to win over the enemy.

No one responded to Phil's pleas except one guardsman who stepped forward and told Phil that, as a college student, he had taken a girlfriend to one of his concerts; he had even bought some of Phil's records. However, after seeing Phil in Chicago, he would never go to another Phil Ochs concert or buy another record.

"Phil was genuinely hurt by that," said Stew Albert, who witnessed the incident. "He really seemed to expect that the troops would refuse to do what they were ordered to do. That *he* could not get them to throw down their arms when he asked them directly to do it, both in a speech and then actually going one-on-one, was really crushing for him. He couldn't understand how they could refrain from such a wonderful opportunity to be such exciting actors in history."

On a more practical level, Phil's hopes were further toppled when the peace plank was defeated by a 1,567–1,041 delegate vote. When he heard of the defeat, Phil was certain that America was a lost cause.

———

On August 28, Hubert Humphrey was officially nominated as the Democratic Party's candidate for the fall presidential election. The delegate vote, however, was only a weak epilogue to one of the most horrific days in the history of American electoral politics.

The day was supposed to be the biggest day of Festival of Life activities, beginning with a series of afternoon speeches in Grant Park and culminating in a march to the convention center, where there was to be a mass protest of Humphrey's nomination. The police department, aware of the Yippie plans, circulated flyers saying that the march would not be permitted. To ensure that it would not happen, police and guardsmen circled Grant Park, sealing off demonstrators from the rest of the city.

The main activities took place at the park's bandshell, where David Dellinger, Allen Ginsberg, Dick Gregory, and a host of others delivered speeches. When it was his turn at the microphone, Phil played "I Ain't Marching Anymore," which may not have set off another round of impromptu draft card burnings, but which nevertheless received one of the biggest ovations of the afternoon. The lyrics to the song had now taken on a new meaning to Phil. Betrayed by the system he had hoped to save, Phil was in a revolutionary state of mind.

"Chicago was the formal death of democracy in America," he said in an interview conducted not long after the convention. "I no longer feel any ties of loyalty to the present American society . . . I've gone from being a left social democrat to an early revolutionary mentality. I haven't the total courage or commitment yet to be a full-fledged revolutionary, but that is my direction."

The early portion of the day's festivities passed without incident, but the mood of the demonstrators began to disintegrate when, around three o'clock in the afternoon, a young Yippie scaled a flagpole near the bandstand and tried to bring down the American flag. The police rushed in, dragged the youth off the flagpole, and while arresting him, beat him with their nightsticks. Some of the demonstrators began to throw rocks, bottles, bricks, and sticks at the police, and the day that would come to be known as "Bloody Wednesday" had officially begun. In the ensuing violence, a number of demonstrators were beaten and arrested. Rennie Davis, one of the afternoon's speakers, tried to encourage people to stay calm, and for his efforts he was bludgeoned with a nightstick; the blood-soaked rag used to clean his head wound was eventually run up the park's flagpole.

When order was finally restored, David Dellinger addressed the crowd. He implored people to sit down and stay calm, and not to give the police any reason for breaking up the meeting. He then presented three alternative courses of action: people could join his group, which would be marching to the Democratic Convention and staging a nonviolent demonstration; people could leave the park and do whatever they felt they had to do elsewhere; or they could stay in the park and not demonstrate at all. Dellinger repeatedly stated that his march would be nonviolent, and that anyone seeking a confrontation with police should go elsewhere.

The police had plans of their own. When Dellinger's marchers attempted to leave the park, they were stopped near its entrance and told that they could not go any further. While Dellinger negotiated with police, the would-be marchers sat on the ground, singing songs or chanting mantras with Allen Ginsberg. The impasse dragged on. Finally, when it became obvious that the police and guardsmen had no intention of allowing the demonstrators out of the park, no matter how reasonable or impassioned the Dellinger argument, demonstrators broke rank and began running along the edge of the park, looking for a place to escape. They found a gap in the line of defense near the Jackson Street Bridge, and in no time, thousands of demonstrators were pouring out of the park and heading toward the Hilton.

The police were prepared for this, and in no time the demonstrators found themselves compressed into a small area near the Hilton, a mass of police pursuing them from the rear, a strong line of defense holding position in front of them. Tear gas cannisters were fired, the police moved in from all directions, and thousands of demonstrators, area residents, and people visiting the Loop were suddenly caught in the midst of what was later called a police riot. Countless people were arrested, beaten relentlessly with nightsticks, shoved and knocked down, stomped, or even pushed through storefront windows—all within shouting distance of the hotel housing the convention's delegates. From the melee rose a chorus that would be remembered for years to come: "The whole world is watching! The whole world is watching!"

The convention delegates, aware of what was taking place just outside the security of their hotel rooms and the convention hall, were divided on what course of action to take. Many, sickened by the violence, wanted to call off the convention, relocate it, or postpone it until order and safety could be assured. Senator George McGovern, a last-minute peace candidate, publicly condemned the police actions, while Senator Abraham Ribicoff, in his nominating speech for McGovern, was direct in his criticism. "With George McGovern," he stated to the thousands gathered in the convention hall, "we wouldn't have Gestapo tactics on the streets of Chicago." An enraged Mayor Daley, seated near the front of the hall, shouted over the din at Ribicoff. "Fuck you, you Jew son of a bitch," screamed the mayor of the second largest city in the United States. Unintimidated, Ribicoff looked directly at Daley. "How hard it is to hear the truth," he said.

———

Phil had not rushed out of the park with the thousands of demonstrators. He remained behind with Allen Ginsberg and a group of others, waiting until it was safer to leave.

Nevertheless, he witnessed some of the worst of the violence, narrowly escaping a beating himself when he ducked into a doorway. He was horrified when he watched the events of the afternoon replayed later that evening on television news reports. As he took in the footage of people being beaten senselessly, he was certain that he had enough material for an entire album on the convention itself. The album would be his final statement: after seeing the week's events in Chicago, he had no reason to sing or write anymore. All he had to live for had been beaten down by the very society he had hoped to turn around. He was as dead as the Movement itself.

Chapter Eleven

REHEARSALS FOR RETIREMENT

IN THE MONTHS following the convention, Phil dropped into the deepest depression of his life. He saw no reason to work, especially after his appearance at the Philadelphia Folk Festival, where his customarily supportive audience now booed him off the stage when he tried to sing "I Ain't Marching Anymore." At Andy Wickham's house in California, he sat around lethargically, not up to doing much of anything. He and Karen fought frequently, and he battled with his brother Michael over what he planned to do with his career. Even a brief trip with Wickham to Mexico, which found the two drinking nonstop and visiting the local brothels, failed to lift his spirits.

At the core of his depression was a deep-seeded rage that he directed toward everyone, including himself. He hated the present form of government and its leaders, who he felt were oppressive and murderous. The counterculture, he decided, was a bad joke; people like Jerry Rubin and Abbie Hoffman, though dedicated, had no clues about how to change America. Finally, he was angry at himself for believing that change was possible in the first place.

Despite these feelings, there were occasional signs that the old Phil Ochs, political activist and songwriter, was still around. The internal conflict was especially evident at a large pre-election gathering at the Berkeley Community Theater early in November. Phil, scheduled to sing at the rally, became incensed when a small pig, draped in an American flag, was brought onstage as part of the theatrics.

"He wouldn't perform until someone took the flag off," said Stew Albert, who emceed the event. "He said it was disrespectful. So here he was, saying how he's going to be a revolutionary, and how he feels no bonds to society or government, but he's still against desecrating the flag."

Phil continued to write song lyrics in his notebooks, and while some of the new works, such as a eulogy to Robert Kennedy, didn't pan out, others, such as a poem about the Scorpion, a recent tragedy involving a sunken nuclear submarine, showed great promise:

Sailors climb the tree,
Up the terrible tree.
Where are my shipmates,
Have they sunk beneath the sea?
I do not know much,
But I know this cannot be.
It isn't really, it isn't really,
Tell me it isn't really.
Sounding bell is diving
Down the water green,
Not a trace, not a toothbrush,
Not a cigarette was seen.
Bubble ball is rising
From a whisper or a scream,
But I'm not screaming, I'm not screaming,
Tell me I'm not screaming.
Captain will not say
How long must remain.
The phantom ship forever sails the sea.
It's all the same . . .

It was Phil's ultimate statement of despair, the dark side of "Pleasures of the Harbor." In the wake of Chicago, Phil was feeling suffocated, trapped on the phantom ship that had once been his country. As he told Izzie Young in a *Broadside* interview, he was ambivalent about whether the country, with its corrupt electoral system and violent heritage, was worth salvaging.

"I've always tried to hang onto the idea of saving the country," he said, "but at this point I could be persuaded to destroy it. For the first time I feel this way . . . At a certain point you start losing interest in helping things in America."

But Phil had not lost interest—not entirely. He still felt great sympathy for the innocent people trapped on board the ship, and given the opportunity, he would have tried to save them. For the moment, he was exhausted from his past efforts, and he knew of no new direction to take.

———

J. Edgar Hoover's hatred of the Yippies was hardly news. The FBI Director viewed the Yippies, Black Panthers, the Mobe, and other dissident groups as being dangerous to the State, and he went after them with the same zeal he had reserved for communists a decade earlier. In the months following the Chicago convention, he devoted countless personnel and man hours to finding ground for the arrests of those individuals he deemed to be especially menacing.

He had previously labeled Phil Ochs "potentially dangerous" and "subversive"; by Hoover's thinking, Phil's "conduct or statements showed a propensity for violence and antipathy toward good order and government." After the convention, Hoover took a personal interest in Phil's whereabouts and, in a teletype message to agents in San Francisco, Chicago, and New York, he ordered personnel to locate and interview Phil.

"Ochs is considered one of the principle subjects involved in demonstrations at [the] Democratic National Convention," Hoover wrote in his September 26 directive. "Our investigation [is] aimed at establishing possible violation of Federal antiriot law." At the time, Phil was believed to be in San Francisco, and Hoover instructed his special agent there "to conduct [an] active investigation in [an] effort to locate subject for interview. Do not rely solely on efforts being made by sources. This phase of investigation must receive continued vigorous attention."

For the next three months, the FBI followed every lead in order to, first, locate Phil and, second, find a way to arrest him. Active in the search were agents from New York, Los Angeles, Chicago, San Francisco, Cincinnati, and Milwaukee. Telephone and police records were checked, newspaper clippings files perused; agents labored to trace his movements in the country. Phil's FBI file quickly grew to a thickness of over an inch.

As it turned out, locating Phil took some effort.

On September 26, a New York special agent, via teletype, advised other agents that Phil was "currently in California, presumably in LA area." The New York agent, however, did not end his investigation at this point. Four days later, he again advised other agents that Phil was "reportedly residing in vicinity of Los Angeles, California." A day later, he sent out still another message, noting that Ochs "could probably be located at A & M Records, Los Angeles, for whom subject records."

At this point, Los Angeles agents took over. Through A & M Records, an agent was able to determine Michael Ochs' Los Angeles whereabouts. Michael was contacted on two separate occasions, but he could only tell agents that Phil was indeed out of town, in San Francisco, and that he intended to be returning to Los Angeles soon.

On October 1, agents finally caught up to their quarry:

> PHILIP DAVID OCHS, 1329 Topanga Road, was advised of the identities of the interviewing agents and of the desire of agents to interview him regarding his participation in demonstrations during the Democratic National Convention. OCHS was advised of his rights as contained in the Waiver of Rights Form.
>
> At this point, OCHS advised that he would not discuss his activities with agents.
>
> The interview was then terminated.

The FBI, however, was not finished with Phil. Agents carried on their various investigations of Phil's past, compiling a hefty biography for Bureau records, their labors continuing even after the Washington D.C. office received the following message:

> On October 23, Assistant United States Attorney RICHARD G. SCHULTZ advised he declined prosecution [for violation of antiriot laws] as there does not appear to be a basis for prosecution in this matter. SCHULTZ stated, however, due to the apparent association with JERRY RUBIN and others, he may consider OCHS as a witness and issue a subpoena for his appearance before the Grand Jury in Chicago.

Phil would indeed be called upon to testify in a court proceeding involving Jerry Rubin and others—only he would do so as a witness for the defense, not as a witness for the prosecution.

———

Even in the throes of depression, Phil realized that he would have to work again. He was not wealthy by anyone's definition of the word, and there was still enough of the artist in him to prod him into creating something new. One day that fall, without having given any previous indication that he had any intention of writing or recording in the foreseeable future, Phil surprised Michael by asking him to call Larry Marks about booking studio time for a new recording.

Phil's latest cycle of songs, largely written over a period of two weeks, picked up thematically where *Tape from California* had left off. Whereas *Tape from California* had depicted America in its decline, the new songs focused on a country at the edge of an apocalypse, teetering on the brink of self-destruction through paranoia and violence. With the exception of "The Doll House," which had been written almost a year earlier, all of the songs were rooted in Chicago, although only one ("William Butler Yeats Visits Lincoln Park and Escapes Unscathed") was directly about the convention itself. Gone were any traces of Phil's trademark idealism, now replaced by pessimism bordering on despair.

A new poem, eventually published on the new album's back cover, touched upon not only the themes of the individual songs, but also of the spirit of the entire album:

> *This then is the death of the American*
> *Imprisoned by his paranoia*
> *and all his diseases of his innocent inventions*
> *he plunges to the drugs of the devil to find his gods*
> *he employs the farce of force to crush his fantasies*
> *he calls conventions of salesmen and savages*
> *to reinforce his hopelessness*
> *So the poet swordsmen and their beat generation*
> *must divorce themselves from their very motherland*
> *only for the beast sensation of life or love or pain*
> *our deepest and most religious moments*
> *were on elevators posing as planes.*
>
> *Part two of this earnest epic*
> *finds seaweed lapping against your eyes*

the sailors have chosen the mystery surprise
to join the Flying Dutchman in his search for a green disguise

Still others invade the final colony
to present their tinted tributes to the millionaire assassin
While I stumble through this paradise
considering several suicides
for distant lavendar lovers
or bless the violence of the ridiculous revolution
for self-bronzing brothers
and finally turn away from the tourquoise towers
of this comic civilization
my responsibilities are done let them come let them come
and I realize these last days these trials and tragedies
were after all only
our rehearsals for retirement.

"The songs on [the] album," Phil later explained, "were about the new paranoia, police brutality, the escape into drugs, Chicago itself, people coming to the West—another escape route—thoughts of suicide, thoughts of revolution; and then finally pulling back and saying all this has been our rehearsals for retirement."

"My darkest fear," he continued, "is that we are about to go all through the 'iron head' again—in this case America rather than Germany. Vietnam is almost a prelude to an attempt to annihilate progressive forces."

On *Rehearsals for Retirement*, Phil took no chances that listeners might miss his point: there is virtually no humor in the songs, and his language is brutally direct. As the opening numbers of his first two A & M albums ("Cross My Heart" and "Tape from California") had set the tone for the major themes woven into the overall fabric of the songs, so, too, do the venomous lyrics to "Pretty Smart on My Part," the opening track on *Rehearsals for Retirement*, establish the dark mood running through his most recent album. In "Pretty Smart on My Part," Phil assumes the persona of an American consumed by violence and paranoia:

I can see him a-coming, he's a-walking down the highway
With his big boots on and his big thumb out.
He wants to get me, he wants to hurt me,

He wants to bring me down.
Ah, but sometime later when I feel a little straighter,
I will come across a stranger
Who'll remind me of the danger, and
Then I'll run him over.
Pretty smart on my part,
To find my way in the dark.

This, however, is only the beginning. The language is even more violent in "I Kill Therefore I Am," Phil's nasty indictment of the kind of policeman he had encountered on the streets of Chicago:

I don't like the students now
They don't have no respect
They don't like to work now
I think I'll wring their necks
They call me pig although I'm underpaid
I'll show those faggots
That I'm not afraid.
I am the masculine American man
I kill therefore I am.

As on *Tape from California*, Phil and Larry Marks kept the song arrangements simple, leaving the lyrics exposed and muscular. Phil wanted a harder-edged, rock 'n' roll flavor on the album, and to achieve this, he employed guitarist-bassist Bob Rafkin to fill in behind Lincoln Mayorga's piano.

Mayorga's playing on two of the album's best entries—the title song and "The Scorpion Departs But Never Returns"—is brilliantly understated, casting a calm-before-the-storm feeling to Phil's moody lyrics. This, of course, is precisely the effect that Phil was seeking: in the past, he had been a witness to history, reporting on the events of the day and urging his fellow citizens to action; now, in his new role as prophet of doom, he wanted to paint as stark and ominous a picture as possible:

The lights are cold again, they dance below me
I turn to old friends, they do not know me.
All but the begger, he remembers.
I put a penny down for payment

Gertrude Phin and Jacob "Jack" Ochs on their wedding day. Their marriage would be tempestuous, marked by their general incompatibility and Jack's lifelong battle with manic depression. *(Courtesy of Phil Ochs Estate)*

Philip, age 2. *(Courtesy of Sonny Ochs)*

Michael and Philip.
(Courtesy of Phil Ochs Estate)

Philip and Sonia.
(Courtesy of Sonny Ochs)

A visit to the local photo booth produced pictures of Philip (left), and Philip
and his best friend, Dave Sweazy (right). *(Courtesy of Phil Ochs Estate)*

Philip, playing clarinet at a local talent show. At age 15, he had already established his musical talent. *(Courtesy of Phil Ochs Estate)*

Phil's high school graduation photo. He chose to attend the Staunton Military Academy in Virginia after seeing an advertisement for the school in the *New York Times. (Courtesy of Michael Ochs Archives/Venice, CA)*

Michael (left) and Phil.
(Courtesy of Michael Ochs Archives/Venice, CA)

The only known photo of the Sundowners. Jim Glover (left) taught Phil how to play guitar. Glover went on to become part of the successful folk duo Jim and Jean. *(Courtesy of Michael Ochs Archives/Venice, CA)*

Phil, playing guitar at Faragher's, the Cleveland club that gave him his first big break in the music business. *(Courtesy of Michael Ochs Archives/Venice, CA)*

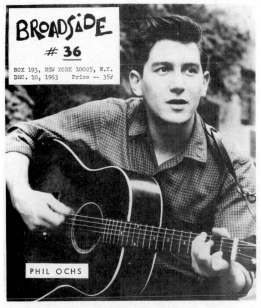

BROADSIDE
36
BOX 193, NEW YORK 10025, N.Y.
DEC. 10, 1963   Price -- 35¢

PHIL OCHS

IN THIS ISSUE: TWO SONGS BY PHIL OCHS
"THAT WAS THE PRESIDENT"
"IT MUST HAVE BEEN ANOTHER COUNTRY"

Shortly after moving to New York, Phil became a regular contributor to *Broadside* magazine, which promoted the careers of many of the country's best new folksingers. *(Courtesy of Sis Cunningham)*

Alice. *(Courtesy of Phil Ochs Estate)*

Phil, playing with Meegan in their Greenwich Village apartment. *(Photo by Alice Ochs. Courtesy of Phil Ochs Estate)*

Phil and Meegan. *(Photo by Alice Ochs. Courtesy of Phil Ochs Estate)*

Three of folk
music's brightest
young talents:
Tom Paxton (left),
Phil, and Eric
Andersen (seated),
at the Newport
Folk Festival.
*(Photo by Dave
Gahr.)*

Alice, Phil, and Paul Krassner at Newport. *(Photo by Dave Gahr.)*

"I Ain't Marchin'": an early publicity photo for A & M Records. *(Courtesy of Michael Ochs Archives/ Venice, CA)*

Phil on the sidewalks of Greenwich Village. *(Photo by Dave Gahr)*

Phil, posing outside
Carnegie Hall before his
first sold-out performance.
(Photo by Arthur Gorson.
Courtesy of Arthur Gorson
and Michael Ochs
Archives/Venice, CA)

With Andy Wickham (right). *(Courtesy of Michael Ochs Archives/Venice, CA)*

Arthur Gorson, Phil's manager during his most productive years. *(Courtesy of Arthur Gorson)*

An early notebook draft of Phil's song "Tape from California." *(Courtesy of Phil Ochs Estate)*

The "War Is Over" rally in Los Angeles. One of the largest anti-war demonstrations of its time, the rally ended with police attacking protesters in Century City. *(Courtesy of Michael Ochs Archives/Venice, CA)*

Phil at a New York press
conference announcing
the formation of the
Youth International
Party. *(Courtesy of
Michael Ochs
Archives/Venice, CA)*

The cover of *Rehearsals
for Retirement*, issued
shortly after the
Democratic National
Convention in Chicago,
1968. *(Courtesy of
A & M Records)*

"Critic of the Dawn": Phil, performing in Lincoln Park during the Chicago convention. *(Courtesy of Michael Ochs Archives/Venice, CA)*

"Welcome to Chicago": The police and National Guard turned the streets of Chicago into an armed camp during the Democratic National Convention in August 1968. *(Courtesy of Michael Ochs Archives/Venice, CA)*

The troubadour as gunslinger: Phil's decision to perform onstage in a gold lamé suit proved to be one of the most controversial choices of his music career. *(Courtesy of Phil Ochs Estate)*

FRIENDS OF CHILE PRESENTS

AN EVENING WITH SALVADOR ALLENDE

THE FELT FORUM
Madison Square Garden
May 9, 1974 at 8:00 P.M.

WITH
Arlo Guthrie
Phil Ochs
Pete Seeger
Melvin Van Peebles
Gato Barbieri
The Living Theater
Ambassador Harald Edelstam
La Cantata
by Victoria & The Open Theater
The Poetry of Pablo Neruda
Films and surprise guests

(Courtesy of Deni Frand)

With Bob Dylan at the "Evening with Salvador Allende" benefit concert. *(Photo by Chuck Pulin/ Star File)*

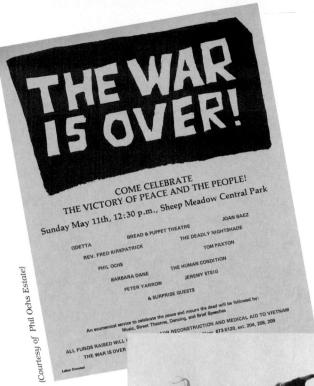

THE WAR IS OVER!

COME CELEBRATE
THE VICTORY OF PEACE AND THE PEOPLE!
Sunday May 11th, 12:30 p.m., Sheep Meadow Central Park

JOAN BAEZ
BREAD & PUPPET THEATRE   THE DEADLY NIGHTSHADE
ODETTA
REV. FRED KIRKPATRICK   TOM PAXTON
PHIL OCHS
                    THE HUMAN CONDITION
BARBARA DANE   JEREMY STEIG
PETER YARROW
& SURPRISE GUESTS

An ecumenical service to celebrate the peace and mourn the dead will be followed by:
Music, Street Theatres, Dancing, and Brief Speeches

ALL FUNDS RAISED WILL ... FOR RECONSTRUCTION AND MEDICAL AID TO VIETNAM
THE WAR IS OVER ... ... 673-5120, ext. 204, 208, 209

Labor Donated

Performing "There But for Fortune" with Joan Baez at the "War Is Over" rally in Central Park. *(Photo by Dave Seelig. Courtesy of Phil Ochs Estate)*

Phil was determined that Sammy Walker (left) would be the next Bob Dylan. *(Photo by Julia Fahey. Courtesy of Sammy Walker)*

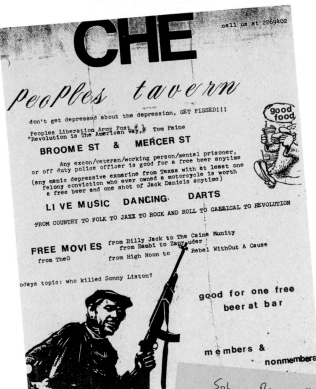

An advertisement for John Train's ill-fated tavern.
(Courtesy of Ed Sanders)

John Train's account of
his attack on Che.
(Courtesy of Ed Sanders)

Soho Bar attacked   by John Train

A drunken Phil Ochs smashed 5 windows of a bar called 'che'

He had bought 80% of the bar but during negotiations had been thrown out repeatedly by his own partner Robert Bonic.

Bonic signed a letter of intent with Sept. 15. If he recieves $32,000 Phil Ochs is the official owner pending S.L.A. approval.

Ochs was so drunk earlier in the evening he threatened several lady customers when they complained that the juke box was too loud.

His own bouncer then decided to lock him out. It was a monumental battle. Before Ochs could climb thru the broken glass he was halted by 4 police cars. They took him into custody, but after hearing the full story they released him without charges

Phil Ochs a Suicide at 35; Singer of Peace Movement

By ROBERT E. TOMASSON

Phil Ochs, the folk singer, guitarist and lyricist whose music provided some of the strongest notes of protest against the Vietnam War in the early 1960's, committed suicide yesterday morning at his sister's home in Far Rockaway, Queens, the family reported.

"Phil had been very depressed for a long time," a family friend said. "Mainly, the words weren't coming to him anymore."

Mr. Ochs, who was 35 years old, had been living with his sister, Sonny Tanzman, since December, according to a family friend. He died by hanging.

By the time Mr. Ochs made his first appearance in Carnegie Hall, he had gained a reputation as "a troubadour of the new left."

"The voice is spare . . . guitar playing is rudimentary, and the melodies of his songs are erratic mixtures of brilliance and mediocrity," Robert Shelton wrote in The New York Times.

An Urbane Writer

"But Mr. Och's appeal is in his rebel stance, his iconoclastic wit, his self-burlesque and his obviously literate way with word play and philosophy," the folk-music writer said of the performer, who was then 26.

His early songs — "Nobody Buys From the Flower Lady," "Cross My Heart, I Hope to Live," "The Ballad of William Worthy," "Outside of a Small Circle of Friends" and "The Bells" established Mr. Ochs as a major lyricist of urbane song writing.

Joan Baez and Bob Dylan, both superstars of folk music, both sang his songs.

Mr. Ochs preferred to be called a topical singer rather than a folk singer. By the time he broke into professional playing cabarets in Greenwich Village, he had a repertory of more than 60 songs, virtually all of which had a social punch line or question.

"Talking Cuban Crisis" and "50-Mile Hike," were among the songs he sang when he appeared at the Thirdside on West Third Street in 1963.

Mr. Ochs was born in El Paso. His father, a doctor, moved the family to upstate New York when Phil was a few years old. When he was a teen-ager, the family moved to Far Rockaway.

He graduated from the Staunton Military Academy in Virginia and attended Ohio State University for three years, majoring in journalism.

"He wanted to publish something, they said no. So he left," Mr. Ochs's sister said yesterday. "From there, he went to the Greenwich Village coffeehouses."

Mr. Ochs's lyrics quickly began to supersede his reputation as a singer. Some of his other songs include "Changes," "Love Me, I'm a Liberal," "I Declare the War Is Over" and "Talking Vietnam."

His lyrics in the early 1960's

Phil Ochs

represented, as those of perhaps no other song writer of the time a bitter, unequivocal pacifist view that on more than one occasion provoked brawls in both coffeehouses and concert halls.

Early Protest Song

IN 1963, his song "I Ain't Marching Anymore" was one of the first of the protest songs of the Vietnam war:

For I flew the final mission in
the Japenese skies
Set off the mighty mushroom
roar
When I saw the cities burning,
I knew that I was learning
I ain't marching anymore.

He also wrote romantic lyrics. But as with his protest songs, they had a markedly passive quality, a view of uncontrollable events that had occurred and seemed destined to be repeated.

In my rehearsals for retirement.
Had I known the end would end in laughter
Still I tell my daughter it doesn't matter . . .

In many ways, *Rehearsals for Retirement* is Phil's penultimate topical album, an extended tone poem addressing society's specific maladies rather than individual news stories. All of the elements addressed in Phil's earlier topical albums—the racism, brutality, warfare, apathy, and cruelty—are present on the new offering, but on *Rehearsals*, Phil reaches for a larger picture than the daily headlines. An epoch, he suggests, is coming to an end.

Phil, however, can no longer pretend to have a reporter's sense of objectivity; he is not even capable of an editorialist's restraint. The fall of America spells the spiritual death of its people, including Phil. For the cover of the album, Phil had a tombstone made, and the marker says it all:

PHIL OCHS
(AMERICAN)
BORN: EL PASO, TEXAS 1940
DIED: CHICAGO, ILLINOIS 1968
REHEARSALS
FOR
RETIREMENT

The album, then, is as much a personal statement as it is a commentary on contemporary society. Significantly, his most personal album to date was also the first recording that he made in a state of depression, and in "My Life," he actually provides a picture of the pain that he mentioned earlier in "Crucifixion":

My life was once a joy to me,
Never knowing I was growing every day.
My life was once a toy to me,
And I wound it, and I found it ran away.
So I raced through the night
With a face at my feet,
Like a god I would write,
All the melodies were sweet

And the women were white.
It was easy to survive,
My life was so alive.

My life was once a flag to me,
And I waved it and behaved like I was told.
My life was once a drag to me,
And I loudly, and I proudly, lost control.
I was drawn by a dream,
I was loved by a lie, every surf on the sea
Begged me to buy.
But I slipped through the scheme
So lucky to fail.
My life was not for sale.

My life is now a myth to me,
Like the drifter, with his laughter in the dawn.
My life is now a death to me
So I'll mold it and I'll hold it till I'm born.
So I turned to the land
Where I'm so out of place
Threw a curse on the plan
In return for the grace
To know where I stand.
Take everything I own,
Take your tap from my phone,
And leave my life alone,
My life alone.

In retrospect, *Rehearsals for Retirement* is one of the most har-rowing recordings ever issued in pop music, as unflinchingly honest as John Lennon's *Plastic Ono Band* or Neil Young's *Tonight's the Night*. Unfortunately, pop-music audiences will venture only so far into the psyches of their heroes, and when *Rehearsals for Retirement* was released, it was ignored by critics and fans alike. The few reviews that the album managed to get were generally favorable, with review-ers happy that Phil had not abandoned his voice-in-the-wilderness approach.

"It is surprising and encouraging to find one of the original anti-war folk protestants not only sticking to his viewpoint but producing excellent new material," offered one critic. "[Ochs] has been attacked as a nihilist and anarchist (which he is not) and has had many of his albums banned by radio stations. His latest, *Rehearsals for Retirement*, is going to be treated the same way, but quite undeservedly."

Phil's lack of commercial appeal was noted by other reviewers as well: "*Rehearsals for Retirement* is Phil Ochs' sixth album. Like the others, it will sell little more than 20,000 copies, and like the others, it is a classic which people will dig up when Ochs is 'discovered' one of these days."

A dismal failure at the cash register, *Rehearsals for Retirement* was pulled from circulation only months after its release, giving the tombstone on the album's cover a more ominous meaning. As a recording artist, Phil Ochs was in serious trouble.

———

Phil continued to enjoy success as a performing artist, although his audiences, mostly holdovers from the old days, were more responsive to such relics as "There But for Fortune," "Changes," or "I Ain't Marching Anymore" than to the newer entries from the past two or three albums. "Crucifixion" could still bring down the house, as could "Outside of a Small Circle of Friends," which had achieved cult classic status from its play on FM radio stations.

The failure of *Rehearsals for Retirement* haunted him. He had been so certain that he'd hit upon an important personal statement with the album that he was crushed when others failed to share his enthusiasm for the record. Even his friends rejected him. Shortly after the release of the album, Phil turned up unannounced at Paul Rothchild's home, a copy of *Rehearsals* under his arm. Rothchild was hosting a cocktail party at the time, but he invited Phil in. This proved to be a mistake when, undaunted by his imposing upon the social occasion, Phil announced that he was playing his new album and dropped it on the turntable. Rothchild disappeared and, moments later, the electricity in the house was cut off. There would be no playing of the album.

Andy Wickham found the incident hysterically funny, but Phil was bruised by it. In the old days, people couldn't wait to hear one another's new album. It was all business now, and in Phil's case, the business was not very good.

In his present state of mind, Phil found performing a difficult chore. The old standbys were losing their flavor—to the extent that it was not uncommon for him to forget his own lyrics during a concert. On, occasion, he would have someone hold up a songbook while he played the longer songs, particularly "Crucifixion," while on other occasions, when he was singing and forgetting the words to shorter numbers, he would just muddle on through, hoping his audience would forgive his temporary lapse of memory.

One place he was always welcome was Carnegie Hall. He knew that he would be cheered there, no matter what he chose to play, and his April 11, 1969, Carnegie Hall concert—his fourth consecutive SRO performance at the hall—was no exception. Phil had been living on the West Coast for some time, but fans on the East Coast still regarded him as one of their own. Inspired by their warmth, Phil put on one of his better shows in recent months, mixing the usual crowd-pleasers with virtually all of *Rehearsals for Retirement.* His New York audience, Phil was pleased to note, were as unhappy about the recent presidential election as he was.

Phil's artistic crisis, in almost every respect, reflected the changes occurring everywhere in the music business. Folk music, having enjoyed its moment of national mainstream popularity, had once again become a specialized interest. Popular music as a whole was shifting its focus. The Band, with its breakthrough inaugural work, *Music from Big Pink*, was now the darling of the critics, spawning a new school of country and rhythm-and-blues-flavored albums. Bob Dylan's most recent offering, *Nashville Skyline*, had found Dylan reinventing himself again, this time in country digs.

The changes had profound effects on Phil's career, leaving him without a workable niche. There was no longer a market for topical music, and Phil's three attempts at pop music had been, at charitable best, only marginally successful. He could go on earning a living on the concert circuit, but neither he nor his audiences wanted him to become a nostalgia item or museum piece that plays the same songs indefinitely. To survive, he had to find a way to pick up his sagging recording career.

Phil deeply resented the pressures that he felt to be both an artistic and commercial success, and he poured out his bitterness in a new song entitled "Chords of Fame":

> *They'll rob you of your innocence,*
> *They will put you up for sale.*
> *The more that you will find success,*

The more that you will fail.
I've been around and I've had my share
And I really can't complain.
But I wonder who I left behind
The other side of fame.
So play the chords of love, my friend,
Play the chords of pain.
But if you want to keep your song,
Don't, don't, don't
Play the chords of fame.

It was a familiar lament, expressed by almost every artist who ever felt as if he or she had sold out, even in the tiniest way, to achieve fame and fortune, or by those who refused to compromise and paid a dear price for holding onto their integrity. Critics had always praised Phil for refusing to compromise his standards, but this offered him no consolation. He desperately wanted to release the hit single that had eluded him throughout his career, and to his dying day he could not believe that "Changes" had not topped the charts. Joan Baez had charted a hit with "There But for Fortune," and Peter and Gordon had scored a minor success with "Flower Lady," but this gave Phil little satisfaction. Instead, he would remember the near-misses—how Peter, Paul and Mary were going to record "Changes," or how the Byrds had considered recording "Flower Lady"—and he would wonder what might have happened to his career if their versions of his songs had taken off.

Longtime friend Erik Jacobsen noted that Phil never gave up hope that one of his albums would break through.

"We had a standing bet," he said. "We bet a thousand dollars—which, at the time, was a pretty large amount for us—on his first album. He said it would sell a million, and I bet against him. We didn't put a time limit on it, so it became an ongoing joke throughout our entire relationship. I would bring it up—'Where's my thousand?'—and he would say, 'Once one of my things pops through, they're all going to sell a million.' It was one of our ongoing jokes, but I never collected."

Phil's despair was even more apparent in "No More Songs"—another song written in 1969. In interviews published after the Chicago convention, Phil had hinted that he was reaching the end as a song-writer, that events in recent history had destroyed any hopes he had

felt as an American and an artist, but "No More Songs," with its funeral dirge melody and despondent lyrics, brought these feelings
home with unnerving clarity:

> *Hello, hello, hello*
> *Is there anybody home?*
> *I only called to say I'm sorry.*
> *The drums are in the dawn*
> *And all the voices gone,*
> *And it seems that there are*
> *No more songs.*

In the song's third verse, Phil wrote convincingly of the utter loneliness that the artist feels when his message goes unheeded:

> *Once I knew a sage*
> *Who sang upon the stage.*
> *He told about the world*
> *His lover.*
> *A ghost without a name*
> *Stands ragged in the rain,*
> *And it seems that there are*
> *No more songs.*

Despite the air of finality in his song's lyrics, Phil was not prepared to surrender his career. He continued to fill his notebooks with
fragments of song lyrics, and if only a few of the new songs ever saw
the light of day, it was due more to Phil's exacting standards than
to his giving up on himself. "No More Songs" was a warning, not a
declaration—a self-examination that, in time, would look like a
confession.

———

Although his behavior was not yet comparable to the erratic and
alarming behavior characteristic of his later life, Phil was beginning
to worry his friends. He was drinking more than ever, and he had
picked up a Valium dependency after he was prescribed the drug to
help calm his nerves. Neither incapacitated him, but both could make
him unpleasant to be around.

Phil had been using Valium since his Greenwich Village folk scene days, but always in small doses. He would typically take a Valium tablet and break it in half—or even in fourths—and use the small dose to help control his nervousness and stuttering during concerts. Only people actually seeing him take the drug would have known he was using it at all, and as a rule, he looked at Valium the same way he regarded other drugs—as substances that could hinder, rather than open, the mind.

Nevertheless, after moving to California, Phil stepped up his intake of Valium, and his dependency became more apparent. On one occasion, while he was having breakfast with David Blue at Schwab's Drugstore, Phil flew into a rage when he discovered that he was out of Valium and the druggist refused to sell him any; he settled down only after Blue offered him some of his supply.

Alcohol was an entirely different matter. As a casual drinker, Phil was fun to be around, but when he was drinking heavily, especially if he was in a depressed state, he could be unreasonable and contentious and, on rare occasions, violent.

One of the more bizarre episodes associated with his drinking during this period occurred at a party hosted by comedian Tom Smothers. The party, thrown in honor of the folksinger Donovan, was overflowing with entertainment figures. As Phil wandered through Smothers' enormous estate, he could not help but be put off by all the glamour and wealth surrounding him, especially at a time when Hollywood celebrities were making a lot of noise about supporting the starving Vietnamese refugees. To top off his party, Tom Smothers was giving away a door prize of an enormous wicker basket filled with fruit, cheese, and imported wine. Phil won the raffle for the prize, but when he went up to claim it, he surprised the party's guests by delivering a long, rambling monologue about Vietnam, the well-fed and the starving, and the incongruity of the party. Then, to punctuate his statements, he placed the door-prize basket into the swimming pool, where it sank without further ceremony.

"I was seized by a host or something at the party," he said later. "Normally, I'd never do anything like that. I was as amazed as anyone else."

Amazed, perhaps, but unrepentant: when discussing the incident, Phil compared it to one of Abbie Hoffman's Yippie actions. Hoffman, said Phil, was the kind of guy who would walk into a police station and kick in the glass of a trophy case, just to get arrested. He saw his actions at the Smothers party in a similar vein.

"It was really a protest against myself," he explained. "I could see myself at some point making enough money and living like that . . . with that big pool and all, and throwing that party. It scared me."

What Phil failed to mention—or perhaps even notice—was that his behavior at the party was as offensive to Tom Smothers as Abbie Hoffman's antics had been to him at his earlier Carnegie Hall concert. Such behavior, out of character for the old Phil Ochs, was nevertheless significant: in the months following the Chicago convention, Phil began to display, for the first time in his life, indications that he might have inherited his father's manic depression. For the moment, the signals were so subtle that neither friends nor family would take much notice of them, but, in hindsight, there is little doubting that the convention triggered the manifestation of an affliction that would torment Phil for the remainder of his life.

Chapter Twelve

GUNFIGHT AT CARNEGIE HALL

THERE SEEMED to be no escaping the Chicago convention. Rather than let the unfortunate events of that August week in 1968 slip shamefully yet quietly into history, the powers that be decided to push the issue even further by staging what is now regarded as one of the most outrageous court proceedings in American history. On paper, the Chicago Conspiracy Trial, as the case came to be known, involved eight activists—Abbie Hoffman, Jerry Rubin, David Dellinger, Tom Hayden, Rennie Davis, Bobby Seale, John Froines, and Lee Weiner—all accused of conspiring to cross state lines "with the intent to incite, organize, promote, encourage, participate in, and carry on a riot." In reality, the trial was a transparent attempt by authorities to dismantle the antiwar and black power movements by placing some of their most visible leaders behind bars. On a smaller scale, the city additionally hoped to save face by showing, in open court, that the police violence was somehow justified.

The trial was nothing if not theater of the absurd, heightened exponentially by a system determined to punish its wayward children and, in the process, re-establish an appearance of order. It mattered not that the state had, at best, a flimsy case; or that the national media, still sickened by the bloodshed on the streets of the Windy City during convention week, had little sympathy for either side and viewed the trial as a circus; or that the seventy-four-year-old man presiding over the trial, Judge Julius Hoffman, though known as a strict jurist, was about as poor a choice as could have been selected to control the inevitable courtroom theatrics of a Jerry Rubin or Abbie Hoffman, or even the legal maneuvering of William Kunstler and Leonard Weinglass, the attorneys for seven of the eight defendants.

The tone for the trial was set early when Bobby Seale requested that he be allowed to act as his own attorney. Seale's attorney, Charles Garry, had undergone emergency gall bladder surgery, and when Judge Hoffman refused Garry's request for a six-week postponement while he recovered, Seale demanded the right to represent himself in court. Hoffman refused, and after a series of heated exchanges, during which Seale complained of racist treatment, Hoffman ordered court marshals to bind and gag the black activist so the trial could proceed. Hoffman's decision proved to be a serious tactical error: the media immediately sided with Seale, and from that point on, portrayed Judge Hoffman—and, by extension, the state—as being ham-fisted tyrants willing to resort to any measure, including Draconian punishment, to silence its opposition.

————

Phil had been contacted early in the year about appearing at the trial as a witness for the defense, and his time on the witness stand was illustrative of the trial's farcical nature. Phil, who had been deemed an important participant in the events in Chicago by the FBI, which worked closely with the authorities in establishing the case, was actually disappointed that he had not been one of those indicted. Like other leaders that had been left off the list, or who came to be known as unindicted co-conspirators, Phil was insulted that he had not been considered important enough to be charged with others.

Even so, Phil had mixed emotions about the trial when he traveled to Chicago in December to give his testimony. After a year's depression over the events in Chicago and the subsequent presidential election, Phil was ready to vent some frustration. On the other hand, he had been following the trial closely and was smart enough to know that, theatrics aside, the trial could wind up being nothing but another exercise in futility.

When Phil took the stand, he hardly looked the part of the wild-eyed revolutionary committed to the destruction of civilized society. If anything, he looked like an aging college student. Nor did he come across as contentious or disrespectful, although he might have been forgiven had he acted in such a manner, given the prosecution's barrage of objections to almost any one of his answers, and Judge Hoffman's continual stacking of the judicial deck in favor of the state. At one point, Phil nearly lost his temper when Hoffman, in admonishing Phil for not answering quickly and directly enough, said, "You are a singer, but you are a smart fellow, I'm sure."

"Thank you very much," Phil responded, looking straight at the judge. "You are a judge, and you are a smart fellow."

Typical of the trial, Phil's testimony was continually interrupted, which at times created disjointed, humorous dialogue:

> MR. KUNSTLER: Did you have any role [in buying the pig and bring-
>   ing him to the city]?
> PHIL OCHS: Yes. I helped select the pig, and I paid for him.
> MR. KUNSTLER: Where did you find the pig?
> PHIL OCHS: I don't remember the exact place.
> MR. KUNSTLER: Mr. Ochs, can you describe the pig which you
>   finally bought?
> MR. FORAN: (prosecutor): Objection.
> JUDGE HOFFMAN: I sustain the objection.
> MR. KUNSTLER: Was it a pig or a piglet?
> MR. FORAN: Objection.
> JUDGE HOFFMAN: I sustain the objection.
> MR. KUNSTLER: Did you buy the pig yourself or with other people?
> PHIL OCHS: I bought the pig with Jerry Rubin.
> MR. KUNSTLER: And did anything happen in connection with that
>   pig subsequently, at a time when Jerry Rubin was present?
> MR. FORAN: I object to the form of question, Your Honor. It is
>   leading and suggestive.
> JUDGE HOFFMAN: I sustain the objection.
> MR. KUNSTLER: Would you state what, if anything, happened to
>   the pig?
> PHIL OCHS: The pig was arrested with seven people.

And so it went, with Judge Hoffman and the prosecution forcing a plodding line of questioning that only underscored the outrageous nature of the trial, and defense attorneys deftly sidestepping the worst of the legal potholes and moving ahead, entering into the court record whatever they could. Phil remained patient throughout the questioning, even when the proceedings became so absurd that they might have driven others to distraction. Phil spoke of the fragmentation of the Youth International Party and its plans to stage a festival of life during the week of the convention; he detailed his involvement in the Pigasus episode. He talked of the violence he witnessed on the streets. Finally, toward the end of his second day on the stand, he recited—but was not allowed to sing—the lyrics to "I Ain't Marching Anymore."

Compared to the testimony of other witnesses at the trial, Phil's testimony was remarkably subdued. William Kunstler would later comment about how impressed he was with Phil's contribution.

"I met many people in Chicago," he said. "During that trial I learned many ugly things in this country, but I don't think I had a more shining moment than when I had the honor and privilege to take Phil Ochs through his direct examination."

———

In analyzing the Yippies' failure at the Democratic convention, as well as Richard Nixon's election a few months later, Phil was convinced that Nixon had become president because, first, he was able to make people believe that the election was a good vs. evil proposition, and, second, because both the demonstrators and the Democratic Party had lost touch with America's working class—the very people they were supposed to be representing. Although he was loath to do so, Phil had to give Nixon his due: he had been brilliant in recognizing the political climate and acting on it.

"Nixon," he maintained, "got across his image. 'It's us against them. I mean, no matter what you think of me, I'm a regular, straight American guy, and if you're not going to have me, you're going to have some hairy freak, with dope in the streets and the destruction of the country. So take your choice.' That's the game he played, and played very effectively."

The choice was easy for most Americans to make. The working class had always been a hardworking, patriotic lot, and given the choice between continuing the American tradition and supporting revolutionary change, working stiffs would always vote for the safety of the status quo. The Democratic Party had failed to recognize this, as had the activists who had gone to Chicago.

The more Phil thought about it, the more convinced he became that his own artistic future hinged upon his appealing to a working-class base. He needed to find a way to reach a larger cross-section of the public and deliver his message to them. In turning it over in his mind, Phil kept returning to his old idols—John Wayne, Audie Murphy, James Dean, and Elvis Presley. All had realized hero status in their lifetime.

Elvis intrigued Phil the most. He was a true working-class hero, a truck driver turned King of Rock 'n' Roll. He had taken American forms of music—rhythm and blues, country, gospel, and even folk—and adapted them to his own style. He had reached unparalleled success, yet in recent years his career had fallen on hard times. He seemed to have lost his way, but now he was returning with a vengeance.

As luck had it, Michael had secured four tickets to see Elvis Presley's comeback show in Las Vegas, and he offered the tickets to Phil, who flew to Nevada with Karen, Andy Wickham, and Andy's girlfriend Frances. The show was everything Phil could have dreamed it to be, with Elvis putting a new, glittery spin on his standards. He was older and thicker around the middle than the young man Ed Sullivan had once refused to show below the waist, but he was still an electrifying presence, rising from the ashes of his career and knocking them dead in the entertainment capital of the United States.

Phil was bowled over by the show, and he was certain that, in Elvis Presley, he had found a model for his own comeback.

———

But first, there had to be a new album—something to present the new Phil Ochs . . .

In recent months, Phil had written a handful of new songs that continued to explore the intensely personal songwriting that he had presented on *Rehearsals for Retirement*. Some of the numbers, like "Bach, Beethoven, Mozart, and Me," which described the domestic life he and Karen shared with Andy and Frances at their Los Angeles home, and "Basket in the Pool," an account of the fiasco at the Smothers party, were straightforward autobiographical readings. For "Boy in Ohio," Phil returned to specific scenes of his youth:

> *Creek was runnin' by the road*
> *And the buckeyed sun was a-shinin'*
> *I rode my bike down Alum Creek Drive,*
> *When I was a boy in Ohio.*

The English teacher, he didn't care.
He challenged us to checkers,
And once in a while we'd swap a joke,
When I was a boy in Ohio.

Inspired by the Elvis concert, Phil returned to his own roots, and the days when he would listen to Hank Williams, Lefty Frizzell, Faron Young, and Webb Pierce. "Gas Station Women" was the kind of country-and-western song, complete with sappy lyrics, double entendre, and wordplay that could have been appreciated in any truckstop in America's heartland:

Everything is going wrong,
Everything is bad.
There's no one I can talk to
When I am feeling sad.
She broke my heart a million ways,
I'm losing all my friends.
The boys down at the factory,
They wonder where I've been.
So fill 'er up with love, please,
Won't you mister.
Just the high test
Is what I used to say.
But that was before I lost my baby.
I'll have a dollar's worth of regular today.

The move into country-and-western music, Phil later explained, had been partially influenced by a trucker's strike. "The whole way they dealt with the truckers," he said, "was to play them that country music. There are waves of restlessness sweeping through these kinds of people, which is why they find themselves in the awkward position of being like the students they were hating five years ago."

Phil would also use a country-and-western sound, complete with fiddles and a country-swing tempo, in "Chords of Fame," one of the highlights on the new album, and he would continue to explore America's obsession with automobiles and mobile lifestyles in "My Kingdom for a Car," a tongue-in-cheek work that effectively contrasted the guarded sense of place in "Boy in Ohio":

I've found my freedom here
And I've been flying down
That highway of gold.
My shirtsleeves are rolled
My Colt Forty-Five is cold
I go fast till I'm going faster.
Look how far we've come
Look how far.
A car, a car,
My kingdom for a car.

Phil wanted Larry Marks to produce the album, but this time around it wasn't going to happen. Marks had been a reluctant participant in the *Rehearsals for Retirement* project—he was considering leaving the business to work in the movies—and he now turned down Phil's request to produce the new record. After considering other prospective producers, Phil decided to go with Van Dyke Parks, an iconoclastic singer-songwriter-producer who was considered to be one of the finest—and quirkiest—young minds in the business. Parks had co-written a number of songs with Brian Wilson of the Beach Boys, including the hit "Heroes and Villains," and he had recently produced Arlo Guthrie's album, *Washington County*. Phil thought Parks would be ideal for what he wanted to do on his new recording.

"I was working exclusively at Warner Brothers," Parks recalled. "I liked Phil a lot, and we had mutual friends. Phil wanted to continue to surround the guitar with more instruments, and I was interested in that. I was interested in the possibilities of production."

According to Parks, Phil was "very intense" during the two days it took to record the album. As on *Pleasures of the Harbor*, Phil found himself sharing studio space with a large team of musicians, technicians, and even a group of backup singers. Lincoln Mayorga was on hand to contribute to a fourth consecutive album, and special guest musicians included Elvis' guitarist, James Burton, and guitarists Ry Cooder and Clarence White; Bobby Wayne, a veteran country singer who had worked with Merle Haggard, chipped in harmony vocals.

"My Kingdom for a Car" and "Gas Station Women" might have been, by Phil's estimation, the cornerstones of the album, reflective of his new career direction, but the spiritual center of the new recording was "Jim Dean of Indiana," a lengthy biography-in-song reminiscent of Phil's earlier "Joe Hill." In fourteen verses, accompanied

226 / *There But for Fortune*

only by Lincoln Mayorga's mournful piano, Phil gave a complete accounting of James Dean's life, ending with his placing a flower on the movie star's grave.

Most haunting, at least from a historical perspective, was the inclusion of "No More Songs," which was placed at the end of the album. The song itself was ominous enough, with Phil's dark hints of his own demise, but Phil raised the song's stakes by bringing in Jim Glover to sing the background vocals, as if to bring his career around full-circle. "No More Songs" proved to be frighteningly prophetic: it would be the last song on the last studio album released in Phil's lifetime.

Much to the displeasure of A & M officials and his manager-brother, Phil insisted on calling his new album *Phil Ochs' Greatest Hits*. The title, said the company, would be misleading, since all of the material on the album was new. Phil emphatically disagreed.

"It started out as a joke," he said. "I was trying to think of an album title, and I thought, 'Wouldn't it be funny if I put it out as *Greatest Hits*, since I never had any hits.' It would also be a spoof of the industry, because everybody keeps putting out 'greatest hits' and 'best ofs'—you know, repackaging their songs again and again."

But this was not the end. For the cover photograph, Phil posed on an empty stage, holding an electric guitar and wearing a gold lamé suit custom-made for him by Nudie Cohen, the tailor who, years earlier, had made an identical suit for Elvis Presley. The suit, Phil said, was intended to be both a spoof and a homage.

"I recently came to the conclusion that Colonel Parker knows more about organizing America than Angela Davis or SDS," he explained. "He understands the American mentality. In terms of change in America, you have to reach the working class, and to me, Elvis Presley, in retrospect, is like a giant commercialization of the working-class singer. [He is] also a true integrationist in terms of bringing black music and country music together, which is why his strength is so long-lasting. His gold suit was Parker's idea of the super-gross carnival treatment, a cheap ikon of all America has to offer."

To finalize the parody, Phil appeared on the album's back cover, wearing a black leather jacket and looking every bit the image of James Dean. *50 Phil Ochs fans can't be wrong*, said the cover—a blatant reference to an earlier Elvis album. Unfortunately for Phil, the back-cover gag hit closer to home than either he or his record company would have liked. *Phil Ochs' Greatest Hits* sold the fewest of any of Phil's albums, and it, like *Rehearsals for Retirement*, suffered the indignation of being discontinued before a lot of record-buyers knew the album was out.

———

Despite opposition from Michael and others, Phil was absolutely, convinced that he was onto something big with his new Elvis–gold lamé suit–*Greatest Hits* obsession. He had the entire concept worked out in his mind: to effect significant change in America, you had to be part Elvis Presley and part Che Guevara.* As a topical songwriter and political activist, Phil had long ago established his revolutionary credentials; what he needed to do now was make the Elvis connection. The *Greatest Hits* album had begun the process. The next stop would be to take the show on the road.

The plan was simple: a tune-up performance at Doug Weston's Troubadour, and then on to New York and Carnegie Hall, to be followed by a limited tour of the States. The shows, as Phil saw them, would be an explanation of his *Greatest Hits* persona to those who might have missed the point.

The Troubadour show hinted of things to come. Phil still had enough of a following to pack the club, but his audience was at a loss as to how to react when he walked onstage, decked out in a gold lamé suit and flanked by a rock 'n' roll band consisting of Lincoln Mayorga on piano, Bob Rafkin on guitar, Kenny Kaufman on bass, and Kevin Kelly on drums. The Phil Ochs that everyone knew and loved was evident in such songs as "I Ain't Marching Anymore," "Pleasures of the Harbor," and "Changes," but this Phil Ochs seemed to be losing an artistic battle with a newer model who played extended medleys of Buddy Holly and Elvis Presley songs.

"I thought it was Phil's way of acknowledging his roots and showing his versatility," commented Paul Krassner. "It was like presenting a multiple personality in one performance. The gold lamé suit came out of the same artistic freedom as 'I Ain't Marching Anymore'—you couldn't separate them on that level."

---

* The Elvis Presley-Che Guevara idea had been Andy Wickham's. He and Phil had been shooting pool one evening, when Phil joked about what would happen if Elvis and Che teamed up as a nightclub act. Responded Wickham: "What would happen if you became a combination of Elvis Presley and Che Guevara?" The idea grew from there.

Ron Cobb admitted that he initially had difficulty drawing the connection between Phil Ochs the folksinger and the man that he saw in the gold lamé suit, but he liked the show in any event. "It was very comparable to Dylan's coming out in polka-dot shirts and using electric guitars," he said. "It was a big shock when Dylan did that. Phil went further with Buddy Holly and all this stuff. People just didn't know what to make of it. There was a lot of tense silence while the performance was going on, and people would yell for old requests, but it was kind of hard to ask Phil to sing 'There But for Fortune" when he's wearing a gold suit. No one quite knew what he was all about. His audience thought it was a complete contradiction, but anyone who knew Phil knew that it was totally consistent with him. Phil was really giving of himself—what he was and where he was— and you had to buy the complexity and see the connections. I thought it was all quite valid."

Cobb's assessment represented a minority opinion. Some of the Troubadour audience shared his enthusiasm for Phil's latest musical direction, but the majority was either befuddled by the show or angered by what appeared to be an artist's reckless disregard for his audience. Phil, quite naturally, was too stubborn to be swayed by any form of criticism, positive or negative. The real test would be Carnegie Hall.

———

Ron Delsener, the top concert promoter in New York City, handled the arrangements for the two Carnegie Hall shows, scheduled for Friday, March 27, 1970. Advertisements for the concerts featured a photograph of Phil's new look, complete with the gold lamé suit and electric guitar. Phil might have looked ludicrous posing as a rock 'n' roll idol, but the posturing did nothing to slow ticket sales. New York still loved Phil Ochs.

The shows got off to an shaky start when the sound crew turned up three hours late, putting Phil in the awkward position of having to go onstage without conducting a sound check. This, as it turned out, would be the least of his problems. The crowd reacted with a mixture of laughter, applause, and derision when Phil took the stage in his gold lamé suit, and the overall humor of the audience deteriorated from that point on. Catcalls peppered the downtime between songs; audience members demanded to hear the *real* Phil Ochs. It was bad enough that Phil insisted on dressing in a lame-looking out-fit, but people were not about to applaud his rendition of "Okie from Muskogee," which smacked of the kind of right-wing, hard-hat mentality they had to deal with on the street every day.

Phil plowed ahead, hoping to somehow win over the crowd. Dylan had been booed at the '65 Newport festival and he had been right; Phil would be right in his new career direction. Or so he believed.

Such emotions aside, Phil was hurt and embarrassed by the hostile audience response. His mother and sister had come in from Far Rockaway to see the show, and others, such as Jerry Moss, Doug Weston, and Jerry Rubin, had flown cross-country for it. Some of his closest friends from the city were in attendance. It had to be embarrassing for them to hear the booing and heckling.

The show hit bottom just before what normally would have been the intermission. Throughout the concert, the band would leave the stage while Phil performed a number or two alone with his acoustic guitar. During one such break, Lincoln Mayorga was approached backstage by a plainclothes police officer.

"You've got to go out there and tell him to end the concert," the cop told Mayorga. "We've had a telephone bomb threat."

Unfortunately, Mayorga was instructed to tell Phil to avoid offering any reason for bringing an end to the show, since doing so might create a panic situation.

"I went out onstage and Phil came over and started tuning his guitar at the piano," Mayorga recalled. "He was moving pretty slow because he was in a strange, spacy place. And I said to him as quietly as I could, 'Phil, the police have just told me that we have to bring this concert to a close. There's been a bomb threat.' He didn't say anything or really acknowledge what I said. He just smiled this strange, broad, shit-eating grin that was typical of him, and continued tuning his guitar. Then he went back to the microphone, acting completely oblivious to what I told him, and rambled on and on about this and that. Then, before he went into the next number, he came back and tuned his guitar once more. This time he said to me, 'Are you prepared to die for rock 'n' roll?' I was nervous at the time—I was looking under the piano for explosives—but even then it struck me as a very, very funny line."

Phil was not about to simply terminate the concert without explanation. Instead, he directed the band through several more numbers, all played at nearly twice their normal speed. The crowd howled its disapproval, and when Phil finally ended the concert abruptly and without explanation, he was pelted with programs hurled by angry patrons. Phil rushed outside and tried to explain what had happened, but few people leaving the theater were buying his excuses.

The midnight show was not immediately cancelled, and while Carnegie Hall was checked out for the presence of a bomb, Phil retreated to the Carnegie Tavern for dinner with his mother, sister, Jerry Rubin, and a handful of friends. Phil openly admitted that the first show had been a nightmare, but he would not consider the suggestion, posed by one of his friends, that he cancel the second show and use the bomb scare as an excuse. Phil knocked back several drinks, along with some uppers that he hoped would help get him through the next performance. He would do the show, and there would be no argument about it.

Midway through his meal, Phil was approached by a group of angry kids who had attended the first performance. "How can you charge money to put on a show like that?" the group's spokesperson demanded, complaining that the program had been short and substandard.

Phil, who had always enjoyed good person-to-person rapport with his audience members, was genuinely shaken by the group's appearance.

"Give me your names," he said, "and I'll get you into the second show."

A list was drawn up, and Phil walked over to the Carnegie Hall box office to deliver it. He returned to his family and guests, confident that the matter had been settled. However, ten minutes later, the group was back. The list, they told Phil, had been torn up.

Phil stormed out of the Carnegie Tavern and returned to the box office. The second show had been sold out, and no one was at the ticket window. Enraged, Phil pounded on the glass. When no one answered, he pounded harder on the window, putting his fist through the glass and cutting the tendons in his right thumb. People in the lobby cheered as Phil held up his damaged hand, his blood gushing everywhere, including on his gold suit. Phil Ochs the revolutionary was back.

"He cut his hand very badly," recalled Lincoln Mayorga. "I remember him running from the box office, west on 57th Street, south on Seventh Avenue, and east on 56th, leaving a trail of blood down the street, up the steps to the stage entrance, and up to the dressing room."

A doctor was called and Phil's thumb was treated. However, with the bandage on his thumb, Phil could not finger-pick, which only created more anxiety about the second show. To soothe his nerves, Phil had a couple more drinks, and by the time he hit the stage for the midnight show, he was drunk and feeling confrontational, more determined than ever to convert his audience.

The shows themselves, despite the negative reaction from the crowd, were well conceived. People would remember the Buddy Holly and Elvis medleys, or the Conway Twitty and Merle Haggard numbers, as if Phil had played very little else, but in truth the shows featured a healthy sampling of the *Greatest Hits* album ("Basket in the Pool," "Jim Dean of Indiana," "Chords of Fame," "Gas Station Women," "My Kingdom for a Car," and "Boy in Ohio"), as well as favorites from the past ("I Ain't Marching Anymore," "Outside of a Small Circle of Friends," "Pleasures of the Harbor," "Crucifixion," "Tape from California," and even "The Bells"). The band, although by no means a polished unit, played gamely behind Phil, who often had trouble hitting the high notes, fell behind in the songs' tempos, forgot or slurred lyrics, and otherwise sang with a thick, hoarse voice. If Phil let his audience down that night, it was not because he wore a gold suit or planned an inferior program; he let them down because he was in no condition to perform.

He was, however, prepared to engage in a dialogue with fans and critics alike, and his between-song patter was as compelling as anything he performed. Phil spoke of his music, calling the first verse of "Jim Dean of Indiana" the best verse he had ever written, and he lambasted the Nixon administration, particularly Vice-President Spiro Agnew; in one of the more outrageous non sequiturs of the evening, he lumped the Kennedys with Joe Pyne during his performance of "Crucifixion." The audience, initially as combative as the group from the first show, took him to task at every point, cheering wildly when he played an old standard and booing unmercifully any time the band stepped onstage.

Somehow, Phil managed to keep his temper. It was their right, he told them, to voice disapproval, but they really ought to consider what he was trying to do.

"The trick is," he said, "with wearing a suit like this, is the same trick as living in America today, which is how to come to terms with wealth."

"Strip!" a woman in the audience shouted.

"No, no," Phil replied in an even tone. "I could never do that, for it would be cheap. I prefer to maintain my dignity as an American citizen." The remark drew laughter. "I will never strip," Phil went on. "So I will now try to wear this gold suit and sing a song of significance. I'll try to have wealth come to terms with responsibility."

The show became a protracted tug-of-war, with Phil gaining and losing ground at regular intervals, the music becoming secondary in importance to Phil's determined attempts to get his audience to understand what he was really trying to accomplish. In the past, Phil had been able to keep audiences on his side by sheer charm and the power of his convictions. He had played and sung poorly before, and he had forgotten his lyrics, but his personality had always won the day. People appreciated the fact that his heart was in the right place, even if he had left his voice at home.

At Carnegie Hall, the battle was waged into the wee hours of the morning. At three o'clock, when Phil finally reached the end of the show and had walked offstage, the hall management cut the stage's electricity before he could perform an encore, giving Phil one more opportunity to bond with his audience.

"I want power!" he began to chant when he walked back onstage for the planned encore. The crowd quickly joined him. "We want power! We want power! . . ."

After a few minutes, the electricity was restored and Phil closed out the evening with three songs—a cover of Elvis' "A Fool Such as I," the evening's second reading of "Outside of a Small Circle of Friends," and, as the coup de grace, a cover of Chuck Berry's "School Days." The crowd ate it up. By the time he had finished, many audience members were dancing in the aisles. "It became a total magic moment," Phil later recalled.

Arthur Gorson was in attendance that evening, and he agreed that Phil eventually brought the crowd around.

"It was a battle," he said, "and it took him until the encores. He had to beat the audience into submission. He had to stop and lecture them, and Carnegie Hall tried to turn off the electricity, and he played with bloody hands and all the rest . . . but he got his point. At the end of the day, the audience understood something of what he was trying to do, and they called for more. It was like a bullfight."

The day after the show, David Frost called Phil and invited him to be a guest on his talk show the following Monday. Phil was elated. He had been struggling to get on television for years, and with the exception of an occasional appearance on small local programs, or a turn or two on news programs, he had been ignored by the medium. The invitation had additional meaning, coming as it did on the heels of the Carnegie Hall show: perhaps others were catching on to what he was doing.

Sadly, such feelings were temporary. After taping a twenty-minute segment of the show, during which he performed his Elvis medley in his gold suit, Phil took to the road for a series of concerts similar to the one he had given at Carnegie Hall. Audiences were neither as accepting nor forgiving as the one he had encountered during his second show at Carnegie, and the tour flopped horribly. Phil was scorned in Boston and Philadelphia, and fared even worse when he returned to the West Coast for a show in Berkeley. People weren't buying his explanations about his new musical direction, and the concerts became ordeals. In the weeks following the Carnegie Hall shows, Phil lived in a state of constant agitation, which he tried to offset with excessive drinking and the use of drugs.

"He was physically abusing himself very badly on that tour," said Lincoln Mayorga. "He was drinking a lot of wine and taking uppers. It was a funny combination. The wine was pulling him one way and the uppers were pulling him another way, and he was kind of a mess. There were so many pharmaceuticals around—so many pills. I'd never seen anything like that."

Phil paid his price for all the substance abuse after his show in Philadelphia. He had just finished his concert when he collapsed in his dressing room. "He was moaning and groaning and saying he felt it was all over," recalled Mayorga, who was frightened by the experience. "He said that he was being pulled this way and that way, that it was all over, and that never, ever again would he abuse himself the way he had on this tour."

The plug was mercifully pulled on the tour before Phil could embarrass himself or damage his career any further. Phil, however, was not yet ready to hang up the gold suit entirely. Incredibly, he approached Jerry Moss with the proposal that A & M release the Carnegie Hall shows as a live album. Moss flatly refused to do anything of the sort.

Michael Ochs was also opposed to releasing the concert as an album and, as always, he was not hesitant about offering his opinions to his brother. "Phil and I argued like crazy," he said. "I thought the [gold suit] concept worked better on paper than it did on record. As a tangential idea, it was great. And I agreed with something that Andy Wickham said: 'You gotta give Phil credit for the balls it took to do that.' I said, 'I give him credit. It's real bravery to actually go that far to pull off the idea.' But, to me, it was a matter of not knowing when to quit.

"At the time, one of my best friends worked as the head of underground promotions for A & M. I said to him, 'Do me a favor. Make some acetates of the show and take them around to all the FM stations you hit. See what their reaction is.' He did, and the reaction was totally negative. I told Phil about it and he said, 'They're all wrong, they're all wrong.' He just wouldn't drop it. And I said to Phil, 'I think it would really hurt you. *Greatest Hits* put you as Presley on the cover and it bombed—and it was a *good* album, damn it. If you put the *Gunfight* album out, it will kill your career. You'll never come back from it.' He said, 'You're full of shit,' and stormed out. Then he went to Jerry Moss and came back and said, 'Jerry said the same thing. He's as dumb as you.' I said, 'Good. Thank God Jerry Moss said that.' "

Jerry Yester, a friend of Phil's, saw the toll that A & M's refusal to release the album exacted from Phil.

"It broke his heart," said Yester. "He played it for me when he first finished it, and he was so excited by it. Then I talked to him about a month later and he said, 'A & M's not going to release it.' He was just crushed by it."

Phil returned to Los Angeles, badly beaten by the failure of the gold-suit tour. He had no idea what he would do next—or *if* he would do anything next. As far as he was concerned, his career was finished.

Chapter Thirteen

TRAVELS AND TRAVAILS

PHIL HAD always believed that he would die at a young age, and he now began to contemplate his death, especially by suicide. It was not yet the obsession that it would become, but it was something that he could easily call up and consider, often in an eerily detached way. The tombstone on the cover of *Rehearsals for Retirement* had been no exaggeration: he constantly spoke of how he had died with America in Chicago. He elaborated on it at the Carnegie Hall shows, where he announced the death of Phil Ochs, speaking of himself in the third person as if he could stand back and look at his life with a totally objective view.

He swore he would never perform again. He saw no reason to rehash the same old material, and in his latest prolonged bout of depression, he could hardly write a single line, let alone an entire song, in his notebooks. With enough money in the bank to carry him indefinitely, Phil reasoned that he could stay away from the stage and recording studio for as long as he wanted.

The big plan, he told friends, was to travel and see the world. He had seen a large portion of Europe when he was performing, but his professional obligations had kept him from exploring the countries in any depth. Now, with time and money at his disposal, he vowed to check out every country in the world before he died.

He began his quest at the end of the year, when he visited France, Holland, England, and Ireland with friends Jerry Rubin and Stew Albert. Leaving the United States lifted his spirits. As Albert recalled, Phil was an ideal tourist, whose enthusiasm rubbed off on everyone around him.

Rubin and Albert had their own agenda on the trip—to bring the

Youth International Party to Europe—and they held press conferences and met with leftist organizers and activists wherever they went. Phil, still burned out from politics in general, turned down numerous invitations to become involved, either through television appearances or by giving benefit concerts. In Paris, he passed up the chance to appear with Rubin and Albert on television, going instead to the movies while his friends taped the show. In Holland, the group connected with members of the *Kraubauterzen*, a radical Dutch organization similar to the Yippies. Phil was amazed and pleased to learn that one of their members had been elected to a local city council.

Ironically, the Americans' politics were considered mild in comparison to their European counterparts. In England, a group of British and Australian activists accused Rubin and Albert of selling out by agreeing to appear on *The David Frost Show*, which was currently broadcasting live in London. Rubin, Albert, and Brian Flanagan, a British activist also scheduled to appear as a guest on the show, struck up a deal with the radicals: the three of them would do a portion of the show as if they were serious guests, and then, after about fifteen minutes, they would allow the radicals to "take over" the program. Phil was asked if he wanted to participate in the overthrow, but he declined to have anything to do with it. He still felt loyal to Frost for giving him a shot on his program only a few months earlier, and he was not about to do anything that might embarrass him.

The takeover went off as planned. At the appointed moment, the English and Australians stormed the stage, shouting obscenities and political slogans, and creating bedlam in the studio. One activist kissed Frost on the mouth, proclaiming it a moment for gay liberation. Hashish joints were broken out and smoked. As Rubin had hoped, the cameras caught all of the action, including one funny moment that found David Frost watching the whole affair from the front row of the studio. The police were finally called and the troublemakers chased from the studio, but not before all involved had become local heroes.

"We were like the Beatles," remembered Albert, noting that the story had run on the front page of a number of local papers. "We couldn't go anywhere without being recognized."

While in London, the group, including Phil, met with Bernadette Devlin at a local tavern. The entourage hoped to spend some time in

Belfast, but before heading into Ireland they wanted to speak to Devlin about the country's volatile political climate. The trip itself was uneventful, the group spending a week in Ireland and maintaining a low profile until Rubin and Albert's limited visas expired and they had to leave.

————

The European trip was merely a temporary break from the lethargic rut that Phil's life had become. Back in Los Angeles, he fell back into his routine of lying around the house and watching television, stepping out to go to breakfast, lunch, or the movies, or hanging out with Doug Weston at the Troubadour. His relationship with Karen was at an all-time low. Andy Wickham and his girlfriend had moved out and, not needing the big house in Hollywood Hills, Phil moved to a more modest, less expensive place in the city, at 8812 Rangeley Avenue.

Michael Ochs had all but given up on his brother's career. The two had been bickering about it for the better part of two years, but with Phil flatly refusing to record or perform, there was little that Michael could do to help him. To protect Phil's financial interests, Michael set up an account with a New York accounting firm, which paid Phil's bills and gave him an allowance to live on. For some reason, the arrangement confused Phil to no end: until the day he died, he would assume that Michael controlled his money when, in fact, he had access to his own earnings at all times. The misunderstanding, which Michael did little to clarify, turned out to be useful later on, when Phil's binge-spending might have otherwise run him into the ground financially.

One of Phil's closest friends and confidants during this rough period was Doug Weston, who served Phil drinks and listened to his stories and complaints on a nightly basis. Like Andy Wickham, Weston remained supportive of Phil throughout the bad times, withholding judgment and encouraging him in small ways, and when he asked Phil to come out of his semi-retirement and play a week's worth of shows at the Troubadour, Phil readily accepted.

This time, there were no gold suits or rock bands, no Elvis medleys or Conway Twitty covers. The shows presented a career retrospective, from "I Ain't Marching Anymore" to "Jim Dean of Indiana," and all points in-between, with Phil performing by himself on an acoustic guitar. People were impressed. "It was a wonderful performance—special, authoritative, and truly exciting," wrote a *Los Angeles Times* critic, who admitted up-front that he had not been fond of the gold-suit shows. "It was a mature performance by a singer who has a great deal to sing about. Hopefully, he will never be silent for long."

What the critic could not have known is that Phil regarded his Troubadour appearances as gestures of friendship. He and Weston had grown so close that it is possible that Weston was the only person on the West Coast who could have talked him into performing. Although Weston secretly hoped that Phil would use the Troubadour gigs as a springboard to concerts elsewhere, Phil treated the week as a one-shot deal.

On occasion, the two would get together away from the Troubadour, sometimes to go rowing at a nearby lake, other times to go on short excursions outside of Los Angeles. One time, Phil decided that he wanted to go to the desert for a day or two; a little time away from the city, he told Weston, might serve as inspiration to his sagging creativity. Weston was all for the idea, and they set off for a lodge in the middle of the desert, Phil complaining all the way about Weston's driving. After checking into the lodge and having dinner, Weston suggested that they go for a ride in the desert.

"We went for a little drive," Weston remembered, "until we were about five miles away from where we were staying. And I said, 'Doesn't the desert look beautiful? Let's park the car, get out, and walk.' We started walking, but we hadn't gone very far when Phil said, 'Where are we?' He had taken twenty steps from the car and he couldn't see it any longer, so he started thinking that he was going to get lost in the desert because it was night. I said, 'Don't worry, Phil, I know how to get back.' We walked around for a while, and we went up and down sand dunes and things like that. He got more and more paranoid. He had seen some ancient black-and-white movie about these guys getting lost in the desert, and the further we walked, the more paranoid he became."

The experience was not a total loss. As soon as they returned to the lodge, Phil took out a sheet of paper and wrote the lyrics to a new song—his first in more than a year. The song, an account of his being lost in the darkness, never developed beyond that initial writing stage, but Phil took it as a positive sign. Maybe there was hope after all.

———

By mid-1971, Phil had found a new political obsession: the Allende government in Chile. Salvador Allende, a physician and social reformist, had accomplished what political theorists believed to be the impossible when he became the first communist leader to rise to power through free democratic elections. To Phil, Allende was the most compelling political story since the Castro-led revolution in Cuba—not to mention the kind of peaceful revolution he had dreamed about for the United States—and the more he read about the government, and America's opposition to it, the more convinced he became that he had to witness some of this history firsthand.

Phil's first call went to Jerry Rubin, who was also interested in what was happening in Chile. Rubin was eager to visit the country with Phil, but to Phil's disappointment, he suggested that Stew Albert come along. Phil, who hoped to use the occasion to strengthen a friendship that had been flagging since the Chicago convention, knew all too well that this would not be possible if Albert was in the picture, since Rubin had a tendency to act out whenever he had an audience.

"It was a kind of paranoia showing through," said Albert, acknowledging that he felt the tension almost as soon as he and Rubin met Phil in Chile. Phil and Stew had known each other for nearly a decade, but they had never been especially close. Ironically, their friendship deepened, even as Phil and Rubin grew farther apart. "We really became friends," Albert later commented, "because we shared a common dream [of] socialism and liberation."

In Santiago, the three toasted their first night in Chile in the dining room of an elegant hotel, where they treated themselves to huge steaks and delicious red Chilean wine. Afterward, they settled back and smoked Cuban cigars. The wealthy people around them, they decided, were part of a dying social order, and it was only a matter of time before they would be replaced by the more deserving working class—the people behind Allende's peaceful revolution.

Phil loved the country, and over the next few weeks, he, Jerry, and Stew were introduced to every type of Chilean character imaginable, on the streets and in out-of-the-way places.

"We were everywhere," Albert recalled, "[in] the jungles, mines, caves, factories, basketball games, film and TV studios, newspaper offices, the desert . . . We met all kinds of characters, worthy and otherwise: trade union hardhats [with] red stars on their hats, Communist Party bureaucrats, businessmen working currency scams, underground guerillas preparing for the coup, anarchist students on strike against the socialist faculty, hippies smoking weak grass in public places, CIA agents disguised as *Time* magazine, and the very wretched of the shanty-town earth, who called Allende 'Comrade President' and offered not the finest, but the most generous wine."

Of all of Phil's experiences in Chile, none would compare to the events that took place on August 31, beginning with a chance encounter and ending with his being taken into a copper mine deep in the Andes. The day opened with Phil, Jerry, and Stew taking one of their routine strolls through the streets of Santiago. While on the walk, they spotted a handsome young Chilean with curly black hair, holding a guitar and leaning against a car, talking to a woman. Rubin wanted to stop and chat, and the Chilean, speaking in broken English, introduced himself as Victor Jara. The woman, an Englishwoman and former ballet dancer, was his wife.

Although none of the Americans had heard of him before, Victor Jara was one of the most beloved populist figures in Chile—a folksinger and political activist not unlike Pete Seeger in the United States. Jara had been instrumental in Allende's rise to power, but he was not one to give a blanket endorsement to any single individual or political party, and for this he had made many enemies in both the governing Communist Party and its opposition, represented largely by the military. Jara's main political activity now consisted of his traveling around the country, singing and drumming up support for the *Union Popular*, which made him a folk hero among his countrymen.

Phil, who had initially been reluctant to meet the young folksinger, was utterly mesmerized by him after they had talked for a while. Stew Albert had his own theory for why this was so: "I think Victor Jara was a role model for Phil. He *did* what Phil wanted to do. He was nationally famous, he had played a part in electing a president, and he had all these connections. If you had said to Phil, 'What would you like to be in the United States?' he probably would have said, 'I'd like to be the American Victor Jara.' Phil really did identify with him."

On the day of their meeting, Jara was scheduled to give a brief concert during the halftime of a basketball game between a local college basketball team and a pickup team of copper miners. In what

Phil called "the best serendipity of the trip," Jara invited the Americans to join him. Phil, said Jara, could sing a song or two of his own.

"Great!" Phil scribbled in the diary that he was now carrying with him everywhere. "What a break—everything—the mines, the Andes, a Chilean experience away from all this bureaucratic driftwood."

The trip, commencing at dusk, took two hours by bus. Phil grabbed a seat next to Jara, and throughout the bus ride, the two traded stories about their respective careers. Jara, Phil learned, had recorded six albums and had visited the United States; he had played a number of shows in California.

Numerous delays stalled the trip, but Phil was too taken by the company and the scenery to care. The mountains, with their snow-capped peaks, reminded him of California, and he was awed by the sunset refracting light off breathtaking beauty everywhere. Night fell, and just when Phil began to wonder if the bus might be lost in the middle of nowhere, the lights of a city appeared on the horizon.

The basketball game took place in a large sports complex—complete with basketball court and an Olympic-sized swimming pool. The complex, placed in the midst of modest, dorm-style housing units, struck Phil as being the ultimate irony. The halftime concert went well, with Jara singing first and Phil doing two songs afterward, Jara translating after every verse and chorus.

The experience, similar to those of a decade earlier in Hazard, Kentucky, moved Phil deeply. "I sang for the workers," he noted in his diary. "They seemed to like it—I guess they catch spirit—but not words."

After a meal and a walk in the thin mountain air, which left Phil puffing and vowing to work himself back into better physical condition, the group decided to visit a nearby copper mine. Jara, observing an elevator taking workers down, deep into the earth, turned to Phil and shook his head. "They look like wild animals in a cage," he said sadly. Phil, who was apprehensive about going down into the mine in the first place, slipped on his helmet and examined the rocks stained red and green from the copper.

Down in the mine, Phil and the others talked to the workers, including a group of student volunteers, and walked for miles along tracks set in the mine's many tunnels. Jerry Rubin was immediately drawn to a film crew shooting a documentary of the mine, and he and Albert were interviewed for the film. The visit, originally intended to last an hour and a half, dragged on. After four hours, Phil grew bored and, to the amazement of everyone around him, pulled out a novel.

"He was *reading*," said Stew Albert, still chuckling at the memory over two decades later. "Some of the Chilean miners were looking at him as if he was this crazy *gringo*, absolutely out to lunch."

More likely, Albert continued, Phil was feeling claustrophobic and was using the novel as a way of settling his nerves and giving the appearance that he was quite at home in the mine. The confinement of the tunnels, along with the weak lighting and damp air, would have done in a lot of city boys.

The group left the mine just as the sun was breaking. A long ride back to Santiago awaited them, but before leaving, Victor Jara treated everyone to a breakfast of warm, baked bread, and cheese and meat sandwiches. To Phil, who was famished from the day's activities, the meal was as rewarding as the thick, rare steaks he had enjoyed back in Santiago at his hotel's restaurant.

———

The weeks passed quickly. Phil and Victor Jara appeared together on national television, and for the first time in months, Phil enjoyed keeping an active schedule. Chile, he decided, was paradise.

On September 2, Phil met a young American named David Ifshin, with whom he would share some of his most memorable—and harrowing—travel experiences. Ifshin, a former student-body president at Syracuse and president of the National Student Association, was in Chile to attend an international student conference. He had seen Phil perform a couple of years earlier, at the Democratic convention in Chicago, and he had briefly met Phil in April at an antiwar demonstration in Washington. D.C.

The Washington D.C. experience had left each sour on the other. Phil remembered Ifshin as the "neurotic, fast-talking, intelligent Jewish American radical" who "was fighting to speak when I wanted to sing at [the] last big Washington march," while Ifshin "kind of thought Phil was an asshole at that point."

"There were a lot of speakers," Ifshin remembered of the rally, "and I was just one insignificant person invited to speak. A lot of people had been boffed around the schedule, and Phil was getting impatient about having to wait, so he asked me if he could sing before I spoke. I said that it was no problem with me. Well, Country

Joe and the Fish were preceding me, and the person running the podium said, 'No, we can't have two singers back-to-back. It's got to be Country Joe, then you as the speaker, and then Phil Ochs.' Phil was really pissed off and began to create a little bit of a scene, and I said, 'Look, this is not my doing. I'd be happy to let you speak next, so quit ragging me about it. I'll do whatever they tell me. It's up to them.' "

In Chile, the two were finally able to work out the misunderstanding and, in the process, become good friends. Ifshin had an irreverent sense of humor that Phil was delighted to discover one evening while they were sitting in the hotel bar and getting pleasantly drunk on Chilean wine.

For weeks, Jerry Rubin had been getting on Phil's nerves, sometimes by acting in what Phil considered to be an inappropriate manner, sometimes just because the two had been traveling together too long and were getting tired of each other. Rubin, who was perhaps second only to Phil when it came to complaining about real or imagined illnesses, had come down with what was probably a minor upper-respiratory infection shortly after his arrival in Chile, but as the weeks passed and the ailment showed no sign of going away, Rubin was convinced that he had caught something more serious— perhaps even life-threatening.

"Phil was just disgusted," Ifshin recalled. "He was convinced that Jerry was really overacting. He wouldn't let any doctor in Chile touch him because he was convinced that no doctor in the country would be able to take care of him, so he wanted to go home because he couldn't get adequate medical care. We were sitting at the bar, and Phil was bitching about what a big baby Jerry was about all this, about how Mr. Revolutionary—Che Guevara with war paint—gets a cold and thinks he's dying and wants to Medivac back to the States. So I said—in *jest*—'We ought to find somebody to dress up like one of those witch doctors and send him up there with a big jar of leeches.' I was just kidding, but Phil got real serious. 'We gotta do it,' he said. 'We gotta do it.' He wanted to go out and get somebody."

Nothing ever came of the prank, but Ifshin's suggestion sealed their friendship.

By mid-September, Phil was reaching the end of his patience with Rubin. He and Jerry argued all the time, often about unimportant matters, and it was clear to both that their time together on the trip was reaching the end. Rubin was ready to move on, either to another country or back to the United States, whereas Phil was considering a side trip to Argentina. Phil's plans took a definite shape when a group of Uruguayans visited David Ifshin and invited him to speak at a university rally in Montevideo on October 8—the anniversary of Che Guevara's death.

Ifshin, who knew virtually nothing about Uruguay or its politics, saw the invitation as an ideal opportunity to visit another country.

"Look," he told the Uruguayans, "I'm not really that important. In my judgment, the guy you should really care about is Phil Ochs. He's somebody who will really have an impact."

The Uruguayans had never heard of Phil, but they agreed to have him participate at the rally. "If he's your friend," they told Ifshin, "you can bring him too."

Phil was excited about the prospects. The new plan now had him heading down to Argentina, where he would spend a few days with Ifshin before they traveled to Uruguay for the rally. He had no way of knowing, as they made their plans, that they were about to embark on the adventure of a lifetime.

———

Before leaving Chile, Phil visited the Alacumbra Desert where, on the spur of the moment, he took some mescaline and spent the day marveling at the natural beauty around him and ruminating about his lot in life. At first, the drug frightened him and he worried that he might pass out, but, as he noted in his journal, he was able to settle down after a while:

> Go with time—don't fight against it—flow—in the moonscape a hard crust—the purest, cleanest spot in this corrupted world— a selfish man would never come here—after about 2 hrs, start to feel better—gain confidence—actually feel my strength returning—almost ecstasy—realize how I am divorced from my sensations—in LA now I would be sitting in Schwab's eating pork & reading about assholes & trivia—in America you learn to love killers—Wayne—Murphy—killers hide behind beauty . . .

In the desert valley, Phil began to believe that he was part of nature. He removed his clothing and, lying naked on the ground and feeling the sun wash over his body like a cleansing force, he tried to encourage himself to take better control over his life. "I must push myself to the limit," he vowed. "If lying naked in the middle of the valley of the moon won't inspire you, perhaps you weren't meant to be a songwriter. How can I overcome my stupid fears?"

After nightfall, Phil spent a couple more hours in the desert, looking out at the stars and continuing his self-examination. For all of his questions, he had very few answers.

————

Phil flew to Buenos Aires at the beginning of October. Jerry Rubin and Stew Albert had left Chile a short time earlier, and with David Ifshin off on his own, hitchhiking his way to Argentina, Phil found himself without a traveling companion for the first time since he had arrived in South America. Being alone didn't faze him. By now, he was a comfortable tourist, open to exploring anything and everything a city had to offer. In Buenos Aires, he hit the streets with a fervor, sightseeing and checking out the city's restaurants and movie houses.

The past couple of weeks had been rough. Although he and Rubin had parted amicably, the tension between the two had been, at times, almost unbearable. To make matters worse, Phil was battling physical ailments that left him feeling worn out and irritable. A bad reaction to a small-pox vaccination brought on a nasty fever, and if that weren't bad enough, Phil had to contend with the effects of a case of the clap that he'd caught while visiting a prostitute in Santiago. Phil was in poor physical condition to begin with, bloated from months of excessive drinking and eating all the wrong foods, and by the time he flew to Buenos Aires, he had promised himself that he would make an effort to work himself back into shape when he returned to the States.

David Ifshin caught up to Phil in Buenos Aires a couple of days after Phil's arrival in the city. Phil immediately insisted on taking Ifshin to see *Gone with the Wind*, a movie that the younger American had somehow never managed to see, and the two went on to spend the better part of a week touring the city by day and sitting around and talking late into the evening. In Chile, Phil had introduced Ifshin to his nightly routine of huge salads, steaks, wine, and cigars. Phil loved nothing more than to settle back in an old stuffed chair, the smoke from a Cuban cigar swirling around him, while he regaled Ifshin with tales from his past.

"He would tell me these great stories which, to me, were just legendary, about being in the Village in '62 and '63, about what it was like being with Bob Dylan the night he first wrote and played 'Mr. Tambourine Man' for him. He told me long stories about the gold suit. I'm sitting there with my jaw dropped, trying to maintain my equilibrium. It was great to see Phil in Argentina, because it was just the two of us. In Chile, hanging out had been a matter of convenience, but in Argentina we became even better friends."

The rally in Uruguay amounted to more than either Phil or David Ifshin had bargained for. Neither knew much about the country's political picture, and both assumed that, as Americans, they would be protected if any problems arose while they were in the country. They could not have been more mistaken.

The rally was held in a large auditorium at the university, with about three hundred people in attendance. Ifshin spoke first, impressing Phil with his simple, humble manner. Then it was Phil's turn. He had just begun to sing when he was interrupted by the sounds of gunshots outside the auditorium. The rally, it turned out, was not only illegal, but it was the first one held since a shootout between students and police had resulted in the deaths of six students and one cop. The army now surrounded the university, and their gunfire was being answered by students positioned throughout the campus.

Phil could not believe it was happening. The shooting, the tear gas, the heavily armed soldiers positioned behind trees—the entire scenario struck Phil as dreamlike. It was, in his own words, "like living in a newsreel—right in the middle of the volatile South American politics you always read about."

"There was nowhere to go," recalled David Ifshin, "so Phil and I sat behind a turned-over table in this courtyard. Phil, being a movie buff, immediately flipped into this scene out of *Butch Cassidy and the Sundance Kid*. He was warming up to the occasion, and he said to me, 'Wait till Rubin hears about this. He'll be incredibly jealous that he didn't come with me.' Meanwhile, there were bullets being shot around—some of which, I think, were relatively serious."

The gunfire eventually ceased, and the army began negotiating with the students for a settlement of the conflict. The government wanted the rally to break up and the students to take down a banner honoring dead Tupamaro rebels. Phil, of all people, could not understand why the students refused. "Why don't the students just take down the sign and get it over with?" he wondered.

The negotiations took forever, with neither side willing to compromise. Phil, growing impatient during the lull in the fighting, suddenly decided that he had to have a cigar. Problem was, Phil had stashed his gear, including his precious supply of Cuban cigars, in the university president's office, which was now occupied by rebel students who had been exchanging gunfire with the troops. Phil, for reasons that David Ifshin would never understand, did not see this as a deterrent.

"I'm going to get a cigar," he announced.

"Phil," Ifshin replied, "you'll get killed if you go out there."

Phil just grinned. "A Cuban cigar," he informed Ifshin, "is worth dying for."

Years later, Ifshin laughed at the memory. "And Phil," he said, "who was not Captain Courageous, in the one heroic moment of all our years, began to run across this courtyard, kind of crouched over. I shrugged and ran behind him."

They reached the office without incident, and Phil was able to grab his cigars, along with the rest of his possessions. "Comfort in the middle of anarchy," Phil noted laconically of his victory.

A few hours later, the opposing factions arrived at a settlement. Everyone was to assemble outside. Students with identification would be allowed to leave; anyone without the proper papers would be arrested. Phil and Ifshin were assured by their hosts that, as guests of the university, they would have no trouble leaving the campus.

Such assurances proved to be unfounded. Outside, Phil and Ifshin were searched and their passports confiscated. Phil tried to explain that he was an American folksinger, that he had recorded seven albums and was well known in the United States of America. Ifshin, likewise, attempted to explain his background. Their words meant nothing. As soon as the authorities saw the passports, they ordered Phil and Ifshin arrested, and the two were then led away at machine-gun point and driven to a prison where they were booked, checked in, and relieved of their possessions.

Ifshin, who had heard horror stories about South American prisons, feared the worst. "I figured I was here forever," he said, describing his prison cell as a hellhole. "And Ochs is gone. I figure, 'Poor Phil, he ain't gonna survive twenty-four hours of this, much less if we're here for months or, God forbid, longer.' "

Phil and Ifshin were detained overnight. On several occasions, they were summoned for questioning. Their captors, finding Phil's cigars and noting Ifshin's dark complexion, originally figured that the two were Cubans who had been brought to the university as outside agitators. The Tupamaros, they explained to Phil and Ifshin, were serious enemies of the state; they did not invite tourists to entertain or speak to students.

Repeated interrogations did nothing to resolve the issue. Phil and Ifshin stuck to their stories. Finally, just when it seemed to Ifshin as if they were going to be stuck in their run-down cells indefinitely, he and Phil were taken, in shackles and at gunpoint, to the Montevideo airport. They were walked to a plane, relieved of their handcuffs, given their possessions, and, without further ceremony or explanation, put on a flight to Argentina.

The two celebrated throughout their flight to Argentina. "Strange to feel so happy to be on a plane," Phil wrote in his diary, noting that he and Ifshin were enjoying an "incredible feeling of liberation."

"What a great story," Phil said to Ifshin. "We got out alive. We're going to be able to really tell people what a great time this was. Jerry Rubin, eat your heart out. We're going to have a great steak and see a movie, and then we're going to see our friends."

They were going nowhere: as soon as they stepped from the plane in Buenos Aires, they were arrested and handcuffed again, and led away to another prison.

––––––

By this point, the spirit of adventure was wearing thin, and both Phil and David Ifshin were feeling more than a little frightened. Their Argentinian prison cells, Ifshin was horrified to discover, made their accommodations in Uruguay look comfortable. The two were kept apart, in tiny cinder-block cells with no beds or mattresses—only a naked lightbulb hanging from the ceiling.*

Although he found the prison conditions dehumanizing and de-

* Ifshin made the mistake of trying to disconnect the lightbulb in his cell, and was beaten when he was caught by one of the prison guards.

pressing, Phil was now growing impatient with the routine. The questions were always the same, and the authorities had no grounds to hold them prisoner. Phil angrily demanded to see a man he knew at the American embassy, but he was put off; similar demands for his possessions were ignored. To Ifshin's utter amazement, Phil even went so far as to complain about his cell guard, who insisted on listening to a transistor radio playing what Phil considered to be bad rock 'n' roll.

"It was the ultimate insult to Phil," Ifshin recalled. "Here I was, thinking about how we could get out of this alive, and Phil's bitching about the music."

Unbeknownst to Ifshin, Phil's actions had been carefully calculated. He had spoken to other prisoners—people held on political grounds—and he feared that he and Ifshin would be held indefinitely and without any contact with the outside world unless he acted the role of the outraged American. He was shaken by the fact that Ifshin had been beaten by a guard, and for all of his bluster, he was very worried. "Despair is really setting in," he confessed in his diary.

Phil never did speak to his contact in the American embassy. Instead, he and Ifshin were informed that they were being expelled from the country that afternoon. They would be put on a plane and flown to La Paz, Bolivia, where they would be free to go their own ways.

Ifshin panicked. He, too, had spoken to some of the political prisoners around him, and he had been cautioned that a popular solution to dealing with dissidents was to send them to Bolivia. These people, Ifshin was told, had a bad habit of disappearing without a trace. "Whatever you do," the prisoners instructed Ifshin, "don't go to Bolivia."

Phil and David, of course, were not given a choice of travel itineraries. At the appointed time, they were loaded into a police car and escorted to the airport. As the car sped through the streets of Buenos Aires, its siren blaring, Ifshin passed along to Phil what he had learned about Bolivia from the prisoners. "We've got to have a plan," he said, "because this could be it. We can't leave the country for Bolivia."

In no time, the two had hatched a plan. Once at the airport, Phil would create a diversion; in the resulting confusion, Ifshin would sneak away and, using Phil's American Express card, purchase tickets to Lima, Peru. Ifshin's role was going to be difficult, since he would have to pull off the purchase without showing the ticket counter that he was handcuffed and shackled, but given the circumstances, they had no other option.

Phil turned in a performance worthy of an Oscar.

"Help!" he shouted, instantly drawing a crowd. "We're being kidnapped. We're going to be killed by these fascists. Please. We're innocent."

The scheme worked as conceived. While Phil and Ifshin's captors turned their attention to Phil and tried to convince the people around them that Phil was a dangerous criminal and enemy of the state, David Ifshin slipped off to a Braniff ticket counter, flipped the credit card on the counter, and ordered two tickets to Lima. He almost got away with it. At the last instant, just as the tickets were being issued, a guard caught sight of Ifshin standing at the counter. He ran to the scene and began talking to the Braniff worker in rapid Spanish.

"This fellow here says you're under arrest," the ticket man said to Ifshin. "You can't leave."

"Look," Ifshin begged, "I'm an American citizen and you're an American carrier. Give me the goddamn tickets." Unfortunately for Ifshin, in pleading his case he was banging on the ticket counter, and his handcuffs showed. The man at the counter looked at Ifshin's wrists and shook his head.

"I think you'd better go with him," he said, indicating the guard.

Meanwhile, Phil was having better luck at his end. His cries for help had attracted the attention of a member of the British embassy in Argentina, and after some discussion, the Argentinian guards agreed to allow Phil and Ifshin to purchase tickets to Peru. As it turned out, the flight they were on was scheduled to go on to Lima after a brief stop in La Paz.

Phil and Ifshin rejoiced.

"We thought we'd pulled it off," Ifshin remembered. "We got out, they took the handcuffs off, and we were put on this plane. Phil and I sat down next to each other. Phil was ecstatic."

"Never was I so glad to see a garish Braniff plane," Phil wrote in his journal. "Total sense of relief—get a couple of drinks, peanuts, sandwiches—so good to be in the secure, dark sky."

But security, as Phil and Ifshin had repeatedly discovered during their adventures in South America, was very tenuous. Midway through the flight, the pilot left the cockpit and made his way down the aisle, stopping at Phil and Ifshin's row.

"What did you two guys do, kill somebody?" he asked.

Phil and David looked at each other. "Why?" responded Ifshin.

"Well," said the pilot, "this guy came on and said to make sure you both deplane in Bolivia. There are police waiting for you." Earlier, before the plane had left Argentina, Phil and David had watched an Argentinian official enter the cockpit of the plane, but since they had not been removed from the aircraft, they had assumed that their problems were behind them. It now appeared that they were in as much trouble as ever.

Phil and Ifshin told the pilot their story. They informed him of who they were and what they were doing in South America, and then briefed him on their troubles in Uruguay and Argentina. They were not communists and they weren't spies, they insisted; the entire episode had been a huge misunderstanding.

To their great relief, the pilot believed them and sympathized with their troubles.

"This kind of stuff happens," he said. "When we land, just stay on board and you'll be fine. They can't board an American carrier."

The plane landed in La Paz, and as soon as it had come to a stop, it was greeted by heavily armed soldiers in jeeps. Phil and Ifshin stayed on board as instructed, and from their window they could see the soldiers looking over every passenger leaving the plane. Phil, worrying that they might board the aircraft despite international law, walked to the back of the plane and locked himself in the bathroom— as if that would have prevented his capture had the military chosen to come aboard. Ifshin slid down in his seat, hoping that no one outside could see him.

The holdover in La Paz lasted the better part of a long, tense hour, but passengers eventually began to return to the plane for the final jaunt to Peru. As before, the soldiers checked everyone passing their checkpoint, but at no time did they attempt to come aboard the plane.

This time, there were no celebrations. Both Phil and David Ifshin were so unnerved by their experiences that they fully expected to be taken into custody as soon as they arrived in Lima. After all, they had been arrested after their flight from Uruguay to Argentina, and the authorities had been pursuing them from that point on. They easily could have called ahead and asked that the Americans be detained when they attempted to go through Customs.

In Peru, the two waited in the long Customs line and, for once, neither was in any hurry to reach the front. Everyone in the airport looked like the enemy. Ifshin could have sworn that he had seen one of the Customs officials back in Argentina. Both scanned the people standing around, waiting for someone to point them out. They felt totally exposed in a line that didn't seem to move.

Ifshin was the first to reach the front.

"Why are you here?" the Customs officer asked.

"To visit," Ifshin replied. "Tourism."

The Customs officer stamped Ifshin's passport and waved him through. "Have a great stay in Peru," he said.

———

What had started out as a vacation had turned into a three-month lesson in totalitarianism. Neither Phil nor David Ifshin dared to assume that they were safe in Peru, and though they checked into a hotel and spent several days as tourists in Lima, they were constantly dogged by the fear that somehow, in some way, authorities in Argentina, Uruguay, or Bolivia had contacted people in Peru about having them arrested.

Such fears, they learned, were justified. The day after arriving in Lima, David Ifshin looked up several Peruvian students he had met at the conference in Chile. He told them of his and Phil's problems in Uruguay and Argentina.

"Don't go back to your hotel," the students warned Ifshin. "They're going to figure out where you are very quickly, and they're going to come back and get you. The police forces all work together here."

Back at the hotel, Phil, unaware of Ifshin's conversation with the students, was busy trying to call his contact at the American embassy in Argentina. He eventually heard from Ifshin, who told him of his conversation with the students. The Peruvians, Ifshin informed Phil, were checking to see if the authorities were still looking for them, but in the meantime, it might be best if he checked them out of the hotel. Phil needed no further persuasion.

The students confirmed their suspicions. "The police know you're here and they're going to look for you," they told Ifshin.

Avoiding the police was not terribly difficult, as long as Phil and David stayed on the move. Rather than stay in the city indefinitely, they decided to catch a train, and then a bus, to the ancient Inca ruins of Machu Picchu, which they explored with an American couple and their young daughter. Phil, who was not fond of Peru, enjoyed the distraction from their problems.

They still had to figure a way out of the country. The airport in Lima was risky because, in all likelihood, authorities would be waiting for them there. Ifshin favored a trip up the Amazon, which would be time-consuming but safer. Before leaving Lima, he had called the president of the National Student Association and detailed his and Phil's plight to her.

"If I vanish again," he told her, "I'm in serious shit here. I may be killed."

Now all he wanted to do was get out of South America alive, no matter how difficult the task.

Phil, however, had reached the end of his endurance. He was exhausted from their travels and was due back in New York for a concert. He couldn't bear the thought of an arduous journey up the Amazon.

"I can't take it anymore," he complained to Ifshin. "I just gotta go back."

The decisions were reached: Ifshin would travel alone up the Amazon, while Phil would catch a train back to Peru and take his chances at the airport.

To Phil's amazement, no one was waiting to arrest him. He boarded the plane as easily as he might have caught a flight in the United States. A free man, he settled back in his seat, trying to take his mind off the long flight ahead.

Chapter Fourteen

HERE'S TO THE STATE OF RICHARD NIXON

THE TRIP to South America rekindled Phil's interests in political activism. For all his commentary about giving up on America, he had never quit following the political goings-on in the country—particularly anything having to do with the Vietnam War—and he still found it difficult to turn down worthy benefit performances. Nevertheless, the events in recent years had left him dispirited. After the Chicago convention, he had questioned whether any kind of activism was capable of changing the system; after four students were slain by the national guard at Kent State in 1970, he wondered if the risks of exercising one's free speech were worth the risks to one's personal safety. The government, Phil concluded, would stop at nothing to preserve its agenda.

The dictatorships in South America, where strong-arm politics could be seen on the streets everyday, helped Phil adjust his thinking. In the United States, people had been beaten and imprisoned for their political beliefs, and some had even been killed, but the country had to slide a whole lot further before it reached what Phil had witnessed at the university in Montevideo, where students and the army were literally exchanging gunfire over the principle of free speech. The main objective, he decided, was to stop America's backslide.

Immediately after flying back to the States, Phil gave a concert at Hunter College in New York, where he spoke of his troubles in South America and dedicated a song to David Ifshin, who still had not turned up in the United States and was now presumed missing. For Phil, the Hunter College gig was an eye-opener in more ways than one. He'd had to practice for hours the day before the show just to relearn his own songs, and even as he stood backstage, minutes before going on, he worried that he would forget his lyrics. He made it through the show without a problem—thanks, in no small part, to a student in the front row, who held up a songbook like cue cards—but he was less than thrilled that his old songs still received the biggest response.

"I can't believe it," he told his audience. "I'm a nostalgia item."

The main problem, Phil admitted to friends, was a case of writer's block that he could not overcome. Not a single new song had risen out of all his adventures in South America, and the lyric fragments in his notebook always seemed to lead him down blind alleys. With all the talk of the 1972 presidential election, now only a year away, the best Phil could produce was a reworking of "Here's to the State of Mississippi," now called "Here's to the State of Richard Nixon." The updated version was virtually identical to the previous one, with Phil substituting the words "Richard Nixon" for "Mississippi" ("Here's to the State of Richard Nixon," "Richard Nixon, find yourself another country to be part of"). The retooled edition featured only one new verse:

> *Here's to the laws of Richard Nixon.*
> *Where the wars are fought in secret,*
> *Pearl Harbor every day.*
> *He punishes with income tax*
> *That he don't have to pay.*
> *And he's tapping his own brother*
> *Just to hear what he would say.*
> *Oh, corruption can be classic*
> *In the Richard Nixon way.*
> *Here's to the land*
> *You've torn out the heart of.*
> *Richard Nixon, find yourself*
> *Another country to be part of.*

That audiences loved the song gave Phil little satisfaction, at least in the beginning. Like its predecessor, "Here's to the State of Richard Nixon" had its place as a political statement, but it offered no real sense of artistic accomplishment. Reworking old songs only reinforced his status as a nostalgia item.

———

While in New York, Phil was reunited with Jerry Rubin, who was now living in Phil's old Prince Street apartment. The tension they had felt in South America still lingered between them, and as much as he would have liked to have talked about his experiences after Rubin's departure, Phil avoided the topic whenever the two of them were together. The wounds, Phil determined, were going to take time to heal.

Rubin was now seeing a lot of John Lennon, who had moved from England to New York and was presently battling the government for the right to stay in the States. The immigration service claimed that Lennon should be deported because of a previous marijuana bust in England, but this was the least of the government's reasons for wanting Lennon out of the country; in reality, the Nixon administration was in a lather over Lennon's outspoken political views, especially on Vietnam, and the former Beatle still exacted enough influence to cause officials concern.

When Lennon heard that Phil was in New York, he expressed interest in getting together with him. He had recently written three protest songs, which he hoped to run by Phil for his opinion. Jerry Rubin and Stew Albert set up a meeting.

Phil had met Lennon years earlier in England, during the heyday of the Beatles, and the meeting had been awkward. Lennon had never heard of Phil, and he received him the way he might have greeted a fan. This time around, Lennon was much more accommodating— almost solicitous at times—as he played Phil a new song that he had written about John Sinclair, a Michigan poet and radical activist who had recently been given a heavy prison sentence for offering two marijuana cigarettes to an undercover agent. Lennon, who knew all too well about the way the government was using drug busts, real or trumped-up, to silence dissidents, wanted to give the case national publicity in his song.

Phil loved the song—so much so that he volunteered to sing it at his next show. Lennon, in turn, invited Phil to participate in a marathon "Free John Sinclair" rally being staged in Ann Arbor, Michigan, on December 10. The rally had great promise: some of music's biggest names, including Stevie Wonder and Bob Seger, were to perform alongside the likes of Allen Ginsberg, Ed Sanders, Jerry Rubin, David

Dellinger, and Bobby Seale. Phil embraced the opportunity to join the cast.

The meeting with Lennon was a huge success. Phil played two of his own songs ("Joe Hill" and "Rhythms of Revolution"), with Lennon joining in on Dobro, and the two discussed politics and topical song-writing. In one humorous exchange, Phil tried to explain the background of the Wobblies to Lennon, who could not get beyond his amusement over the IWW group's nickname.

Phil honored his promise to play the Lennon song at his next concert. He was surprised when there was no immediate reaction to his mention of either John Lennon or John Sinclair, but the song received a standing ovation when he finished singing it. Apparently, people still liked a good song and a good cause. The "incredible response," Phil noted with pleasure in his journal, "was very much a throwback to the old days."

———

Shortly after seeing Lennon, Phil was visited by a friend from the old days—Bob Dylan. The years had smoothed over the ragged edges of their differences, and the two were finally able to sit and talk without the competitive edge that had all but ruined their friendship just a few years earlier.

The opening moments of their reunion, however, were rather tentative. Dylan, wearing sunglasses and a white fur hat, struck Phil as being restless, ready to bolt at any moment. Phil, on the other hand, was hung over from his Thanksgiving festivities the day before, and it took all the effort he could muster just to walk to the kitchen and gulp down vitamins and tomato juice. As an icebreaker, Phil played several of his more recent songs for Dylan, who responded by complimenting Phil's voice and playing one of his own new numbers, a song about Lenny Bruce.

Before long, each was telling the other about recent events in his career. Dylan spoke of his visit to Israel earlier in the year, complaining that he couldn't even escape his popularity in a foreign country. His music was playing everywhere.

"You were lucky not making it so big," he told Phil, meaning it. "There's no one to protect me from the fans and the media. The media is always trying to use you, and strange people come to my front door.

They know too much about me." He kept changing, he said, to hold people at arm's reach. "I did *John Wesley Harding* to create room for myself."

Although, in some respects he would have gladly traded places with Dylan, Phil sympathized with his friend's trials and could even joke about avoiding some of the traps of celebrity. "Hey," he quipped, "I'm no fool. I knew what was coming."

The conversation meandered into every conceivable topic. Dylan spoke of his involvement in George Harrison's concert for Bangladesh, which had been held a few months earlier at Madison Square Garden and found Dylan making a rare public appearance at the star-studded benefit. They talked about John Lennon. Dylan went on and on about D. B. Cooper, America's latest outlaw celebrity, who had hijacked a plane and escaped by parachuting out over Washington state.

Phil struggled to focus on the conversation. He paced the room nonstop, fighting dizziness. His hangover was killing him, and the juice and vitamin pills were having no effect. In desperation, he started drinking Worcestershire sauce straight from the bottle. When that failed, he excused himself and went for a walk, first to a drugstore for tranquilizers, then to a bar for a couple of beers.

"What an awful way to be," he wrote later in his journal. "Even risking seeing Dylan again for these stupid drinks."

If Dylan was put off by Phil's behavior, he showed no sign of it.

"All you Irish poets are dead of drink by the time you're thirty-five," he told Phil, meaning it only half-seriously. He had no way of knowing how close his remark would come to the truth.

———

The John Sinclair benefit, staged before an audience of fifteen thousand in the University of Michigan's Crisler Arena, was in its own way the kind of festival that organizers had intended for the Chicago convention three years earlier. The New Left, broken and left for dead over the past few years, were coming together for another worthy cause—that, and John Lennon's first onstage appearance in the United States since the breakup of the Beatles.

Allen Ginsberg opened the evening with some mantra chanting and an improvised song to John Sinclair. He was followed by Bobby Seale, who gave the first of the evening's many impassioned speeches. The Sinclair case might have been the specific occasion for the gathering in Michigan, but the speakers tried to use the forum to unify the remnants of the counterculture for more activities in the future. There was a presidential election coming up in less than a year, Jerry Rubin reminded the audience, and this rally was just the starting point for an all-out effort to defeat Richard Nixon.

Phil was the fifth to go on. He had been nervous about doing the show, but he was loosened up by the warm reception from the crowd. The stage monitors had been set up in such a way that Phil could hear his voice but not his guitar, and the performance became a struggle. By his own estimation, he did a "bad job on 'Changes,' " but he redeemed himself on "Here's to the State of Richard Nixon," which earned him a standing ovation.

The program, stalled on numerous occasions by lengthy setup times, ran for over eight hours and featured many high points. Ed Sanders delivered a performance that was part poetry and part song, and Stevie Wonder had people on their feet during his abbreviated set. The evening hit its emotional peak when John Sinclair addressed the audience via a telephone call projected over the hall's public address system. Sinclair, who had already spent over two years in prison for an offense that, at this point, was usually getting people suspended sentences or lengthy probationary periods, and who had repeatedly been denied bail while his case awaited appeal, reduced the Ann Arbor crowd to tears when he talked directly to his child.

John Lennon and Yoko Ono concluded the evening by singing a selection of their new protest songs, including numbers about the Attica prison riot, the civil unrest in Ireland, radical activist Angela Davis, and, finally, John Sinclair. The audience, perhaps expecting a few Beatles songs to be thrown into the mix, disappointed Phil with its reaction to the new material. "Response not as big as I thought it would be," he noted in his journal.

The trip to New York worked wonders on Phil's state of mind. Although Los Angeles was now his official residence, Phil would always consider New York City his hometown: "Always get a rush when I come back here," he had written in a positively giddy journal entry the day he returned to the city.

Two or three weeks in town always rejuvenated him and filled him with new resolve. On this particular trip, he had been reconnecting with old friends, as well as making new ones. His performances, as a rule, had helped him move beyond the embarrassment of the gold-suit tour, and the Sinclair benefit brought back memories of days that seemed so distant in his past. By the time he was heading back to California, he was feeling alive again.

"In state of euphoria," he exclaimed in his journal on the day he left to return to Los Angeles. "What a great trip to NY . . . ending what could be my best year—productive—happy—great traveling."

The difference between the Phil Ochs in New York and the one in California was noticed by a number of his friends and family members, but never as bluntly as in the assessment provided by Michael Ochs. Phil's move to Los Angeles, said Michael, was a fatal choice, based mostly on his desire to be near him and Andy Wickham.

"He never should have followed me to LA," he said. "Whenever I don't want to get into a lengthy conversation with people who ask me, 'What killed your brother,' I'll say 'LA.' It's that simple. He had too much energy for Los Angeles."

————

While in New York, Phil had resolved to cut back on his drinking when he returned home, but his good intentions evaporated almost as soon as his plane touched down on the tarmac at the Los Angeles airport. For years, Phil had been a streaky drinker, going for long periods without touching anything but an occasional glass of wine or beer, followed by periods of very excessive drinking, during which he could be irrational and combative. He had now been drinking heavily for the better part of a year. It finally caught up to him on December 12, the day after his arrival in LA.

His problems had actually started the evening before. Karen had mistaken the date of his return, and Phil was livid when she was not at the airport to pick him up. The ensuing fight, one of the worst of Phil's and Karen's relationship, spilled over into the next day. After an evening of nonstop drinking, Phil resumed the argument, berating Karen in front of guests, and before long, Phil was, by his own admission, "totally out of control." In a white-hot rage, he began "beating her viciously like a madman," stopping only when friends separated them. Phil rushed from the house, got in his car, and started racing down Sunset Boulevard. He had not gone far when he crossed over the street's center line and slammed head-on into a car coming from the opposite direction. The tremendous force of the collision heaved him forward in his seat, slamming his face into his car's steering wheel and knocking out teeth.

For a few moments, the accident seemed almost surreal to Phil. He felt a pain in his chest, which made it difficult for him to breathe, and he determined immediately that he had lost some teeth, yet none of it seemed to matter. He tried to get out of his car, but the door had jammed shut. Outside, an elderly man—the driver of the other car—stumbled out into the street.

The police arrived and arrested Phil for felonious drunken driving. He was taken in handcuffs first to a hospital, where he was cleaned up, and then to the police station, where he was booked and locked in a holding cell. The initial shock from the accident wore off and pain set in. Phil felt the stubs of his broken teeth with his tongue; he looked down at his bloody clothing. This, he decided, was very serious: he would probably lose his driver's license, and in all likelihood he would be sued by the other driver. Every time he tried to lie down or get up, he could hear a cracking sound in his chest.

As the hours passed, he grew more and more depressed. Just two days earlier, he had been onstage in Michigan, singing in front of thousands of people; now he was in jail, a bloody mess waiting for someone to bail him out. In Ann Arbor, he had enjoyed all the privileges of stardom; he now had to wait in line just to use a pay phone to call his brother to get him out of jail.

Michael eventually showed up and Phil was released. Michael was shocked when he saw Phil's condition, but as he recalled, Phil didn't seem too concerned.

"He was grinning from ear to ear," said Michael. "He said, 'Look, I've lost all my teeth.' It didn't seem to bother him at all."

Michael drove Phil to a hospital for a full examination. X-rays indicated that Phil had cracked a rib. He was bandaged and sent home to ponder what lay ahead of him as the result of the accident.

In the end, he came out of it better than he could have ever imagined. The other driver threatened to sue, just as Phil had feared he would, but it turned out that he was also drunk at the time of the accident. Not only was the lawsuit dropped, but charges were dropped as well. Phil retained his driver's license and bought another car.

Phil held onto a reminder of the accident: the steering wheel of his old car, marred by the indentations of his teeth. He placed it on the mantel in his apartment, displaying it like a ghoulish trophy that was both darkly comical and ultimately depressing, a symbol of what his drinking had cost him.

————

The accident left Phil emotionally battered and unwilling to do anything but slog along in a routine that would have driven others stir-crazy. Over the four months following the accident, Phil spent much of his time vegetating at movie theaters, drinking at the Troubadour, going to boxing matches, playing cards with friends on Friday nights, zoning out in front of the television, and eating himself into the worst physical condition of his life. He had barely broken in a new car when he was involved in yet another accident, though this one was not his fault. Depressed and bored, Phil again entertained thoughts of suicide—these more serious than before. "Everything is in various levels of pain," he wrote in his journal. In another even more alarming entry, he confessed that "I was going to slit my wrists but I didn't know whether to cut sideways or up & down."

Finally, in March, after a winter of inactivity, he started showing signs of coming to life again. The presidential primaries were starting up, and Phil was determined to contribute whatever he could to help elect a candidate who would put an end to the Vietnam War. His participation, however, was tinged in cynicism. He had heard enough campaign rhetoric over the years to be skeptical of it now, and he had no intention of involving himself in any of the plans being made for the forthcoming national political conventions. When he spoke of George McGovern, his candidate of choice, he could barely mask his disdain for the entire electoral process.

"I give critical support to McGovern," he declared, although not entirely convincingly. "I'm not a fan of the Democratic Party. I'm a socialist. The Democratic Party is a capitalist party, and McGovern's a reformist capitalist."

McGovern, said Phil, was a basically decent guy with some admirable programs for change. As a peace candidate, he was worth the vote. "If McGovern wins," Phil predicted, "he'll definitely end the war—probably in thirty days, definitely in ninety, and for that reason alone he's worth supporting. And he's going to save more Vietnamese lives, which is most important."

During the primaries, Phil sought the advice of a number of

friends, including Jerry Rubin, who was making plans for demonstrations at the Republican National Convention in Miami, and David Ifshin, who was deeply involved in the McGovern campaign. No course of action appealed to Phil, and he finally decided to wait until after the conventions to actively work for a candidate—*if*, in fact, he was going to become involved at all.

Lee Housekeeper, one of Phil's closest friends during this period, believed that Phil's indecision was largely due to political ambivalence. Phil talked a lot about being a socialist and giving up on his country, and he fancied himself to be a supporter of most liberal causes, but from the many hours that he spent with Phil, Housekeeper was convinced that Phil was not necessarily the political animal he made himself out to be. "He was a closet conservative," said Housekeeper.

It was through Housekeeper that Phil obtained his first songwriting assignment in the motion picture industry: writing the theme song to *Kansas City Bomber*, a movie starring Raquel Welch. Phil loved to watch roller derby and professional wrestling on television, and when Housekeeper became involved in the scoring of *Kansas City Bomber*, he figured Phil would be an ideal candidate to write the film's title song.

Eager as he was to compose the song, Phil was not accustomed to writing on demand. In the past, he had always relied on some kind of inspiration, no matter what the source, to move him to write. From the onset, "Kansas City Bomber" gave Phil fits, constantly reminding him of how firmly his writer's block gripped him. He struggled with the lyrics, and when he had finally put together several verses, he was hard-pressed to come up with a melody to match them. What he once could accomplish in an hour or less now rolled into day after day of hard work. When he eventually finished the song, he went to the studio and cut a demo, using his friend, Mickey Dolenz of the Monkees, to sing background vocals.

"Kansas City Bomber," which might have fit comfortably on Phil's *Greatest Hits* album, was neither an admirable work nor an embarrassment. No one was going to mistake the song for "Changes" or "Crucifixion," but it worked as intended—as atmospheric music to be played while a movie's credits were shown on the screen:

> *She's the Kansas City Bomber,*
> *Let her roll, let her roll,*

Let her fly through the fury of the race.
The cry of the crowd
Is the keeper of her soul.
You can tell it by the rage upon her face.

————

Phil's hopes of seeing the world received a major boost when Ron Cobb asked if he wanted to join him on an all-expenses-paid tour of Australia. Cobb's cartoons had been used in student and underground newspapers in Australia, establishing him as a kind of countercultural folk hero, and a group known as the Aquarius Foundation contacted him about speaking on a campus circuit tour. Cobb favored the idea, but he was also nervous about it.

"I wasn't really sure what I was getting into," he said, "so I thought of having Phil along to cover for me and sing. I said to him, 'Phil, why don't you come on this tour with me? You said you wanted to see the world. Here's your chance to see Australia.' It turned out that there was a lot of interest in having Phil come to Australia, so a package deal was made."

Robin Love, the tour's organizer, characterized the tour as "very low-key"—the kind of affair put together on a shoestring budget. "Both were prepared to come out for practically no money at all," she said, noting that it would have been impossible to bring them over had they been at all demanding. Ron and Phil were paid a weekly honorarium for their work, and they were put up in student housing or in the homes of organizers' friends.

Just getting the tour off the ground seemed to be a Herculean task. The Australian government, less than enthralled about the country's hosting what they considered to be a couple of radicals, dragged their feet in issuing visas. Rather than wait in Los Angeles, Phil and Ron decided to visit Tahiti while their visas were being worked out.

They almost didn't make it out of Los Angeles. Phil had prepared himself for the long transoceanic flight by drinking himself into a stupor, and when an airline official saw him slumped in a chair in the airport terminal, rumpled and barely able to function, he refused to allow Phil on the flight. Ron Cobb intervened on Phil's behalf, and the two were summoned to another official's office. Phil did little to ingratiate himself when he entered the office and immediately dropped a bottle of wine on the floor. Somehow, almost miraculously, Cobb was able to convince the official that Phil was harmless, that in all likelihood he would be sleeping for the greater percentage of the flight—which, in fact, he did.

Phil came around when the plane was approaching Tahiti. Then, just as the aircraft was about to touch down, he came up with a wild new scheme: he was going to protest the flight. He and Cobb were flying on UTA, and Phil decided that, to protest the French nuclear testing in Polynesia, a sit-in on the plane might be in order.

Cobb looked at Phil as if his friend had lost his mind. "Do you want to spend the rest of your life in Tahiti?" he asked, thinking to himself that it probably wasn't the worst thing that could happen to them.

Fortunately, Phil abandoned his spontaneous protest, and the two went on to spend an uncomfortable week in Tahiti, staying at a cheap hotel without air conditioning and tooling around the island in a beat-up truck. Cobb was shocked by how much Phil was drinking. He always seemed to be drunk, and it was taking its toll on him physically. He had developed a rash all over his body, and he would claw at himself furiously, never once considering that his health might improve if he put the bottle away.

Despite the anxiety over the visas and Phil's drinking, there were memorable moments. Cobb recalled an evening when he and Phil were returning by motor launch from Mooréa. They had flown to the island earlier in the day, and had spent their time there snorkeling and lounging on the beach. The trip back proved to be the highlight of the side trip. "We were standing on the back of the boat," Cobb remembered. "It was a pitch-black night and the stars were all out in the middle of the Pacific. Phil was in a great mood, hanging off the back of the boat and smoking a cigar. We were thundering along in the blackness, talking about all sorts of things."

The delays in leaving Tahiti appeared to last forever, but finally, at the last possible instant, on the day that Phil and Ron were to open the tour at the University of Sydney, the visas were issued and the two were allowed to enter the country. Phil, true to form, drank throughout the flight to Australia, and he was barely functional when he arrived in Sydney.

"He kind of stumbled off the plane, looking absolutely appalling," recalled Robin Love, who greeted Phil and Ron at the airport. "I found out later that he had been drinking solidly since before he got on the plane, and he was in very bad shape. There was a fairly well-known Australian groupie who had gone out to the airport because she was interested in Phil. She took one look at him and left without introducing herself."

Although he seemed to be in no condition to perform, Phil assured Robin that he would be able to do the show. All she had to do, he said, giving her a copy of his songbook, was sit in the front row and prompt him if he forgot the words to one of his numbers. This was not the kind of professionalism that Robin had had in mind when she invited him to Australia, but she was pleasantly surprised a couple of hours later when Phil walked onstage.

"He did fine," she said. "He muddied up some of the verses in 'Crucifixion,' and started singing the same verse over again, but he got through the concert. I was in a panic, thinking 'What have I gotten myself into?' but apart from stumbling on 'Crucifixion,' he was fine. It was a very popular tour, and he never, ever gave a performance that was unprofessional. People loved him."

What neither Ron Cobb or Robin Love knew then, but would recognize in hindsight, was that Phil was entering the manic side of his manic depression. The excessive drinking, the extraordinary bursts of energy, the inability to concentrate on a task for any noteworthy period of time, the irrational (and sometimes delusional) behavior— Phil would display all of these characteristics off and on for the remainder of his life, whenever he was in a manic state, but Robin and Ron had not seen Phil this way before. All they could see was that he was drunk as often as he was sober, and they attributed his stranger behavior to alcohol.

Ron had problems of his own. When he had first been asked to do the tour, he had invited a girlfriend to meet him in Australia. Because the woman was very active in a Los Angeles abortion clinic— one of the test clinics in the city—Ron reasoned that she could lecture about her experiences as part of the tour. However, Ron and the woman broke off their relationship just before Ron and Phil left the States, which led to a decidedly uncomfortable scene when she joined them later in Australia. The tension and culture shock—and Ron's obvious affection for Robin—provoked the woman's early departure, but not before all parties involved had made themselves thoroughly miserable.

The developing romance between Ron and Robin left Phil the odd man out, and for his sexual gratification in Australia he visited local brothels, engaged in a couple of one-night stands, and even had two brief affairs—one with the wife of a local politician. Robin was put off by Phil's demands that she find him a date or drop him off in a red-light district, but she did her best to accommodate him. "I was drawing a fine line between being strongly disapproving and trying not to be puritanical," she recalled.

One person Phil insisted on seeing while he was in the country was Tina Date, who had married and moved back to her native land since Phil had seen her last. For most people, the visit would have been ill-advised and awkward, but Phil thought nothing of spending three days with Tina, her husband, and their two children. Although it was obvious to all that Phil still had great affection for his former girlfriend, Phil stayed on his best behavior, and when he finally left, he promised Tina that he would never bother her again.

The tour rolled along, a mixed success, blessed by some excellent performances and cursed by roughshod publicity that kept the attendance low at several of the stops. Beside performing and sight-seeing, Phil had to concern himself with the fate of "Kansas City Bomber." Through phone calls to Lee Housekeeper, Phil learned that the film's producers had liked the demo but wanted a more polished version for the movie. Phil, who still believed that the song would open up a whole new career for him in the movies, promised to put together a new recording while he was in Australia. For a backing band, he enlisted the services of Daddy Cool, a popular Australian rock group, but their initial remake turned out worse than the original. Phil and Ron both agreed that it ran much too slow, and that another recording would have to be made.

As both Ron Cobb and Robin Love would recall, traveling with Phil was both a pleasure and a terror. As a tourist, Phil could be an utter joy, meeting with people and paving the way for his two fellow travelers, who tended to be less gregarious around strangers. On the other hand, Phil's drinking and unpredictable behavior could be un-nerving. Ron and Robin conspired to find ways to keep him from driving, but on those occasions when they failed, he would sit behind the wheel, clutching a beer, driving aggressively and drinking at the same time, scaring his passengers half to death.

"It was very frightening," said Cobb. "He would drive very, very fast and constantly pass other cars, and he would be leaning over the back seat, talking and drinking. He would go through a six-pack and he would have to stop to get another one. It was a constant battle to get him not to drive."

After a time, Ron and Robin suspected that Phil was suffering from something more than a drinking problem. On a couple of occasions, Phil experienced what appeared to be anxiety attacks, during which he would stutter and scratch and complain that he was losing the feeling in his arms.

The most serious of these manifestations occurred near Melbourne. Phil, Ron, and Robin, along with a couple of carloads of friends, had gone into the hills to look for psychedelic mushrooms native to the area. Phil ingested two of the mushrooms, but rather than have a pleasant experience similar to the one he'd had after taking mescaline in South America, he began to panic as soon as the drug took effect. In his diary, he entered a brief description of the experience: "Am running myself ragged here—don't feel too good—sure enough—here comes another attack—very sudden & strong."

His panic was intense. He had to have water, he screamed; he was growing faint, his heart was beating too rapidly, and he was losing sensation in his arms and neck. The group did its best to calm him, but his anxiety only increased. Alarmed by Phil's behavior, and fearing that he might indeed be having a heart attack, people scrambled to their cars and raced down the highway, looking for a place to stop for help.

The group finally spotted a farmhouse on the side of the road. A woman stood in the yard, hanging clothes on a line. A small child rode a tricycle nearby. The woman's eyes widened when she saw three cars roar into the yard, scattering her chickens and geese.

"I'll never forget the expression on her face," said Cobb. "She must have thought the Manson family had arrived. We just flew into this yard—three cars—and all doors flew open and we all ran for the hose. Someone turned on the water, and Phil stuck the hose in his mouth and started pacing back and forth, with someone following him, massaging his neck."

Both Ron Cobb and Robin Love would find some humor in the scene two decades after it occurred, but when it was actually happening, they feared for the worst. To everyone's great relief, Phil calmed down after drinking the water, and the group was able to move on without further incident.

Altogether, Phil spent two months in Australia, excluding a week-long sidetrip to Tasmania and New Zealand. The tour, running from mid-June to mid-August, took him to every major city on the continent, including Sydney, Melbourne, and Perth, but he always seemed to have something on his mind that kept him from totally enjoying himself. He worried about the fate of "Kansas City Bomber" throughout his stay in Australia. Lee Housekeeper had told him that there was talk of finding someone else to write the theme, and with the prospects of losing the job dogging him relentlessly, Phil pushed to salvage the effort. The song, one of the most insignificant he would ever record, suddenly meant the world to him, as if he had wagered his entire future on its reaching fruition. On two occasions, while he was traveling on the tour and was hundreds of miles from the studio, he went to the bother and expense of flying to the studio, only to rejoin Ron and Robin a short time later. Nothing worked. One time, when he showed up at the studio, he learned that his time had been handed over to someone else. On another occasion, he wasted the better part of a day trying to get in sync with the band. He finally put together a tape that he could live with, but the effort was ultimately for nothing: the studio turned down Phil's version and gave the theme-writing assignment to someone else.

The tour ended and it was time to move on. Phil hoped to work his way up to Vietnam and eventually connect with Jane Fonda for a tour of the battle-torn country, but it never happened. In Hong Kong, a thief broke into Phil's hotel room while he was out to dinner and stole all of his valuables, including his money, leaving him with only the cash he carried in his wallet and his American Express card. Disheartened, he purchased a ticket to Los Angeles and flew home.

———

While in Australia, Phil had kept close watch on the presidential election campaigns. Demonstrators had turned up at the conventions, including a powerful display at the Republican National Convention in Miami, staged by antiwar groups and disenfranchised Vietnam vets, but there had been no repeats of the violence in Chicago four years earlier.

What really captivated Phil's interest was what initially appeared to be a minor break-in at the Democratic Party headquarters at the Watergate Hotel in Washington D.C. Phil read about it in the Australian newspapers, and he was interested enough in the incident to cut out photographs of the burglars and paste them in his Australian scrapbook-diary. The entire affair smelled fishy to him, and from the beginning he suspected that it amounted to much more than a botched burglary.

How the break-in would affect Nixon and the Republican Party in the November elections remained uncertain. What Phil did know, however, was that there was a lot of work ahead. Nixon maintained a substantial lead over George McGovern in the newspaper and television polls, and if he was re-elected, there was no telling how much longer the war in Vietnam might go on.

Phil's eventual involvement in the McGovern campaign came in response to a request by David Ifshin, who was now working for the Democratic National Committee. After his return from South America, Ifshin had become heavily involved in campaign politics, and he had proven to be adept in campaign strategy and tactics, especially in the area of voter registration and finance. By the autumn of 1972, workers for the Democratic Party and for George McGovern were at odds, and Ifshin, among others, was concerned about how to mate state and local interests with the presidential campaign, and thereby unite the party. Ifshin helped develop a strategy in which thousands of volunteers would canvass a city, distributing campaign literature for all Democratic Party candidates to every residence, all in an effort for a huge party victory in the November elections.

Ifshin used Phil as the bait in his plan: any volunteer who would walk a precinct and distribute campaign literature for the entire party would be given free admission to a Phil Ochs concert.

Phil liked Ifshin's idea when he presented it to him, and in the weeks preceding the election, he gave performances in such cities as Madison, Milwaukee, Indianapolis, and Kansas City. The campaign volunteers were natural audiences for his political commentary, particularly "Here's to the State of Richard Nixon," which, given the election ahead and the newspaper headlines about Watergate, became a kind of campaign rallying cry. For someone who had sworn off performing just a few months earlier, Phil was now delivering first-rate concerts, even if he was drawing on material that seemed to have been written a lifetime ago.

The music left lasting impressions on people, occasionally in unexpected ways. "There was a haunting moment that I'll always carry with me," offered David Ifshin. "We were in this empty hall in Indianapolis. We had to give a concert there that night. Phil was sitting at a piano, and he sang 'Jim Dean of Indiana.' There might have been nine people in the hall, but it was one of the most moving moments I can recall, just knowing Phil and what he'd been through and the whole James Dean thing. I still get shivers thinking about that."

Phil's efforts on behalf of George McGovern, although positive in the sense that they kept him occupied when he otherwise might have been wasting away in Los Angeles, ultimately had little effect on the outcome of the election. In November, President Richard Nixon was re-elected by the widest margin of victory in U.S. presidential election history.

———

The death of J. Edgar Hoover did not write an ending to the FBI's interest in the country's political dissidents. If anything, the Bureau seemed determined to honor the legacy of its late leader. The FBI in Los Angeles filed numerous reports on Phil Ochs throughout 1972, including a detailed account of his automobile accident and an update of his arrest record; a sketch of his travel abroad; an updated biography; and periodic verifications of his address and employment. His drug use and excessive alcohol consumption were duly noted, as were many of his political associations and activities. He was still branded a "subversive" because of "his participation and gratuitous entertainment services as a folk singer at various militant left-wing activities as recent as April 1972, coupled with the fact that he was reportedly one of the four founders of the Youth International Party as an organizer." On July 27, in a standard annual report to the Secret Service, acting FBI director L. Patrick Gray III continued the Bureau's official classification of Phil Ochs as potentially dangerous to the president.

———

Although "Kansas City Bomber" never made it to the big screen as the title song to the film, Phil pushed A & M to release it as his first single in five years. This proved to be a mistake. When released in 1973, "Kansas City Bomber," backed by "Gas Station Women," became the biggest bomb of Phil's career, ignored by radio stations and record buyers alike.

Convinced that his career as a recording artist was terminally ill, if not already dead and buried, Phil decided to try his hand at journalism again. The demand was certainly there: over the past decade, he had published a sizeable volume of his essays and reviews, and editors of music publications and underground newspapers were constantly asking him for work. For Phil, the most obvious starting point was the *Los Angeles Free Press*, where he had friends on the staff and would be given free reign over what he could write about.

His first three contributions to the paper, published in February and March of 1973, might have appeared to be odd choices of subject matter, but in retrospect, each piece is also revealing of the author's state of mind. The first, "The Last Ten Best List," finds Phil getting his feet wet again, expounding on his choices of the ten-best movies of the year. Present in the work is the self-effacing style characteristic of Phil's best stage patter:

> For years now I have lived off my reputation as the best dressed entertainer in Hollywood. But I realize now I have certain re-sponsibilities here in the sodomized Seventies to do more. Un-beknownst to the general public, behind this glossy exterior lurks a fanatic student of the cinema. I see most of the films that are released each year, and I notice several I admired were left off many reviewers' lists. Here is a perspective on the year in no particular order.

And with that stated, he was off, serving up opinions on some of the year's best known films (*Cabaret, The Godfather, Deliverance, Lady Sings the Blues*) and some of its hidden treasures (*Bad Company, Across 110th St., The Harder They Come*). The most interesting entry on the list was *Kansas City Bomber*, proving if nothing else that Phil, if not exceptional in his personal taste, could be forgiving of past transgressions. As journalism, the piece was no better than his writ-ing at Ohio State—chatty and opinionated—but it was hardly the kind of work one might expect from someone of his experience and reputation.

He was much better in his next installment, a profile of wrestler-actor Mike Mazurki. Showing the eye for anecdote and detail present in the best of his songs, Phil tells the story of a journeyman who, at one time, had wrestled five nights a week in New York City, including Madison Square Garden, and who had also acted in films with John Wayne, Tyrone Power, Dick Powell, Burt Lancaster, and other well-known leading men; all told, he had wrestled in four thousand matches and appeared in over one hundred movies. Yet here he was today, running a little bar and grill in a decaying section of Los Angeles, noticed only by those with strong memories:

> Underneath the soul sucking smog of LA lie the lonely shadows of eight million prisoners of fame, many sentenced to solitary confinement. There is little organic connection between people here, no sense of neighborhood, and very little past associations.
>
> Who knows who is living next to you? It could be Nixon's brother, it could be a lighting man for *2001*, it could be your second cousin. No one dares to ask. Some have been dead for years and nobody even knows . . .

As one in danger of suffering the same fate, Phil was writing from a vulnerable position, never quite showing his own hand while remaining sympathetic but not patronizing to Mazurki.

He revealed even more of himself in his third *Free Press* contribution, an interview with Los Angeles mayoral candidate Tom Reddin. This piece, like his earlier one on movies, might have been a disposable bit of journalism had it not been for one important bit of history: Reddin had been Los Angeles' chief of police at the time of the Century City demonstration in 1967. Phil admitted in his introduction to the published interview that he was "curious to find out what kind of guy [Reddin] was," and while the overwhelming proportion of the conversation focused on campaign issues, the police violence at the Century City demonstration flitted at the edge of Phil's consciousness, distracting him to such an extent that, on two separate occasions, he had to excuse himself and leave the room while he took a drink of water and settled down from an obvious anxiety attack.

"Mr. Reddin was very kind to me and was surprisingly patient considering his tight campaign schedule," Phil wrote. "As we shook hands my insides were climbing the wall, but I plunged in."

Phil's knowledge of the Los Angeles political climate was evident throughout the interview and, like a veteran reporter, he knew how to ask the tough question with the appropriate balance of respect and sense of journalistic mission. That much was clear when Phil finally got around to asking about the Century City rally:

Q. I want to get into a touchy area. I suppose the most critical view of you would be in your handling of the Century City demonstration. What is your perspective on it?

A. Naturally, I've spoken about this a number of times. At Century City we had the one and only major confrontation between the people and the police. During that confrontation, the police department learned a great deal and the demonstrators learned a great deal as evidenced by the fact that since that time there have been no further confrontations on that scale.

Now we had information that there were specific plans for violence, that there were threats against the President's life. We knew how the parade was going to come to a stop, how they were going to storm the front of the hotel, and on and on, a great number of things that concerned us.

Q. Let me put it this way. I was in the crowd that was stationary in front of the hotel. My criticism is: when the police charged into the crowd, causing a melee, didn't that put the President's life in more danger?

A. We would never endanger the President's life. He was inside the hotel in the banquet room . . . we were protecting him rather than endangering him. (Reddin at this point visibly began to get angry.) I really don't want to debate this with you. I've answered your question and I don't think that pursuing it is going to do either one of us any good.

Q. Okay.

A. Just go back and pick up old copies of the *Free Press*. I was the front page subject for the next three or four months as a result of that. I don't want to go over it again.

Over the next few years, as Phil's career plummeted into oblivion, a number of his friends, including editors and reporters, suggested that Phil turn to journalism as a second career. The three pieces in the *Los Angeles Free Press*, along with articles he would write for the paper later in the year, indicated that Phil still possessed the professional tools of a good reporter. What he did not possess was the ability to stay focused. That would become clearer in the months to come.

Phil needed to perform again, if for no other reason than to replace his dwindling bank account. He was not poor by any means, but he was getting nothing to speak of from his royalty accounts, and his sporadic performances earned him less than he needed to keep up with his spending. Michael, who had formed Michael Ochs Management in early 1973, wanted to book Phil on a coast-to-coast tour. Phil wasn't certain he was ready to play at all.

His friends worried about his well-being. Not only was he shying away from work, but he was living a very unhealthy lifestyle, eating poorly and getting very little exercise. He was drinking so heavily that even he was becoming alarmed. A violent altercation with Karen had brought their relationship to an ugly, unceremonious ending. At the rate he was going, Phil was headed toward disaster, perhaps even fulfilling his own prophecy of dying at an early age.

Phil finally relented and instructed Michael to schedule a limited tour of the country's biggest cities, opening on the East Coast and working its way westward. This time, however, there would be no discussion about Phil's playing large venues. Michael wisely booked him into clubs and coffeehouses, beginning with a two-show stint at Folk City in New York.

As Phil himself might have predicted, the tour was a mixed success. Most of the shows sold out, and the reviews, almost without exception, were favorable. As always, Phil used the stage as his soapbox, expounding at length about Watergate and the corrupt Nixon administration. It was now time for people to become active again, he insisted, although he acknowledged, rather sourly, that the world had grown apathetic in the seventies.

"There may be some of you who won't believe this," he said sarcastically to one of his audiences, "but people actually used to march in the street carrying signs. Of course, now we've got our downers and our gurus to keep us happy."

His statement was honest and symbolic of what Phil knew to be true: the parade was passing him by. All he needed for confirmation of this was a quick reading of his concert review headlines: "Ochs Still Marching to the Drums of the '60s," "Phil Ochs: A Bit of Nostalgia," "Sixties' Phil Ochs is Alive and Singing." A Chicago critic, in a positive notice, observed that "seeing Phil Ochs . . . was a bit like watching a vivid documentary on the 1960s—an experience simultaneously entertaining, interesting, and more than a little sad."

Throughout the tour, Phil was forthright, to the point of being almost apologetic, about the writer's block that had kept him from producing new material. "I've been sitting too long in California," he told an audience in Philadelphia. "I've been living there for five years and I've been singing off and on, but not that steadily because I've been having trouble writing. So I decided to come out and sing anyway, loosen up my vocal chords and get back into the easy feelings I used to have when playing the guitar in the hope that some songs will come."

Fans were sympathetic—to such an extent that, in California, a reporter began an "Inspire Phil Ochs" campaign in the *Berkeley Barb*. Taking the lead, A & M Records, printed and distributed buttons with the slogan emblazoned on them, all with the hope of making light of what was becoming a serious situation. Sadly, none of it helped. New songs were not forthcoming.

———

The tour had its golden moments, not the least of which occurred early on, in New York, when Phil appeared with Dave Van Ronk and Patrick Sky on a WBAI radio concert. Phil had been seeing a lot of Van Ronk while he was in the city, and Van Ronk invited Phil to join him and Sky on the scheduled "Free Store" concert.

The program, known to Ochs fans as the "Drunken Folkies Show," harkened back to the Greenwich Village days of the mid-sixties, when the folksingers would gather at the Kettle of Fish and spend evening after evening discussing music, arguing politics, playing cards, drinking, and showing off their newest compositions, or to Phil's own days as a guest on WBAI's all-night radio show, when he and Arthur Gorson would pop into the studio and talk for hours about politics and the folk scene. Now, the atmosphere in the studio was easygoing, with the three singers sitting on stools and bantering back and forth, much to the pleasure of the studio audience. All three had been drinking heavily prior to the show, but the alcohol consumption, rather than detract from the program, seemed to spur them on. After Phil played "Flower Lady," Van Ronk needled him about the subject of his song.

"There was a Cadillac parked over on Houston Street, waiting for her every night after she'd sold her flowers," he told Phil. "She would hobble out of the restaurants, and by the time she was south of Bleecker, her walk would improve considerably."

The good-natured parrying went on for hours. Van Ronk, in particular, enjoyed the occasion. He and Phil had debated regularly in their Greenwich Village days, and it was always stimulating and entertaining to work up a spirited debate with Phil.

"We enjoyed arguing with each other," Van Ronk noted two decades later, adding that there was always an element of humor in their discussions. "Phil was a clever debater, and you crossed swords with him at your own risk. However good you were, there was no guarantee that you were going to pull out of that argument with your skin on your back."

The highlight of the evening was Phil's disagreement with Van Ronk on Nixon and Watergate. Phil believed that Nixon was heavily involved in the Watergate break-in and coverup, and he was convinced that when the word became public, Nixon would be impeached by the Senate.

Van Ronk begged to differ. "You underestimate the cowardice of the United States Senate," he countered.

Phil clung to his belief that justice would ultimately prevail. The main test was getting the word out. "I hereby accuse Richard Nixon as being the man behind Watergate," he said. "I believe this is the first time over the mass media that this has been said. Richard Nixon was the guy who planned Watergate. I hereby would like to start a little movement here in New York City to impeach Richard Nixon. Spread the word around, tell everybody you know, call up your pals on the West Coast and let's get the word out, because the straight media is too chicken."

For good measure, Phil and Van Ronk placed a bet on the air, Phil wagering that Nixon would be impeached and leave office in disgrace, Van Ronk betting that Nixon would survive his term. Years later, Van Ronk laughed at the memory. "I think I owe Phil a hundred bucks," he quipped.

Although Nixon left office before he faced impeachment, Phil turned out to be remarkably astute in his interpretation of the Watergate story and its implications. He was obsessed with the story from the beginning, spending countless hours watching television news reports, reading newspaper accounts, and filing clippings on Watergate in scrapbooks. His idealism had been sparked once again, and in the weeks following his radio debate with Van Ronk, he continued to formulate his hope for a grassroots movement to impeach Nixon.

"I think it's very important right now to mobilize," he told Studs Terkel when the tour brought him to Chicago and to Terkel's highly acclaimed radio show. "I think we're coming out of a kind of deep sleep with the breaking of the Watergate scandal. There was tremendous activism in the Sixties, which was effectively blocked, I think, by the two administrations—Johnson and Nixon. I think what Nixon was about was the creation of a total police state, step by step: the repression of the press, of individuals . . . step by step, taking away all the advances that have been made. But he got too arrogant and went too far and it exploded with Watergate. At that point, people had stopped being activists and had developed a sense of despair, frustration, and mainly impotence, and had, I guess, become very self-disinvolved, either by going to the countryside, or drugs, or self-examination, yoga, gurus, or what-have-you."

These same people, Phil insisted, were ready to reclaim their country. A song like "Here's to the State of Richard Nixon," written long before the facts of Watergate had been known to the public, was now a tool for mobilizing people, and this gave Phil his pleasure while he was on his tour. He would find a way to live, however uncomfortably, with his status as a nostalgia act as long as there was the tiniest chance that he could still move people to action.

Chapter Fifteen

AN EVENING WITH SALVADOR ALLENDE

IN LATE SEPTEMBER, Phil flew to Africa for what he hoped would be a two-month period of restful travel and relaxation.

The past couple of months had been hectic, with Phil staying as active as he had been since his move to California. He had enjoyed a brief tour of Canada, and had performed at several political rallies and demonstrations, including an August 25 benefit for the Gainesville Eight. He continued to publish an occasional piece of journalism, contributing an excellent essay on Watergate to the *Los Angeles Weekly News* and an article on movie star Bruce Lee to the *Los Angeles Free Press*. His public commentary, whether written or spoken, remained outwardly cynical, yet the mere fact that he was working steadily and carrying a new political torch seemed to suggest that the ghost of the old Phil Ochs was lurking about, waiting for the right moment to nudge him back into another creative cycle.

Phil looked forward to his trip to Africa. Once again, his traveling companion would be David Ifshin, who had left the United States after the 1972 elections and settled onto a kibbutz in Israel. Phil and David had corresponded on an irregular basis, and in one of his letters, Phil had proposed that he and Ifshin travel through eastern Africa together. Ifshin was all for it. According to the plan, they would tour parts of the continent separately and then meet on a designated date in Kenya.

Phil's itinerary included visits to Ethiopia, Kenya, Tanzania, Malawi, and South Africa. The countries in Africa always seemed to be in a state of transition, and Phil was hopeful of seeing firsthand the kind of revolutionary spirit he had witnessed two years earlier in South America. He was especially interested in Idi Amin, whose iron reign in Uganda was being widely reported in newspapers around the world. Phil desperately wanted to travel to Uganda and, with any luck, actually meet the dictator face-to-face.

Africa invigorated Phil. He loved much of the music he heard, and he was fascinated by the sound of the various languages and dialects. The people impressed him as being some of the most gentle souls he had ever encountered. In no time, he had met and befriended a number of native musicians, and in a rare seizure of inspiration, he decided to record a couple of songs with them. He called Jerry Moss at A & M and asked him to set up studio arrangements in Nairobi.

Phil hoped to deduct his travel expenses on his next year's income tax returns, and with this in mind, he scheduled a handful of concerts in different cities across Africa. In Dar-es-Salaam, he would be appearing as the headliner in a benefit for the Institute of Adult Education. He also booked performances at the University of Witwatersrand and at a hotel club in Johannesburg.

Dar-es-Salaam proved to be his undoing. One evening, while walking alone on the beach, he was attacked by three men, who jumped him from behind, strangling him and beating him to unconsciousness before robbing him and leaving him for dead. He was found early the next morning, still unconscious, and was taken to a nearby hospital. His vocal chords had been ruptured while he was being choked, and to Phil's horror, he could no longer sing the upper three or four notes in his vocal range. The sweet-sounding quality in his voice now sounded raspy and harsh. Doctors were guarded in their prognoses: his voice might return on its own in time, but he was warned not even so much as attempt to sing for the time being.

Phil stayed in the hospital for several days, during which he replayed the mugging over and over in his head. He was certain that he had never seen his assailants before, but he found it difficult to believe that he was simply the victim of random violence. He was especially bothered by the fact that he had been strangled. The people attacking him could have easily incapacitated him and robbed him without choking him. Did they know he earned his living as a singer? Had they been hired by someone to strangle him?

The more he considered it, the more convinced he became that the attack might not have been a random act. He had always feared that he would be killed onstage, perhaps by someone hired by the government to do the job. He never doubted that he was being watched by the FBI, just as he was certain that his international movement was being monitored, perhaps by the CIA. There were, of course, no definitive answers—only additional questions, including the big one that begged to be answered: How would all this affect his career? For the time being, there was no way of knowing.

———

Despite the mugging in Dar-es-Salaam, Phil was determined to complete his tour of Africa. He was still due to meet David Ifshin, and with any luck at all, his voice might return by the time of his scheduled concert in Johannesburg.

Phil hooked up with Ifshin on the appointed date. David had not seen Phil since their work on the McGovern campaign, and he was shocked to see how badly Phil had let himself go over the past year.

"I vividly remember waiting for him outdoors as his plane landed in Nairobi," said Ifshin. "He'd been strangled by muggers and he was really out of it. He had deteriorated badly from our adventure in South America. Almost the first thing he said was, 'We're going to have to control the drinking. You gotta help me stop on this trip. All I want is one beer a day.' Well, compared to our prior drinking in South America and the United States, one beer a day was like total abstinence."

For the most part, Phil was able to restrict himself to just a beer or two a day, and his self-discipline helped make the trip a pleasant one. On his first night in Nairobi, Phil was in a sour mood, blaming his mugging on Ifshin by suggesting that it never would have happened had David been there to protect him. Ifshin let Phil vent his frustration, and as the evening grew longer it was like old times again, with each filling in the other on the recent events in his life.

Ifshin rented a Volkswagen Beetle, and he and Phil made their way around Africa, driving the tiny car all over Kenya and Tanzania, visiting out-of-the-way sites near Lake Victoria and exploring the Serengeti Plain. Phil still wanted to go to Uganda, but Ifshin refused to humor him. He had Israeli stamps all over his passport, he told Phil, and he was not about to enter a hostile country and risk the kind of tribulations they had endured in South America—or worse.

Phil befriended people wherever he went. As Ifshin recalled, one of the high points of the trip was an evening spent, at the invitation of one of their new friends, in a tiny Kenyan village far away from the amenities of modern civilization, where Phil, David, and a small group of Africans sat in a hut, shared good African beer, and talked long into the night.

"Phil and I were at the height of our adventure," said Ifshin. "We were way out in this tiny village, the only two Westerners around, talking to these wonderful people. There was only one lantern burning, and you could hear lions roaring in the distance. Phil was talking and our friend was translating back into Swahili. We were talking about the States and they were just fascinated by it. Finally, one of them turned to our friend and said, 'Have you actually been to America?' And our friend said, 'Yes, I went to school in Oregon.' 'Were you in New York?' 'Yes.' 'Weren't you terrified?' Phil thought that was hysterical, and he loved telling the story afterwards."

For all of his talk about enjoying the rugged safari lifestyle, Phil preferred to stay in his own private room in city hotels. Ifshin, on the other hand, was quite the opposite. He loved nothing more than to roll up in a sleeping bag or parka and sleep under the stars. Throughout their travels in Africa, the two alternated between camping and staying in hotels. They would camp for several days at a time, until Phil could stand sleeping in a tent no longer, at which point they would head for more comfortable lodging.

This arrangement ultimately led to their most harrowing experience in Africa. They had been camping on the Serengeti Plain for several days, and Phil, tired of sleeping on the ground and wanting a good meal, demanded that they spend a night or two in a nearby tourist lodge. Ifshin agreed. However, when they arrived at the lodge, they discovered there were no rooms available. Rather than immediately head out in search of a campsite, they decided to repair to the lodge's bar for a few drinks. Both were delighted to find several airline stewardesses sitting in the bar, and Phil, perhaps sensing other rooming accommodations in the works, turned on the charm, regaling the stewardesses with stories about his African safari.

Ifshin watched the scene with amusement. "Phil had been bitching like crazy about this trip," he said, "but suddenly he becomes Jungle Jim, holding forth on our adventures in the bush. I just played along with it."

Nothing came of the meeting with the stewardesses, other than Phil's compromising his one-drink resolve. After a few hours in the bar, both he and Ifshin were drunk, and they now had to negotiate unfamiliar terrain in search of a campground. Ifshin, as always, took the wheel of the Volkswagen, winding the car down narrow dirt roads in pitch-black darkness while Phil resumed his customary role of navigator/back-seat-driver. They had not been driving for long when they found themselves face-to-face with an enormous African buffalo blocking the road. Ifshin honked the car's horn and flashed its lights, but the animal refused to budge.

"It's only a buffalo," Phil sneered. "Get out and shoo him away."

Ifshin was doing no such thing. He had read Hemingway's accounts of his experiences in Africa, and he remembered how Hemingway had written that the buffalo were the most dangerous animal on the continent. If the buffalo decided to charge the Volkswagen, both he and Phil would be in serious trouble.

"*You* get out and shoo the fucker away," Ifshin told Phil. "I'm staying in the goddamn car."

To everyone's relief, the buffalo eventually lost interest in the intruders and wandered off without further incident.

Phil and David drove on, stopping at what appeared to be the first available campground. Both were exhausted and still feeling the effects of their evening of heavy drinking. In a matter of minutes, Ifshin had pitched the tent and the two had collapsed inside.

Their rest was short-lived. "About one or two in the morning," Ifshin remembered, "I heard this huge, slashing sound. Something was alive outside, and it just passed the tent. I got the flashlight, stuck my head out the tent, and I saw lions everywhere. It reminded me of how, when you're a kid and you're camping out in your backyard, you're totally convinced that there are lions there, even though you're only twelve feet from the house. Well, this was real. We had lions out there."

As they would later learn, Phil and David had not selected a campsite for the evening; instead, they had pitched their tent in a clearing where tourists often gathered to observe lions passing through the area.

Ifshin shook Phil awake and alerted him to what was going on just outside their tent. Phil wanted to make a mad dash for the car, but Ifshin was reluctant to move. From one of his conversations with tourists, David had learned that, when confronting lions, people were generally safe if they stayed quietly where they were; lions were attracted to motion. A rush to the car would only invite trouble. To make matters worse, David had locked their gear in the Volkswagen, so any attempts to run to the car would be slowed down while Ifshin unlocked it.

"Phil's teasing me about all this, but he was really serious," said Ifshin. "Phil's attitude was that I should run out there, open the door, get the car started, get the heater going, and back the car to the tent so he could get in. I'm saying, 'No way, Phil. I'm not going to do this.' Well, the lions went away and we had a sleepless night. As I recall, that was our last night camping out."

———

The two were soon heading back to Nairobi and Phil's recording session. Phil was extremely interested in trying to create a new sound that combined some of the reggae rhythms that Andy Wickham had introduced to him, with the African beats that he had been hearing on his trip. In the studio, he experimented with native musicians on all kinds of sounds and rhythms, yet for all his efforts the final product was not deemed marketable enough to be issued anywhere outside of Africa.

The single, while interesting in an historical sense, added nothing of real significance to the Phil Ochs canon. "Bwatue," the A-side, found him singing in Lingala and backed by the Pan African Ngembo Band. On "Niko Mchumba Engamba," the single's flip side, Phil sang in Swahili. He sounded awkward in either language, and both of the numbers had an amateurish quality that made them sound more like small-time, self-produced efforts than the music of someone who had been working professionally for more than a decade.

Phil's vocal chords had not healed over the passing weeks, yet he remained determined to honor his performance dates in Johannesburg. Shortly after recording the single, he and Ifshin went their separate ways, Ifshin returning to Israel, Phil going on to Uganda, where he failed in his attempts to win an audience with Idi Amin.

In retrospect, Phil would have done well to skip Johannesburg. Not only was he putting himself at risk by ignoring his doctors' advice that he rest his voice, but he also embarrassed himself his first night there by giving one of the worst performances of his career. He knew from the onset that the show was going to be difficult. His throat burned when he tried to sing, and to soothe it, he drank beer throughout the show, with disastrous results. Obviously drunk and out of control, Phil slurred his words, knocked over his drink, and, at one point, fell off his stool. Then, as if this wasn't enough, he topped off his performance by tumbling off the edge of the stage, leaving his audience with less-than-favorable impressions of his forty-minute set.

"Phil Ochs, a once shining light on the American folk scene, was reduced to a mere flicker last night in a performance that rates as possibly the most embarrassing I've had the misfortune of reviewing," offered a critic for the *Johannesburg Star*. Another reviewer, an unabashed Ochs fan, shared the audience's sense of betrayal. "I am more than ready to accept a casual approach as being relevant to the folk scene," he wrote, "and would be the first to reject a slick, cabaret presentation as being ill suited to the genre. But not even the greatest of performers should be allowed to get away with what smacks of contempt for the audience."

Phil met with reporters the next day and tried to engage in some damage control. "Yeah, I was pretty crazy last night," he admitted, explaining that he normally did not drink onstage. He told reporters of his troubles in Dar-es-Salaam, and how he had hoped the beer might help his voice. He apologized for the inadequate show and vowed to do better in his next performance.

Bad as it was, the show was only a signal of worse times ahead—and Phil knew as much. His writer's block had stalled his recording career, but Phil had always held out hope that the Muse would return. Now, with his voice so badly damaged, he couldn't even sing the old songs, let alone work on anything new. Unless things changed, his career was finished.

———

Phil returned to the States, beaten and dispirited. Beside the crushed vocal chords, Phil came back with a stomach ailment that he was certain he had contracted in Africa, perhaps as the result of an insect bite, and that left him with prolonged periods of constipation and unbearable stomach cramps. He consulted with doctors for treatment of his ailments, but no one could rid him of his problems.

His physical afflictions did not keep him from closing out the year with a highly publicized, fourteen-show engagement at Max's Kansas City in New York. Sam Hood, Phil's friend from the Gaslight days, was now involved with the club, and Phil agreed to do the shows more as a favor to Hood than from any burning desire to perform. Poet-rocker Patti Smith, a hometown favorite, was signed on to open for Phil.

The shows, beginning on Christmas and running through New Year's Eve, were enormously successful. Each performance was sold out, and management added seats, assuring the club new attendance records. The Phil Ochs–Patti Smith billing brought in a wildly divergent crowd, the Ochs factions regarding Smith as little more than a smart-ass, momentary fad, the Smith crowd sneering at Phil as a washed-up has-been representative of an era when people were actually foolish enough to believe that political activism could change the world. Such reaction was hardly surprising, since the artists themselves were both less than thrilled about appearing together.

Ironically, the shows netted Phil some of his best reviews in ages. Each night, Phil would explain his mugging in Africa, as if that might excuse the rough moments in the program, and then he would go on to give a performance that included selections of his best known songs, covers of songs by Ewan MacColl and Johnny Cash, and even an encore number that found him changing into his infamous gold lamé suit. This time around, the outfit was greeted with applause and good humor.

Phil had reasons for resurrecting the gold suit. After years of trying, he had finally convinced A & M to release his Carnegie Hall–gold-suit concert on record. According to the agreement, the album would be issued in Canada only, and if that test market succeeded, it would be subsequently released in the United States; if, however, the album faired poorly in Canada, it would be pulled from circulation without any further discussion about putting it out in the U.S.

As released, *Gunfight at Carnegie Hall* never stood much chance. To be effective, it should have been a two-record set, offering the diversity of the original shows. This, of course, was too much to expect, given Phil's poor sales figures and the expense of producing a two-record set, but the heavily edited version robbed listeners of the up-and-down effect of the shows—the sense of Phil's winning and losing his audience. The best of the stage patter was preserved, as were the Elvis Presley and Buddy Holly medleys, the Conway Twitty and Merle Haggard tributes, and a handful of Phil's better received numbers ("I Ain't Marching Anymore," "Pleasures of the Harbor," and "Tape from California"), but the concert, as presented on album, lacked the cohesiveness of the actual performances, which featured a better mixture of originals and covers. As it stood, the only way the album could be fully appreciated would be to play it in conjunction with Phil's *Greatest Hits* album—and even then, much of the effect would be missing. Gunfight at *Carnegie Hall* would never be released in the United States during Phil's lifetime.

———

On September 11, 1973, a military coup, backed by CIA-trained officers, overthrew the Allende government in Chile. Salvador Allende had been murdered in the presidential palace, and in the aftermath of the coup, thousands of Chileans had been butchered or tortured by the new fascist regime. The new government, led by General Augusto Pinochet and supported by the United States, proved to be both brutal and corrupt, but in the eyes of the American officials, the objectives of overthrowing communism and defeating Allende's movement to nationalize the country's copper mines were far more important than humanistic concern for people sacrificed in the process.

Phil had been in Africa at the time, and it wasn't until he returned to the States that he heard the details of the coup. He needed no prodding to hate the Nixon administration's foreign policy, and he was cynical enough to believe the United States to be capable of anything. He was, however, enraged when he learned how his friend Victor Jara had been tortured to death in the Santiago Stadium in front of thousands of people. The military had cut off his hands and dared him to play his guitar and sing; when he continued to sing, they knocked out his teeth and taunted him to sing again. Finally, when it was apparent that nothing would silence him, they shot him dead. His widow found his remains a week later, stacked in a pile of dead bodies in the morgue.

A fantastic rush hit Phil when he heard the news. "Something's gotta be done about this," he declared, and a plan came to him in an instant: he would stage a huge concert, featuring some of the most popular entertainers in the business, all in an effort to raise public awareness of what had happened in Chile. Any money earned from the benefit could go to helping the people in Chile. With any luck, additional funds could be secured from a recording of the concert— much the way George Harrison had aided Bangladesh refugees with the recording of his benefit concert.

Phil's head was spinning with ideas. He ran into Pete Seeger and Arlo Guthrie, who were now performing concerts together, and they were immediately receptive to his plans for the show. He sounded the idea off friends, who encouraged him to follow through. The concert, they agreed, could be one of the most significant events of the year.

———

One day, not long after he started putting together his plans for the concert, Phil bumped into Arthur Gorson at Max's Kansas City. Arthur had done very well for himself after he and Phil had broken off their partnership, and like so many people who were now seeing Phil after a long absence, Arthur was surprised by Phil's poor physical condition. Phil spoke of his mugging in Africa, but when Arthur heard him sing "Here's to the State of Richard Nixon," he could not see Phil's voice as being so damaged that he could no longer record or perform. In fact, Arthur liked the song so much that he offered to produce it as a single.

The studio session yielded three worthwhile new works. "Here's to the State of Richard Nixon" was kept simple—just Phil and his guitar—with an identical arrangement as the earlier "Here's to the State of Mississippi." The other two numbers were also remakes, each presented in dramatically altered form. "Power and the Glory," never recorded to Phil's satisfaction, was set in a drum-and-fife arrangement, topped off with powerful background vocals that made the song sound even more like an anthem than its original folk arrangement; Phil had every reason to be enormously proud of the work. The other remake, "I Ain't Marching Anymore," although interesting for its new arrangement, was less successful. For this song, Gorson brought in a bagpipe player, who literally marched around the studio in circles while playing a musical line that was woven into the song.

Phil liked the idea of reissuing some of his older songs with brand-new arrangements, and he began to talk seriously about cutting an album consisting of the three newly recorded songs, along with perhaps new renditions of "Changes" or "Crucifixion," and selections of his favorite songs by other artists. This, however, was something for future consideration. For the time being, he had a benefit to work out, which meant assembling a team of organizers.

Arthur Gorson was a good place to start. Phil was well aware of his former manager's exceptional organizational skills, and he was typically passionate when outlining his plans to Arthur. Gorson, Phil was happy to learn, was excited about assisting with the show.

Through Arthur, Phil was put in touch with Deni Frand, a dark, attractive twenty-six-year-old with a rich and varied résumé that included a job as a securities analyst and film distributor; she had also worked as a volunteer in the McGovern campaign, which had intensified her interests in politics. When Arthur told her about Phil's concert plans, Deni was very interested in getting involved, though she knew very little about recent history in Chile. Prior to meeting with Phil, she took a crash course on the coup by reading through every *Time* and *Newsweek* she could find.

As she recalled, her initial meeting with Phil was not exactly what she had expected. In fact, she wasn't even able to pick him out of a small group present at the bar where they met.

"We agreed to meet at the Lion's Head," she recalled. "I had never seen Phil in person, although I had seen record covers, and he did play at my high school's senior prom the year my sister graduated. I called a friend who was worshipful of Phil and said, 'I'm going to meet him. What do I look for?' And he said, 'Look for someone who looks like Ralph Nader.' So I went into the Lion's head, looking for this lean Phil, and there was nobody who looked like that. There was a couple sitting at the bar, an old man sitting at a table, and then there was this fat guy in a checkered shirt sitting alone. It didn't look right. I finally had the nerve to approach him, and of course it was Phil. He started to describe this 'Evening with Salvador Allende' concert that he wanted to put on, and he asked me to run it. It was very quick."

Deni was impressed by Phil's intensity. At a time when people were angry with the government but were equally cynical about the fruits of political activism, Phil came across as a fresh, if somewhat imposing, presence. "Phil used to say to me, 'Unless you're prepared to die for something, it's not worth doing.' It scared me initially, but his passions became contagious, and after a while I truly believed it. That stuck with me for a long time. He believed . . . he *truly* believed."

After signing on with Phil, Deni contacted Cora Weiss, a dynamic organizer with an extensive history of political activism. A woman of seemingly boundless energy, Cora had been involved for years in Women's Strike for Peace, an organization initially founded to protest atmospheric testing of nuclear weapons. In time, the organization had set its sights on the Vietnam war, which ultimately led to Cora's being the only woman to co-chair the National Mobilization to End the War in Vietnam. She had been to Vietnam on a number of occasions, and as the result of a trip to the country in December 1969, she had created an organization dedicated to acting as a liaison between American families of servicemen, prisoners of war, and the Vietnamese government.

"Basically," she commented, looking back on a career of activism that also included work in the civil rights movement, "I was the mother of three young children, who cared desperately about the reputation of our country and the future for my children. I simply could not tolerate this absolutely unnecessary, probably illegal, and totally immoral war. I used to spend twenty-four hours a day working against it."

Rounding out the organizing team was a Chilean refugee named Claudio Bedal, whom Phil had met three years earlier during his trip to South America. Claudio, now living in New York, had heard that Phil was organizing the benefit, and had called to volunteer his services. Phil was delighted. Having a Chilean refugee on the staff gave his project an air of authenticity. Claudio was still connected with rebel factions in his homeland, as well as with leftist organizations in other countries; his participation in the benefit gave the Friends of Chile, as the group was now calling itself, both a symbolic and a real connection to the fallen Allende government.

The organization's first order of business was to find an office and begin the fundraising. A friend of Cora's offered them, free of charge, a tiny, one-room office on the eleventh floor of an office building at 777 U.N. Plaza—directly across from the United Nations—and in such cramped quarters the real effort began.

"We sat in a room that was meant for half a person," said Cora Weiss. "Phil would order a Chinese buffet lunch on a steam table, and it would come with a white tablecloth." Shaking her head and laughing, she added, "Nobody has ever sent a white tablecloth or steam table to this building since then.

"That was the dream room as well as the doing room," she continued. "Phil had his dreams—his grand plan—and it never occurred to us to say *no*. We simply encouraged each other."

Phil's biggest ambition was to stage the show at Madison Square Garden's Felt Forum. The hall did not come cheaply, and Phil desperately needed seed money for a down payment on it, as well as for other operating expenses. Claudio was a friend of millionaire François De Menil, who donated three thousand dollars for start-up funds.

Over the ensuing weeks, Phil was utterly shameless when it came to soliciting money for the cause. He would hit up everyone he knew for any kind of donation they could give him, large sums or small, and no method of persuasion was beneath him. He needed to realize his dream.

———

To help finance the concert, Phil played a handful of concerts in every type of venue imaginable, from small coffeehouses to New York's Avery Fisher Hall. His audiences were now getting a double dose of politics—Watergate and Chile—along with the shows, and Phil made a point of taking up a collection for the Chile benefit at the end of each performance.

"He would come back with bags of money—change and dollar bills—stuck in all kinds of places," said Deni Frand, "and we'd count it and package it and bring it to the bank. He was on the road a fair amount of the time, but the concert was always on his mind. He was obsessed with it."

Phil wanted to have a hand in every aspect of the production, and he demanded to know every detail about the planning of the event. He would call the office from wherever he was on the road, getting updates from Deni or Cora, offering suggestions about how the show could be promoted, and providing new information about possible performers for the bill. His energy, prodigious to begin with, had shifted to a frenetic new level—to the extent that he could only calm himself by taking Valium or by heavy drinking. The show *had* to be a success.

Unfortunately, potential concert-goers failed to share his enthusiasm for the project, and ticket sales moved at a crawl. Phil had succeeded in booking the Felt Forum, but neither the purpose of the program nor its announced list of performers moved people to visit the box office. Phil tried to raise the ante by attracting marquee names, but he found it impossible. Frank Sinatra, one of Phil's early choices, wasn't interested. Joan Baez, a natural for the concert, was already performing that evening, as were others that Phil contacted.

With the concert date closing in and only about one-fourth of the hall's tickets sold, Phil faced the prospect of losing huge sums of money on his benefit.

His luck began to change as the result of a chance encounter.

He was in the Village one evening, attending a Buffy Sainte-Marie show at the Bottom Line, hoping to sign her onto the Allende show lineup, when he ran into Bob Dylan.

"I know that voice," Dylan said, walking up to Phil. "What's happening, man."

"I'll tell you what's happening," Phil replied, and with that, he was off, talking a mile a minute, giving Dylan every detail of his upcoming "Evening with Salvador Allende" benefit.

"Remember that song you wrote," Phil continued, "where it said, 'It's much cheaper down in South American towns/Where the miners work almost for nothing'? Well, how'd you like to work for nothing and sing that one song for this goddamn rally?"

Dylan was not immediately sold on the idea.

"Look," Phil said, "I'll give you four numbers. If you want to talk to me, you can reach me at one of these four telephone numbers."

Phil tried not to raise his hopes too high. Persuading Dylan to perform was probably too much to expect, but he also realized that if the reclusive singer was to sing so much as one song at the show, the "Evening with Salvador Allende" would be a guaranteed success. While he awaited Dylan's response, Phil ran himself to a state of exhaustion, appearing all over New York, on radio shows and political rallies, promoting the concert with a zeal that wore him down physically.

He finally crashed one evening while he and Deni Frand were en route to a radio station at Columbia University.

"He was very, very drunk," Frand said. "We were taking a cab, and while we were driving, he kept reaching in his pocket and putting things into his mouth. I thought it was candy. Finally, I grabbed a-hold of what he had. He had been taking Valium. When we got to Columbia, he fell out of the cab and rolled onto the island on Broadway. I was very worried. I thought he was going to die."

Claudio Bedal, who was supposed to meet them at Columbia, suddenly appeared at the gate leading to the university. Deni, now frantically trying to revive Phil, screamed for help. Claudio only laughed as Deni pounded on Phil's chest and tried to give him mouth-to-mouth resuscitation.

Deni was shocked by Claudio's behavior, which seemed anything but sympathetic or helpful. "He started screaming Phil's name," Deni recalled, "as if to gather a crowd around him, so people would see Phil lying half-dead in the street. That was very upsetting to me."

Phil eventually came around and, after vomiting on himself, stumbled to his feet. The scheduled time for the radio show had come and gone, leaving Deni with the unenviable duty of piling Phil back in a cab and escorting him back to his apartment.

———

Phil heard from Dylan a week after their meeting at the Bottom Line. Dylan remained noncommittal about appearing at the Allende concert, but he asked if he and Phil could get together at Phil's Prince Street apartment.

The two talked for hours, Phil giving Dylan the history of Allende's rise to power and the military coup that had brought him down. Dylan, who knew very little about these events, listened intently. Whatever he had felt about Phil in the past, especially about his politics and topical songwriting . . . however reluctant he was to lend his name to political causes, no matter how worthy . . . all dissolved as Phil delivered an impassioned plea, capped by a shattering, verbatim reading of Allende's inaugural address.

A mutual friend, present at the meeting, was overwhelmed by Phil's presentation. Dylan, she said, had come to New York City to take painting lessons, and he had hoped to keep a low profile while he was in town, but after running into Phil at the Bottom Line and seeing the trouble he was in, Dylan was fairly certain he would do the show. Phil's speech became one of the deciding factors. "He was so passionate," the friend said of Phil. "He read this speech, and it was just so moving."

Even then, Dylan still would not make an absolute commitment. What he did tell Phil was that he was ninety-percent certain that he would appear at the concert. Phil interpreted that to mean that he would be playing, but that Dylan didn't want to be advertised as a scheduled guest. Ecstatic about the prospects, Phil told people working on the benefit about Dylan's probable involvement—hoping, no doubt, that rumors would leak out to the press and potential ticket buyers.

Not everyone was as thrilled as Phil about the prospects of Dylan's appearing at the concert. The "Evening with Salvador Allende," they reminded Phil, was intended to be a political event. Dylan's presence would distract people from that purpose.

"Phil was determined to have Dylan at the Allende concert," said one organizer, "because that would sell it out and make it a success. Phil was always more an artist than a political organizer. He was oblivious to the argument that, to really make the concert a success, we needed a popular outpouring of people with a social conscience, all coming to the Felt Forum to support Allende. We needed people sympathetic to this cause. Phil only saw the words 'sold out' and celebrity endorsement."

Phil, of course, also saw Dylan's involvement as pulling him from the fires of financial disaster. Shortly before talking to Dylan, Phil had heard from promoter Ron Delsener, who had encouraged him to cut his losses by pulling out of the show. Phil, stubborn as always, refused to entertain the notion. The concert, he insisted, would go on as scheduled.

His critics may have been correct in assuming that Dylan's presence in the lineup would move the program away from the political and into the entertainment arena, but Phil's commitment to the political cause was genuine. His ads and handbills for the event looked more like political handouts than the promotion of a concert, and he refused to compromise what he thought was the integrity of the benefit when his friends urged him to change the poster for the sake of ticket sales. Then there was the issue of the kind of problems that his involvement in the concert might cause him. The government could not be happy with the project. People associated with the show could feel the heat as the result of their contact with Chilean rebels, or from their attempts to secure a visa allowing Allende's widow to enter the country and attend the show.

"There was a sense of vulnerability," said Deni Frand, "because you knew you had the FBI around, or the CIA around. You had others who were not exactly on your side. It was a *real* feeling. We didn't manufacture it."

Arthur Gorson agreed. "We had the feeling that we were under constant surveillance," he said. "Our phones were tapped. I had people watching my house from across the way."

Phil drew a measure of satisfaction from knowing that his concert was gaining the attention of his enemies. At that point in time, the CIA's involvement in the overthrow of Allende and the instatement of

Pinochet was only beginning to come to light, and Phil had every intention of using his "Evening with Salvador Allende" as a forum for expanding public knowledge. If he was being watched, it was by people and organizations that had the most to lose.

The day before the show, Bob Dylan called the Friends of Chile office, looking for Phil. He had yet to finalize his appearance at the concert.

"When's rehearsal time?" he asked.

Phil started calling everyone he knew. Bob Dylan, he announced, would be appearing at the benefit. A few hours later, tickets had been purchased for every seat in the house.

———

The show itself was almost anticlimactic.

"I think I was the only one who wasn't drunk," Arlo Guthrie quipped, pointing to one of the main reasons for some of the evening's sloppy performances. Any thoughts of releasing the concert as an album were scratched fairly early in the proceedings, when it became clear that many of the artists were not up to their usual standards. Nevertheless, as a political statement—as a means of drawing attention to the situation in Chile and the United States' involvement in it—the show was wonderfully effective. "Once again," noted Guthrie, "the folksinging contingent came to respond to an intolerable situation."

Phil was completely out of sorts throughout the show. He had drunk himself into a stupor by the time the concert began, and he was angrily vocal about the way the program's focus had shifted to Bob Dylan.

"Okay, okay, Bob Dylan's here," he said to the audience, trying to calm the enormous ovation that greeted Dylan when he was introduced at the beginning of the program. "We've gotten over that—we're over the starfucking. We're not here to see Bob Dylan. We're here to see Salvador Allende."

Such an admonishment, though admirable in its intention, smacked of hypocrisy, and no one was more aware of it than Phil. He had been the one to use Dylan as a trump card to encourage ticket sales, and even backstage at the concert, he paraded Dylan around like a prize steer.

"He loved the starfucking," Deni Frand commented. "He would

very much have liked to have been starfucked, too. That was unfortunate. He screamed at everybody about it."

As Cora Weiss remembered, Phil had dangled the prospects of Dylan's appearing at the concert in front of audiences for weeks prior to the show—all in an effort to fill the hall. "He didn't have the faintest notion that Dylan was going to show," said Weiss, "and he couldn't promise it because he didn't want to be a liar. But he teased it just enough so he could pack the house."

The evening had plenty of memorable moments, beginning with Pete Seeger's opening performance, in which the folksinging community's elder statesman sang "Guantanamera" and "Mary, Don't You Weep." Dave Van Ronk followed with an intense reading of "He Was a Friend of Mine," one of the most popular songs in his repertoire. Melanie contributed a standout performance, and Arlo Guthrie brought the crowd to its feet when he played a stirring new number, "Victor Jara," which gave the details of the Chilean folksinger's life and death. The evening's most bizarre moment arrived when the Beach Boys' Mike Love, performing as a solo act, walked onstage and tried to engage the politically charged audience into a singalong version of "California Girls"; he was nearly booed off the stage.

Politics ultimately won the evening. Actor Dennis Hopper, activist Daniel Ellsberg, and former attorney general Ramsey Clark took turns reading at the podium; Joan Jara, Victor's widow, accompanied by their two children, delivered a riveting speech about the coup, complete with a description of how she had had to look through a pile of corpses to find her husband's body. Short films about Salvador Allende were shown, even as his widow, Isabelle Allende, watched from her place in the audience.*

The Living Theatre turned in the evening's most controversial performance with a work entitled "Meditation on Political Sado-Masochism with a Text on Violence and Police Repression." The short piece depicted a graphic torture scene, in which a prisoner is stripped naked, slung across a pole, and shocked repeatedly by an electrode inserted in his rectum, the play ending with the theater troupe chant-

---

* There had been a struggle to get Isabelle Allende into the country, the State Department allowing her entry on the condition that she refrain from making any public speeches during her visit. To circumvent the order, Allende gave her speech to her secretary to read.

ing "There is no end to the play," and the audience responding, "Except revolution!"

The piece, said Deni Frand, almost didn't make it to the stage. "The people who ran Madison Square Garden were not going to allow The Living Theatre to go onstage naked. At the last minute, they told me, 'Forget it. It they don't cover themselves up, we're not going to allow them onstage.' I said, 'Listen, these are artists and this is their art form. You can't tell them how to perform. You wouldn't go to Picasso and say, "Very nice picture, but you should have some red in the corner." ' They finally relented and let them go onstage, and they did this very powerful bit of theater."

Dylan's performance, in comparison to the Living Theatre's, was almost an embarrassment. By the time he appeared on the stage, the concert was running two hours overtime, and Dylan was both very drunk and terribly nervous. Many of the evening's performers joined him onstage for the final few songs, but in this instance, the extra voices only detracted from the music, which now sounded like a tavern singalong at closing time. Phil, who had managed to avoid singing anything during the show, sang harmony on "Blowin' in the Wind."

The quality of the performance did not matter to the audience, which was ecstatic just at the sight of Dylan onstage, or to Phil, who had pulled off the biggest gamble of his life. For so long, his life had lacked a strong sense of purpose. He had doubted himself as a performer and songwriter; he had watched his self-esteem slip away. Now, for a few golden hours, he felt vibrant and useful again. He was convinced that he could never top this high.

Sadly, he was absolutely correct in his thinking.

Chapter Sixteen

THE DOWNHILL SLIDE

IN THE WEEKS following the Allende concert, Phil concocted plans for all kinds of similar events. In the warm afterglow of the concert, he was quick to forget the long hours and anxiety that had driven him to exhaustion during the planning of the event; all he could remember were exuberant feelings—the lift he felt when he saw people banding together for a good cause. He had enjoyed being an organizer and ringmaster. In such a role, he didn't have to worry about creating or performing new songs.

His post-Allende-concert plans ran the gamut, from the staging of similar concerts in other cities in the United States to, perhaps strangest of all, a gigantic Concert of Death, in which the world's most pressing concerns were to be addressed in a series of songs, images, and short theatrical skits.

"It was going to be the biggest 'anti' thing that you could do," Deni Frand remarked of Phil's Concert of Death plans. "Every single bad thing was going to be thrown into one concert. It was going to be an almost violent demonstration of all the world's problems."

Phil, however, was unable to focus on any individual idea for any notable period of time. Ideas rushed by like speeding trains, and Phil could only watch and feel the energy as it all passed him by. This was especially evident when he and Bob Dylan talked seriously about staging a joint tour of the country. Dylan had enjoyed the Allende show more than he had anticipated, and in the days following the concert, he and Phil sketched out plans for going on the road and playing small clubs and halls for charity. Phil called Ron Delsener with the intention of enlisting his help in arranging such a series of shows, but when the time came for all of them to meet and firm up the details, Phil was a no-show. They met later on the day of the scheduled meeting, at a party at Cora Weiss' house, but by then it was too late. They Dylan-Ochs tour never got off the ground. A year later, Dylan modified Phil's idea into his highly publicized Rolling Thunder Revue tour—an entourage that did not include Phil.

Phil did manage a reprise of the Allende show, at least to a limited extent, at the Troubadour in Los Angeles. The two-show extravaganza, known to Ochs fans as the "Phil Ochs and Friends" concerts, found Phil acting again in his familiar master-of-ceremonies role, leading a group of friends in an engaging evening of songs, readings, and comedy performances, the proceeds of the shows earmarked for his Friends of Chile fund. The two shows, however, did not feature the dramatic political content of the earlier "Evening with Salvador Allende" benefit in New York, and the atmosphere in the Troubadour was much more playful. Even club owner Doug Weston got into the act, making his performance debut by reciting T. S. Eliot's "The Love Song of J. Alfred Prufrock" and playing triangle when Phil sang "The Bells"—all to the delight of SRO audiences. As it turned out, Weston's rather reluctant trip to the stage was all part of an arrangement to get Phil back onstage. According to the agreement, Phil would perform only on the condition that Weston take a turn at the microphone. Phil held up his end of the agreement by playing a selection of his greatest hits, but in the end, the shows belonged to an eclectic roster of performers that included Loudon Wainwright, David Blue, Roger Miller, Peter Asher, Peter Tork, Ed Begley, Jr., and just about anyone else who wandered into the club and had the talent to step onstage for a number or two. The shows may not have carried the political impact of the earlier Allende concert, but they were memorable nonetheless. Phil would never again enjoy himself onstage to such an extent.

———

For all his activism and planning, Phil was saddled with a feeling of emptiness after the Allende show. What was he going to do now? Staying busy provided temporary relief, but as the weeks passed, dark moods became more and more prevalent. His mind, fragile to begin with, seemed to be on a wild, nonstop pendulum swing between his hopes for the future and his despair that it held nothing in store for him.

"It was hard to believe," said Deni Frand, who was still seeing a lot of Phil during the period. "One night, we were sitting in a coffee-house next to the Greenwich Theater. We were actually having a fun time. We were watching some guy devouring a watermelon, and it became so contagious that we were devouring watermelon ourselves, like in a whole, wonderful watermelon orgy. But then Phil went into this litany that he repeated all the time; 'What am I going to do? What am I going to do?' He used to say, 'Today is so bad that tomorrow couldn't be better' because he couldn't see beyond how depressed he was today. There would be these moments when we'd laugh and have a good time, and part of me would say, 'Well, I'll keep laughing and we'll keep having fun. Maybe tomorrow we'll laugh again.' It's like any patient who's very ill: take it one day at a time."

Arthur Gorson, all too familiar with the range of Phil's emotions, pinpointed the Allende concert as a turning point. "Prior to the show," he said, "Phil was foundering and couldn't do anything. He didn't have much of a reason or direction. Suddenly, he came back to life. That was part of the genius of Phil: he was such an amazing catalyst. He was all mad passions and ideas, and it was a big high. Things were happening. It was straight downhill after the Chile concert."

Deni Frand's feelings for Phil had deepened substantially over the months, and she now took it upon herself to watch over him, especially since it had become clear that his growing depression was beginning to impair his good judgment. Phil's drinking had escalated to the point where Deni worried about how it was affecting him. He was letting himself go. He was bathing infrequently, and walking around the city in filthy clothing. Desperate to turn him around, Deni invited Phil to stay at her apartment, but the arrangement produced very little improvement. Phil would stagger in at all hours, stinking of alcohol and vomit and urine. He didn't seem to notice or care.

"When he was at my apartment," Frand remembered, "it was frightening because he had no regard for himself at all. He was filthy and slovenly, and it was real hard to love him and take care of him. I used to have to throw out his clothes. They were so disgusting that I couldn't even wash them."

Deni decided to employ Phil's enormous interest in politics as a means of inspiring him to some kind of useful activity. Former attorney general Ramsey Clark, whom she and Phil had met during the planning stages of the Allende benefit, was running for the Senate, and Deni reasoned that Phil might be jolted back to life if he involved himself in Clark's campaign. Phil liked Clark, and after a little prodding from Deni, he agreed to play a benefit concert for him.

The show, held at the Village Gate, attracted only a handful of people by the time Phil was scheduled to go on. Embarrassed for Clark, Phil stepped outside the club and invited passersby to come in and see the concert. His efforts were less than a rousing success, but he did manage to pull in enough people to keep the evening from being a total disaster.

Phil offered a short speech before his performance, telling his audience that he had worked as a volunteer for Eugene McCarthy and George McGovern.

"I should never have campaigned for McCarthy," he offered, "because he was no good, and I shouldn't have done it for McGovern." He paused a beat to let his words sink in. "And I should never do it for Ramsey Clark." Another pause. "Ramsey Clark shouldn't be senator from New York. He should be president of the United States."

It was vintage Phil Ochs—passionate, committed, and sincere, willing to put his name on the line in support of an underdog. Other, more successful performances followed, even though they had little effect on the outcome of the race. Clark would lose the election, but he would never forget Phil's efforts on his behalf.

"He was a do-er," said Clark. "I remember one time down here, when he played for probably an hour. When he was finished, he said, 'Let's go over to another place.' It didn't have anything to do with the campaign, so I said, 'That's a commercial establishment. We can't go in there and take over for fundraising.' He still wanted to go. He wanted to crash this nightclub and take it over. That's the kind of guy he was."

———

By the end of 1974, Phil had grown weary of New York and was ready to head back to Los Angeles. A change, he figured, might stimulate him into correcting some of his nasty habits, particularly his drinking. In recent months, he had been drinking heavily on a daily basis—to the extent that he was beginning to get a town-drunk reputation among those who saw him frequently. As a rule, Phil could be a lot of work to deal with when he was in one of his manic cycles; if he was drinking during one of these periods, he could be almost impossible. An angry, bitter side of him often surfaced when he had been over-served, and his drunken diatribes could get on people's nerves and spoil what might have otherwise been a pleasant evening. Phil recognized, as well as anyone around him, that he needed to straighten himself out.

Once in Los Angeles, Phil looked up Andy Wickham and Lee Housekeeper. Wickham still served as Phil's sounding board and occasional foil, and the two would spar over every political or social topic that came up in their conversations. Although Housekeeper liked to engage in political discussions with Phil, the time he spent with Phil was important on another level: through his friendship with Housekeeper, Phil quit drinking and began to work himself back into decent physical condition.

It had begun simply enough, during a chance encounter on the street. Housekeeper suggested that Phil swing by sometime in the near future for a swim in his pool, and Phil did. In no time, he was a daily visitor. He purchased a secondhand woman's bicycle, and every morning—sometimes before Housekeeper was awake—he would pedal over to Housekeeper's house, take a swim, and relax on the patio with the daily newspapers. He and Housekeeper would then go for long bike rides around the city. In the passing weeks, a healthier version of Phil Ochs began to appear.

The renewal of the friendship also found the two resuming a favorite pastime—their hunt for the Great Los Angeles Hamburger. The search had begun a year or two earlier, when Lee and Phil had gone out regularly to lunch. Both enjoyed hamburgers, and they decided that it might be entertaining to see if they could find the best the city had to offer.

Phil approached the project with typical fervor. He purchased a scale, which he loaded into his bicycle basket and brought with him whenever he and Lee were going to lunch. Phil would dutifully weigh and measure a restaurant's hamburger, entering the figures in a pocket notebook that he kept specially for the hamburger search. In the interest of fair play, Phil insisted that the burgers be served exactly the same way, no matter where they went. He and Housekeeper would down the sandwiches, and like culinary Siskels and Eberts, they would discuss the merits and demerits of the hamburgers, with Phil scribbling the final judgments in his notebook.

The hamburger search, however, was nothing in comparison to a new Ochsian obsession: backgammon. Lee was a better-than-average player, and Phil, intrigued by the game, asked him to teach him how to play. Phil was a very quick study, and within weeks of being introduced to the game, he was giving Housekeeper all he could handle whenever they played.

"Phil would come over to the house in the morning," said House-keeper, "and he would want to play backgammon. He couldn't beat me, and it became very frustrating to him. His goal in life was to master that game. He considered me a master, but I was a Grade C player at best. Finally, just about the time that he went back East and went through that final madness, he wound up beating me."

Housekeeper was impressed by Phil's enthusiasm for the game, as well as by his relentless pursuit of perfecting it; as Phil's level of play improved, so did Housekeeper's. Phil attacked backgammon the way he had once approached learning to play clarinet.

"He literally did nothing but play that game," reflected House-keeper. "It was not inconceivable to me that, on a good day, Phil could have beaten a master. He certainly worked hard enough at it. But did he enter any big tournaments? No. Did he play any major players? Not that I know of. Did he work harder at it than anybody I've known in life? Yes."

The backgammon sessions proved to be revealing of Phil's state of mind at the time. Although Phil rarely let his guard down in public, he did confide in Housekeeper during their daily meetings.

"Something that started to come up, right around the time we started playing backgammon together, was his depression. I was sur-prised by his willingness to talk about it. He told me that he was thinking of suicide, and asked if I would get him some pills or drugs. This was really my first experience with anything like this, and I dealt with it in a rather cavalier way—and I regret it. I just made a joke out of it, hoping it would go away. I would say, 'Well, if you're going to do it, why don't you do something more spectacular, something suiting your personality and place in life? Why don't you just fly to Wash-ington, take over a plane, and dive into the White House?' That isn't even a joke now, but I didn't know what to do then. It didn't seem that bad. He was suffering from some depression at the time, but he was still keeping his schedule of showing up at my house every day."

In retrospect, Housekeeper could see Phil's behavior as the be-ginning of his final descent into his darkest days, but when they were actually talking and playing backgammon, he had no way of knowing how serious Phil was about taking his own life. If anything, Phil seemed to be getting his life back under control.

————

Los Angeles had a mixed effect on Phil. There was little question that, apart from his occasional bouts of depression, he was now in better spirits than when he had been in New York, and his exercise regime, coupled with an extended period of abstinence from drinking, had produced positive, noticeable results. He had avoided another New York winter—always a plus to Phil—and he felt an energy he hadn't experienced since the weeks immediately following the Allende show.

Nevertheless, Phil realized that he was accomplishing nothing of artistic merit in Los Angeles. He and Jim Glover had appeared together on the *Midnight Special* television program, but apart than that, he had done nothing professionally during his time in the city. Even the *Midnight Special* performance acted as a reminder of his failure to move forward in his career. Phil had wanted to play "Here's to the State of Richard Nixon" on the show, but NBC officials balked at the selection. The old Phil Ochs might have stood up to the network executives, much the way he had confronted the television people during the *Hootenanny* controversy a decade earlier, but the present Phil Ochs, long out of the hub and no longer inclined to try to salvage his career, simply shrugged off the network objections and played another number.

————

Phil was back in New York by springtime. An ending to the Vietnam War had finally been negotiated, and Phil decided that something noteworthy had to be done to mark the occasion. One of the first people he spoke to about his intentions was Cora Weiss, who was equally enthusiastic about staging an event commemorating the end of the war.

"It was important," Weiss remembered, "because we recognized that every important act in history had to have a comment, just as every paragraph has to end with a period before you begin a new paragraph. Those 'periods' took the form of demonstrations. Those were the grammar marks of history. One could not go on to a postwar period without marking the end of the war."

Phil whipped himself into a frenzy during the organization of his third—and final—"War Is Over" rally. At this point, he was experienced enough in organizing political rallies and demonstrations to know what worked and what did not, and in his enthusiasm for the planning of an event, he could be quite dictatorial in assigning tasks to volunteer workers. Such a position, noted Cora Weiss, was not embraced by the mid-seventies version of the Movement.

"The Movement was never egalitarian," she pointed out, "but it did not believe in hierarchy and authority, either. Phil sat in on the organizing meetings, and he was being impossible because he was very authoritarian."

Part of the problem, Weiss explained, could be attributed to the time crunch that everyone was feeling prior to the rally. The war had officially ended on April 30, and the group decided to hold the rally on Mother's Day—eleven days later—which gave them almost no time to organize a major event. Phil oversaw every detail of the event's planning, staying up for days on end, eschewing alcohol and running on raw energy alone. David Livingston, the head of a local union, had donated office space at 13 Astor Place, and Phil would sit in the Manhattan office "twenty-nine hours a day," calling potential performers and enlisting more volunteers, ordering countless meals of Chinese food, and pushing himself to the point of utter exhaustion. As with the previous "War Is Over" rallies, he designed the event's official poster, although this time around he was forced to find a photograph other than the traditional shot of the sailor kissing the nurse on VE Day. The classic photograph, judged the planning committee, was sexist and could not be used.*

The hard work paid off. On the day of the rally, over a hundred thousand people gathered at the Sheep Meadow in Central Park on a warm, sunny day. Phil's mother, sister, brother, and daughter turned out to see one of Phil's finest moments, as he led Pete Seeger, Harry Belafonte, Joan Baez, Peter Yarrow, Odetta, and others in a massive celebration. Phil and Joan sang a duet on "There But for Fortune," and Phil ran through "The War Is Over" one more time. For

---

* The new poster, featuring a photograph taken by Cora Weiss and Dan Luce, depicted doves landing on the outstretched arms of a Vietnamese woman.

Phil, the event was essentially the flip side of the Allende concert a half-year earlier, a joyous occasion to counteract the seething anger that he had felt over America's involvement in the military coup in Chile.

Even so, the "War Is Over" rally proved to be a mixed experience emotionally for many in attendance—an official closing to an historical imperative that had bound the movement together. "It was festive," noted journalist Jay Levin, a friend of Phil's from the *Free Press* days, "but in the sense of triumph was a bit of a sense of sadness, a sense of 'what happens to all this energy next?' "

Paul Krassner agreed with Levin's assessment. "It was bittersweet," he said, "because you knew of all the deaths and all the destruction that had occurred. In a strange sense, the rally was anticlimactic. A kind of emotional rug was being pulled out from under people because then we had the time to suddenly understand, in retrospect, what was going on in the Movement and in our own lives."

Phil understood all too well what was going on in the Movement and in his own life. The rally had given him a renewed sense of purpose, but this feeling, like the emotional rush that he had experienced after the Allende event, was only temporary. In his day-to-day life, nothing of significance had changed.

———

As always, Phil spent most of his time hanging out—drinking, eating, talking, and scheming. He was soon growing heavy again, and anything positive that he might have gained earlier by exercising and abstaining from drinking was now being quickly reversed. To make matters worse, he was now spending more money than he was receiving in his allowance—especially on food and drink—and he was accumulating hefty bills at Village establishments willing to let him buy on credit.

Paul Colby, owner of The Other End, one of Phil's favorite haunts, was especially patient with Phil's mounting bills. He had only known Phil for only a brief period of time, but he had taken a great liking to him and was constantly badgering him about playing at his club. It didn't matter, he said, if Phil had no new material to sing; people came to hear the hits. Phil could play a couple of shows, earn enough money to pay his debts, and actually be in the position of picking up his career again.

Phil, of course, would not consider any such proposition. If Colby was worried about his bill, he said, all he had to do was call Michael or one of his accountants and it would be paid.

Colby was not alone in trying to coax Phil out of his retirement. Michael was always after him to agree to a tour, and, even more recently, Arthur Gorson was pushing him to re-enter the business. Phil and Arthur had grown very close again, mainly because Arthur was almost as obsessed with backgammon as Phil had been in California. On a typical night, Phil would head over to Gorson's Village apartment, and the two would go for carry-out food at an Italian restaurant downstairs. They would then retreat back to the apartment and spend the evening playing backgammon and drinking. Arthur knew of Phil's debts to Paul Colby and, inevitably, at some point in the evening, he would try to convince Phil to play at the club.

"I was sort of in the middle, trying to negotiate something," said Gorson, "because I wanted Phil to play for his own sake. I thought it would help him back if he would play in an intimate surrounding where there were people who loved him. So I was pressing Phil to talk to Paul and work something out."

In time, Phil was worn down by all the talk, and he posed a bizarre wager to Colby.

"I'll tell you what I'll do," he told the club owner. "I'll play you three games of backgammon. If you win, I'll play your club for nothing. If I win, you have to supply me with a woman, a hotel room, and all the refreshments and booze that I want."

Colby shook his head. "I can't do it," he said. "I'm not a backgammon player."

The two talked it over, and soon they had reached an agreement. Colby could select someone to play as his proxy. Colby had a friend who lived in his neighborhood, a crack backgammon player named Mike Halverian, who would act as Colby's player. Halverian owned an uptown restaurant called Knickers, and Phil agreed to meet him there for the match. Given Halverian's expertise at the game, new rules were drawn up. To win his bet, all Phil had to do was win one of his three games with Halverian.

Phil was certain that he had the bet won the minute he signed the contract drawn up for the match. He fancied himself to be a world-class backgammon player even though, by the accounts offered by those who played him, he was only slightly better than average. In fact, Phil was so confident of his chances that he decided to turn the match into a major event. He would surround himself with friends and family, all of whom would cheer him on as he engaged in his own form of battle royale.

"It was to be a big shoot-out in the tradition of Phil Ochs shoot-outs," recalled Arthur Gorson, who acted as a formal witness to the contract signing. "Phil made it out to be the biggest match since Muhammad Ali and Joe Frazier. He went around drunk, talking about it all the time, when he should have been staying sober and practicing his backgammon."

Phil called everyone he knew and extended formal invitations to the match. Such old friends as Lee Housekeeper and David Ifshin were summoned to the big event that, Phil proudly pointed out, was going to be filmed for posterity. Phil even attempted to get his daughter, who was staying with Sonny in Far Rockaway, to come to the match, but that fell through, supposedly because Meegan had too much homework to attend.

Phil's friends might have done well to stay away, as well. In the days preceding the match, it was clear to those who knew Phil that he was spinning out of control. His drinking had reached an alarming plateau, and he was beginning to display delusional thinking, referring to Halverian as Hassan the Assassin and talking about the backgammon game as if it were a huge grudge match. The bet, which had appalled many of Phil's friends in the first place, had suddenly become a life-or-death scenario to Phil.

For all the buildup, the match was mercifully quick, with predictable results. Phil took a limousine to Knickers, picking up David Ifshin along the way. As Ifshin remembered, Phil had with him a lady friend who was to be part of a unique battle strategy.

"He wanted her to take her shirt off," said Ifshin. "He was going to play a game or two, and then, at the right moment, she would take off her shirt. This was supposed to distract Hassan the Assassin into losing a game.

"Well, this was Ochs at his worst. First of all, the woman had not agreed to even consider it. He badgered the hell out of her in the car, telling her, 'You've got to do it. It's really important.' She was looking at me like 'What should I do?' It was ridiculous."

Phil, who had primed himself for the evening by drinking heavily at a Greenwich Village club, was no challenge for Halverian. The match, by Ifshin's assessment, was a "complete massacre," with Phil barely able to follow the action. Between the first and second games, he stepped outside the club and again tried to persuade the woman, now joined by two of her friends, to take off her blouse. When they all refused, Phil became abusive.

"You say you're artists," he sneered, "but you won't even show your nipples, even though you've shown them at parties I've seen you at. Here you are, at this crucial moment in time, and you're afraid to show Hassan your nipples. So fuck you. You're still my girlfriends, but you're businesswomen. You're not artists."

The women protested, but Phil waved them off.

"Well," he said, "if you're artists, take off your clothes. If you're not, shut up."

He fared no better the second game. Halverian whipped him quickly and easily, and by the time the game had ended, Phil realized that he stood no chance against the superior player. The final game was never completed. Midway through the game, Phil turned over the board and angrily conceded the match. The great backgammon shoot-out had turned out to be little more than target practice.

———

Phil had no intention of honoring the terms of the bet. He had been so certain he would win that he had not given a lot of thought to the price of losing, but when it came time to pay up, he told an angry Paul Colby that he couldn't possibly play at his club. His voice was shot, he said; he had nothing new to offer. Colby, who had heard these excuses many times before, argued that Phil had lost the bet and had to hold up his end of the deal. He had already printed tickets, he told Phil, and there were people looking forward to the show. Phil stubbornly refused to back down. There would be no concert.

Despite his claims that he was finished as a performer, Phil continued to map out projects for the future, many of which fell under the umbrella of a large multimedia corporation that he wanted to form. The company, called Barricade, Inc., was to produce records and movies, manage artists' careers, and perhaps even put together concerts on the scale of the Allende benefit. Phil outlined his plans to Arthur Gorson and, good friend that he was, Gorson listened, even though he worried that Phil's wild mood swings and heavy drinking were taking him "off the deep end."

One idea that both Gorson and Phil found especially appealing was the staging of a huge concert in Peru, to be played high in the

Andes near the Machu Picchu ruins. The initial plans had been hatched shortly after the Allende benefit, when Arthur had been visited by a Peruvian music promoter named Peter Kun. The Peruvian government, Kun told Gorson, was interested in improving its world image, and Kun believed that a concert along the line of the Allende event would be an ideal avenue.

Gorson agreed in principle, though he felt that Kun needed to be more realistic in his overall objectives.

"He thought we were magicians and could get Bob Dylan, Jane Fonda, and everybody else they wanted," said Gorson. "After he went back to Peru, Peter called and said that he'd talked to some people about putting on the concert, and he wanted to know if I could come to Peru immediately. And I did. I was treated to a week in the Peruvian highland. I saw Machu Picchu for the first time and met all these incredible people and Latin American poets. It was as profound for me as Phil's trip to Chile, I'm sure.

"What Peter had erroneously promoted was the idea that we were going to be able to do a giant concert, with all these acts, for money. He had said that we were going to do a big commercial thing, but there was no way that that could happen. There was no money to be made down there. I was presented to the government as the Great White Hope or something—as the guy who was going to bring a big concert there—so I was on the spot. Thinking on my feet, I came up with a way to do the concert. It would be a contrast to the Chile concert, which had been basically triggered by negative events. We would now do a big event that would be a positive affirmation of unity among artists in the Americas. The Peruvian government liked the idea."

Arthur had brought Phil into the planning in the early stages, well before he set out for Peru. Phil immediately latched onto the idea, and in the following weeks, he jumped into the planning with manic energy. This time, however, he was ill-equipped to work on the logistics or finer points of such a complex presentation. In the past, he had always refrained from drinking while putting together major events; during the planning of the Peruvian concert, he was drinking so heavily that Peter Kun advised against his traveling with Gorson to Peru.

"He wasn't in a state to go," Gorson said of Phil, "so they didn't invite him. Peter was afraid that Phil was going to scare people."

Phil's behavior, in fact, was beginning to frighten or annoy nearly everyone he knew. He would walk into a local watering hole, drink himself into a terrible state, and rant and rave about whatever popped into his head. One evening he might ramble on about government conspiracies, especially the way the FBI or CIA were undermining world events; the next night he would go on and on about how he was going to change his name and get Colonel Harland Sanders of the Kentucky Fried Chicken franchises to manage him.*

Another side of Phil—an unpleasant, aggressive side—was taking over. Phil had always loved a good debate, often just for the sake of discussion, but his arguments now were hostile and meanspirited, leaving his friends glancing at one another in amazement. Bartenders were frequently cutting him off or banishing him entirely from their establishments. Paul Colby, for one, informed Phil, after a particularly nasty evening, that he would always be welcome to come into his place for something to eat, but that he would never serve him another drink.

Phil's friends implored him to seek professional help, but their advice was ignored. If anything, Phil's concerns were more for his physical than his mental health. His stomach ailments had flared up once again, but doctors, as before, were unable to find anything wrong with him. In desperation, Phil visited a self-proclaimed witch doctor on Manhattan's Upper West Side, and she offered him a vile-smelling, evil-tasting potion that was supposed to cure him of his problems. Phil could barely keep the liquid down, and he eventually abandoned it when he realized that the potion itself was making him sick and doing him no good at all.

———

By early summer, Phil had lost much of his grip on reality. He continued to sketch out wild plans for his future, especially for the Barricade company, but most of his brainstorming took place in the evening, when he was so drunk and incoherent that he could barely remember, let alone act upon, his ideas the following day.

One idea, however, evolved steadily as the weeks passed. As far as he could see, Phil Ochs was dead and had to be replaced. Ochs had been useful in his time, but he was no longer credible as an artist

* Phil had originally hoped to get Colonel Tom Parker, Elvis Presley's manager, to handle him, but when that fell through, he turned his sights on another well-known Colonel.

or as a person. He had no music left in him, and with the Vietnam War now a regrettable part of history, he had lost his greatest cause. And if all this wasn't bad enough, Phil Ochs, once a nice guy, had become a common drunk who was embarrassing to his friends and family. He needed a new identity—a complete makeover in personality.

He could even use another name.

From such thoughts sprang the improbable existence of Phil's ultimate creation—an antiheroic character named John Butler Train, an alter ego who, when all was said and done, would cost him his life.

Chapter Seventeen

TRAIN

JOHN TRAIN appeared without warning in the early weeks of summer 1975, quickly asserting himself into the Greenwich Village scene like an unwanted stranger who refused to go away. For the next few months, he would anger, confuse, shock, sadden, or frighten nearly everyone crossing his path.

With his huge pot belly, filthy clothing, confrontational attitude, and arsenal of strange weapons, Train could not have been more different from the Phil Ochs of the sixties. Train was Mr. Hyde on the loose—a tortured, violent being incapable of freeing the Dr. Jekyll trapped inside. Train, who took his name from Phil Ochs' big-screen heroes John Ford and John Wayne, as well as from the poet William Butler Yeats, was a kind of cinematic character brought to life. In the past, Phil Ochs had often imagined himself to be a character in an epic motion picture; Train was the fantasy come true. He was a Wild West gunslinger in a postmodern, apocalyptic world—a revolutionary without a country, a rebel without a cause.

In an interview taped in mid-summer, Train explained his origins: "On the first day of summer 1975, Phil Ochs was murdered in the Chelsea Hotel by John Train, who is now speaking. I killed Phil Ochs. The reason I killed him was he was some kind of genius but he drank too much and was becoming a boring old fart. For the good of societies, public and secret, he needed to be gotten rid of."

For all of its bravado, the statement spoke volumes of what Phil Ochs had become, at least in the regions of his own mind. Phil had been suicidal, off and on, for years, yet for whatever reasons he had been unwilling or unable to actually take his own life. His "murder" at the hands of John Train was more than symbolic; it represented no less than a frantic attempt to put an end to a life that had lost its purpose and meaning. Phil had always possessed a high opinion not only of his creative talent but also of its impact on society, but his self-image had fallen substantially in recent years, as his drinking and lengthy periods of inactivity drove him into deeper and deeper depression. Becoming a martyr at the hands of John Train assured Phil of the status of having a heroic figure in the minds of the "public" society that admired his activism, and ended his harrassment by the "private" societies (i.e., the FBI, CIA, mafia, etc.) that wanted him silenced.

Or so Train hoped.

Although Phil insisted that John Train was a separate entity—to the extent of his occasionally insisting that people refer to him as Train rather than as Phil—the character was, in fact, an open, honest representation of the defeated Phil Ochs. Phil had never been afraid of wearing his passions in public, and John Train became a penultimate manifestation. The world was witnessing, in painful clarity, the terrible price one human being would pay for caring too much.

———

Train's emotional compass spun completely out of control, with virtually no sense of direction. One minute—usually when he was in public, drinking at a local bar—he would be angry and confrontational, prepared to fight with anyone who dared to disagree with him; other times, he would be all but catatonic, sitting silently and listlessly in front of a television or movie screen, his eyes following the action but the rest of him registering no response to what he saw. Phil Ochs had never been without comment on whatever he was watching; John Train displayed very little interest at all.

Train's barroom escapades during the summer of 1975 became the stuff of legend. Train would enter a Village tavern or club, drink until he was slurring his words and could barely stand, and invariably he would pick a fight with someone around him. In the early days of the Train manifestation, there was very little chance of his actually becoming physically violent—there was still too much Phil Ochs in him for that—but he would become so loud and overbearing that bartenders and owners would order him to leave. In time, the banishments from some of the bars became permanent.

After being ejected from a bar, Train would wander around the streets of the Village, occasionally trying to enter another establishment, but more often than not retreating to a quiet place where he could either sleep off the drunk or sit silently with a friend. Train was anything but discriminating in choosing a place to sleep: park benches or alleyways were as good as a warm bed. He would simply stagger off to a place where he could be alone and collapse, often after he had thrown up on himself or urinated in his pants. To Train, personal hygiene was a low priority.

If he had been tossed out of an establishment fairly early in the evening, Train would seek company for the rest of the night. One of his favorite companions was Mayer Vishner, a longtime political activist who had an apartment on MacDougal Street. Vishner also suffered from bouts of acute depression, and on a typical night, the two would sit on Vishner's bed, silently watching television for hours on end.

Vishner worked as a substitute disk jockey for WBAI radio in New York, and on one of the occasions when he and Train were sitting around and watching television, he told Train that he had a tape that he wanted him to hear. The recording, sent to WBAI by Sis Cunningham and Gordon Friesen, featured a new singer/songwriter named Sammy Walker.

Train came alive as soon as Vishner put the cassette into his portable tape recorder. Walker's voice and guitar playing sounded strikingly similar to the way Bob Dylan had sounded when he initially arrived in New York. Suddenly, Train wanted to know anything and everything about this young, new talent.

"He responded to the tape immediately," Vishner recalled. "Fifteen minutes earlier, we had been sitting for three hours with no conversation, just staring at that TV. All of a sudden, he had something to do. I told him I had obtained my copy of the tape from Bob Fass [at WBAI], who had gotten it through Sis Cunningham, and I told him that Sis was as close to getting directly to Sam as I could get him. He opened the door and he was gone. I don't think he even said goodbye."

As Sis Cunningham remembered, she and her husband had discovered Sammy Walker almost by accident.

"We were getting tapes from people," she said, "and we'd just put them on the table. We couldn't even play them, because Gordon and I were both sick. Finally, our daughter Jane said, 'Let's play some of these tapes.' When we got to Sammy Walker's, we were so impressed that we sent it to Bob Fass. He kept playing it on the air, and he would call us to say that he was getting phone calls about the guy. When Phil Ochs heard it, he called us up and said, 'Could you arrange for me to meet Sammy Walker?' We set a date and we got Sammy and Phil here."

Sammy Walker, Train learned, had been born in 1952 and raised in Waycross, Georgia. Like many kids his age, he had been a fan of Elvis Presley, but he had become a huge fan of folk music while in high school, when he and friends discovered the music of Woody Guthrie, Bob Dylan, and Peter, Paul and Mary. He had been introduced to the music of Phil Ochs when he was fifteen.

"I had a friend from Stewart, Virginia," he said, "and I used to meet him every year at Myrtle Beach, South Carolina. We used to go to a campground there with our parents. My friend had a tape of *Phil Ochs in Concert*, and he said, 'Listen to this guy.' It was the first time I'd heard it, and I was blown away."

Oddly enough, Walker had met Phil Ochs a few years earlier, when Phil was playing a series of shows in Georgia. Walker, who was earning a reputation for himself on Georgia's club and college circuit, introduced himself to Phil after one of his concerts and told him how much he enjoyed his music.

Train, of course, remembered nothing of the chance encounter. All he knew was that he loved this young man's music and wanted to help further his career. Sammy Walker, he decided, would be Barricade's first big client. He was going to be a star—maybe even the next Bob Dylan.

———

Like Phil Ochs, John Train was a man of a thousand ideas—all converging at the same time and colliding into a jumbled mess inside his mind, all demanding immediate attention from a man who, in his manic state, had the attention span of a child. Train could be brilliant when it came to formulating concepts, but he inevitably faltered on seeing them to fruition.

Of his many ideas, a handful stayed with him long enough to merit some development. He wanted to produce a record by Sammy Walker. He still hoped to pull off the concert in Peru. He continued to make plans for Barricade. He gave some thought to buying a bar— a place where he could drink every night and never have to worry about being thrown out if he got a little rowdy. All of the ideas, in their own way, were plausible enough.

He and Sammy Walker were hanging out all the time. He dragged Walker to all the old Phil Ochs haunts and introduced him to his friends as his big musical discovery. Walker, shy by nature and not much of a drinker, liked Train and appreciated all that he was trying to do for him, though he was hard-pressed to understand why the former Phil Ochs had adapted a new name and was acting the way he was. Train was terribly paranoid, especially when he was drunk, and he would constantly complain, always in the most general of terms, about how he was being pursued by the FBI and the mafia. No one—least of all, Sammy Walker—could convince him otherwise.

Train used several of Phil Ochs' old connections to help launch his new protégé's career. With the assistance of Sis Cunningham and Gordon Friesen, Train was able to secure a recording contract for Walker with Mo Asch's Folkway's Records. Train then contacted Andy Wickham, who was presently working in A & R for Warner Brothers, and within a couple of weeks, Walker had a recording contract with that label, as well.

"I was pretty overwhelmed by it all," Walker admitted. "I'd just come up from Georgia and was wet behind the ears, and within a month Phil had helped me secure two record contracts." Even in retrospect, Walker could only speculate as to why Train had gone to such lengths for him. "Maybe he saw a little of himself, when he was first coming up, in me," Walker concluded.

Train was eager to see Walker through the recording process, and he decided to produce the album himself. Given his state of mind, the decision was certainly ill-founded. Rather than enter the studio with Walker and lay down a dozen tracks in a workmanlike fashion, Train elected to turn the recording session into a big party. He called everyone he knew and urged them to the session, telling them that they would be witnessing the beginning of an important new musical career.

Not surprisingly, the recording session was a disaster. Train turned up drunk and out of control, and the Basement Recording Studio was packed with hangers-on. Walker, nervous about the sessions to begin with, struggled to get through his songs while Train disrupted the process with his drunken, heavy-handed directions, leading an exasperated recording engineer to suggest that the session might go better if Train left the studio.

"It was a sad scene," commented Deni Frand, one of the evening's many invited guests. "Phil cared very much about producing this session. It was very important to him, which is why there was a crowd there. And then he came to the recording session in that state. It was very sad."

Sis Cunningham took over the direction of the recording session after Train had left, and somehow, despite the distractions, a number of songs were put on tape. The next afternoon, a sober, repentant Train showed up at the studio and contributed harmony vocals on Walker's cover of "Bound for Glory," the old Phil Ochs tribute to Woody Guthrie. It was the last time that either Phil Ochs or John Train would appear on record.

———

Train was absolutely convinced that he was being followed by someone hired to assassinate him, and for protection against his enemies, he armed himself with a variety of weapons, including a hammer, knives, a broken-off shovel handle, a meat hook, or a lead pipe. Such weapons, however, brought him very little assurance. He saw the enemy on every street corner; he was afraid to leave a bar for fear of running into a government agency hit man. He hated to walk around alone, so he took to hanging out with people that he met on the street or in taverns. As far as Train's old friends were concerned, the new circle of friends represented nothing but trouble.

"When he was Train," offered Larry Sloman, "he was incredibly effusive. He had this grandiosity to him that was amazing. I remember him showing up at times with the most degenerate kind of street-level scuzz that you can imagine. These were people that he picked up along the way."

"I didn't know who these people were," added Carol Realini, another longtime friend who accused these new drinking buddies of attaching themselves to Train because they enjoyed watching him get drunk and make a fool of himself. "They were just crazies. They were mindless people who exploited him."

Paul Colby had similar memories. "I hated those friends," he said. "It was heartbreaking to watch this talented guy come in, looking terrible and disheveled, half his shirt in and half out, with these two or three guys behind him, walking around the Village and making their reputations with John Train. After he died, one of these guys came up to me and said, 'You weren't his friend. You were one of the guys who hurt him.' I said, 'You son of a bitch. How dare you say I wasn't his friend. *You're* the guy who helped bring him down. You walked around the neighborhood with him, using him to get free drinks at places. I helped him by *not* buying him a drink.

"I loved Phil," Colby continued, "and I told him so. I said, 'Phil, you're hanging out with the wrong guys. These guys aren't helping you. They're all crazy.' Then I said, 'Look, Phil, let me tell you something. I love you and I'll feed you, but you can't buy a drink in here. I won't give you a drink and you're not going to buy a drink.' The last time I saw him, his head was down and he looked awful, and he said, 'You said you'd buy me food if I ever asked for any.' And I said, 'Yes, I did. What do you want?' He said he wanted chicken salad, so I called my waitress and told her to give him a chicken salad sandwich. That was the last time I saw Phil."

Colby witnessed the worst that John Train had to offer, and he worried for his safety. Still, as a businessman, he was concerned about the welfare of his establishment and clientele, and like other proprietors in the Village, he tossed Train out of his place when he was out of line.

"He had a pipe in the waistband of his pants," Colby recalled, "and one day he took it out and raised it above his head as if he was going to hit me with it. I had a German Shepherd at the time, and it went for him but I called him off. I said to Phil, 'You can't come in—not in the condition that you're in. You're disruptive, and I'm not going to let you in.' He destroyed every place he went. Phil was a talented guy, well-liked and respected in the business, until he went nuts and antagonized everybody. Then it was chaos everywhere he went."

For all his reckless behavior, there were indications that Train could control himself when he chose to do so. He remained calm and respectful when he was around older friends, such as Sis Cunningham and Gordon Friesen. Sis and Gordon's apartment became a refuge when Train felt threatened or needed a place to crash. One time, he knocked frantically at their door, obviously terrified out of his wits.

"Somebody's got to hide me," he told Sis and Gordon, "because they're going to kill me." The assassins, he said, were waiting for him in the lobby of the apartment building.

"We tried to help him as much as we could," said Cunningham, who wound up putting Train up for a week on that particular occasion. "We didn't know if he was fantasizing or something, but after he died and we were thinking this over, I believe it was true. We know now that he was under surveillance. The FBI reports showed that.

"He came here a lot, and he would talk to Gordon for hours. Sometimes he'd come here after sleeping in the park. He would be in terrible shape—all dirty, his hair matted, no socks, the tongues hanging out of his shoes. Gordon would tell him to take a shower. He would find him some clean clothes and some socks, and he would put him to bed. This went on time after time after time."

Cunningham believed that Train behaved himself around her and her husband because they were like traditional parent figures. Cora Weiss, on the other hand, believed that Train favored certain places as safe havens where he could go for a few days to dry out and try to pull himself back together.

"Phil used to come visit us a lot," she said. "I lived in Riverdale, and I had a house that was comfortable. When he started to get sick or drank too much, I would find him a doctor. He would go, and he might be good for a couple of days, but it didn't last. He knew that I wouldn't yell at him. He also knew that he couldn't do drugs or drink as much as he wanted at our house. I don't think he tried, either. We had young children around, and it wouldn't have been right."

Carol Realini also noted Train's gentle side when he was around children. Realini had a young daughter who was accorded special treatment, first by Phil Ochs, and later by John Train.

"He was a wonderful, caring person who loved kids," she recalled. "He used to come over and sing to my little daughter. I left him with her a few times, even in his last couple of years. People said I was crazy, but he was my friend, and I understood him and loved him. I didn't fear him. He would sit on the couch and play guitar to my daughter until she fell asleep. He would sing a lot of old Irish folk music, and this whole repertoire of stuff that he loved. I was lucky because he just liked to sit around the living room and play."

———

When Arthur Gorson returned from Peru, the plans for a huge concert in the country seemed as valid as ever. While in Peru, Gorson had met with the country's minister of culture, and the two had agreed to time the concert to coincide with the birthdate of Tupac Amaru, the eighteenth-century Inca descendant who had led an uprising against Spanish rule. According to the plan, the Peruvian government would provide two DC-10s to transport the musicians and crew to the concert site. The government's Intellectual Committee would underwrite most of the costs of the concert. Arthur was especially enthusiastic about the prospects of holding the concert in the mountains and playing before the country's native people.

"I suggested that we mainly aim it at the local Indians," said Gorson, "and not make it a big jet-set thing. We weren't going to publicize it all over the world and have rich kids fly in. It would have been fun to have all these big stars from all over the Americas playing to people who had never heard of them. We would have tried to record it and televise it and raise a lot of money to set up a foundation—the Tupac Amaru Foundation—which would have provided money and facilities for Latin American artists who otherwise didn't have access to instruments and recording facilities."

Gorson was shocked, then, when he came back to the United States, fired up about the project and prepared to launch an all-out effort with Phil Ochs, only to be greeted by a drunken and unruly John Train, who was more interested in filling his head with his crazy ideas for Barricade than in settling down and working out the finer points of the concert in Peru. The more Train drank and rambled on about his plans, the more convinced Arthur became that he had to be excluded from the work on the concert.

Arthur's plans were eventually derailed, not by John Train but by historical events. In August, just as the final details for the concert were being worked out, a bloodless coup in Peru unseated the Velasco government and replaced it with a right-wing militarist regime. A concert in the country was now out of the question.

————

To help promote Sammy Walker's career, Train decided to resurrect Phil Ochs for one final appearance. He approached Mike Porco and proposed an Ochs-Walker concert at Folk City, and Porco readily agreed. There were to be two shows, one at eight and one at midnight.

Train showed up at the club with a claw hammer tucked into his belt. Before the show, he sat at the bar and drank orange-juice-and-rums, watching people come in and take their places at tables. By showtime, he'd had far too much to drink.

"What can I tell you about the shows," offered Mayer Vishner, who attended both segments, "except Sam was great and Phil was drunk. He wasn't consistently awful, but the shows were sloppy and embarrassing. People walked out. It broke my heart. This was a guy who should have been playing Carnegie Hall."

Sammy Walker went on first and played a solid set of the songs he had included on his recently recorded album. At one point, he called Phil Ochs and Sis Cunningham to the stage to sing with him on "Song for Patty," the title song on his album. After taking the stage, Train launched into an extended, incoherent introduction to the song, during which he yammered on about Patty Hearst, Che Guevara, and CIA director William Colby, while Sammy Walker and Sis Cunningham stood by, looking embarrassed.

"I put out a contract on Colby for a hundred thousand dollars," Train declared. "I told Colby he's got a half-year to get out or he's dead. They can kill me but he's dead. He's a dead man now . . . unless he quits, commits suicide, gets a convenient disease, or resigns . . . In the meantime, you will now hear the best song written in the seventies about Patty Hearst—a girl I don't particularly like, but for some reason he likes her. So we'll hear the song."

Train's monologue had people shaking their heads. Phil Ochs had always laced his performances with political commentary, but his stage patter had been sharp and witty; the man now onstage, droning on in a stream-of-consciousness style that defied logic or understanding, was pitiful. Sammy Walker displayed remarkable patience while enduring Train's embarrassing performance, but the fact remained that Train was disrupting an otherwise commendable concert.

Reported Mayer Vishner: "Sam was in the awkward position of having people commiserating with him. He couldn't bask in the commiseration because he didn't want to acknowledge how bad it was to be stuck with Phil."

Train's own shows, particularly the second set, were confrontational. Train, however, could not win over audiences the way Phil Ochs had converted them during his gold-suit concert at Carnegie Hall. Drunk and obnoxious, Train was spoiling for a fight, and he went out of his way to insult the people who came to see him.

"I live outside the law," he boasted. "I've no respect for the law. I've got no respect for any human being alive in this room. I'd kill you all as soon as look at you. Believe me, I will."

The music, sung between Train's long, drunken tirades, was almost beside the point. Some of the old Phil Ochs songs—"There But for Fortune," "Crucifixion," and "Chords of Fame"—were played, but the better part of the two sets was devoted to covers of Johnny Cash songs or traditional folk songs. Somehow, Train managed to make it through the two shows without being dismissed from the stage for his out-of-control behavior. At one point, he picked up Sammy Walker's guitar and angrily flung it against the wall, and on another occasion, he held his hammer aloft as if to challenge anyone who dared to disagree with him. Phil Ochs, he told the people sitting in Folk City, was officially finished.

"Anybody comes up to me tomorrow and says, 'Are you Phil Ochs?'—you get the hammer in the old temple. You're dead, all right? You get a broken arm, a broken leg. That's it. But tonight you get the last of Phil Ochs."

Sadly, most of the audience would have had little objection to his retirement.

———

Train's business interests were faring poorly. Neither of his pet projects, Barricade, Inc., and his proposed revolutionary bar, were panning out as hoped. The ideas themselves were workable, but like just about anything else that Train attempted during this period, they were undermined by his boorish behavior.

"It was a great idea," insisted Arthur Gorson of Train's intention of buying a bar. "It was to be a place where people could have political discussions and drink and carry on. Phil had a barroom thing from the day he came to New York—the romance of bars and the whole romantic notion of being a poet and drinking yourself to death. I remember very clearly that he never thought he'd live to be thirty. The bar was part of this legendary romance.

"We were in a bar culture at that time. New York was quite different from what it is now, and artists' bars in particular were a real life force in the city. You could just go into a bar and there would be people and conversations and fabulous things going on. It harkened back to the early scene around the Kettle of Fish, when there was drinking and rapping and sharing songs, and staggering home to write a song to bring back the next night."

Train had high hopes when he learned that a tavern owner in SoHo was looking for an investor. The bar, located on Broome Street, was a traditional neighborhood saloon, complete with beautiful woodwork and an ample bar. The place had fallen into disrepair, and its owner, Bob Bonick, needed money to restore it. His investment price was thirty thousand dollars.

To Train, the bar's potential was well worth the asking price. As he envisioned it, the tavern would be renamed "Che" and would be every bit as revolutionary as its namesake. Society's outlaws could gather in the bar and play a jukebox full of Frank Sinatra and Tony Bennett records or, on selected nights, listen to live music played on the tavern's tiny stage. It was the kind of watering hole that Train wanted to frequent himself.

Unfortunately for Train, Michael Ochs was opposed to the idea, and he was reluctant to authorize the release of the money from Phil's accounts. Thirty thousand dollars would nearly clean out what Phil had left in his bank account, and with what he had been hearing about his brother's recent behavior, Michael wasn't sure the bar was a good idea. He put off sending the money for as long as he could, but he relented when Train called with a terrifying threat.

"He told me that if I didn't turn over the money, he would kidnap Sonny's kids and hold them for ransom," Michael said. "I had no choice. He was crazy enough to do it."

Che's grand opening, according to one observer, was "a disaster." John Train turned up drunk and in embarrassing form, and proceeded to make a fool of himself in front of a packed house. To Bob Bonick, Train's sloppy behavior should have signified an unhappy future: Phil Ochs had never been known for his social graces; John Train, whether behind the bar or working the crowd, was a social disgrace.

As it was, Bonick could barely tolerate Train and some of his friends. They drank too much and they talked too loud; they played the jukebox at a volume so high that customers were unable to talk to each other. On several occasions, he'd had to ask them to leave. A violent confrontation occurred one evening when Bonick insisted on turning down the jukebox. In retaliation, Train smashed a bar stool through the tavern's front window and went on a drunken rampage, trashing his own bar.

Train later wrote an account of his version of the evening's events. Oddly enough, he blamed Phil Ochs for his problems:

SOHO BAR ATTACKED
by John Train

A drunken Phil Ochs smashed 5 windows of a bar called 'Che.'

He had bought 80% of the bar but during negotiations had been thrown out repeatedly by his own partner Robert Bonic.

Bonic signed a letter of intent until Sept. 15. If he receives $32,000 Phil Ochs is the official owner pending S.L.A. approval.

Ochs was so drunk earlier in the evening he threatened several lady customers when they complained that the Juke Box was too loud.

His own bouncer then decided to lock him out. It was a monumental Battle. Before Ochs could climb thru the broken glass he was halted by 4 police cars.

They took him into custody, but after hearing the full story they released him without charges.

Train's involvement in the bar was short-lived. All of his money had disappeared in the rehabilitating and restocking of the bar, and the place was in dreadful financial shape from the day it opened. Bills could not be met; business dwindled to nothing. At one point, not long after the grand opening, the electricity had been shut off. Within a few weeks, Train had no other choice but to face the truth: he had invested virtually everything he had in a business that needed much more to survive. Che was history.

———

Train held on to the Phil Ochs fantasy of hiring Colonel Harland Sanders to manage him, and he was thrilled when he received a letter from the Heublein Corporation, the parent company of Kentucky Fried Chicken, informing him that a company representative would be flying to New York to discuss the possibilities of its backing Barricade. A few months earlier, Phil Ochs had contacted the company with detailed plans for Barricade, Inc. The letter had been organized and professional enough to convince corporate officials to take him seriously. That he dropped Bob Dylan's name in the letter, saying that he wanted to include him as a Barricade client, probably didn't hurt his case, either.

"Even during that whole manic period, there was a basis of fact in half of what he was saying," Arthur Gorson recalled. "It made sense in Phil's whole scheme of things. He was a great promoter and had incredible entrepreneurial business sense. The whole idea of having a major corporation represent him, and setting up music and publishing and all kinds of things, was attractive enough for Heublein to send somebody from Louisville to check it out."

However, the pending visit from the corporate representative posed a serious problem for Train: in his letter, Phil had written of owning a building that would house Barricade's corporate headquarters and recording studios. Heublein was interested in inspecting such a building.

Rather than tell corporate officials the truth, Train decided to go out and find a building. It didn't matter that he had no way of paying for it—he would obtain the financing from his friends. He looked until he found a warehouse suitable to his needs.

"Phil actually entered into negotiations to buy this building in TriBeCa," said Larry Sloman, who accompanied Train to the site one day. "He actually had the owners of this building convinced that he was going to buy it. He told me that Dylan was going to put up the money. He had all these people who were going to bankroll it. He showed me the floor plans that he had sketched out, and he took me on a tour of the building. He was going to renovate the whole thing. 'This is where the meeting rooms are going to be,' he said, 'and this is where the bar's going to be.' I said, 'Come on, Phil. Get real. You don't have the money to do this.' And he said, 'What do you mean I don't have the money to do this? I can buy and sell you.' 'All right,' I said, 'buy me then.' 'I'll give you a million dollars,' he said. He wrote out a check! He was so grandiose when he got into that John Train mode."

Train was indeed nothing if not grandiose. Not only was he fooling himself about the prospects of obtaining the warehouse, but when it came time for the Heublein representative to come to New York, Train decided to turn the visit into another major event, right down to filming it for posterity. Sammy Walker, as Barricade's first big client, was invited to attend the meeting, as was Arthur Gorson. Train called *People* magazine, which dispatched a reporter and photographer to the event.

The meeting, as one might have expected, turned out to be a total farce. Although he had not purchased the building, Train had hoped to give the impression that he had by bribing a custodian into letting him walk the Heublein representative through the warehouse. The plan might have worked if Train had shown up with money, but he was nearly broke and had nowhere near the fifty dollars that the custodian demanded as "insurance" money.

After trying unsuccessfully to panhandle the money, Train came up with another plan. A group of young men were playing basketball on a court across the street from the warehouse, and Train decided to approach them with the idea of playing a pickup game for fifty dollars.

One can only imagine what passed through the Heublein representative's mind when he arrived at the warehouse and met John Train, obviously drunk, dressed with no socks and standing with his shirttail hanging out, walking around the area and trying ineffectively to pull the whole thing together. Filmmaker François De Menil and his crew filmed the festivities, while the reporter and photographer from *People* tried to make sense of what was turning into a pointless assignment. What was supposed to have been a serious business meeting had all the elements of a three-ring circus.

The Heublein representative hung around until Train attempted to talk him into playing in the basketball game. He politely excused himself, saying that he had to make a phone call or two, and disappeared. There would be no colonels managing Phil Ochs, John Train, or anyone associated with them.

———

People were at a loss over what to do about John Train. Michael Ochs had heard the stories of Train's exploits, and he began to investigate the possibility of having his brother committed to a psychiatric hospital, where he would at least be receiving the medical attention he so obviously needed. Others, particularly Jerry Rubin, encouraged Train to voluntarily check into a hospital or clinic. Friends, afraid of or disgusted by Train, banished him from their apartments, leaving him more isolated than ever.

One friend—Larry Sloman—encouraged Train to use his creativity to make something out of even the worst of his experiences.

"He was living at the Chelsea Hotel," recalled Sloman, "but when he'd come downtown, he would always hang out at Prince Street. It was like another home for him because it was his old apartment and we always welcomed him there. It was such a schizophrenic thing. When he was John Train, he was the most arrogant, out-there maniac you could imagine. Then, when he was feeling depressed, he was this meek, gentle little lamb—and shy. He didn't want to say anything.

"I kept prodding him: 'You gotta do something, Phil. You gotta try to work through this. You can still do it—you can write songs.' He kept saying that he couldn't. 'What am I going to write about?' he'd say. So I said, 'Why don't you write about what you're going through?'

"One day, I asked him if he had written any songs, and he said, 'Actually, I've been trying to write some about myself, like you said.' 'Let me hear them,' I said, and he picked up a guitar and started playing. The songs were amazing: all about John Train and Phil Ochs and this whole mishmosh identity that he had, all this kind of confused, schizophrenic thing that he was living through. They were unbelievable fragments of what could have been an amazing Phil Ochs album. His voice was not beautiful, but the melodies were gorgeous. It was a brilliant attempt to chronicle what this character had been going through."

The lyrics to the songs were the startling confessions of a man who had disappeared down the rabbit hole of his own imagination:

> *John stands for Kennedy, Butler stands for Yeats,*
> *Train stands for hobos at the missed silver gates.*
> *They won't understand what I've done.*
> *They've even taken away my gun.*
> *I must be public enemy number one.*

Sloman taped the songs that Train sang in the Prince Street apartment that day, and in time, copies of the tape began to circulate around Greenwich Village. People hearing the songs were struck by the raw honesty of the music. Train held nothing in reserve, as was apparent in his "Ballad of John Train," a revealing number that indicated Train's knowledge of just how far he had fallen:

> *Phil Ochs checked into the Chelsea Hotel.*
> *There was blood on his clothes, they were dirty.*
> *I could see by his face that he was not feeling well.*
> *He'd been to one too many parties.*
> *He walked in the lobby, a picture of doom.*

It was plain to see he'd been a-drinkin'.
I had to follow him to his room
To find out what he was thinkin'.
Train, Train, Train,
From the outlaw in his brain
But he's still the same refrain.

He walked in his room and he fell on the floor,
Hangin' in his hangover.
Now the act from the stage he plays on the street,
Handing out piles of money.
His audience now is the bums that he meets.
Is he a phony or funny?

Train's self-perception—as highly romanticized outlaw—came through in most of the songs. Had they ever been formally issued on record, the new numbers would have stood as a compelling coda to *Rehearsals for Retirement*. If, in *Rehearsals*, Phil Ochs had allowed his audience the opportunity to witness his despair and spiritual death, John Train had taken him one step further; the newly written songs reflected his season in hell, from which there was no possible return.

———

Train's fancies of being an outlaw were by no means without merit. As the summer went on and he fell deeper and deeper into his own delusions, Train was indeed living outside the margins of society and, eventually, the law. He was no longer just an unsavory eccentric; he had become dangerous to himself and to others.

As a rule, the people who knew him feared that he would be beaten, or perhaps even killed, by one of the strangers that he insulted or picked a fight with. Friends knew how to handle him, but strangers, seeing the weapons, coupled with Train's aggressive demeanor, might have taken violent exception to his behavior.

Such concerns proved to be well founded. On several occasions, Train goaded a bar patron into a fight. He was invariably beaten up, but never too badly. The punishment had little effect on him: if anything, he wore the cuts and bruises like battle scars.

His troubles with the police were another matter. In early August, after another night of heavy drinking, Train lost control of the car he was driving and plowed into a row of parked cars. When the police arrived at the scene, they found him standing in the street, covered with blood. They immediately called an ambulance, but when they tried to take him to the hospital, Train became abusive and violent. It was no better at the hospital. In his short time there, Train tried to hit the doctors and nurses taking care of him.

He was eventually transferred to the police station, where he was booked, under the name of John Train, on a variety of charges, including assault and driving without a license or proper registration. Unrepentant, Train screamed that he was the victim of police brutality and demanded the phone call guaranteed him by the law. The police contacted Deni Frand on his behalf.

"I got a call in the middle of the night," Frand remembered, "and a man was saying, 'Do you know John Train?' I hung up. They kept calling me back and asking about John Train, but it didn't connect for a while. Finally, the man said, 'This is the police. John Train is here and he said to call you.' "

Deni called Claudio Bedal, and the two drove to the police station. They found Train in a drunken rage, shouting about how he had been beaten by the police and was going to sue them, and demanding that Deni and Claudio call a lawyer. Instead, Deni called Michael Ochs in California.

"Let him stay in jail," Michael told her, refusing to wire bail money. Michael had been receiving daily reports about Train's activities, and he was almost relieved that he had been arrested without having seriously injured himself or someone else. With any luck, Michael reasoned, a judge would send Phil to a psychiatric hospital for observation.

It was not to be. The next morning, a cleaned-up and sober John Train stood in court and contritely offered to pay for any damages from the previous evening's accident. He had been going through some tough times, he told the judge, but he could promise that he would not repeat his actions. The judge lectured him for a while and then dismissed the case.

Train had learned nothing from the experience, and Deni Frand, for one, was put off by his cavalier attitude toward his legal difficulties.

"He had a nice time in jail," she said. "When he came out, he was wearing a red bandana around his neck, telling me about all the wonderful people he had met in jail. He said they all were going to work for him at Barricade."

Train had another run-in with the law only a few days later. Since he could no longer drive in New York, Train hired a limousine to take him around. Train, however, had no money, and after several days of escorting him around Manhattan and not being paid for it, the chauffeur demanded that Train pay his bill before going out again. Train argued that the driver and limo service would be paid by Barricade in due time, but this was not good enough. The chauffeur refused to budge until he'd seen some money. When Train became angry and refused to leave the car, the driver picked up his radio and called the police.

Once again, the police struggled to keep Train under control. All he had to do, they said, was pay his bill and he could go on his way. Train was hearing none of it. When he persisted and was nearly arrested, Train shouted for his lawyer—Ramsey Clark. The police called Clark at home, and the former attorney general told them that he would pay the bill. Train was released, but his brief use of the limousine service was over.

Ramsey Clark cared a great deal about Phil Ochs, and like many of his friends, he was stumped over what he could do to help this John Train character, who had an uncanny knack for getting into trouble.

"I saw quite a bit of him," said Clark. "There was one period, maybe three or four Sundays in a row, that he came by every Sunday morning. He was getting to be in worse shape, and I finally got a fellow named Kenny Jackson to work with him. I thought Kenny had all the skills that were needed. He was an ex-con who'd been through the drug and alcohol thing, and he had been a founder of the Fortune Society. He'd been there, he'd seen problems with powerful men, and he empathized with them. Kenny had an office on Hudson Street, and I asked Phil to come up and meet us. When he came over, he was carrying a long-handled spade, and I left him in Kenny's care. I was gone for a protracted period of time—I was moving around all the time—and when I came back, Kenny told me, 'Well, he got away.' He really cared about Phil, and he was a master of working with people, but he couldn't keep up with him."

———

Very few people could keep up with Train. They begged him to get psychiatric help, but he always refused. He distrusted doctors, he said, and he hated psychiatrists even more. Although he realized that something was wrong and he needed help, he was convinced that medications were not the solution to his problems.

Suddenly, just when it seemed as if his life couldn't sink any lower, he was thrown out of the Chelsea Hotel and found himself without a place to live. In desperation, he called Jean Ray, now living in California, to see if he could move into her unoccupied apartment on Thompson Street. She agreed to let him stay there for a short time.

Train quickly established himself as a loud, unruly tenant who, on several occasions, came home drunk in the wee hours of the morning and, unable to open the door to his apartment, simply broke it down. The lobby door received similar treatment. When other tenants in the building complained, the landlord called Jean Ray and told her that she would have to forfeit the apartment if Train didn't leave. Jean tried to talk Train into moving elsewhere, and after several unsuccessful calls, she called one of her New York friends, a young woman named Wendy Winsted, and asked her to change the apartment's locks.

Wendy went to the apartment when Train was out. The door had been broken down, and she let herself in. The place was a shambles, overrun by roaches feeding on garbage piled everywhere. Newspapers and clothes were scattered throughout the rooms. A Sony Camcorder, the only item of value in the apartment, sat on the floor in the corner of the living room. From the looks of it, the place hadn't been cleaned since Train moved in. Wendy instinctively began to tidy up after Train. She then called a locksmith and arranged to have the locks changed the next day. As she was leaving the apartment, she decided to take Train's videocamera to store at her place. As it was, anybody could have walked into the apartment and stolen it.

Train was anything but appreciative about the gesture, even when Wendy called and told him that she had his videocamera. When she tried to explain the situation, Train lost his temper and told her that she had better come over immediately with the machine. "Don't take care of me, bitch," he said when she brought over the camera. "I'll take care of myself. Don't try to take care of me or I'll knock your teeth down your throat."

The scene was worse the next day. The locks had been changed on the apartment and Wendy was about to leave when a menacing and angry John Train showed up unexpectedly, armed with a crowbar. Wendy tried to call the police, but Train broke down the door and tore the phone out of the wall. He threw her across the room and charged after her. In the ensuing attack, Wendy was badly beaten by a man who, the day before, had threatened to kill her. She finally escaped and ran out of the apartment, Train giving chase until she managed to lose him in an alleyway.

Train was arrested and taken to the police station. As before, Michael refused to post bail and, as before, Train was subsequently released when he appeared, remorseful and rational, in front of a judge. Not only did he live outside the law, but by all indications, John Butler Train was above it, as well.

———

With nowhere to stay, Train crashed wherever he could—in doorways and stairwells, in boiler rooms and basements, in the park, or, on occasion, with friends such as Sis Cunningham and Gordon Friesen. He had virtually no money, and he often had to resort to panhandling for money for food, or visiting nearby missions for a free meal.

Recalled one friend: "One day, very early in the morning, I saw him sitting on the curb near West Fourth Street and Bleecker. The Judson Memorial Church had a little office across the street, where they used to have Welfare advocates who helped street people. When I saw Phil sitting on the curb, I said, 'What are you doing?' He said, 'I'm waiting for them to open so they'll give me money for breakfast.' That's where he was at. I mean, we took him in from the street, from lying in the gutter in his own piss and vomit."

"The last time I talked to him," noted another friend, "was at an outside cafe. I forget how I got in touch with him, but he said that he would meet me there. It was in the summertime, and everybody was sitting there in their shirtsleeves. Phil showed up in a heavy winter overcoat, barefooted and filthy and loaded down with newspapers. All he would talk about was how the FBI was hunting him."

Finally, after what must have seemed like an eternity, Jerry Rubin was able to persuade Train to check into Gracie Square Hospital for psychiatric treatment. His stay, however, was brief. After being admitted and receiving a thorough checkup, Train reported to what was supposed to be a group therapy session. The meeting, for reasons unknown to Train, was being conducted in Spanish, and he left shortly after it began, telling the moderator that he needed to use the bathroom. Wearing only a hospital gown, Train left the hospital and walked to Arthur Gorson's apartment, where he borrowed a fresh change of clothing.

New York, Train concluded, had become intolerable. He had no place to live, and he had alienated almost all of his friends. He wasn't even welcome in most of his favorite places. It was time to head back to California.

Coming up with the money for airfare proved to be a challenge. Michael refused to send him money, and no one in New York seemed to have—or seemed to be willing to lend him—the funds necessary for his airfare. He eventually contacted Robin Love, who had married Ron Cobb, and who now owned a small restaurant in West Los Angeles, and bullied her into getting him an airline ticket.

"He called from New York and wanted me to send him a ticket from New York to Los Angeles," Love remembered. "He said it had to be first class because he could get free drinks. We were really poor in those days, and we didn't have credit cards. I said, 'Look, I haven't got enough money for a first-class ticket. I can get you an economy ticket. That's all I've got in my checking account.' He was really angry and was clearly crazy. I knew I'd never see the money again, but I still went down to the local travel agency, wrote a check, and bought him a one-way economy ticket from New York to Los Angeles. It was waiting for him at the airport."

————

Train wasted no time establishing his presence in Los Angeles. Ron Cobb, who had driven to the airport to meet him, gasped when he saw what had become of Phil Ochs. Train's hair was greasy and barely combed, and he had stitches on his face from his automobile accident in New York; his shirt, improperly buttoned and hanging out of his pants, was covered with food stains. Strangest of all, he stepped from the plane brandishing a lobster claw. The airline, Train explained, had refused to allow him to bring a weapon aboard, so he had brought along the lobster claw for protection.

As they drove back to Ron and Robin's apartment, Train talked a mile a minute, telling Cobb how Michael Ochs was out to ruin his life, and how he wasn't going to let that happen. He was putting together an enemies list, and he was going to see that each one of his enemies was taken care of—perhaps by his friends in the mafia. The more Train talked, the more alarmed Cobb became at his anger and aggression.

At the apartment, Train started in on Robin, bitterly accusing her of not coming up with the money that he needed to travel first class. It would have been different, Train said, if she had given the phone to Cobb when he had called. When Ron tried to defend Robin, Train waved him off. The argument went nowhere, and after a while Train let it drop.

When it came time for Robin to report to the restaurant, all three piled into Cobb's car. Robin, by her own admission "terrified" of John Train, was further unnerved when they reached the restaurant.

"Phil walked in the back door and came through the kitchen," she recalled. "I was cooking that night, and there were knives set out. Phil kind of eyed the knives. I was very frightened of him. He was not the warm, sweet, gentle Phil that I knew. He was weird. He wanted some drinks, so we gave him wine, which sort of distracted him from the knives until I could move them out of sight."

Train wanted to visit Doug Weston, and after hanging around the restaurant for a while, Cobb drove him to the Troubadour. On the way, however, Train insisted that Cobb stop back at his apartment, so he could retrieve his weapon for the evening: a samurai sword. Given Train's state of agitation, Cobb had little choice but to follow his instructions and hope for the best.

"He went looking for Doug with the samurai sword, storming through the Troubadour," said Cobb, "and when he came striding into the building, looking like he did, people scattered."

Fortunately, Weston had handled his share of unruly bar patrons in his day, and he was not intimidated by Train. As soon as he saw the sword, Weston told his guest that he would have to check it at the door. Train turned it over without incident. Weston might not have feared Train, but he also recognized that something terrible had happened to his old friend. "At that point in time," he later commented, "Phil was no longer Phil Ochs. He was John Train, and he was no longer sane."

It so happened that Van Morrison, one of Train's favorite performers, was playing at the Troubadour that evening, and Weston invited Train to stay for the show. Train loved Van Morrison's classic album, *Astral Weeks*, and he hoped that Morrison would perform "Madame George," his favorite song on the album. When it became clear that Morrison had no intention of playing the number, Train stood up and loudly requested that he sing it. Morrison refused. Train stormed out of the room and headed toward the men's restroom. Once there, he began to trash the place, ending his tirade by pulling the sink out of the wall. He left the Troubadour in a blind fury.

He was picked up by the police a few hours later, when he was found sleeping on a lawn in Beverly Hills. In the life of John Train, man of action and hero of a thousand imaginary movies, it had just been another day.

————

Train had threatened to kill his brother when Michael refused to bail him out of jail in New York, and while Michael was reasonably certain that Train would not follow through on his threats, he had reason to worry. Knowing that it was only a matter of time until Train found himself in serious trouble in Los Angeles, Michael called Train's friends and begged them not to give him bail money if he was arrested. Not that it took much persuasion on Michael's part: most of Train's friends were familiar with his recent problems in New York, and they dreaded the prospects of his stopping by for a visit. Michael had a strong ally in Ron Cobb, who also wanted to see Train committed for psychiatric observation. Just keeping Train out of trouble, Cobb recalled years later, was a full-time job.

"Everybody was constantly trying to *manage* him," said Cobb. "We were all trying to humor him, talk to him, get him in the car, talk him out of this and talk him out of that. It was just incredible."

Their efforts to keep Train out of trouble were not always successful. On one occasion, he visited the A & M offices and, after terrorizing office employees with his samurai sword, demanded that Phil Ochs be released from his contractual obligations with the company. A & M was not about to dispute his demands. Phil Ochs had never been a moneymaker for the company, and he had not given them an album of new material in half a decade. He was given his release.

On another occasion, Train was found passed out in a car outside the Troubadour. When the police saw the weapons in the car, they promptly arrested him and took him to the station.

This time, Train had a difficult time finding someone willing to bail him out. Michael had been successful in his campaign of talking people into leaving Train in jail, and one by one, they all refused to give him money when he called. Train persisted until he found someone—an A & M employee—willing to act as a character witness at his arraignment. The next day, in a scene that had become all too familiar, Train was released by a judge who appeared to believe that a good scolding was all that this celebrity really required.

Train's enemies list had expanded substantially overnight. Michael was now Enemy Number One, and Train vowed to kill him. He visited each of the people who had turned him down, and while most of them lied to him about Michael's calling them about keeping him in jail, Lee Housekeeper and Ron Cobb both looked him in the eye and told him the truth.

"We all stood accused of trying to destroy him and trying to keep him in jail," said Cobb. "I had to tell him that's exactly what we were trying to do. He came over and said, 'Were you trying to get me committed?' And I said, "Yes.' 'Well,' he said, 'you're on my enemies list.' So I said, 'I'm sorry, Phil. We think you need help and there's nothing I can do about that. You'll just have to put me on your list.' He just changed the subject."

Michael ran into Train a few nights later, at a party that he had put together for Three Dog Night. Fortunately, Train was reasonably sober, and rather than attack Michael, he refused to talk to him or to Doug Weston. As far as he was concerned, he no longer had a brother.

———

Los Angeles, Train decided, was worse than New York. Now that he had no record company and wasn't speaking to his brother or most of his friends, he had no reason to stay. He would be much better off on the East Coast.

However, he wanted to visit his daughter before leaving. He wasn't sure if he would ever set eyes on her again, and it was suddenly all-important that he say goodbye. He called Alice in Marin County and told her that he wanted to see her and Meegan, and Alice invited him to come up and stay with her.

Train closed down his apartment and packed all his possessions—including his notebooks and scrapbooks dating back to his youth—into a truck. A Troubadour bartender named Marty had volunteered to drive the truck to New York. Train, however, did not have the money to finance the move, and he nearly lost everything he owned, including his valuable archival materials. Marty drove until he ran out of money, and then he called Doug Weston for advice on how to get the truck the rest of the way. When neither Weston or Train came up with the cash needed for the trip, Marty put the truck in storage, where it sat until Michael retrieved it after his brother's death.

————

Alice was stunned when she saw her former husband standing in her doorway, a hammer wedged between his belt and his massive belly, telling her that his name was now John Train. He had no friends or family, he said—no family outside of Alice and Meegan, that is.

Meegan was thrilled to see her parents together again. She had always had a difficult time accepting their breaking up, and she nurtured the hope that someday they might be reunited. To a child, the brief reunions were difficult to understand.

"One of the dynamics of my parents' relationship," she volunteered, years later, "was they always slept together when they saw each other. They had an incredible lust for one another, and in the deep sense, I think they did love each other. But they were both very selfish and impatient, and they had no interest in a long-term relationship. The fact that they slept together was very misleading for me because I always felt that they were getting back together, that this time my dad was going to stay."

There was no doubting that things were different this time around. Despite his heavy drinking—he had now taken to buying a quart of orange juice, emptying three-quarters of the carton, refilling it with vodka, and carrying it with him wherever he went—Train spent a lot of time with Meegan. One day, they went on a family picnic, and on another he took her to the flea market, where he purchased a secondhand set of the *Encyclopaedia Britannica* for her. He also bought her a cat that he named Rimbaud. It was a peaceful time, with Train and Alice getting along without the usual outbreaks of bickering.

"I think he knew that he wasn't going to see me again," said Meegan, "because he never called me again. I spent many years thinking about that—how he could die without saying goodbye—but he *did* say goodbye. That's what that trip was all about. He was sending me off into the world with art and literature, in the form of a cat and used encyclopedias, trying to prepare me for when he wasn't going to be there. I think he knew on that trip that he was going to die."

In the few days that he spent with Alice and Meegan, John Train started to disappear and the old Phil Ochs began to reappear. Phil wanted something stable in his life, even if for a short while, and staying with his former wife and daughter took him back to a time that, while far from perfect, at least had a promise for a future. Neither John Train nor Phil Ochs could presently make such a claim.

———

When Train finally returned to New York, he learned that Bob Dylan was planning to tour the Eastern part of the country with a troupe of performers that he was calling the Rolling Thunder Revue. According to the plan, the Rolling Thunder Revue—which featured such performers as Dylan, Joan Baez, and Roger McGuinn—would appear unannounced in smaller venues, playing for the joy of making music more than for the certainty of making big money.

Train loved the idea, which reminded him of the discussions he had carried on, as Phil Ochs, with Dylan a year earlier. He desperately wanted to be a part of the group, but he knew, as did Dylan, that there was no way he could be included. At one time, there might have been room for Phil Ochs, but John Train was far too volatile to be added to the tour.

The exclusion, which effectively illustrated the extent to which Train had alienated his friends and colleagues, finished off what little remained of John Train. His boisterous, grandiose front was punctured by the realization that he was ultimately a failure. Train gave way to Phil Ochs.

One day, quite unexpectedly, Jerry Rubin found Phil standing at his door. Rubin was glad to see that it was Phil, and not John Train, coming to visit him, yet at the same time he was surprised to see the depressed state Phil was in. He invited him in and listened as Phil lamented the damage he had done to his friendships. Rubin assured him that his fears were unfounded; his friends, he said, recognized that there was something wrong with him and would be more than willing to forgive him. To prove his point, Rubin dialed Ron Cobb's number in Los Angeles.

"Guess who's here?" he asked Cobb, handing the phone to Phil.

"Ochs here," said Phil, using his familiar telephone greeting. "I guess I've been kind of strange . . ."

Chapter Eighteen

NO MORE SONGS

PHIL WOULD never escape the rampages of John Butler Train.

Train had caused extensive damage, although, contrary to Phil's beliefs, the worst of the harm was to Phil himself. Most of his friends were capable of dismissing his self-destructive behavior as manifestations of mental illness, and very few had written him off entirely. People still loved him, and when the old Phil Ochs reappeared, beaten and horribly repentant, they were willing to forgive him and help him in any way possible.

Phil could not see this. He was too embarrassed by the John Train episodes—too burdened with the crushing weight of remorse—to consider the compassion and generosity of those closest to him. In his mind, there was no turning back, no reclaiming his former self, no chance for redemption.

He knew what he had to do.

———

His first attempt at suicide ended in failure. One day, while no one was around, Phil tried to hang himself from a banister in the Prince Street apartment. But he had grown so heavy, and the banister was so weak, that the wood gave way and he crashed to the floor. Rather than be frightened by the incident, Phil joked about it to his friends.

One of his daily rituals could be quite unnerving. He would pace back and forth in the apartment, muttering to himself, worrying about his future.

"What am I going to do?" he would say to anyone who was

around—usually Larry Sloman, who was now subletting the apartment. "What am I going to do . . . what am I going to do? I can just see the headlines: *Folksinger Found Dead in His Apartment.*" He would go on from there, improvising his obituary with talk of how this folksinger named Phil Ochs had hanged himself in his Prince Street apartment. Sloman, aware of Phil's earlier attempt to end his life, knew that Phil was serious.

In fact, most of Phil's friends were aware of his death wish. He talked incessantly about suicide, often in a distant, detached way, as if he were etching out details for a scene in a movie. Although worried about his well-being, Phil's friends were encouraged everytime they saw him: one more day had passed without his acting on his threats. Perhaps, they reasoned, he would come around in time.

What those around Phil did not—or could not—understand were the dynamics of Phil's depression. By Phil's thinking, he had died a long time ago: he had died politically in Chicago in 1968 in the violence of the Democratic National Convention; he had died professionally in Africa a few years later, when he had been strangled and felt that he could no longer sing; he had died spiritually when Chile had been overthrown and his friend Victor Jara had been brutally murdered; and, finally, he had died psychologically at the hands of John Train. There was nothing left for the former Phil Ochs, no motivation for his return. John Train had been a final, desperate attempt to create a life within a life—to perhaps create someone or something to write about—but Train, borne on the wings of a manic binge, was a bloodless, soulless entity so at odds with the host he possessed that he was destined to fail. There was too much inherent goodness in Phil for Train to succeed. When Phil eventually (and inevitably) re-emerged, he had no life to come back to—at least in his own mind. He had no prospects, no future, no hope. His only certainty was death.

———

On October 23, Phil turned in his final public performance at a surprise birthday party for Mike Porco at Folk City. To the amazement of nearly everyone in the Village club, Phil made his parting shot a memorable one.

Porco had been one of the constants throughout Phil's adult life. He had given Phil a chance shortly after his arrival in New York, and he had revelled in his success; during the hard times, he had been an ever-listening and sympathetic ear. He had poured John Train many a light drink, he had cut him off entirely, and he had gone so far as to toss him out of the bar . . . but he had never closed the door entirely. Porco loved Phil the way he might have loved a wayward son, and in return, Phil felt a loyalty to Porco that he reserved for very few. Not even paralyzing depression could keep him from attending his friend's party.

The evening's festivities, eventually captured in part in Bob Dylan's film *Renaldo and Clara*, boasted of many high points. Dylan was preparing to launch his Rolling Thunder Revue tour, and his troupe's appearance at Folk City took on the feeling of a dress rehearsal. Dylan had hoped to stage his Rolling Thunder concerts in a loose, easy environment, and this was an ideal occasion to test the show.

Folk City was packed on the night of the party. The Dylan entourage and film crew, along with various hangers-on, were enough to fill the small club, but for this occasion, anybody who had ever played Folk City seemed to have shown up, turning the party into a grand reunion. For Phil, the event was a bittersweet experience, his happiness in seeing old friends tinged by his sadness in knowing that he was no longer a part of them. He could glance around and see people blessed with promising futures. Dylan was riding high on the well-deserved success of *Blood on the Tracks*. Joan Baez could still fill a hall. Bette Midler, relatively new to the scene, was establishing herself as a force to be reckoned with. Phil wandered through the club, talking to people and marveling at the music being made on the club's tiny stage.

Early in the evening, Phil announced that he wanted to perform a few songs. He had arrived at Folk City without a guitar or any intention of doing anything other than enjoy the party, but he was soon caught up in the festivities. Others, however, were leery of Phil's intentions. He had been drinking heavily, and that, along with memories of John Train's last appearance at Folk City, had people wondering if Phil would wind up embarrassing himself and Porco. Still, it was impossible to refuse his request.

By the time it was his turn to go onstage, Phil was so drunk that he could hold himself up only by leaning against a wall. Nevertheless, he was determined to play. As he fumbled around, looking for a guitar to borrow, Phil became involved in a scene that, in a peculiar sense, spoke volumes of his relationship with Dylan, as well as of his career itself. Seeing that Phil needed a guitar, Dylan offered his own for his friend to use. Phil, however, was more interested in borrowing the cowboy hat that Dylan was wearing that evening. Dylan was reluctant to turn over the hat, but Phil persisted. "Bobby," he pleaded, "give me the hat. I want the hat."

The scene, as depicted in *Renaldo and Clara*, left an indelible impression on those who witnessed it.

"It's the story of Phil's life," remarked Mayer Vishner, a mutual friend who saw the irony in the encounter. "It would have been fine if Phil had taken the guitar, but he wanted the hat—as in crown, as in tiara, as in title. He wanted to be Elvis; he wanted to be Dylan. He wanted the hat, but he should have taken the guitar."

When Phil finally stepped to the stage, carrying a borrowed guitar and wearing Dylan's cowboy hat, he looked like a wreck. People held their breath, wondering how he was going to make it through his performance. Such concerns were quickly put to rest. Not only was Phil capable of playing and singing, but he astonished everyone in the room with an emotional welling that seemed to rise from a long-neglected place. People listened in amazement as Phil sang, first, "The Blue and the Gray," an old Civil War song, and then "Jimmy Brown the Newsboy." "Too Many Martyrs" followed.

"There was a punctured quality to his singing," said Larry Sloman, who was present at the performance and working on a book about the Rolling Thunder tour. "It was so poignant because you could see that he was defeated, but the way he was singing the songs was so soulful and emotional. I was standing next to Bob [Dylan] during the whole set. We were standing in the back, and Bob was going, 'Oh, man, I can't believe he's doing that one. Oh, man.' Phil was amazing."

At one point, as he was nearing the end of his set, Phil panicked when he saw Dylan moving out of the room.

"Don't go, Bobby," he called out, sounding desperate.

"I'm not going anywhere," Dylan assured him. "I'm just getting a drink."

Phil then surprised Dylan by playing a stirring version of Dylan's "Lay Down Your Weary Tune." It was both a tribute and an autobiographical statement. When he finished, the Folk City audience rewarded him with one of the biggest ovations of the evening.

As Phil left the stage, Dylan made certain that he got his cowboy hat back.

———

Phil hung around New York in December, staying for a time at the Prince Street apartment and eventually taking up with a woman who looked after him much the way Deni Frand had taken care of him a year earlier. His energy had disappeared. He attended the Rolling Thunder Revue's "Night of the Hurricane" concert at Madison Square Garden, but he showed no inclination toward working himself. That part of him was gone. He continued to worry his friends with his talk of suicide, but such talk had become so routine that most of his friends doubted that he would follow through on his threats.

In the post-Train months, New York had become a difficult place. Phil had always enjoyed a large support group in the city, but he was convinced that he had permanently alienated everyone around him. The city's tremendous energy level, once a source of inspiration, now seemed imposing. Its circle of musicians, artists, and writers only reminded Phil of his own creative demise. He needed to get away for a while.

He left in January. A friend drove him to Sonny's house in Far Rockaway. Phil explained to Sonny, somewhat apologetically, that he wanted to stay for only a few days, and Sonny assured him that he was welcome to stay as long as he wanted. She had never seen him looking so deflated. Ironically, she had recently hosted Meegan for an extended stay at the house, taking care of her while her mother worked through some personal problems; now she was taking care of Meegan's father.

Sonny's efforts to help her brother were valiant, but she was neither a psychiatrist nor attuned enough to Phil's world to make a significant difference. Sonny hated big cities, the music business milieu, and the kind of lifestyle that Phil had lived in New York and California; she had nothing but contempt for what she considered to be excessive living. She had always appreciated her brother's artistic integrity, but she could never understand why anyone would go through hell to attain the kind of stardom that Phil so desperately desired. To Sonny, nirvana was a home in the woods and the simple life with her children.

Her main concerns with Phil were twofold. First, she hoped to nurture him back to physical and mental stability. Once she had accomplished that, she wanted to guide him back toward performing and recording again. Phil was in terrible shape, but Sonny refused to see him as a lost cause.

Phil proved to be both an ideal and a challenging houseguest. In his depressed state, Phil was quiet and lethargic, and at times it appeared to Sonny as if he was going out of his way to avoid being an imposition to her and her two sons, David and Jonathan. As in New York, Phil preferred to stay in and watch television or—better yet, if the boys were around—play cards for hours on end at the kitchen table. He was not interested in going out, or in playing or listening to music.

"He was just totally, totally passive," Sonny recalled. "He didn't want to do anything but play cards. That was the constant. Sometimes I'd get angry at him and say, 'You've got to do something physical. You can't just sit around like this. It's only going to make you feel worse.' Finally, I got him to walk over to my mother's house every now and then. She lived about eight blocks away."

Sonny was well aware of Phil's suicidal thoughts, but she questioned his resolve. Such talk, she reasoned, was a cry for help, and whenever the topic came up between them, she would try to address the issue without acting too alarmed.

"I would try to joke about it," she remembered. "I would joke about the different methods. I'd say, 'Well, you know, suicide's pretty rough. How are you going to do it? You don't have a gun, so you can't shoot yourself. You could take pills, but that's way too slow.' " She would go on and on, listing every method that came to mind, the litany dragging on until the thought of suicide came across as being impossible and absurd. The conversation always came to the same conclusion. "I guess you'll just have to live," Sonny would say.

And Phil would simply shrug and retreat back into himself.

Or deal another hand of cards.

Like his father three decades earlier, Phil had become a presence around the house, a soul lost in the netherworld of his own dark thoughts.

"It was like he was being mugged along the way by ghosts he never saw," said Ramsey Clark, who saw Phil in his final months, and who admitted surprise at Phil's passive, resigned state. "Phil was one of the last people you'd ever expect to give up on anything. I figured he'd be the last one onstage, singing when the ship went down. He loved life passionately."

———

In retrospect, there is no way of knowing what Phil expected to come out of his visit to Sonny's house in Queens. From a pragmatic standpoint, he was sparing himself the brutality of another long New York winter; he had room and board, as well as someone to take care of him. He was not interested in returning to Los Angeles any more than he had any use for staying in New York, and by moving in with Sonny, he was retreating to a safe part of the past and distancing himself from the realities of John Train. With Sonny, he could stay alive without really having to live.

Nevertheless, life with Sonny, for all of her admirable efforts, was depressing to Phil. He was uncomfortable in a domestic setting, especially when his nephews bickered back and forth as teenage boys often do, or when everyone was gone and he was left on his own in the middle of suburbia. Aside from his occasional forays to his mother's house, Phil refused to set foot outside of his sister's house, even to run small errands. If he ran out of cigarettes, he would wait until Sonny returned from work, and he would borrow cigarettes from her until she went out and replaced his supply.

Phil had very few visitors while he was staying in Far Rockaway, but those who saw him were concerned about his welfare. He seemed unhappily out of place.

"It's far-fetched to place Phil Ochs in that setting," commented a friend who visited him at Sonny's. "It's just a given that if you're a cosmopolitan New Yorker, just *being* in Far Rockaway or the Bronx or Brooklyn—any place but Manhattan—is a bummer. You might go there to visit someone, but you certainly wouldn't want to live there.

"The day I was there, Sonny had some friends over, and people were playing music. Sonny, of course, kept urging Phil to join in, but he was sitting in a corner, in a world of his own, ignoring me or whoever else came in. He looked like a little old lady. This was not the Phil Ochs that we knew—no relation at all—and I couldn't help but feel that it was a negative thing for him to be there, even though, at the time, it seemed like a great idea. It was better than seeing him lying in the gutter, no two ways about it. At least he was in a nice, clean place, and he was getting fed. But in terms of feeding his soul, you couldn't have put him in a worse place."

In retrospect, Sonny expressed reservations of her own about the effectiveness of Phil's stay with her. She was quick to admit that she was ill-equipped to handle what would have been a challenging case for a clinical psychiatrist, but she was helpless to do anything but improvise on a day-to-day basis. She tried to make Phil feel at home by fixing up a room with his possessions, and she went out of her way to give him as much room as he needed. She could not, however, force him to seek professional help, and her efforts to get him out of the house, other than to visit their mother, were dismal failures.

One particular trip especially stood out in her mind. "In February," she said, "I brought him to the country, but it wasn't much of a visit. He stayed at my friend Marie's house at the bottom of the hill. You could tell that he was miserable."

As the weeks passed and Phil showed no signs of improvement, Sonny grew increasingly concerned about the odds of her brother's taking his life. If she returned home from work and did not immediately see Phil seated in his familiar place at the kitchen table, she would go on a room-to-room search of the house, fearing the worst and hoping for the best. If he failed to turn up, she would call her mother and ask if he was there. Invariably, that is where he would be.

In her heart, Sonny knew that her relief over his safety was only temporary. For all her efforts, Phil still controlled his ultimate destiny.

———

Throughout the winter, the daily card games remained Phil's only true source of pleasure. He loved Sonny's boys, and David, at fourteen, and Jonathan, at eleven, were at ideal ages to have an adult male around the house. David, in particular, idolized Phil, and he was always after him to play a few songs. Phil was reluctant, but he found it difficult to turn the youngster down. They arranged a deal: Phil would play a song for every five hands of cards that he lost. David was thrilled with the arrangement. With all the cards they were playing, it was a good bet that Phil would be singing fairly often.

———

Although he rarely saw any of his old friends, Phil stayed in touch with a handful of people from his past. Michael called from time to time, usually to check in on Phil and to try to persuade him to consider performing again. Jerry Rubin would call to offer support and, on occasion, the details of another type of treatment.

The most frequent caller was Andy Wickham, who was now suggesting that Phil might be better off moving back to California. Wickham, with his no-nonsense approach to dealing with Phil, could still reach him to a certain extent. Phil looked forward to hearing from him, and he was delighted when Wickham called late in March and announced that he was coming out to see him.

Wickham's arrival brought Phil back to life. The two went restaurant-and-bar-hopping, just as they had done when Phil lived in Los Angeles; they talked about anything that popped into their heads. One night, while visiting a local tavern, they learned that Walter Seeley, a retired boxer whom Andy admired, lived in the area, and they paid him a spur-of-the-moment visit. Wickham's serendipity was just what Phil needed.

Unfortunately, such activity was only a temporary respite and did not move Phil to further action. Shortly before leaving, Wickham repeated his idea that Phil should return to Los Angeles. Phil shrugged, but promised to give the notion some consideration.

He never saw Wickham again.

———

Seeing Phil's change in moods while Wickham was in town, Sonny tried to talk her brother into getting out more often. With spring setting in and the weather improving, Sonny hoped that the warmer temperatures would encourage Phil to go for walks or, better yet, take an occasional trip into Manhattan. To Sonny's delight, Phil seemed at least marginally receptive to the idea. They attended a B. B. King–Bobby "Blue" Bland concert at the Beacon Theater in New York, and another time they went to see *One Flew Over the Cuckoo's Nest*, a movie featuring Jack Nicholson, one of Phil's favorite actors. The choice of films, with its insane-asylum setting and its theme about the struggle to maintain individuality in a rigid society, might not have been the best selection, as Sonny herself later admitted.

Sonny had reason to feel guardedly optimistic. After what seemed like a lifetime of nagging, she had finally convinced Phil to consult with a local psychiatrist, and while she was generally opposed to chemical treatments for psychological disorders, Sonny was happy when Phil told her that he had received a prescription and was taking medication for manic depression.* Then, on April 3, while hosting a party for a group of friends and co-workers, she was able to talk Phil into playing several numbers. His voice was far from perfect, but Sonny's guests were thrilled nevertheless to hear him running through such chestnuts as "There But for Fortune" and "Changes" again.

Phil appeared to be encouraged by the enthusiastic response. After playing the songs, he walked slowly up the stairs leading to his room and sat down on the edge of his bed. Jonathan followed him up and sat down next to him.

"Maybe there's hope," Phil told his nephew. "Maybe I'd better start practicing again."

Two days later, Sonny accompanied Phil to Manhattan to shop for a new guitar. She had heard of Phil's comments and she wanted to offer her support while he seemed to be open to the possibility of performing again. Phil had a standing invitation to play at a coffeehouse near Columbia University, and only a couple of weeks earlier, he had received an invitation to play at a folk festival in Europe. Phil had rejected all of these requests, but in light of his remarks two evenings previous, Sonny hoped that he might reconsider.

They visited a number of guitar shops, but they came up empty. Phil was looking for the exact model of guitar that he had used when he first started playing in the Village clubs, but no one had it in stock. Disappointed, Phil returned to Far Rockaway. There would be no further discussion about comebacks.

———

Sonny's birthday was upcoming on April 12, and she thought it might be nice to celebrate the occasion at her place in upstate New York. Phil hated the idea. He had been thoroughly miserable when he had

---

* She later discovered that Phil had not been telling the truth.

"I was on his case about it," she said. "Everyday, I would say to him, 'Did you take your medication?' and he would say, 'Yes.' After he died, I found the container and there wasn't one pill missing. Phil hadn't taken a single pill."

gone there in February, and he could see no reason to return. Sonny held her ground. A change of scenery, she insisted, would be good for everyone.

"What are you getting me for my birthday?" she teased, hoping to snap Phil out of his mood.

Phil just laughed.

On Tuesday, April 6, Phil returned to Manhattan to have dinner with Jerry Rubin and Ron Cobb. Phil still seemed depressed, but Ron thought he was in better shape than when he had seen him last. At least he was now joking about suicide.

At Rubin's apartment, Phil took a seat on the window ledge.

"How about this?" he said to Jerry and Ron, dangling his leg out the window. "What do you think it would be like to jump out this window?"

The morbid humor continued throughout the evening. Every time Phil thought of a different way to commit suicide, he brought it up to Jerry and Ron. Neither was amused. Rubin, as always, tried to talk Phil into seeking professional help, while Cobb tried to talk him into joining him and Robin in California.

At the end of the evening, after dropping Rubin off at his apartment, Ron Cobb and Robin Love walked Phil to a subway station, where Phil was going to catch a train back to Far Rockaway.

"Come on back and stay with us," they urged Phil, now more out of habit than from any sense that he would accept their invitation.

To their surprise, he agreed. "I'll do it," he said.

While they waited for the train, Phil began to joke again about committing suicide.

"What do you think, Cobb?" he said. "What about the third rail? Is that the way to go?"

Cobb, long accustomed to the game, shook his head.

"No, Phil," he replied. "It's too painful, and it might not work."

At that moment, the train roared into the station. As Phil stepped into the subway car, he turned to Ron and Robin.

"Yeah," he conceded, "hanging is the only way."

Michael called his brother on Wednesday.

He had phoned every week since Phil had moved in with Sonny, mostly to offer moral support, and he and Phil had played verbal ping-pong on the topic of suicide for so long that Michael had become adept at steering Phil away from the topic.

Phil, however, never failed to pose one specific question whenever they talked.

"Do you think my songs will survive?" he'd ask.

Michael always assured him that they would.

On this occasion, Michael informed Phil that he would be traveling to New York the following Monday. He wanted to talk to Phil about the possibility of booking a small tour. Phil agreed to meet him—that is, he told Michael, if he was still alive.

———

At two o'clock on Thursday morning, Sonny found Phil standing in the kitchen, leaning against the refrigerator, his arms propped against the top of the appliance and his head resting on his arms. He was staring off into space, obviously deep in thought.

"What are you thinking about?" Sonny asked.

Phil didn't volunteer an answer.

In years to come, Sonny would be absolutely convinced that this was the moment when Phil was reaching his decision.

———

Phil visited his mother the following afternoon. They talked for a long time, walking along the beach, Phil speaking of the happy days of his youth. Gertrude was surprised. She had not seen her son in such a peaceful state in a long time. He appeared to be almost happy.

———

Friday, April 9, began as a typical schoolday morning. Sonny prepared to go to work in her teaching job at the junior high school, while Jonathan dressed for school. The only change in the routine was David, who had talked his mother into letting him stay home for the day.

One can only imagine what was running through Phil's mind at this point. If, as Sonny believes, he had already made the decision to take his life on that day, he now had a problem: he couldn't kill himself with David in the house. He would have to wait.

The opportunity arrived later in the morning, shortly before ten o'clock, when David left the house to visit a friend next door. He was gone for only a few minutes, but it was time enough. Phil took one of the chairs from the kitchen table into the bathroom, stood on it, and fashioned a noose out of his belt. Whatever was passing through his head on his final moments on earth will never be known—he left no note. He slipped the belt around his neck, wedged it into the top of the door, and kicked away the chair.

———

When David arrived back at the house, he immediately noticed the missing chair and ran to the bathroom, where he was horrified to see the belt still swinging at the top of the bathroom door. Frightened out of his wits, he rushed to the phone and called his mother at work.

Sonny raced from the school, arriving at her house at the same time as the police. David, totally traumatized, stood out in the yard. The police insisted on entering the house first, and after a few minutes, Sonny was summoned to identify the body.

"They had him laid out on the floor of the room right next to the bathroom," she recalled. "He looked very peaceful, like he was resting."

For Phil, the painful, intolerable depression had finally come to an end. There would be no more suffering, no more self-doubt. He had finally found safe haven.

AFTERWORD

Sonny, who hated funerals to begin with, made arrangements to have Phil's body cremated. The decision did not rest well with Michael, who had hoped to come to New York to see his brother one final time, but Sonny wanted to avoid having Phil's suicide exploited by the media or fans any more than was unavoidable. As it was, the news of Phil's death was reported on the radio and in newspapers from coast to coast.

The obituaries, although mixed in their assessments of Phil's artistic importance, were generally kind. The *New York Times* called Phil a "folk singer, guitarist and lyricist whose music provided some of the strongest notes of protest against the Vietnam War," while the *Chicago Sun-Times* praised him as a sensitive troubadour devoted to social and political change. "You saw his face on television screens, singing at major and minor civil rights and antiwar rallies, lending cultural affirmation to what we know was right," the Chicago paper stated, adding that "as a troubadour he affected the collective consciousness of an era." *New Times* magazine, in a write-up that would have pleased Phil, praised his later, nonpolitical work: "Ochs was also a talented and sensitive melodist, whose abilities transcended the pamphleteer's, and whose ambitions encompassed art as well as politics."

Friends and family members were left to sort through their feelings and deal with what Phil's life and death meant to them. Anger, sadness, guilt, futility, and resignation—all visited the survivors. Suicide had left its inevitable aftermath. For many, it would take years to heal.

————

One day, not long after Phil's death, Sonny received a parcel in the mail. She had been unable to bring herself to return to the funeral parlor, and thus had not claimed Phil's ashes after his cremation. The package in the mail contained the remains of her brother. Neither Sonny nor Michael knew what to do with the ashes, so Sonny simply placed the box on top of her refrigerator, where it sat for months, awaiting its final destination.

Andy Wickham eventually posed a solution. He was going to the United Kingdom, and he offered to scatter Phil's ashes in Scotland, Phil's adopted second homeland. Wickham arranged a modest ceremony, which found the Pipe Band of the Queen's Own Highlanders playing "The Flowers of the Forest" while Andy released Phil's ashes from a turret of the Edinburgh Castle.

————

On April 29, 1976, Bella Abzug, congresswoman from New York and a speaker at Phil's final "War Is Over" rally in Central Park, asked to read a statement into the *Congressional Record*. Her statement read:

> Mr. Speaker, a few weeks ago, a young folksinger whose music personified the protest mood of the 1960s took his own life. Phil Ochs—whose original compositons were compelling moral statements against war in Southeast Asia—apparently felt that he had run out of words.
>
> While his tragic action was undoubtedly motivated by terrible personal despair, his death is a political as well as an artistic tragedy. I believe it is indicative of the despair many of the activists of the 1960s are experiencing as they perceive a government which continues the distortion of national priorities that is exemplified in the military budget we have before us.
>
> Phil Ochs' poetic pronouncements were part of a larger effort to galvanize his generation into taking action to prevent war, racism, and poverty. He left us a legacy of important songs that continue to be relevant in 1976—even though "the war is over."
>
> Just one year ago—during this week of the anniversary of

the end of the Vietnam War—Phil recruited entertainers to appear at the "War Is Over" celebration in Central Park, at which I spoke.

It seems particularly appropriate that this week we should commemorate the contributions of this extraordinary young man.

———

Phil's death set off a flurry of FBI reports and memos in Los Angeles, New York, and Washington D.C.

On Tuesday, April 13, 1976, an agent in Los Angeles sent a letter, via AIRTEL, to the Bureau offices in New York and Washington D.C.:

"The Los Angeles Times," daily metropolitan newspaper, dated 4/12/76, carried a UPI article, datelined New York, captioned 'Phil Ochs, 35, Folk Singer and Viet War Protester, Kills Self." Article reveals OCHS hanged himself in his sister's house on Friday 4/9/76. Sister and location of her home not revealed.

In the same memo, the Los Angeles agent asked the New York agent on the Ochs case to check with the Bureau of Vital Statistics, to "verify subject's death and advise Los Angeles."

On April 26, the New York agent responded with a memo that was delivered to both the Los Angeles and Washington D.C. offices. The agent provided Sonny's address, as well as the name and address of her former husband. Also included was a clipping of the New York Times article on Phil's suicide.

Other memos, all dealing with Phil's death and what the Bureau should do about it, criss-crossed the country.

On May 5, a memo signed by FBI director Clarence M. Kelly was forwarded to the director of the United States Secret Service. This FBI document deemed Phil to be "potentially dangerous because of background emotional instability or activity in groups engaged in activites inimical to U.S."

Phil had been dead for nearly a month.

SOURCE NOTES

In researching the life of Phil Ochs, I relied upon countless sources, from the testimony of his family members, friends, and acquaintances (acknowledged elsewhere in this volume), to his detailed scrapbooks, diaries, and notebooks. Taped interviews and concerts were very valuable, as were the seemingly endless newsclippings, magazine articles, books about Phil and the sixties, concert programs, and songbooks that I consulted. In documenting my sources, I tried to give as complete and accurate information as possible, but on several occasions, usually when I obtained information from Phil's scrapbook clippings, this was not possible. In those instances, I cite the scrapbook, along with whatever information was available.

PROLOGUE

"a driven man" Text of speech given by Ramsey Clark at Phil Ochs' memorial service at Madison Square Garden, courtesy of Sonny Ochs.
"the world's a little . . ." Text of speech given by Stew Albert at Phil Ochs' memorial service, courtesy of Sonny Ochs.
"So many people . . ." Sonny Ochs, notes from Phil Ochs' memorial service program, courtesy of Sonny Ochs.

CHAPTER ONE: BOY IN OHIO

Much of the background information about the Ochs family and Phil Ochs' childhood was obtained from author interviews with Sonny Ochs, Michael Ochs, and, to a much lesser extent, Meegan Ochs. A lengthy interview with Fanny Ochs, conducted and supplied by Sonny Ochs, also proved invaluable. Phil Ochs' scrapbooks, including his photographs and handwritten captions, were helpful.

"I suppose . . ." Taped interview with Fanny Ochs, courtesy of Sonny Ochs.
"He was . . ." Author interview with Sonny Ochs.

"My mother . . ." Ibid.

"I cannot . . ." Ibid. All other citations in this passage are from this source.

"My father . . ." Ibid.

"Take these . . ." Ibid.

"He was incredibly . . ." Author interview with Michael Ochs.

"It was absolute . . ." Author interview with Sonny Ochs.

"Over my . . ." Ibid.

"You have exceptional . . ." Musical evaluation in Phil Ochs scrapbook.

"I had . . ." Author interview with Sonny Ochs.

"I had never . . ." Phil Ochs, "White Milk to Red Wine," Staunton Military Academy yearbook, Phil Ochs scrapbook.

CHAPTER TWO: THE SINGING SOCIALISTS

"Phil knew . . ." Author interview with Jim Glover.

"I wasn't really . . ." Rusty Wilson, "Former OSU student/folk singer's life remembered," *The Lantern*, April 9, 1984.

"Well, we gotta . . ." Author interview with Jim Glover.

"Your song shows . . ." Phil Ochs scrapbook.

"Everybody came through . . ." Studs Terkel's WFMT (Chicago) radio show, May 31, 1973, courtesy of Studs Terkel.

"I don't think . . ." Author interview with Dave Van Ronk.

CHAPTER THREE: BOUND FOR GLORY

"Earth Shoe groupies": Author interview with Arthur Gorson.

"What you had . . ." Author interview with Sonny Ochs.

"Call it . . ." Author interview with Sis Cunningham.

"Malvina Reynolds . . ." Ibid.

"The three of us . . ." Ibid.

"He would dig . . ." Gordon Friesen, "Phil Ochs: A Book Review," *Broadside #141.*

"When I asked . . ." Ibid.

"a Will Rogers . . ." Advertisement for Phil Ochs performance, Phil Ochs scrapbook.

"His social protest . . ." Bob Fraund, "Folk-Singing Bug Bites Our Man Bob," *Ft. Lauderdale News*, April 5–11, 1963.

"He was up . . ." Author interview with Erik Jacobsen.

"I don't know . . ." Author interview with Sonny Ochs. All other citations in this passage are from this source.

"I'm playing . . ." Ibid. All other citations in this passage are from this source.

"C'mon and take . . ." Phil Ochs, "Power and the Glory," © 1963 Appleseed Music, Inc.

"Here's a land . . ." Ibid.

"Now they sing . . ." Phil Ochs, "Bound for Glory," © 1963 Appleseed Music, Inc.

"a dress rehearsal . . ." Robert Shelton, *No Direction Home: The Life and Music of Bob Dylan* (NY: Ballantine), p. 197.

"a convention . . ." Author interview with Dave Van Ronk.

"There was a definite . . ." Author interview with Tom Paxton.

"Dylan's crowning moment": Anthony Scaduto, *Dylan* (NY: New American Library, 1973), p. 172.

"I loved . . ." Author interview with Arlo Guthrie.

"They laid him . . ." Phil Ochs, "Too Many Martyrs," © 1963 Appleseed Music, Inc.

"Well, I've seen . . ." Phil Ochs, "Talking Birmingham Jam," © 1963 Appleseed Music, Inc.

"A lot of them . . ." Author interview with Harold Leventhal.

"something funny . . ." Author interview with Sis Cunningham.

CHAPTER FOUR: WHAT'S THAT I HEAR?

"A lot of people . . ." Phil Ochs, as quoted in the concert's program, Phil Ochs scrapbook.

"I think . . ." Author interview with Alice Ochs.

"it seemed . . ." Phil Ochs, "That Was the President," © 1963 Appleseed Music, Inc.

"Phil was absolutely . . ." Author interview with Sam Hood.

"I wasn't just . . ." Ibid.

"William Worthy isn't . . ." Phil Ochs, "The Ballad of William Worthy," © 1963 Appleseed Music, Inc.

"Dick Gregory has . . ." Undated William Worthy letter to Phil Ochs, Phil Ochs scrapbook.

"I wouldn't . . ." Author interview with Michael Ochs.

"social realism": Author interview with Sis Cunningham.

"I organized . . ." Author interview with Arthur Gorson.

"We met . . ." Author interview with Tom Paxton.

"Minin' is a hazard . . ." Phil Ochs, "Hazard, Kentucky," © 1963 Appleseed Music, Inc.

"We were hot . . ." Author interview with Arthur Gorson.

"Let's drink . . ." Phil Ochs, "No Christmas in Kentucky," © 1963 Appleseed Music, Inc.

"beatnik type": Phil Ochs FBI file, courtesy of Sis Cunningham and Gordon Friesen. All other citations in this passage are from this source.

"Phil Ochs . . ." n.a., "Musical News Significant But Not Worth Extra Edition," *Northwest Arkansas Times*, June 5, 1964.

"In his first . . ." Josh Dunson, "Topical Songs," *High Fidelity*, Phil Ochs scrapbook.

"There is great . . ." Myre Buttle, "An Interview with Phil Ochs, Topical Song Writer," *Hootenanny*, June 1964.

"Some of the . . ." Author interview with Len Chandler.

"It was a real . . ." Author interview with Henry Diltz.

"We were young . . ." Author interview with Dave Van Ronk.

"We were goosing . . ." Author interview with Len Chandler.

"Van Ronk used . . ." Author interview with Tom Paxton.

"This was . . ." Author interview with Arthur Gorson.

"Ironically . . ." Phil Ochs, "Requiem for a Hootenanny," *Boston Broadside*, March 4, 1964.

"Alice . . ." Author interview with Michael Ochs.

"One good song . . ." Phil Ochs, "The Need for Topical Music," *Broadside #22* (March 1963).

"the commercial . . ." Phil Ochs, "Topical Songs—History on the Spot," Phil Ochs scrapbook.

"Whether topical songs . . ." Ibid.

"The stuff you're writing . . ." Anthony Scaduto, *Dylan* (NY: New American Library, 1973), p. 205.

"the sound . . ." Phil Ochs, "What's That I Hear?" © 1963 Appleseed Music, Inc.

"had somehow lost . . ." Robert Shelton, *No Direction Home: The Life and Music of Bob Dylan* (NY: Ballantine, 1987), p. 294.

"The Festival's . . ." Paul Wolfe, "Newport '64," *Broadside #53* (December 1964).

"Professor Silber . . ." Phil Ochs, "An Open Letter from Phil Ochs to Irwin Silber, Paul Wolfe, and Joseph E. Levine," *Broadside #54*.

"It was very . . ." Author interview with Len Chandler.

"We turned . . ." Ibid.

"Here's to the State . . ." Phil Ochs, "Here's to the State of Mississippi," © 1964 Appleseed Music, Inc.

"Oh, here's . . ." Ibid.

"a continuation . . ." Phil Ochs, liner notes to *The Broadside Singers* (BR 303).

CHAPTER FIVE: I AIN'T MARCHING ANYMORE

"Oh I marched . . ." Phil Ochs, "I Ain't Marching Anymore," © 1964 Appleseed Music, Inc.

"It's always . . ." Ibid.

"Call it 'Peace' . . ." Ibid.

"This borders . . ." Phil Ochs, liner notes to *I Ain't Marching Anymore* (EKL-287).

"The fact that . . ." Ibid.

"I was taking . . ." Ibid.

"win any fans . . ." n.a., "I Ain't Marching Anymore," *Wichita Eagle*, March 14, 1965.

"one of the finest . . ." Ibid.

"you have to be . . ." n.a., "I Ain't Marching Anymore," *Denver Post*, March 14, 1965.

"Don't be fooled . . ." Ibid.

"And so . . ." Phil Ochs, liner notes to *I Ain't Marching Anymore*.

"I didn't know . . ." Author interview with Arthur Gorson.

"It's the right . . ." Ibid.

"revolution in songwriting": Ibid.

"I've never met . . ." Ibid.

"*Someday . . .*" Ibid.

"*First snow . . .*" Phil Ochs, "First Snow," © 1983, Phil Ochs Estate. First published in *Broadside #147.*

"*I knew Phil . . .*" Author interview with Jack Landron.

"*some very good lines*": Sis Cunningham and Gordon Friesen, "An Interview with Phil Ochs," *Broadside #63.*

"*like tenth-rate Dylan*": Ibid.

"*It's going to give . . .*" Ibid.

"*He was very . . .*" Author interview with Paul Krassner.

"*a slab of mortar . . .*" Ibid.

"*A demonstration . . .*" Ibid.

"*They responded . . .*" Ibid.

"*a reverse kind . . .*" Carl Schoettler, "Singer Stirs Up Fuss, Ridicules Red Charges," Phil Ochs scrapbook.

"*I don't want . . .*" Ibid.

"*I cried . . .*" Phil Ochs, "Love Me, I'm a Liberal," © 1965 Barricade Music, Inc.

"*Sure, once I was . . .*" Ibid.

"*Now, for a change . . .*" Author interview with Paul Krassner.

"*Phil Ochs . . .*" n.a., "N.Y. Folk Festival in Solid Bow; 51G Take Despite Name Shortage," *Variety,* Phil Ochs scrapbook.

"*As for the reasons . . .*" Phil Ochs, "Ochs: It Ain't Me, Babe," *Village Voice,* August 12, 1965.

"*The trouble . . .*" Phil Ochs, "Newport: The Short, Hot Summer," *Broadside #61.*

"*It was like . . .*" Author interview with Arthur Gorson.

"*Some people saw fit . . .*" Phil Ochs, "Ochs: It Ain't Me, Babe."

"*It's all music . . .*" Robert Shelton, "Pop Singers and Song Writers Racing Down Bob Dylan's Road," *New York Times,* August 27, 1965.

"*A herd . . .*" Author interview with Patrick Sky.

"*Hey, maybe . . .*" Anthony Scaduto, *Dylan* (NY: New American Library, 1973), p. 262.

"*You ought to find . . .*" Ibid., p. 263.

"*Dylan was always . . .*" Author interview with Len Chandler.

"*In retrospect . . .*" Author interview with Tom Paxton.

"*the one . . .*" Scaduto, *Dylan,* p. 264. All other citations in this passage are from this source.

"*Sit by my side . . .*" Phil Ochs, "Changes," © 1965 Barricade Music, Inc.

"*Scenes of my . . .*" Ibid.

"*Passions will part . . .*" Ibid.

"*He called . . .*" Author interview with Arthur Gorson.

"*I just can't . . .*" Peter McDonald, "Enter Mr. Ochs . . . ," *Gongster,* December 9, 1965.

"*I'm at the point . . .*" and "*As bad . . .*" Karl Dallas, "Dylan said it—'I can't keep up with Phil,' " *Melody Maker,* November 29, 1965.

"*And the night . . .*" Phil Ochs, "Crucifixion," © 1966, 1968 Barricade Music, Inc.

"*In the green . . .*" Ibid.

"*So dance . . .*" Ibid.

"*Images of innocence . . .*" Ibid.

"*a study . . .*" Phil Ochs on Studs Terkel's WFMT (Chicago) radio show, May 31, 1973, courtesy of Studs Terkel.

"*The Kennedy assassination . . .*" Ibid.

"*They say . . .*" Phil Ochs, "Crucifixion."

"*I don't know . . .*" Phil Ochs on Studs Terkel radio show.

"*Phil wrote . . .*" Author interview with Arthur Gorson.

CHAPTER SIX: CHANGES

"*Everyone said . . .*" Author interview with Arthur Gorson.

"*Promotion was . . .*" Ibid.

"*A barber . . .*" Author interview with Sonny Ochs.

"*Mostly, one suspects . . .*" Robert Shelton, "Phil Ochs Makes Debut as Soloist," *New York Times*, January 8, 1966.

"*There's been . . .*" Phil Ochs, between-song patter on *Phil Ochs in Concert* (EKL-310).

"*And I won't . . .*" Phil Ochs, "When I'm Gone," © 1966 Barricade Music, Inc.

"*That's not . . .*" Erin Raudsepp, "Smiling Protester Lives for Today," *The Globe and Mail*, September 14, 1966.

"*Show me a prison . . .*" Phil Ochs, "There But for Fortune," © 1963 Appleseed Music, Inc.

"*vicious, brilliant . . .*" n.a., "Vicious, Brilliant Dynamite from Phil," *Melody Maker*, April 20, 1966.

"*a good sampling . . .*" n.a., "Record Reviews: Phil Ochs in Concerts," *Variety*, April 6, 1966.

"*a fast moving . . .*" n.a., "Phil Ochs in Concert," *Cash Box*, April 16, 1966.

"*Ochs has gained . . .*" Robert Shelton, "Phil Ochs Returns with His Own Songs," *New York Times*, November 25, 1966.

"*The best . . .*" Jack Newfield, "Aesthetics Is In," *Village Voice*, December 1, 1966.

"*I loved it . . .*" Author interview with Arthur Gorson.

"*He was very . . .*" Ibid.

"*We started out . . .*" Ibid.

"*What are you . . .*" Author interview with Michael Ochs. All other citations in the passage are from this source.

"*I was at . . .*" Ibid.

"*What's up . . .*" Ibid. All other citations in this passage are from this source.

"*I'll give you . . .*" Ibid. All other citations in this passage are from this source.

"*I was sitting . . .*" Ibid.

"*If you're . . .*" Ibid. All other citations in this passage are from this source.

CHAPTER SEVEN: THE WAR IS OVER

"*for literary . . .*" Author interview with Jack Newfield.

"*I think . . .*" Ibid.

"He had . . ." Ibid.

"It is we . . ." Arthur M. Schlesinger, Jr., *Robert Kennedy and His Times* (NY: Ballantine Books, 1978), p. 832.

"You think . . ." Ibid., p. 833.

"It was . . ." Author interview with Jack Newfield.

"He was like . . ." Author interview with Ron Cobb.

"Andy Wickham . . ." Author interview with Doug Weston.

"Our friendship . . ." Author interview with Andy Wickham.

"With Phil . . ." Ibid.

"Why are you for . . ." Paul Krassner, *Confessions of a Raving, Unconfined Nut* (NY: Simon and Schuster, 1993), p. 115. All other citations in this passage are from this source.

"What Paul Krassner does . . ." Author interview with Paul Krassner.

"Isn't it true . . ." Krassner, *Confessions*, p. 118.

"Phil stood his ground . . ." Author interview with Paul Krassner.

"The old standbys . . ." Phil Ochs, "Have Faith, The War Is Over," *Los Angeles Free Press*, n.d., Phil Ochs scrapbook.

"It's beyond . . ." Phil Ochs in WBAI (New York) radio interview, October 21, 1967, courtesy of Michael Ochs.

"It sounds . . ." Ibid.

"Silent soldiers . . ." Phil Ochs, "The War Is Over," © 1968 Barricade Music, Inc.

"Call it peace . . ." Phil Ochs, "I Ain't Marching Anymore," © 1964 Barricade Music, Inc.

"So do your duty . . ." Phil Ochs, "The War Is Over."

"One-legged veterans . . ." Ibid.

"The war . . ." Phil Ochs, "Have You Heard? The War Is Over!" *Village Voice*, November 23, 1967.

"We will take . . ." n.a., *Day of Protest, Night of Violence: The Century City Peace March* (Los Angeles: Sawyer Press, 1967), p. 5.

"Angry artists . . ." Phil Ochs, "The War Is Over."

"My son . . ." *Day of Protest*, p. 18.

"The police were swinging . . ." Ibid., p. 11.

"The cops . . ." Author interview with Paul Krassner.

"The police . . ." Author interview with Ron Cobb.

"Phil just couldn't . . ." Ibid.

CHAPTER EIGHT: PLEASURES OF THE HARBOR

"We made . . ." Author interview with Larry Marks.

"He was an unsophisticated . . ." Author interview with Ian Freebairn-Smith.

"a little awkward": Ibid.

"In a way . . ." Ibid.

"It was a real . . ." Ibid.

"He was indefatigable . . ." Author interview with Larry Marks.

"He spoke . . ." Author interview with Lincoln Mayorga.

"We actually used . . ." Ibid.

"I don't know . . ." Phil Ochs, "Cross My Heart," © 1966 Barricade Music, Inc.

"But I'm gonna . . ." Ibid.

"Millionaires and paupers . . ." Phil Ochs, "Flower Lady," © 1966 Barricade Music, Inc.

"He wanted . . ." Author interview with Ian Freebairn-Smith.

"There but . . ." Phil Ochs, "There But for Fortune," © 1963 Appleseed Music, Inc.

"And the flower lady . . ." Phil Ochs, "Flower Lady."

"[It] came out . . ." Phil Ochs on Studs Terkel's WFMT (Chicago) radio show, May 31, 1973, courtesy of Studs Terkel.

"Look outside . . ." Phil Ochs, "Outside of a Small Circle of Friends," © 1967 Barricade Music, Inc.

"Smoking marijuana . . ." Ibid.

"But I've had . . ." Phil Ochs, "I've Had Her," © 1966 Barricade Music, Inc.

"Do you have . . ." Phil Ochs, "Miranda," © 1966 Barricade Music, Inc.

"The tune . . ." Author interview with Lincoln Mayorga.

"I wanted . . ." Author interview with Ian Freebairn-Smith.

"He had strong . . ." Author interview with Larry Marks.

"They travel . . ." Phil Ochs, "The Party," © 1966 Barricade Music, Inc.

"too overdone": Author interview with Michael Ochs.

"We sat down . . ." Author interview with Larry Marks.

"That's okay . . ." Author interview with Ian Freebairn-Smith.

"It was tricky . . ." Phil Ochs in WBAI (New York) radio interview, October 21, 1967, courtesy of Michael Ochs.

"an attempt . . ." n.a., "Phil Ochs," *New England Scene*, February 1968.

"In the room . . ." Phil Ochs, "Pleasures of the Harbor," © 1966 Barricade Music, Inc.

"an absolute nightmare": Author interview with Larry Marks.

"It was endless . . ." Ibid.

"Phil was unhappy . . ." Ibid.

"In those days . . ." Author interview with Bernie Grundman.

"I would watch . . ." Ibid.

"I remember . . ." Author interview with Larry Marks.

"I had just . . ." Author interview with Ian Freebairn-Smith.

"of no consequence": Ralph Earl, "Pleasures of the Harbor," *Broadside* (Boston), January 17–30, 1968.

"The record jacket . . ." Ibid.

"a memory . . ." Irwin Silber, "The Topical Song 'Revolution,' " *Guardian*, September 28, 1968.

"the most interesting" and *"the more important . . ."* Ibid.

"Ochs deals . . ." Ibid.

"Ochs is destined . . ." Robin Blair, "Protest Is Beauty in New Album by Phil Ochs," *Hartford Times*, July 8, 1968.

"a biting and beautiful . . ." Ibid.

"to move . . ." Tom Phillips, "Janis Gets Mellow," *New York Times*, December 10, 1967.

"a milestone . . ." n.a., "Pop Picks," *Cash Box*, October 7, 1967.

"a lyrical . . ." n.a., "Records," *Florida Times-Union*, February 4, 1968.

"The thing about . . ." Robert Christgau, "Secular Music," *Esquire*, May 1968.

CHAPTER NINE: TAPE FROM CALIFORNIA

"not a disaster . . ." Author interview with Michael Ochs.

"I was very disappointed . . ." Ibid.

"We'll book . . ." Ibid. All other citations in this passage are from this source.

"I was terrified . . ." Ibid.

"Ochs has finally . . ." Jack Newfield, "Notebook for Night Owls," *Village Voice*, October 5, 1967.

"The weather . . ." Phil Ochs on WBAI (New York) radio show, October 21, 1967, courtesy of Michael Ochs.

"Does protesting . . ." Phil Ochs, "Have You Heard? The War Is Over!" *Village Voice*, November 23, 1967.

"They'll do . . ." Leticia Kent, "On a Saturday Afternoon: 'The War Is Over,' " *Village Voice*, November 30, 1967. All other citations in this passage are from this source.

"an amazing event": Author interview with Larry Sloman.

"There must have been . . ." Ibid.

"We fought . . ." Author interview with Michael Ochs.

"They demanded . . ." Author interview with Doug Weston.

"What does . . ." Ibid.

"Leave it up . . ." Ibid.

"I worked . . ." Ibid.

"Sometimes, I suspect . . ." Harvey Siders, "Phil Ochs in Solo Stint on Santa Monica Stage," *Los Angeles Times*, December 19, 1967.

"His charm . . ." Ibid.

"He made me . . ." Author interview with Michael Ochs.

"He was wrong . . ." Author interview with Doug Weston.

"Jack and Jill . . ." Phil Ochs, "The Harder They Fall," © 1968 Barricade Music, Inc.

"Half the world . . ." Phil Ochs, "Tape from California," © 1968 Barricade Music, Inc.

"In my new . . ." Sis Cunningham and Gordon Friesen, "Interview with Phil Ochs," *Broadside #91*.

"In watching an old . . ." Ibid.

"It wants . . ." n.a., "TV Blacklist Too?" *Amusement Business*, February 17, 1968.

"The flower fled . . ." Phil Ochs, "The Doll House," © 1968 Barricade Music, Inc.

"He blamed me . . ." Author interview with Harold Leventhal.

"There were [some] . . ." Sis Cunningham and Gordon Friesen, "Notes," *Broadside #89*.

"The battle in America . . ." n.a., "Yippee," *Berkeley Barb*, April 5–11, 1968. All other citations in this passage are from this source.

"a beautiful shipwreck": Ibid.

"wavering back and forth . . ." Phil Ochs on Studs Terkel's WFMT (Chicago) radio show, May 31, 1971, courtesy of Studs Terkel.

"It was a little . . ." Author interview with Larry Marks.

"He was a real . . ." Ibid.

"The draft board . . ." Phil Ochs, "Tape from California."

"Phil Ochs may . . ." Sherwood L. Weingarten, "On the Record," (Camden, NJ) *Courier-Post*, August 10, 1968.

"most powerful . . ." and *"Ochs mixes . . ."* n.a., "Tape from California," *Billboard*, July 20, 1968.

"Ochs is a master . . ." Mary Campbell, "Records," *Great Falls Tribune*, August 4, 1968.

"I sang in Indiana . . ." Phil Ochs, "James Dean Lives in Indiana," *Village Voice*, May 9, 1968.

"Hubert Humphrey . . ." Ibid.

"We argued . . ." Author interview with Jack Newfield.

CHAPTER TEN: CHICAGO

"best architecture . . ." and *"There's a poetry . . ."* n.a., "Ochs: Pleasures of the Hilton," *Ramparts Wallposter*, August 24, 1968.

"You don't . . ." Ibid.

"The truth is . . ." Ibid.

"Why vote . . ." Author interview with Paul Krassner.

"he was acting . . ." Phil Ochs' FBI file, report dated September 25, 1968, courtesy of Sis Cunningham and Gordon Friesen.

"Jerry Rubin . . ." Author interview with Stew Albert.

"How many . . ." Marty Jezer, *Abbie Hoffman: American Rebel* (New Brunswick, NJ: Rutgers University Press, 1992), p. 158.

"It was very emotional . . ." Author interview with Paul Krassner.

"Will you put . . ." Ibid.

"Phil was genuinely . . ." Author interview with Stew Albert.

"Chicago was the formal . . ." Phil Ochs, in taped interview with Stew Albert.

"With George McGovern . . ." Milton Viorst, *Fire in the Streets: America in the 1960s* (NY: Simon and Schuster, 1979), p. 459.

"Fuck you . . ." Ibid.

CHAPTER ELEVEN: REHEARSALS FOR RETIREMENT

"He wouldn't perform . . ." Author interview with Stew Albert.

"Sailors climb . . ." Phil Ochs, "The Scorpion Departs But Never Returns," © 1971 Barricade Music, Inc.

"I've always tried . . ." Izzie Young, "Phil Ochs Back from Chicago," *Broadside*, November 1968.

"subversive": Phil Ochs' FBI file, courtesy of Sis Cunningham and Gordon Friesen. All other citations in this passage are taken from these documents.

"This then . . ." Phil Ochs, liner notes for *Rehearsals for Retirement* (A&M SP-4181).

"The songs . . ." David Franklin, "Both Sides Now," *Music Now*, March 7, 1970.

"I can see . . ." Phil Ochs, "Pretty Smart on My Part," © 1971 Barricade Music, Inc.

"I don't like . . ." Phil Ochs, "I Kill Therefore I Am," © 1971 Barricade Music, Inc.

"The lights . . ." Phil Ochs, "Rehearsals for Retirement," © 1971 Barricade Music, Inc.

"My life . . ." Phil Ochs, "My Life," © 1971 Barricade Music, Inc.

"It is surprising . . ." Robin Denselow, "Phil Ochs, the anti-cowboy," *Arts Guardian*, August 29, 1969.

"Rehearsals for Retirement . . ." Bob Baker, "Exciting New Ochs Album," *Image*, May 16–29, 1969.

"They'll rob . . ." Phil Ochs, "Chords of Fame," © 1971 Barricade Music, Inc.

"We had . . ." Author interview with Erik Jacobsen.

"Hello, hello . . ." Phil Ochs, "No More Songs," © 1971 Barricade Music, Inc.

"Once I knew . . ." Ibid.

"I was seized . . ." Franklin, "Both Sides Now."

"It was really . . ." Ibid.

CHAPTER TWELVE: GUNFIGHT AT CARNEGIE HALL

"with the intent . . ." Transcript of Chicago Seven testimony.

"You are . . ." Ibid. All other citations in this passage are from this source.

"I met . . ." William Kunstler, in a speech delivered at the Phil Ochs memorial service.

"Nixon . . ." Phil Ochs on Studs Terkel's WFMT (Chicago) radio show, May 31, 1973.

"Creek was runnin' . . ." Phil Ochs, "Boy in Ohio," © 1971 Barricade Music, Inc.

"Everything is . . ." Phil Ochs, "Gas Station Women," © 1971 Barricade Music, Inc.

"The whole way . . ." Bruce Pollock, *In Their Own Words: Lyrics and Lyricists 1955–1974* (NY: Macmillan, 1975), p. 55.

"I've found . . ." Phil Ochs, "My Kingdom for a Car," © 1971 Barricade Music, Inc.

"I was working . . ." Author interview with Van Dyke Parks.

"very intense": Ibid.

"It started . . ." Phil Ochs on Studs Terkel's radio show.

"I recently . . ." Pollock, *In Their Own Words*, p. 55.

"I thought . . ." Author interview with Paul Krassner.

"It was very comparable . . ." Author interview with Ron Cobb.

"You've got . . ." Author interview with Lincoln Mayorga.

"I went out . . ." Ibid.

"How can you . . ." John S. Wilson, "Phil Ochs Fans Are Won Over by Rock," *New York Times*, April 3, 1970.

"Give me . . ." Author interview with Sonny Ochs.

"He cut . . ." Author interview with Lincoln Mayorga.

368 / Source Notes

"The trick is . . ." Phil Ochs, dialogue from *Gunfight at Carnegie Hall* (Mobile Fidelity CD #794). All other citations in this passage are from this source.

"I want power . . ." Ibid.

"It became . . ." John S. Wilson, "Phil Ochs Fans Won Over."

"It was a battle . . ." Author interview with Arthur Gorson.

"He was physically . . ." Author interview with Lincoln Mayorga.

"He was moaning . . ." Ibid.

"Phil and I . . ." Author interview with Michael Ochs.

"It broke . . ." Author interview with Jerry Yester.

CHAPTER THIRTEEN: TRAVELS AND TRAVAILS

"We were like . . ." Author interview with Stew Albert.

"It was a wonderful . . ." n.a., "Ochs Sings His Opinions," *Los Angeles Times*, February 19, 1971.

"We went . . ." Author interview with Doug Weston.

"It was a kind . . ." Author interview with Stew Albert.

"We really . . ." Stew Albert, in a speech delivered at Phil Ochs memorial.

"We were everywhere . . ." Ibid.

"I think Victor . . ." Author interview with Stew Albert.

"the best . . ." Phil Ochs journal entry, August 30, 1971.

"Great! . . ." Ibid.

"I sang . . ." Ibid.

"They look like . . ." Author interview with Stew Albert.

"He was reading . . ." Ibid.

"neurotic, fast-talking . . ." Phil Ochs journal entry, September 8, 1971.

"kind of thought . . ." Author interview with David Ifshin.

"There were a lot . . ." Ibid.

"Phil was just . . ." Ibid.

"Look . . ." and *"If he's your friend . . ."* Ibid.

"Go with time . . ." Phil Ochs journal entry, September 16, 1971.

"I must push . . ." Ibid.

"He would tell . . ." Author interview with David Ifshin.

"like living . . ." Phil Ochs journal entry, October 8, 1971.

"There was nowhere . . ." Author interview with David Ifshin.

"Why don't . . ." Phil Ochs journal entry, October 8, 1971.

"I'm going . . ." Author interview with David Ifshin. All other citations in this passage are from this source.

"Comfort in . . ." Phil Ochs journal entry, October 8, 1971.

"I figured . . ." Author interview with David Ifshin.

"Strange to feel . . ." Phil Ochs journal entry, October 9, 1971.

"What a great . . ." Author interview with David Ifshin.

"It was the ultimate . . ." Ibid.

"Despair is really . . ." Phil Ochs journal entry, October 10, 1971.

"Whatever you do . . ." Author interview with David Ifshin.

"We've got to have . . ." Ibid.

"Help! . . ." Ibid. All other citations in this passage are from this source.

"Never was I . . ." Phil Ochs journal entry, October 10, 1971.

"What did you two . . ." Author interview with David Ifshin. All other citations in this passage are from this source.

"Don't go . . ." Ibid. All other citations in this passage are from this source.

CHAPTER FOURTEEN: HERE'S TO THE STATE OF RICHARD NIXON

"I can't believe . . ." Tape of Hunter College performance, courtesy of Michael Ochs.

"Here's to . . ." and *"Richard Nixon . . ."* Phil Ochs, *"Here's to the State of Richard Nixon,"* © 1971 Barricade Music, Inc.

"Here's to the laws . . ." Ibid.

"incredible response" and *"was very much . . ."* Phil Ochs journal entry, November 24, 1971.

"You were lucky . . ." Phil Ochs journal entry, November 26, 1971. All other citations in this passage are from this source.

"bad job . . ." Phil Ochs journal entry, December 10, 1971.

"Response not as big . . ." Ibid.

"Always get . . ." Phil Ochs journal entry, November 23, 1971.

"In state . . ." Phil Ochs journal entry, December 11, 1971.

"He never should have . . ." Author interview with Michael Ochs.

"totally out . . ." and *"beating her . . ."* Phil Ochs, journal entry, December 12, 1971.

"He was grinning . . ." Author interview with Michael Ochs.

"Everything is in . . ." Phil Ochs, undated journal entry.

"I was going to . . ." Phil Ochs, undated journal entry.

"I give critical . . ." Phil Ochs scrapbook.

"He was . . ." Author interview with Lee Housekeeper.

"She's the Kansas . . ." Phil Ochs, "Kansas City Bomber," © 1972 Barricade Music, Inc.

"I wasn't really . . ." Author interview with Ron Cobb.

"very low-key": Author interview with Robin Love.

"Both were prepared . . ." Ibid.

"Do you want . . ." Author interview with Ron Cobb.

"We were standing . . ." Ibid.

"He kind of stumbled . . ." Author interview with Robin Love.

"He did fine . . ." Ibid.

"I was drawing . . ." Ibid.

"It was very frightening . . ." Author interview with Ron Cobb.

"Am running myself . . ." Phil Ochs, undated journal entry.

"I'll never forget . . ." Author interview with Ron Cobb.

"There was a haunting . . ." Author interview with David Ifshin.

"his participation . . ." Phil Ochs' FBI file, courtesy of Sis Cunningham and Gordon Friesen.

"For years now . . ." Phil Ochs, "The Last Ten Best List," *Los Angeles Free Press*, February 9, 1973.

"Underneath the soul . . ." Phil Ochs, "Mike Mazurki's Spot," *Los Angeles Free Press*, February 16, 1971.

"curious to find out . . ." Phil Ochs, "Tom Reddin as Mayor: Opposes Pot Decriminalization, Freep Press Passes," *Los Angeles Free Press*, Phil Ochs scrapbook.

"Mr. Reddin . . ." Ibid.

"I want . . ." Ibid. All other citations in this passage are from this source.

"There may be . . ." Eliot Wald, "Ochs Still Marching to Drums of the 60s," *Chicago Daily News*, May 30, 1973.

"Ochs Still Marching . . ." Ibid.

"Phil Ochs: A Bit . . ." Bill Pollock, "Phil Ochs: A Bit of Nostalgia," *Los Angeles Herald-Examiner*, June 26, 1973.

"Sixties' Phil Ochs . . ." Mike Grosswold, "Sixties' Phil Ochs Is Alive and Singing," *Times Chronicle*, June 7, 1973.

"seeing Phil Ochs . . ." Wald, "Ochs Still Marching."

"I've been sitting . . ." Grosswold, "Sixties' Phil Ochs."

"There was a . . ." Tape of "Drunken Folkies Show," courtesy of Michael Ochs.

"We enjoyed . . ." Author interview with Dave Van Ronk.

"You underestimate . . ." "Drunken Folkies" tape.

"I hereby . . ." Ibid.

"I think . . ." Phil Ochs on Studs Terkel's WFMT (Chicago) radio program, May 31, 1972, courtesy of Studs Terkel.

CHAPTER FIFTEEN: AN EVENING WITH SALVADOR ALLENDE

"I vividly remember . . ." Author interview with David Ifshin.

"Phil and I . . ." Ibid.

"Phil had been . . ." Ibid. All other citations in this passage are from this source.

"Phil Ochs . . ." Peter Feldman, "Fumble, Mumble, Stumble," *Johannesburg Star*, November 9, 1973.

"I am more . . ." Raeford Daniel, "Phil Ochs Disappoints," n.d., Phil Ochs scrapbook.

"Yeah, I was . . ." Hugh Leggatt, " 'Yeah, man, I was pretty crazy,' " *Johannesburg Star*, November 9, 1973.

"Something's gotta . . ." Frank Rose, "Talking Chile Blues," *Zooworld*, June 20, 1974.

"We agreed . . ." Author interview with Deni Frand.

"Phil used . . ." Ibid.

"Basically . . ." Author interview with Cora Weiss.

"We sat . . ." Ibid.

"He would come . . ." Author interview with Deni Frand.

"I know . . ." Rose, "Talking Chile Blues." All other citations in this passage are from this source.

"He was very . . ." Author interview with Deni Frand.

"He started . . ." Ibid.

"He was so . . ." Author interview with Lola Cohn.

"Phil was determined . . ." Author interview with Mayer Vishner.

"There was . . ." Author interview with Deni Frand.

"We had . . ." Author interview with Arthur Gorson.

"When's rehearsal time?": Rose, "Talking Chile Blues."

"I think . . ." Author interview with Arlo Guthrie.

"Once again . . ." Ibid.

"Okay, okay . . ." Tape of the "Evening with Salvador Allende Concert," courtesy of Michael Ochs.

"He loved . . ." Author interview with Deni Frand.

"He didn't have . . ." Author interview with Cora Weiss.

"The people . . ." Author interview with Deni Frand.

CHAPTER SIXTEEN: THE DOWNHILL SLIDE

"It was going . . ." Author interview with Deni Frand.

"It was hard . . ." Ibid.

"Prior to . . ." Author interview with Arthur Gorson.

"When he was at . . ." Author interview with Deni Frand.

"I should never . . ." Ibid.

"He was a . . ." Author interview with Ramsey Clark.

"Phil would come over . . ." Author interview with Lee Housekeeper. All other citations in this passage are from this source.

"It was important . . ." Author interview with Cora Weiss.

"The Movement . . ." Ibid.

"twenty-nine hours . . ." Ibid.

"It was festive . . ." Author interview with Jay Levin.

"It was bittersweet . . ." Author interview with Paul Krassner.

"I was sort of . . ." Author interview with Arthur Gorson.

"I'll tell you . . ." Author interview with Paul Colby. All other citations in this passage are from this source.

"It was to be . . ." Author interview with Arthur Gorson.

"He wanted her . . ." Author interview with David Ifshin.

"complete massacre": Ibid.

"You say you're . . ." Interview with John Train, courtesy of Michael Ochs.

"off the deep end": Author interview with Arthur Gorson.

"He thought . . ." Ibid.

"He wasn't . . ." Ibid.

CHAPTER SEVENTEEN: TRAIN

"On the first . . ." Interview with John Train, courtesy of Michael Ochs.

"He responded . . ." Author interview with Mayer Vishner.

"We were getting . . ." Author interview with Sis Cunningham.

"I had a friend . . ." Author interview with Sammy Walker.

"I was pretty overwhelmed . . ." Ibid.

"It was a sad . . ." Author interview with Deni Frand.

"When he was Train . . ." Author interview with Larry Sloman.

"I didn't know . . ." Author interview with Carol Realini.

"I hated . . ." Author interview with Paul Colby.

"He had a pipe . . ." Ibid.

"Somebody's got . . ." Author interview with Sis Cunningham.

"We tried . . ." Ibid.

"Phil used to . . ." Author interview with Cora Weiss.

"He was a wonderful . . ." Author interview with Carol Realini.

"I suggested . . ." Author interview with Arthur Gorson.

"What can I . . ." Author interview with Mayer Vishner.

"I put out . . ." Tape of Phil Ochs–Sammy Walker concert at Folk City, Summer 1975, courtesy of Michael Ochs.

"Sam was in . . ." Author interview with Mayer Vishner.

"I live . . ." Tape of Phil Ochs–Sammy Walker concert.

"Anybody comes up . . ." Ibid.

"It was a great . . ." Author interview with Arthur Gorson.

"He told me . . ." Author interview with Michael Ochs.

"a disaster": Author interview with Jack Newfield.

"SoHo Bar . . ." John Train (Phil Ochs), "SoHo Bar Attacked," courtesy of Ed Sanders.

"Even during . . ." Author interview with Arthur Gorson.

"Phil actually entered . . ." Author interview with Larry Sloman.

"He was living . . ." Ibid.

"John stands for . . ." John Train (Phil Ochs), untitled song, © 1976 Barricade Music, Inc.

"Phil Ochs checked . . ." John Train (Phil Ochs), "The Ballad of John Train," © 1976 Barricade Music, Inc.

"I got a call . . ." Author interview with Deni Frand. All other quotations in this passage are from this source.

"I saw . . ." Author interview with Ramsey Clark.

"Don't take care . . ." Marc Eliot, *Death of a Rebel* (NY: Franklin Watts, 1989), p. 260.

"One day . . ." Author interview with Carol Realini.

"The last time . . ." Author interview with Patrick Sky.

"He called . . ." Author interview with Robin Love.

"terrified": Ibid.

"Phil walked in . . ." Ibid.

"He went looking . . ." Author interview with Ron Cobb.

"At that point . . ." Author interview with Doug Weston.

"Everybody was . . ." Author interview with Ron Cobb.

"We all stood . . ." Ibid.

"One of the dynamics . . ." Author interview with Meegan Ochs.

"I think . . ." Ibid.

"Guess who's . . ." Author interview with Ron Cobb.

CHAPTER EIGHTEEN: NO MORE SONGS

"What am I . . ." Author interview with Larry Sloman.

"Bobby, give me . . ." Author interview with Mayer Vishner.

"It's the story . . ." Ibid.

"There was a punctured . . ." Author interview with Larry Sloman.

"Don't go . . ." and *"I'm not going . . ."* Author interview with Mayer Vishner.

"He was just . . ." Author interview with Sonny Ochs.

"I would try . . ." Ibid.

"It was like . . ." Author interview with Ramsey Clark.

"It's far-fetched . . ." Author interview with Carol Realini.

"In February . . ." Author interview with Sonny Ochs.

"Maybe there's hope . . ." Ibid.

"What are you getting . . ." Ibid.

"How about this . . ." Author interview with Ron Cobb.

"Come on back . . ." Author interview with Robin Love.

"I'll do it . . ." Author interview with Ron Cobb.

"What do you . . ." Ibid. All other citations in this passage are from this source.

"Do you think . . ." Author interview with Michael Ochs.

"What are you thinking . . ." Author interview with Sonny Ochs.

"They had him . . ." Ibid.

AFTERWORD

"folk singer . . ." Robert E. Tomasson, "Phil Ochs a Suicide at 35; Singer of Peace Movement," *New York Times*, April 10, 1976.

"You saw . . ." Tom Miller, "Remembering Phil Ochs," *Chicago Sun Times*, April 25, 1976.

"Ochs was also . . ." Arthur Lubow, "Balladeer of the Movement," *New Times*, November 30, 1976.

"Mr. Speaker . . ." Bella Abzug speech, *Congressional Record*, volume 122, part 10.

"The Los Angeles Times . . ." Phil Ochs FBI report, courtesy of Sis Cunningham and Gordon Friesen. All other citations in this passage are from this source.

SELECTED DISCOGRAPHY

SINGLES

"I Ain't Marching Anymore" / "That Was the President." 1966.
"Cross My Heart" / "Flower Lady." 1967.
"Outside a Small Circle of Friends" / "Miranda." 1967.
"The War is Over" / "The Harder They Fall." 1968.
"Kansas City Bomber" / "Gas Station Women." 1973.
"Bwatue" / "Niko Mchumba Ngombe." (In Africa only) 1973.
"Power and the Glory" / "Here's to the State of Richard Nixon." 1974.

ALBUMS

All the News That's Fit to Sing. (1964) "One More Parade" / "The Thresher" / "Talking Vietnam" / "Lou Marsh" / "Power and the Glory" / "Celia" / "The Bells" / "Automation Song" / "The Ballad of William Worthy" / "Knock on the Door" / "Talking Cuban Crisis" / "Bound for Glory" / "Too Many Martyrs" / "What's That I Hear?"

I Ain't Marching Anymore (1965). "I Ain't Marching Anymore" / "In the Heat of the Summer" / "Draft Dodger Rag" / "That's What I Want to Hear" / "That was the President" / "Iron Lady" / "The Highwayman" / "Links on the Chain" / "The Hills of West Virginia" / "The Man Behind the Guns" / "Talking Birmingham Jam" / "The Ballad of the Carpenter" / "Days of Decision" / "Here's to the State of Mississippi."

Phil Ochs in Concert (1966). "I'm Going to Say It Now" / "Bracero" / "Ringing of Revolution" / "Is There Anybody Here?" / "Cannons of Christianity" / "There But for Fortune" / "Cops of the World" / "The Marines Have Landed on the Shores of Santo Domingo" / "Changes" / "Love Me, I'm a Liberal" / "When I'm Gone."

Pleasures of the Harbor (1967). "Cross My Heart" / "Flower Lady" / "Outside of a Small Circle of Friends" / "I've Had Her" / "Miranda" / "The Party" / "Pleasures of the Harbor" / "Crucifixion."

Tape from California (1968). "Tape from California" / "White Boots Marching in a Yellow Land" / "Half a Century High" / "Joe Hill" / "The War is Over" / "The Harder They Fall" / "When in Rome" / "The Floods of Florence."

Rehearsals for Retirement (1968). "Pretty Smart on My Part" / "The Doll House" / "I Kill, Therefore I Am" / "William Butler Yeats Visits Lincoln Park and Escapes Unscathed" / "My Life" / "The Scorpion Departs but Never Returns" / "The World Began in Eden but Ended in Los Angeles" / "Doesn't Lenny Live Here Anymore?" / "Another Age" / "Rehearsals for Retirement."

Phil Ochs' Greatest Hits (1970). "One-Way Ticket Home" / "Jim Dean of Indiana" / "My Kingdom for a Car" / "Boy in Ohio" / "Gas Station Women" / "Chords of Fame" / "Ten Cents a Coup" / "Bach, Beethoven, Mozart and Me" / "Basket in the Pool" / "No More Songs."

Gunfight at Carnegie Hall (1975). "Mona Lisa" / "I Ain't Marching Anymore" / "Okie from Muskogee" / "Chords of Fame" / "Medley: 'Not Fade Away'—'I'm Gonna Love You Too'—'Think It Over'—'Oh Boy'—'Everyday'—'Not Fade Away' " / "Pleasures of the Harbor" / "Tape from California" / "Medley: 'My Baby Left Me'—'I'm Ready'—'Heartbreak Hotel'—'All Shook Up'—'Are You Lonesome Tonight?'—'My Baby Left Me' " / "A Fool Such As I."

Songs for Broadside (1976). "Pleasures of the Harbor" / "That's What I Want to Hear" / "I'm Going to Say It Now" / "Changes" / "On Her Hand a Golden Ring" / "Days of Decision" / "The Marines Have Landed on the Shores of Santo Domingo" / "United Fruit" / "Crucifixion" / "Outside of a Small Circle of Friends" / "What Are You Fighting For?" / "Ringing of Revolution."

Chords of Fame (1976). "I Ain't Marching Anymore" / "One More Parade" / "Draft Dodger Rag" / "Here's to the State of Richard Nixon" / "The Bells" / "Bound for Glory" / "Too Many Martyrs" / "There But for Fortune" / "I'm Going to Say It Now" / "The Marines Have Landed on the Shores of Santo Domingo" / "Changes" / "Is There Anybody Here?" / "Love Me, I'm a Liberal" / "When I'm Gone" / "Outside of a Small Circle of Friends" / "Pleasures of the Harbor" / "Tape from California" / "Chords of Fame" / "Crucifixion" / "The War is Over" / "Jim Dean of Indiana" / "Power and the Glory" / "Flower Lady" / "No More Songs."

A Toast for Those Who Are Gone (1986). "Do What I Have to Do" / "Ballad of Billie Sol" / "Colored Town" / "A.M.A. Song" / "William Moore" / "Paul Crump" / "Going Down to Mississippi" / "I'll Be There" / "Ballad Of Oxford (Jimmy Meredith)" / "No Christmas in Kentucky" / "A Toast to Those Who Are Gone" / "I'm Tired" / "City Boy" / "Song of My Returning" / "The Trial."

The Broadside Tapes 1 (1989). "Ballad of Alfred Packer" / "If I Knew" / "Ballad of John Henry Faulk" / "Spaceman" / "On My Way" / "Hazard, Kentucky" / "The Passing of My Life" / "That's the Way It's Gonna Be" / "Rivers of Blood" / "Remember Me" / "Talking Pay T.V." / "Christine Keeler" / "Spanish Civil War Song" / "Another Country" / "Time Was" / "I Should Have Known Better."

There But for Fortune (1989). "What's That I Hear?" / "One More Parade" / "Too Many Martyrs" / "Power and the Glory" / "I Ain't Marching Anymore" / "Draft Dodger Rag" / "The Highwayman" / "Here's to the State of Mississippi" / "There But for Fortune" / "I'm Going to Say It Now" / "Is There Anybody Here?" / "Cops of the World" / "Ringing of Revolution" / "Santo Domingo" / "Bracero" / "Love Me, I'm a Liberal" / "Changes" / "When I'm Gone."

The War is Over: The Best of Phil Ochs (1989). "Tape from California" / "Flower Lady" / "Half a Century High" / "The Scorpion Departs But Never Returns" / "The War is Over" / "One Way Ticket Home" / "Rehearsals for Retirement" / "Chords of Fame" / "Gas Station Women" / "Outside of a Small Circle of Friends" / "Pleasures of the Harbor" / "Kansas City Bomber" / "White Boots Marching in a Yellow Land" / "Jim Dean of Indiana" / "No More Songs" / "I Ain't Marching Anymore."

There and Now: Live In Vancouver, 1968 (1990). "There But for Fortune" / "Outside of a Small Circle of Friends" / "William Butler Yeats Visits Lincoln Park and Escapes Unscathed" / "The Scorpion Departs But Never Returns" / "Pleasures of the Harbor" / "The World Began in Eden and Ended in Los Angeles" / "The Bells" / "The Highwayman" / "I Kill, Therefore I Am" / "The Doll House" / "Another Age" / "Changes" / "Crucifixion" / "I Ain't Marching Anymore."

Live at Newport (1996). "Introduction: Peter Yarrow" / "Ballad of Medgar Evers" / "Talking Birmingham Jam" / "Power and the Glory" / "Draft Dodger Rag" / "I Ain't Marching Anymore" / "Links on the Chain" / "Talking Vietnam Blues" / "Cross My Heart" / "Half a Century High" / "Is There Anybody Here?" / "The Party" / "Pleasures of the Harbor."

MISCELLANEOUS ANTHOLOGIES AND RECORDINGS

Broadside Ballads, Volume I (1963). "The Ballad of William Worthy."
Newport Broadside (1964). "The Ballad of Medgar Evers," "Talking Birmingham Jam."
New Folks (1964). "William Moore," "There But for Fortune,""Talking Airplane Disaster," "Paul Crump," "What Are You Fighting For?"
The Broadside Singers (1964). "Links on the Chain."

The Newport Folk Festival (1964). "Draft Dodger Rag," "Power and the Glory."

Folksong '65. (1965). "Power and the Glory."

The Folk Box (1966). "The Thresher."

A&M Family Portrait (1967). "Cross My Heart."

Broadside Reunion (1972). "Hunger and Cold," "Changing Hands."

The Bitter End: The First Ten Years (1974). "I Ain't Marching Anymore."

Song for Patty (1975). Harmony vocals on "Bound for Glory."

Interview with Phil Ochs (1976). Taped interviews conducted by Sis Cunningham and Gordon Friesen, originally published in *Broadside* magazine.

Troubadours of the Folk Era, Volume Two (1992). "There But for Fortune."

INDEX

Peter and Gordon, 215
Peter, Paul and Mary, 60, 61, 64, 65, 92, 96,
    99, 120, 215, 316
Pet Sounds (Beach Boys), 120, 150
Philadelphia Folk Festival, 204
"Phil Ochs and Friends" concert, 299
Phil Ochs' Greatest Hits (Ochs), 223–27, 231,
    234, 263, 287
Phil Ochs in Concert (Ochs), 115–17, 119,
    166, 177, 185, 316
Phin, George (maternal grandfather), 14
Phin, Gertrude, *see* Gertrude Phin Ochs
Phin, Harry, 14
Pierce, Webb, 27, 224
Pinochet, Augusto, 287, 295
Plastic Ono Band (Lennon), 212
"Pleasures of the Harbor" (Ochs), 118, 150,
    159–61, 162, 167, 168, 205, 227, 231, 286
Pleasures of the Harbor (Ochs), 128, 129,
    167, 168, 170, 173, 177, 185, 186, 225
    critical response to, 164–66
    recording of, 149–63
Poe, Edgar Allan, 76
Porco, John, 50
Porco, Mike, 50–51, 321, 341–42
"Positively Fourth Street" (Dylan), 106
Powell, Dick, 272
"Power and the Glory" (Ochs), 59–60, 62, 82,
    84, 90, 95, 128, 172, 288
Power, Tyrone, 272
Prendergast, Tom, 50–51
Presley, Elvis, 27, 33, 132, 223, 224, 225,
    226, 227, 232, 237, 286. 311n
"Pretty Boy Floyd" (Guthrie), 186
"Pretty Smart on My Part" (Ochs), 209–10
Progressive Labor Party, 117
Pyne, Joe, 137–39, 231

Rafkin, Bob, 210, 227
Ray, Jean, 4, 46–47, 58, 332
Realini, Carol, 318, 320
Realist, The, 97
Record World, 166
Reddin, Tom, 273–74
"Rehearsals for Retirement" (Ochs), 210–11
Rehearsals for Retirement (Ochs), 208–13,
    214, 223, 225, 227, 235, 329
Renaldo and Clara (film), 342, 343
Reynolds, Malvina, 52–53
Rhodes, Orlando H., 144
"Rhythms of Revolution" (Ochs), 257
Ribicoff, Abraham, 203
Robeson, Paul, 144
Rodgers, Richard, 121
Rolling Thunder Revue, 299, 339, 342, 343,
    344
Rosenberg, Julius and Ethel, 118
Rothchild, Paul, 76, 213
Rothschild, Charlie, 51
Rubber Soul (Beatles), 120
Rubin, Jerry, 5, 97, 169, 170, 182, 183–84,
    194, 196, 197, 204, 207, 219, 221, 229,
    230, 235, 236, 237, 239, 240, 241, 243,
    245, 246, 248, 256, 259, 263, 327, 333,
    339, 348, 350
Rubinson, David, 128–29
Rush, Tom, 119, 122

Sacred Mushroom (club), 40
Sadler, Barry, 141

Sainte-Marie, Buffy, 67, 88, 99, 292
Sanders, Colonel Harland, 311, 325
Sanders, Ed, 130, 195, 198, 199, 256, 259
Sanford Meisner School, 47
Santa Monica Civic Auditorium, 175–76
Scaduto, Anthony, 61
"School Days" (Berry), 232
Schultz, Richard G., 207
Schumann, Robert, 153
Schwerner, Michael, 86
"Scorpion Departs but Never Returns, The"
    (Ochs), 205, 210
Seale, Bobby, 195, 219, 220, 257, 258
Sebastian, John, 79
Seeger, Pete, 33, 38, 52, 53, 61, 63, 65, 66,
    70, 73, 80, 85, 99, 102, 104, 151, 168,
    240, 296, 305
Seeley, Walter, 348
Seger, Bob, 256
Sgt. Pepper's Lonely Hearts Club Band
    (Beatles), 150
Shelton, Robert, 51, 61, 64, 103, 115
She Wore a Yellow Ribbon (film), 178
Silber, Irwin, 84, 85, 165
Simon and Garfunkel, 104, 120
Sinatra, Frank, 291, 324
Sinclair, Hamish, 72, 73
Sinclair, John, 256, 257, 258, 259, 260
Singing Socialists, The, 38–39, 41
Sing Out! 65, 80, 84, 165
Siskel, Gene, 302
Skinner, Alice, *see* Alice Skinner Ochs
Sky, Patrick, 88, 103, 276
Sloman, Larry, 172–73, 318, 326, 327–28,
    341, 343
Smith, Patti, 286
Smothers Brothers, 42, 179
Smothers, Tom, 42, 217, 218, 223
Sobell, Morton, 118
"Song for Patty" (Walker), 322
"Song for Woody" (Dylan), 60
Sopwith Camel, 124
Sound of Music, The (film), 120
Spock, Dr. Benjamin, 145
Star Wars (film), 140
Staunton Military Academy, 26, 27, 28, 29
Steinbeck, John, 72
Stewart, Sharon, 142–43
Student Non-Violent Coordinating
    Committee, 73, 146
Students for a Democratic Society, 195, 226
Students for Kennedy, 73
Sundial, The, 36
Sundowners, The, 39–41, 44, 46, 47
Swayse, Dave, 128
Sweazy, David, 25–26

"Talking Birmingham Jam" (Ochs), 62, 87
"Talking Plane Disaster" (Ochs), 108
"Talking Vietnam" (Ochs), 69
"Talkin' John Birch Society Blues" (Dylan),
    64
Tanzman, David, 345, 347, 351, 352
Tanzman, Jonathan, 345, 347, 349, 351
"Tape from California" (Ochs), 177, 186, 187,
    209, 210, 231, 286
Tape from California (Ochs), 185–87, 208
Terkel, Studs, 42, 278
"That's the Way It's Gonna Be" (Ochs/
    Gibson), 43